OSSAN IDOL! 02

MANGA ◆ ICHIKA KINO
ORIGINAL STORY ◆
MOCHIKO MOCHIDA
CHARACTER DESIGN ◆
MIZUKI SAKAKIBARA

STORY

MIROKU, A 270LB, UNEMPLOYED SHUT-IN, JOINED A GYM, GOT IN SHAPE, AND TRANSFORMED INTO A MIDDLE-AGE HUNK IN NO TIME! SPURRED ON BY THE POPULARITY OF HIS 'LET'S DANCE' VIDEO, HE SETS HIS SIGHTS ON BECOMING AN IDOL. JUST AS MIROKU IS GETTING TO KNOW YOICHI AND SHIJU, WHO HE MET AT THE GYM, THE THREE ARE OFFERED AN IDOL GROUP DEBUT BY MR. LAVENDER, A BIG SHOT PRODUCER IN THE MUSIC INDUSTRY!

CHARACTERS

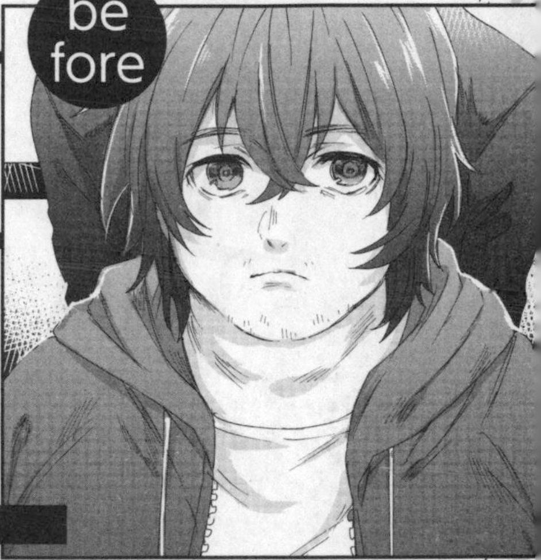
be
fore

MIROKU (36)

MIROKU OSAKI

UNEMPLOYED • SHUT-IN • VIRGIN

INTERNET ADDICT • WEIGHT 270LBS
GIVES OFF WEIRD VIBES

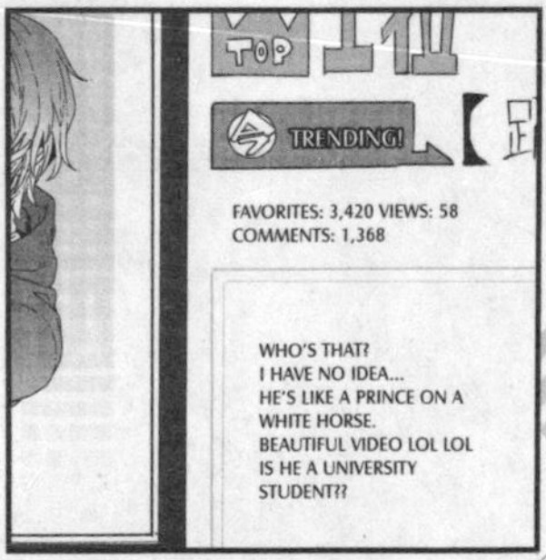
TOP
TRENDING!
FAVORITES: 3,420 VIEWS: 58
COMMENTS: 1,368
WHO'S THAT?
I HAVE NO IDEA...
HE'S LIKE A PRINCE ON A WHITE HORSE.
BEAUTIFUL VIDEO LOL LOL
IS HE A UNIVERSITY STUDENT??

HE PRESSED UPLOAD BY MISTAKE.

AND HIS 'LET'S DANCE' VIDEO WENT VIRAL!!

TURNED INTO A PRINCE ♥

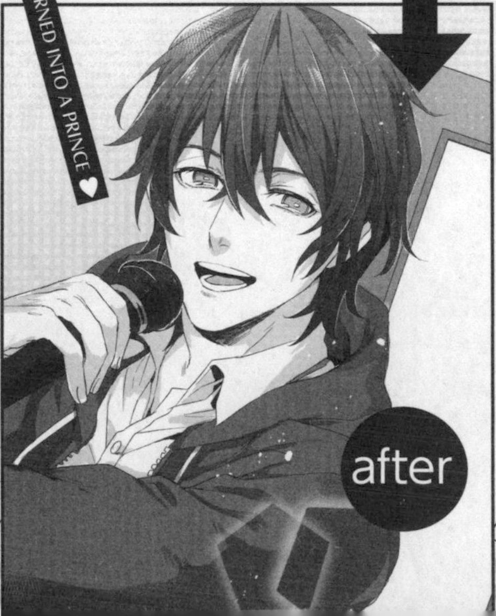
after

YOICHI (41)

YOICHI KISARAGI
HE WAS OVER 300LBS, BUT NOW YOICHI IS THE CEO OF A SMALL ENTERTAINMENT COMPANY. HE AND MIROKU MET AT THE GYM. A GENTLEMAN WHO IS A BIT TOO WORRIED ABOUT HIS MUSCLE MASS.

SHIJU (40)

SHIJU ONOHARA
FORMER DANCER AND HOST, NOW UNEMPLOYED AND LEADING A LIFE ON THE EDGE. SHIJU HAS HIS GOOD SIDE, TOO. HE WAS THE ONE WHO SUGGESTED THAT MIROKU TAKE PART IN THE DANCE COMPETITION.

FUMI

FUMI KISARAGI
YOICHI'S BUBBLY NIECE WHO WORKS AT HIS OFFICE. SHE ALWAYS PUTS HER ALL INTO HER WORK.

KAMO LAVENDER

PRODUCER EXTRAORDINAIRE OF NATIONALLY TREASURED IDOL GROUPS SUCH AS "UGUISUDANI SEVEN."

LET'S GET INTO THE STORY!

OSSAN IDOL! 02

CONTENTS

Chapter 6

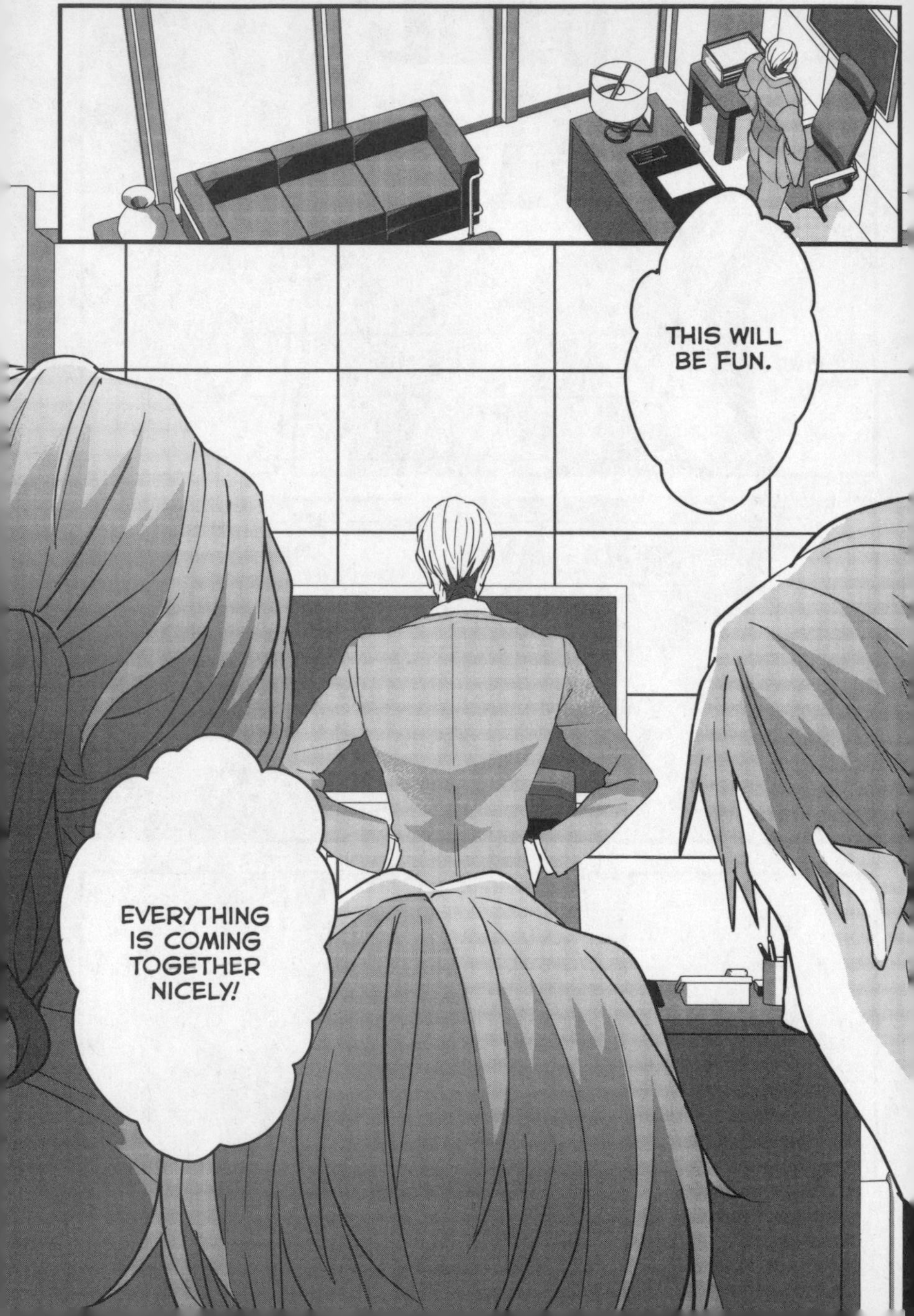

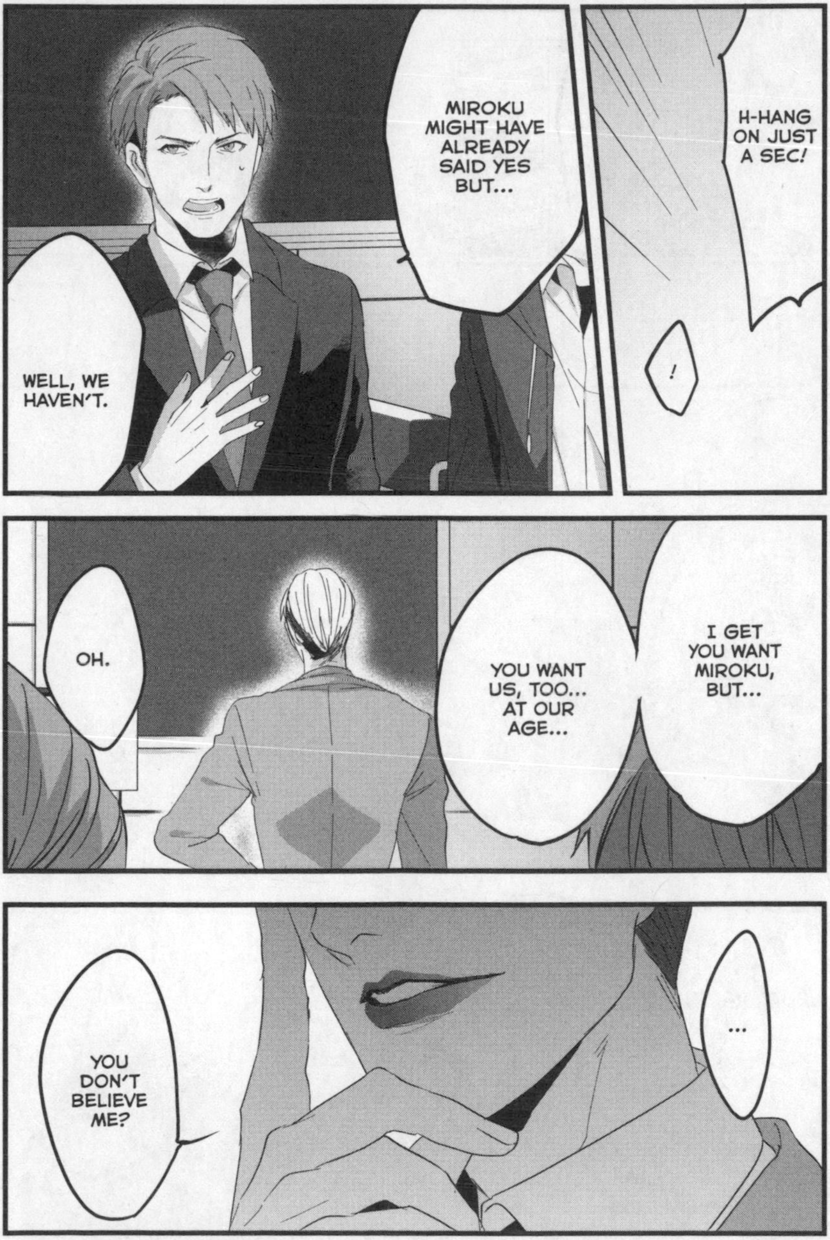
H-HANG ON JUST A SEC!
!
MIROKU MIGHT HAVE ALREADY SAID YES BUT...
WELL, WE HAVEN'T.
I GET YOU WANT MIROKU, BUT...
YOU WANT US, TOO... AT OUR AGE...
OH.
...
YOU DON'T BELIEVE ME?

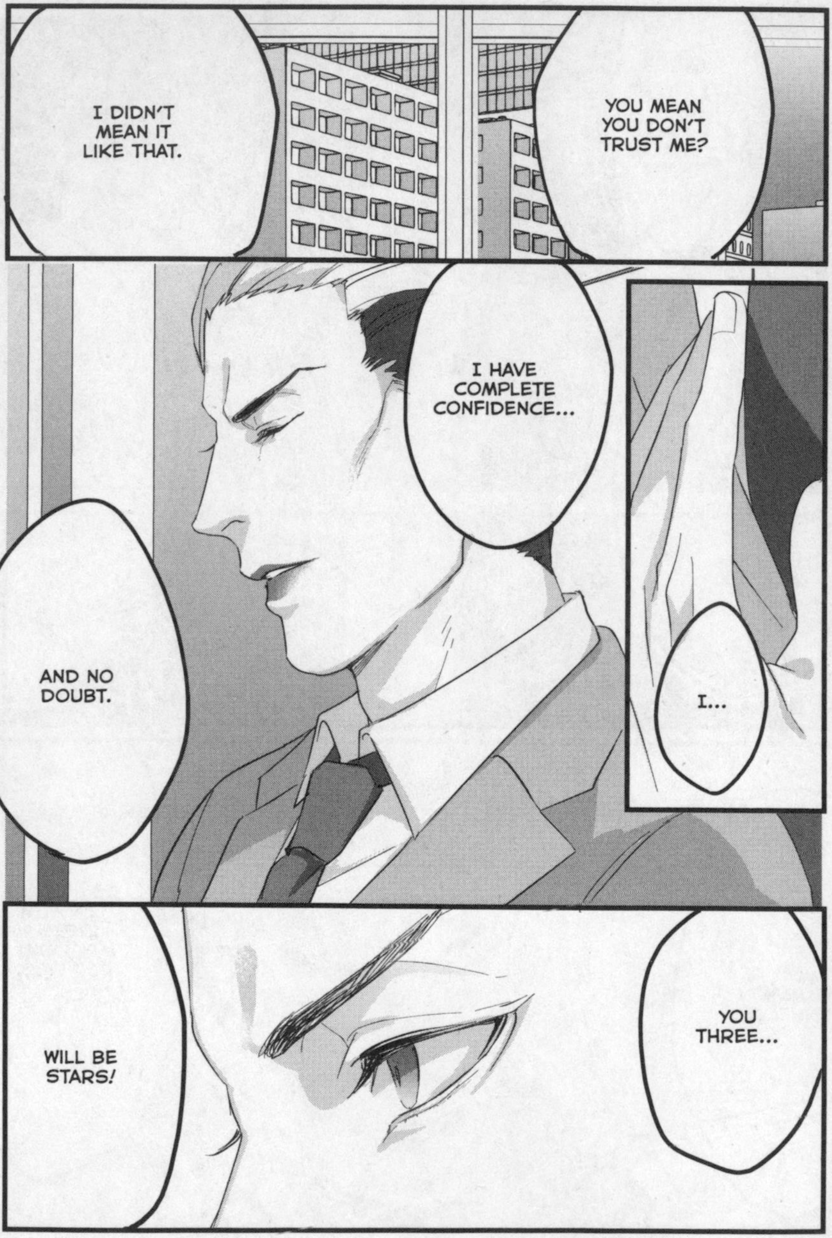
YOU MEAN YOU DON'T TRUST ME?
I DIDN'T MEAN IT LIKE THAT.
I...
I HAVE COMPLETE CONFIDENCE...
AND NO DOUBT.
YOU THREE...
WILL BE STARS!

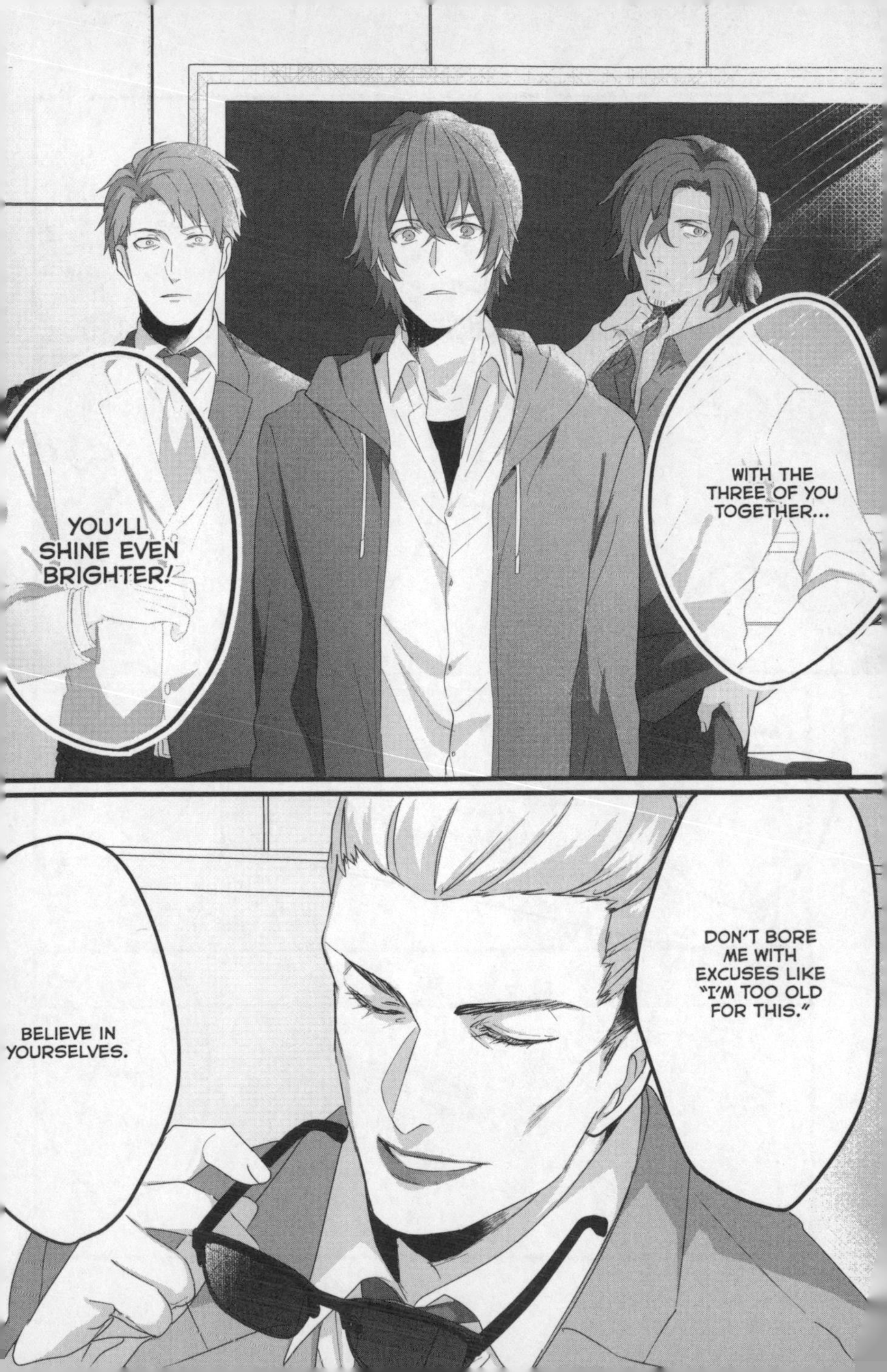
WITH THE THREE OF YOU TOGETHER...
YOU'LL SHINE EVEN BRIGHTER!
DON'T BORE ME WITH EXCUSES LIKE "I'M TOO OLD FOR THIS."
BELIEVE IN YOURSELVES.

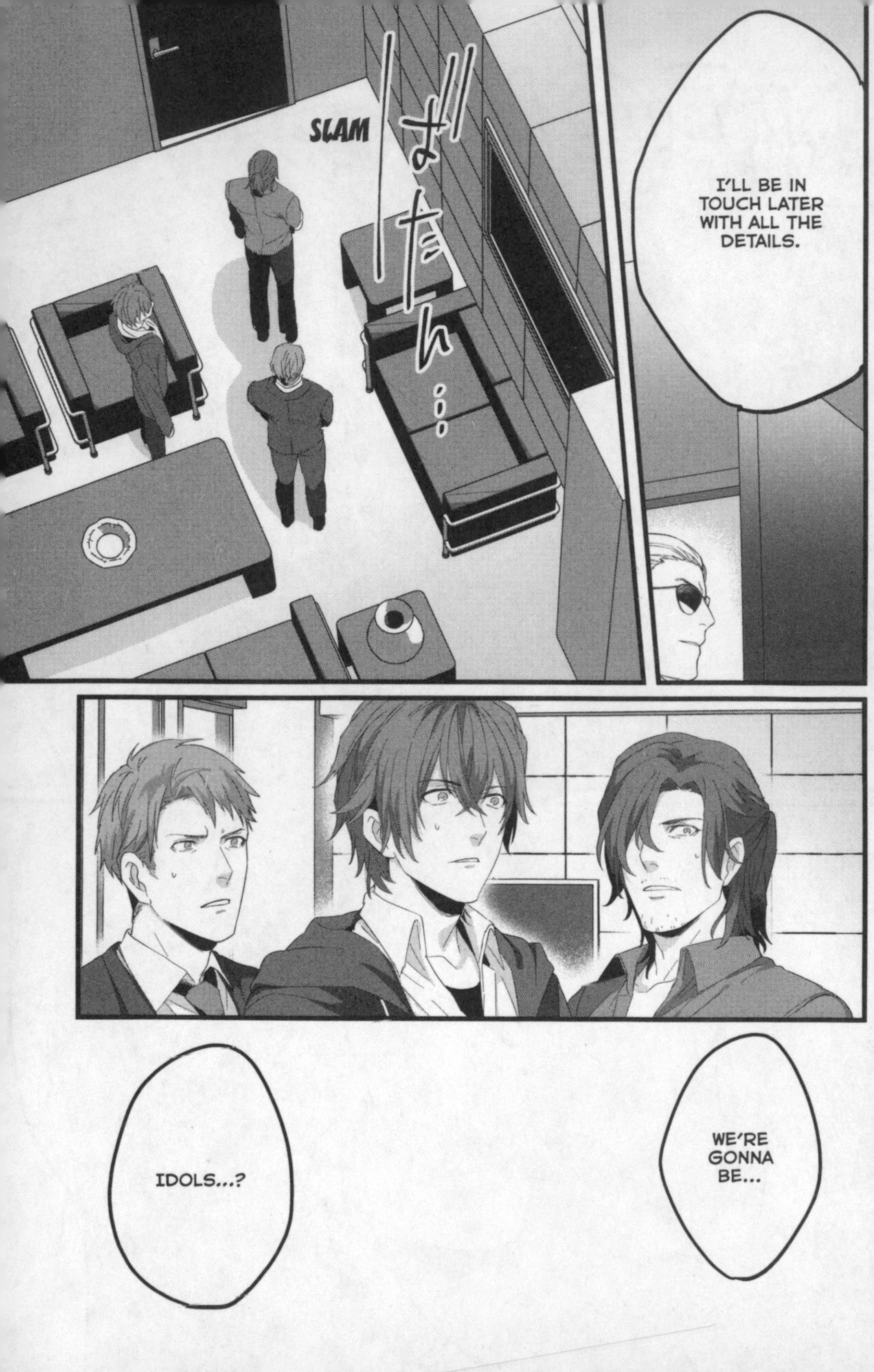
I'LL BE IN TOUCH LATER WITH ALL THE DETAILS.
SLAM
ばたん…
WE'RE GONNA BE...
IDOLS...?

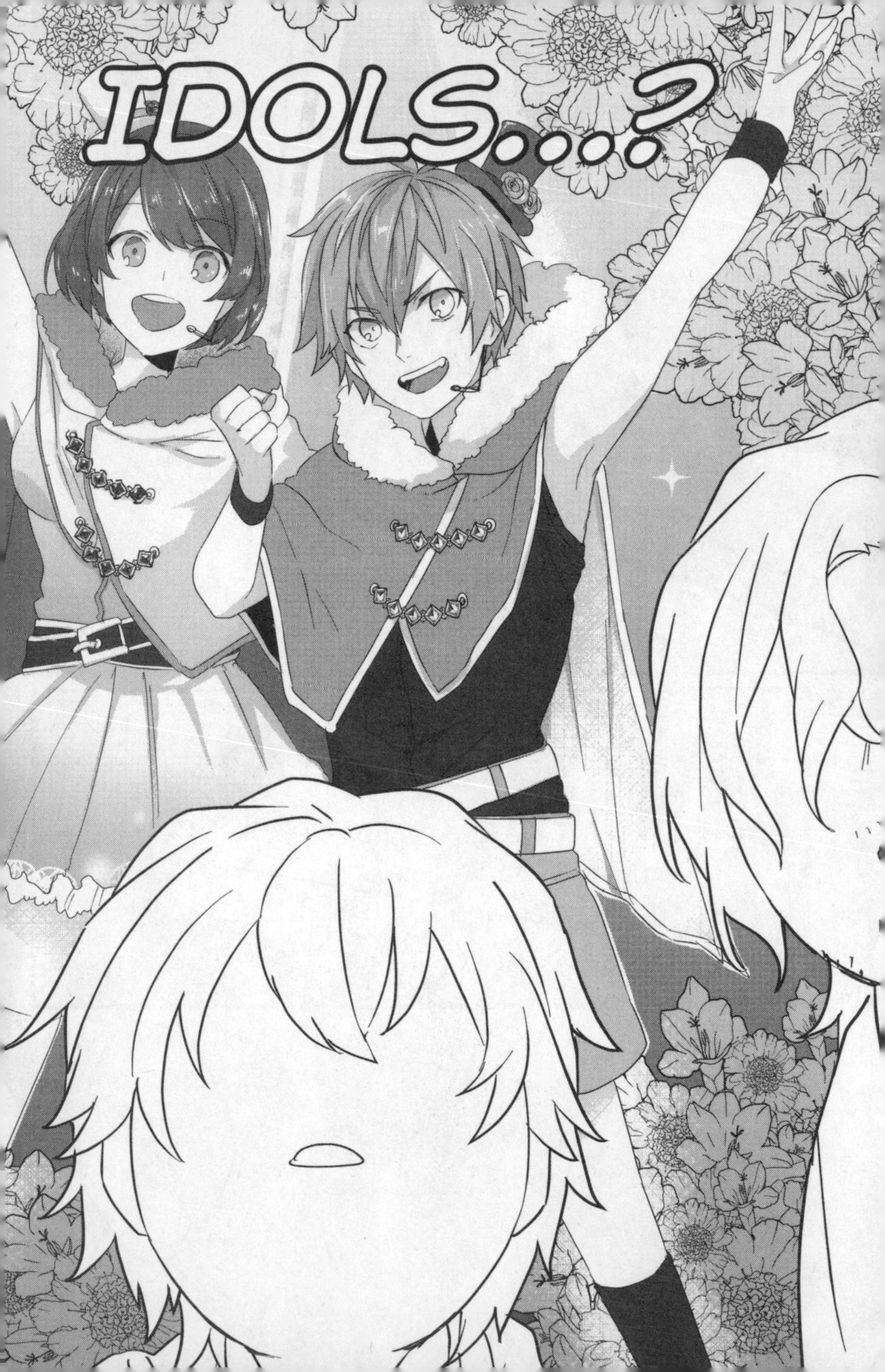
IDOLS...?

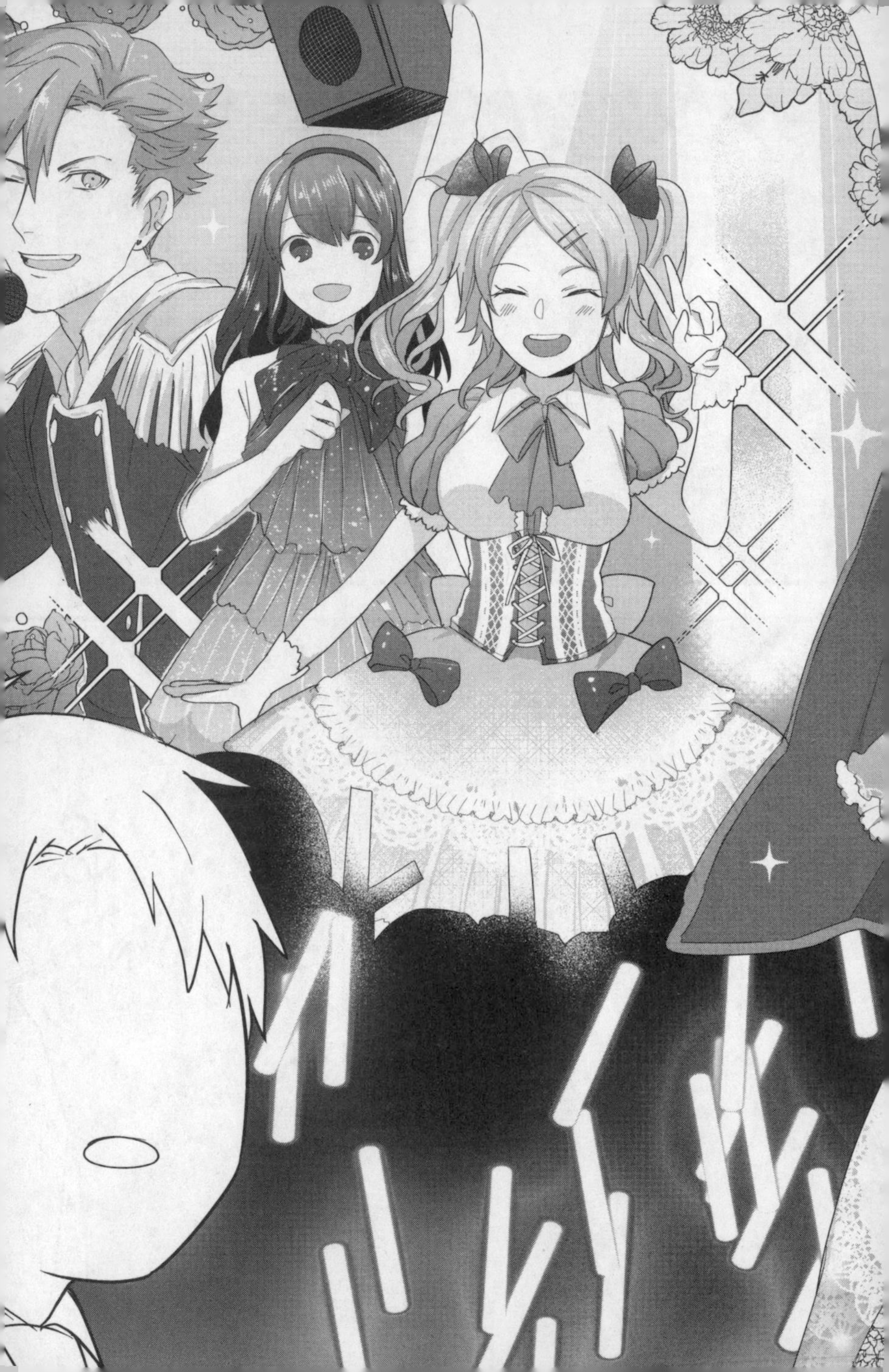

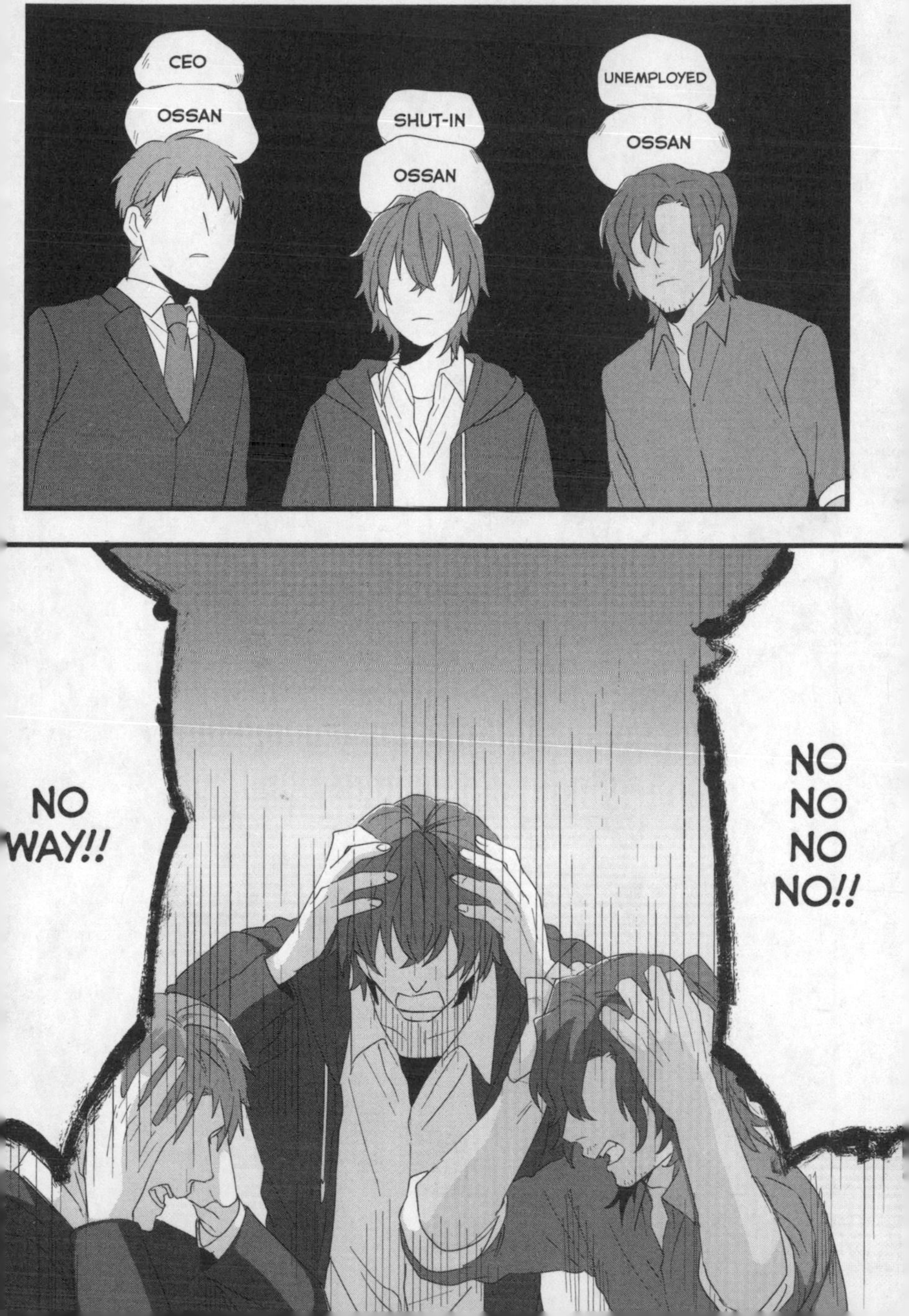
UNEMPLOYED
OSSAN
SHUT-IN
OSSAN
CEO
OSSAN
NO NO NO NO!!
NO WAY!!

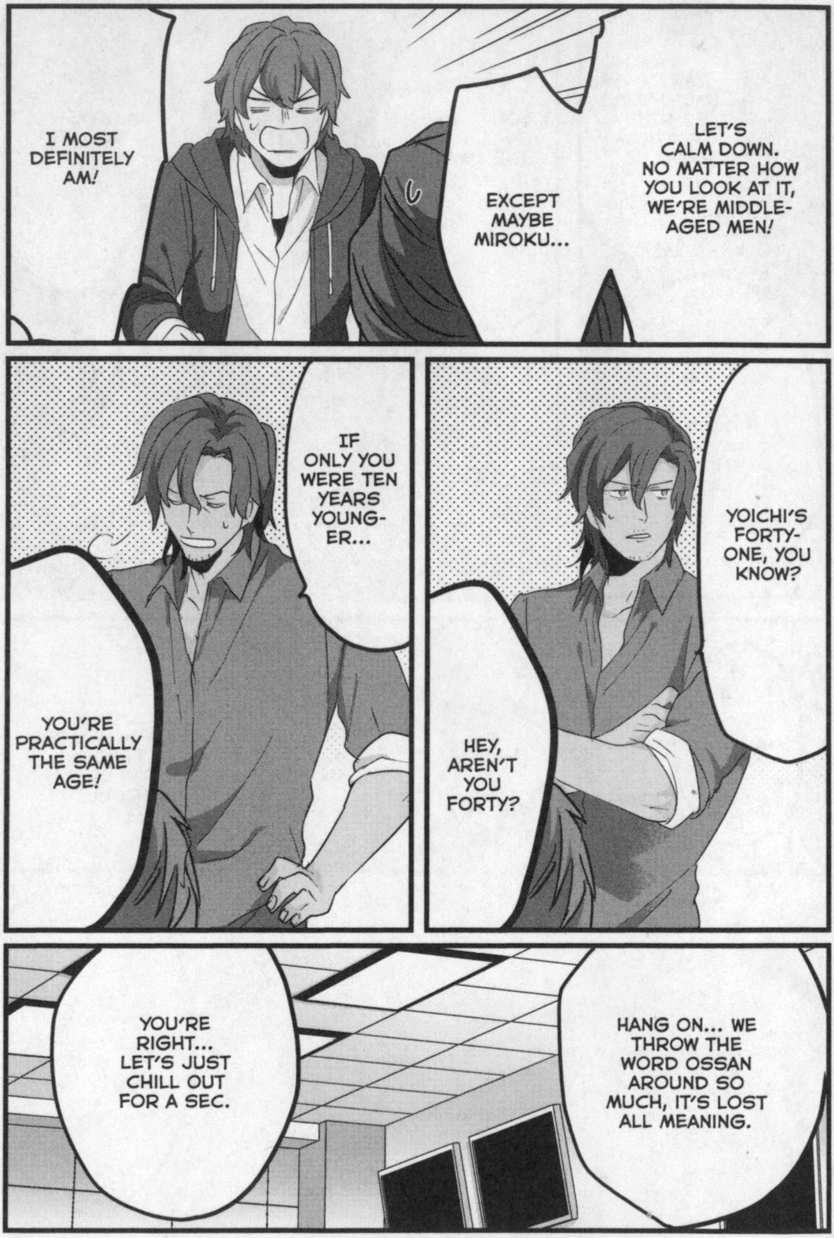
LET'S CALM DOWN. NO MATTER HOW YOU LOOK AT IT, WE'RE MIDDLE-AGED MEN!
EXCEPT MAYBE MIROKU...
I MOST DEFINITELY AM!
YOICHI'S FORTY-ONE, YOU KNOW?
HEY, AREN'T YOU FORTY?
IF ONLY YOU WERE TEN YEARS YOUNG-ER...
YOU'RE PRACTICALLY THE SAME AGE!
HANG ON... WE THROW THE WORD OSSAN AROUND SO MUCH, IT'S LOST ALL MEANING.
YOU'RE RIGHT... LET'S JUST CHILL OUT FOR A SEC.

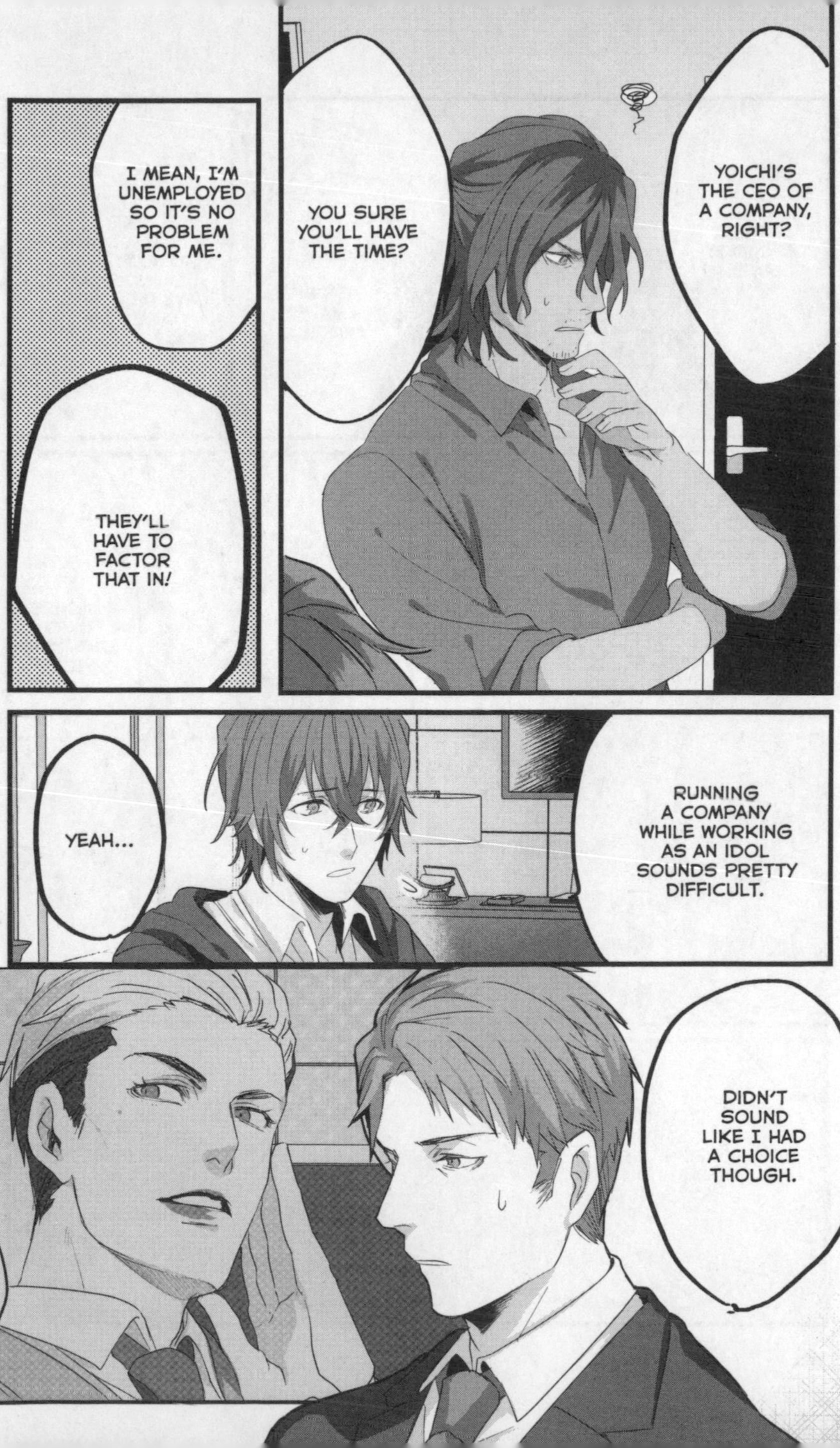
YOICHI'S THE CEO OF A COMPANY, RIGHT?
YOU SURE YOU'LL HAVE THE TIME?
I MEAN, I'M UNEMPLOYED SO IT'S NO PROBLEM FOR ME.
THEY'LL HAVE TO FACTOR THAT IN!
RUNNING A COMPANY WHILE WORKING AS AN IDOL SOUNDS PRETTY DIFFICULT.
YEAH...
DIDN'T SOUND LIKE I HAD A CHOICE THOUGH.

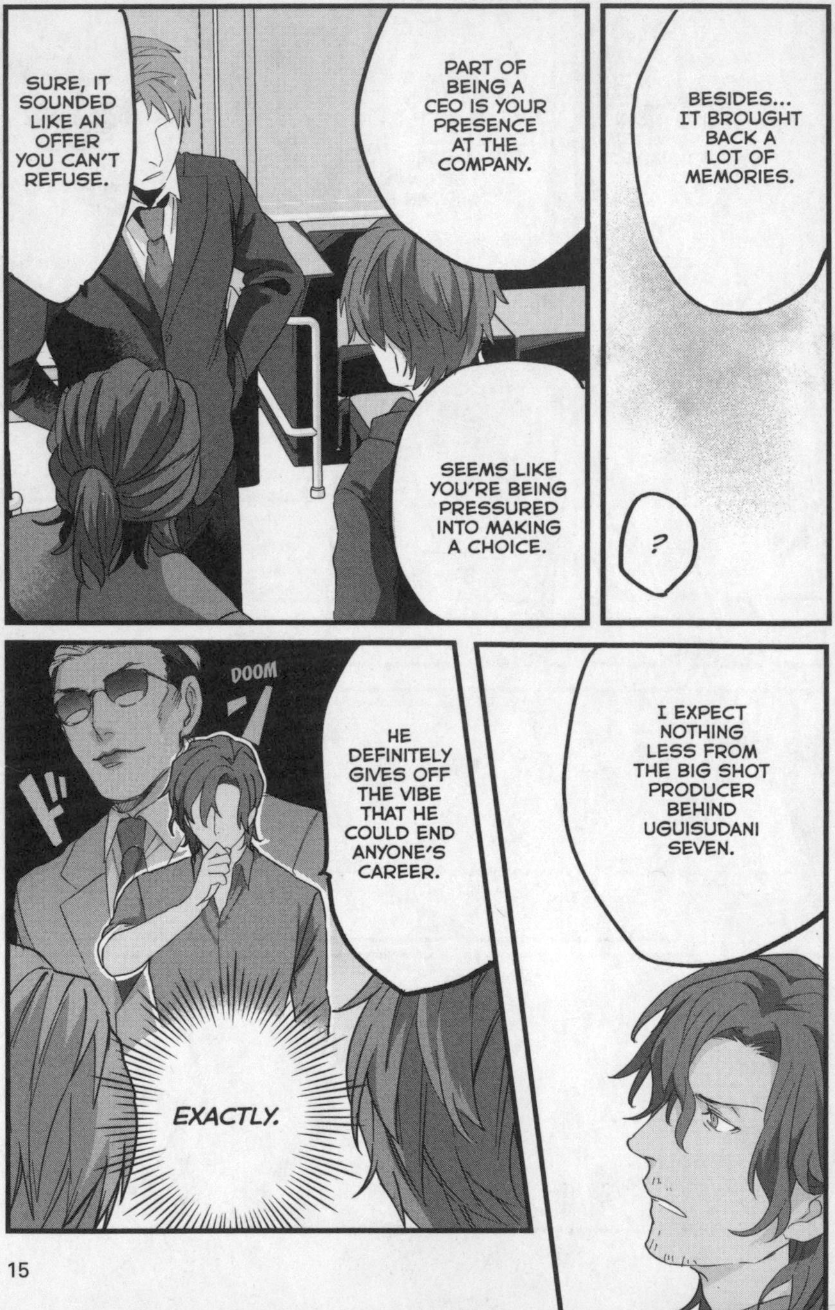
BESIDES... IT BROUGHT BACK A LOT OF MEMORIES.
?
PART OF BEING A CEO IS YOUR PRESENCE AT THE COMPANY.
SURE, IT SOUNDED LIKE AN OFFER YOU CAN'T REFUSE.
SEEMS LIKE YOU'RE BEING PRESSURED INTO MAKING A CHOICE.
I EXPECT NOTHING LESS FROM THE BIG SHOT PRODUCER BEHIND UGUISUDANI SEVEN.
DOOM
HE DEFINITELY GIVES OFF THE VIBE THAT HE COULD END ANYONE'S CAREER.
EXACTLY.

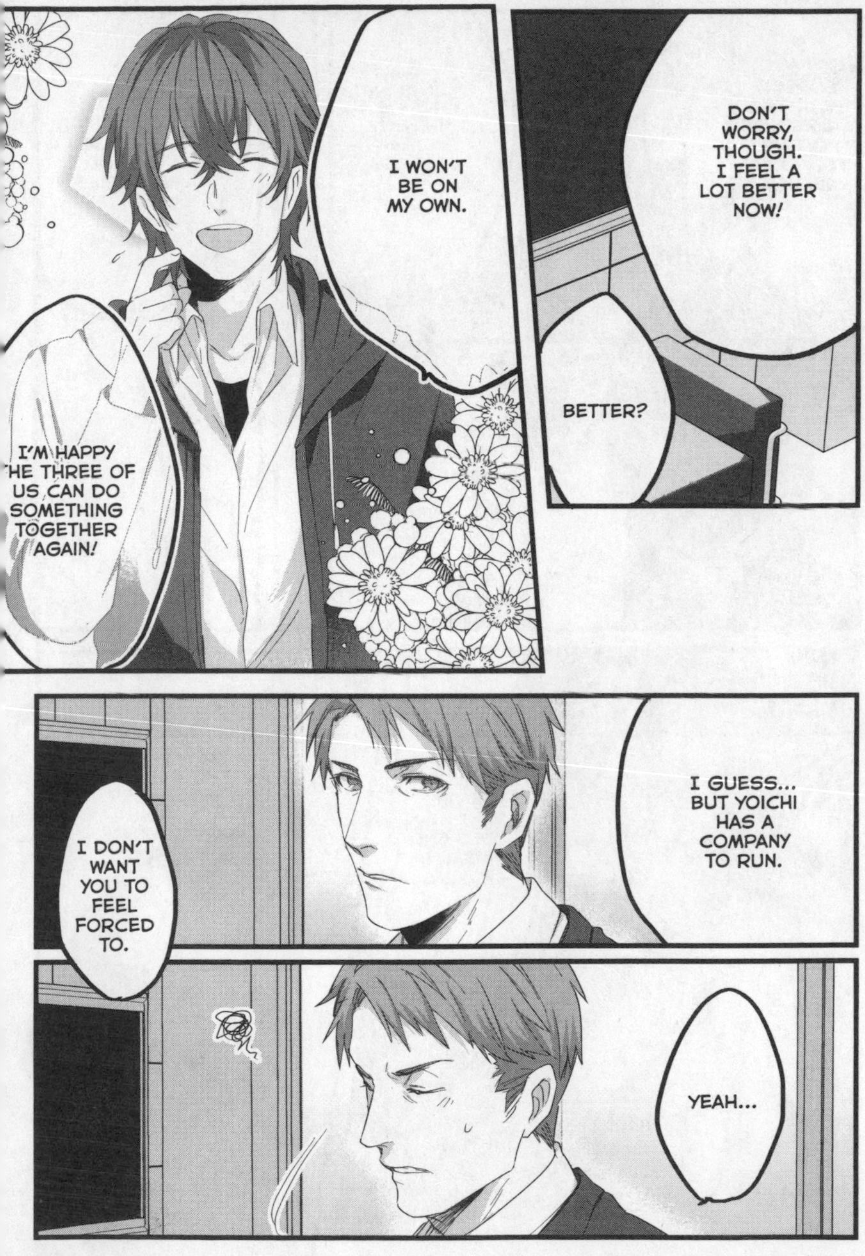
DON'T WORRY, THOUGH. I FEEL A LOT BETTER NOW!
BETTER?
I WON'T BE ON MY OWN.
I'M HAPPY THE THREE OF US CAN DO SOMETHING TOGETHER AGAIN!
I GUESS... BUT YOICHI HAS A COMPANY TO RUN.
I DON'T WANT YOU TO FEEL FORCED TO.
YEAH...

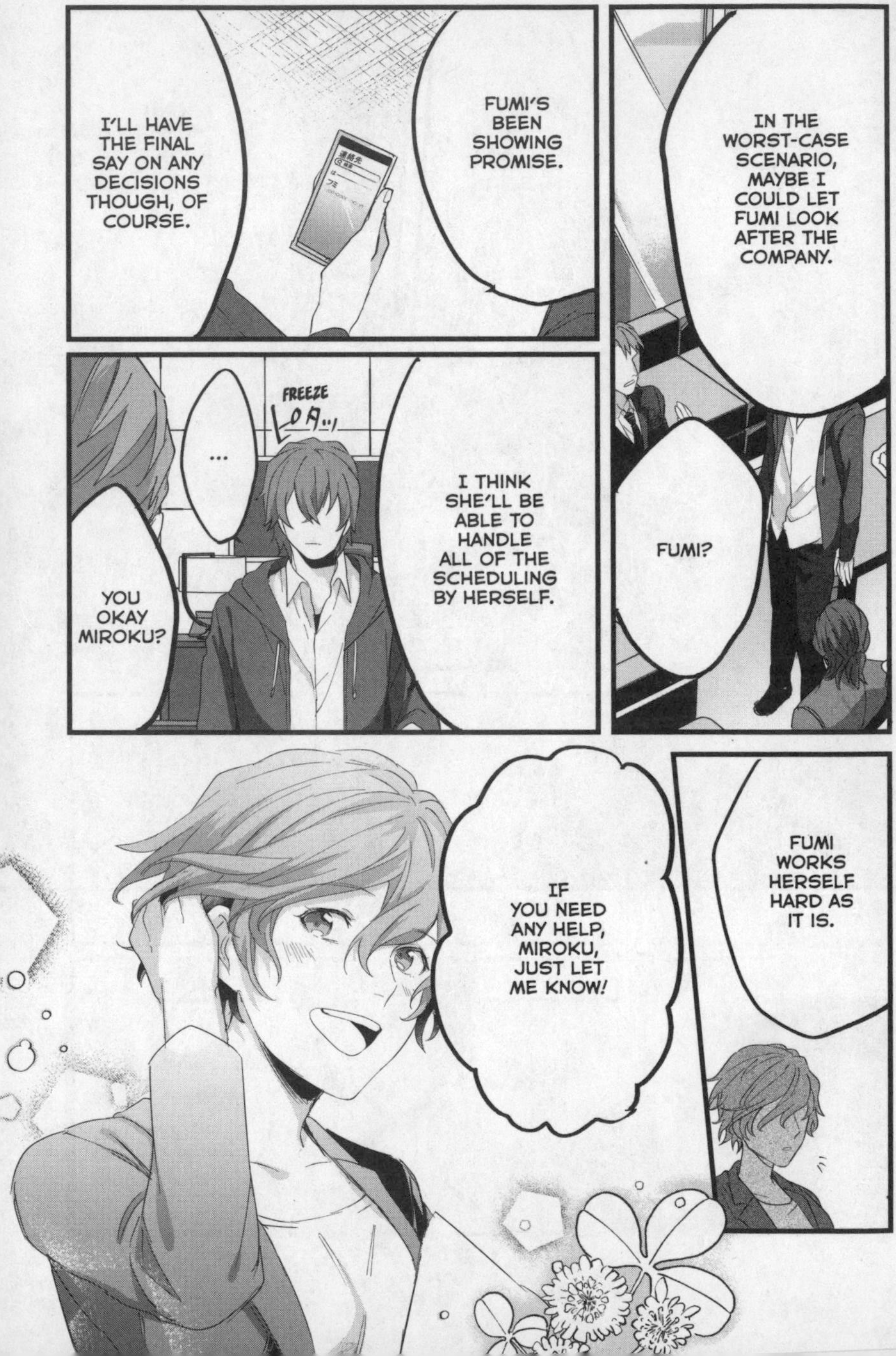
IN THE WORST-CASE SCENARIO, MAYBE I COULD LET FUMI LOOK AFTER THE COMPANY.
FUMI?
FUMI'S BEEN SHOWING PROMISE.
I'LL HAVE THE FINAL SAY ON ANY DECISIONS THOUGH, OF COURSE.
I THINK SHE'LL BE ABLE TO HANDLE ALL OF THE SCHEDULING BY HERSELF.
FREEZE
...
YOU OKAY MIROKU?
FUMI WORKS HERSELF HARD AS IT IS.
IF YOU NEED ANY HELP, MIROKU, JUST LET ME KNOW!

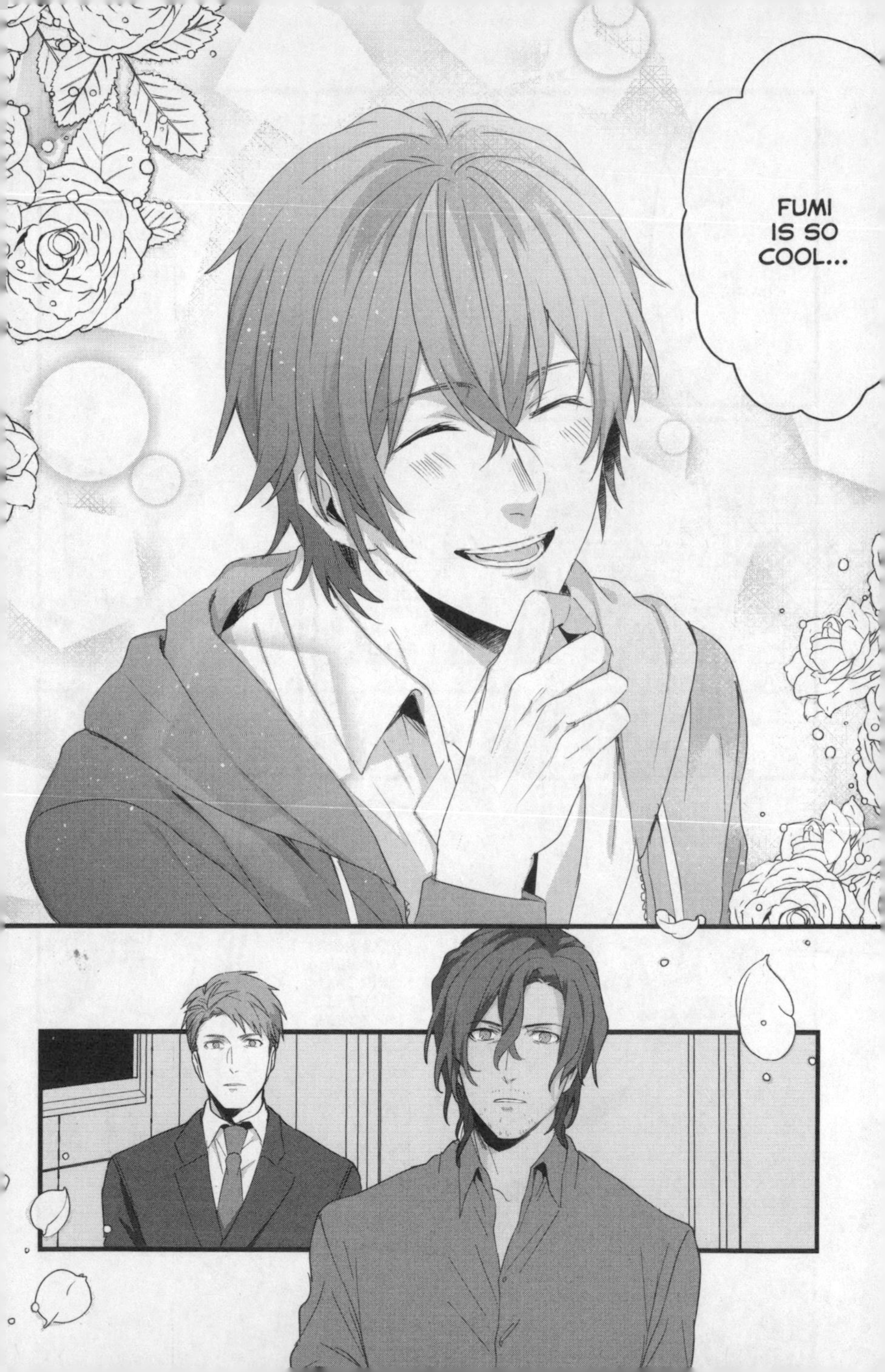
FUMI IS SO COOL...

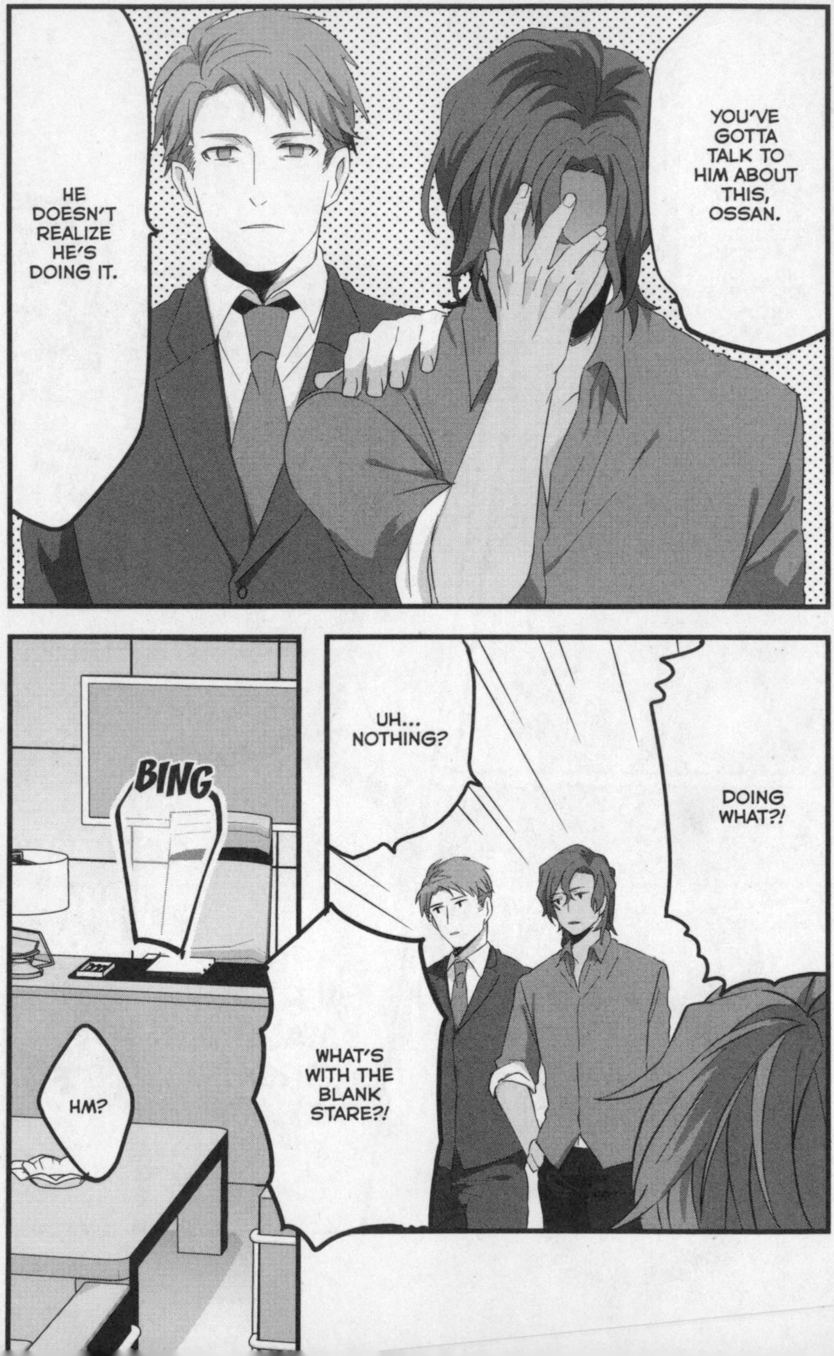
YOU'VE GOTTA TALK TO HIM ABOUT THIS, OSSAN.
HE DOESN'T REALIZE HE'S DOING IT.
DOING WHAT?!
UH... NOTHING?
WHAT'S WITH THE BLANK STARE?!
BING
HM?

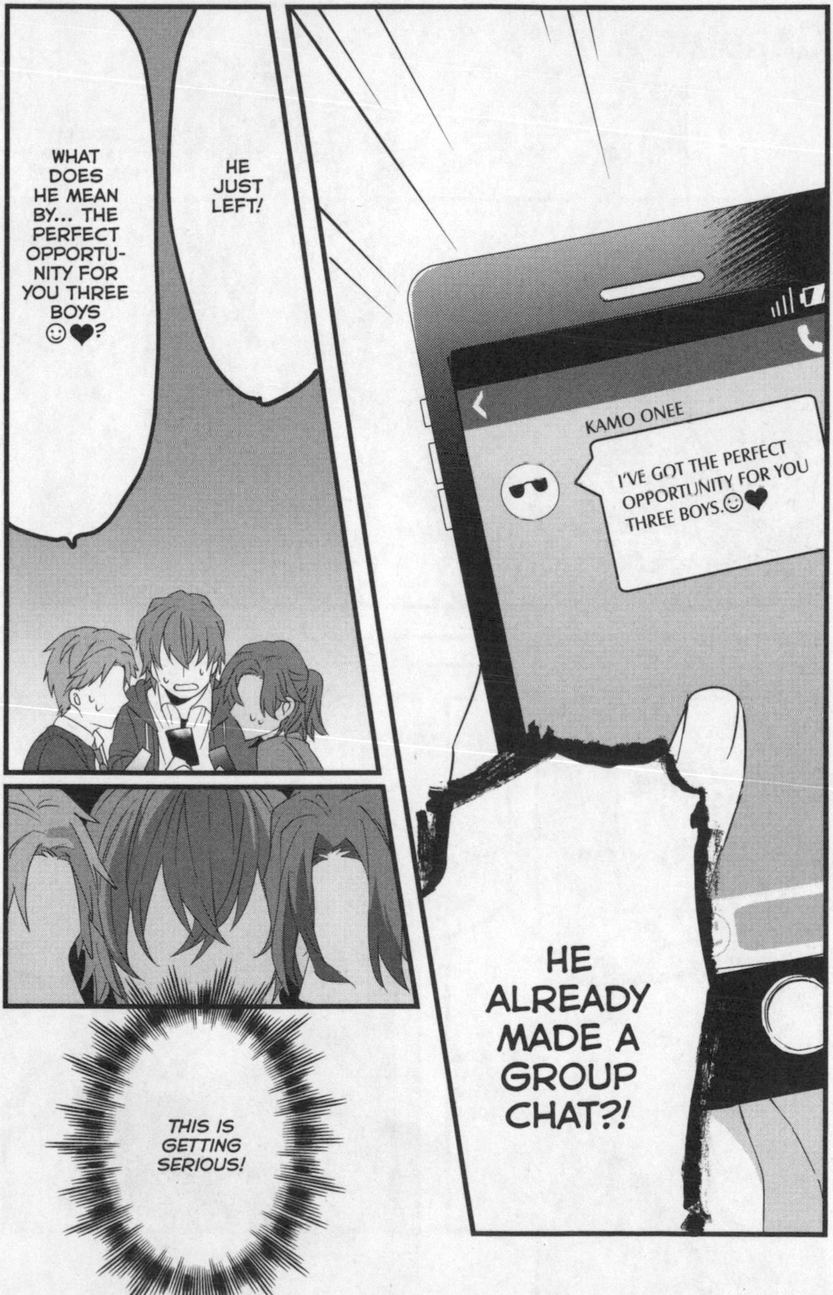
KAMO ONEE
I'VE GOT THE PERFECT OPPORTUNITY FOR YOU THREE BOYS.☺❤
HE ALREADY MADE A GROUP CHAT?!
HE JUST LEFT!
WHAT DOES HE MEAN BY... THE PERFECT OPPORTU-NITY FOR YOU THREE BOYS ☺❤?
THIS IS GETTING SERIOUS!

Chapter 7

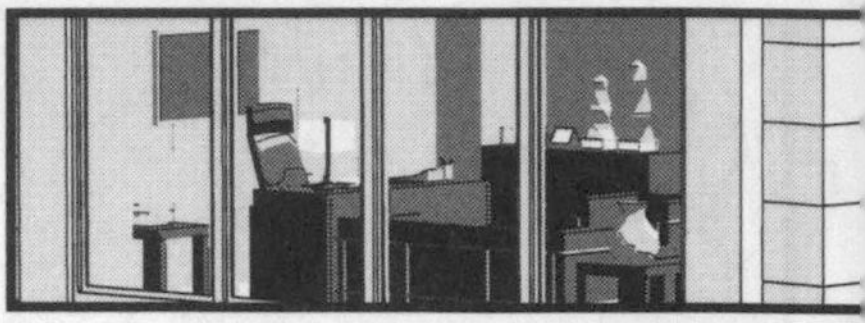

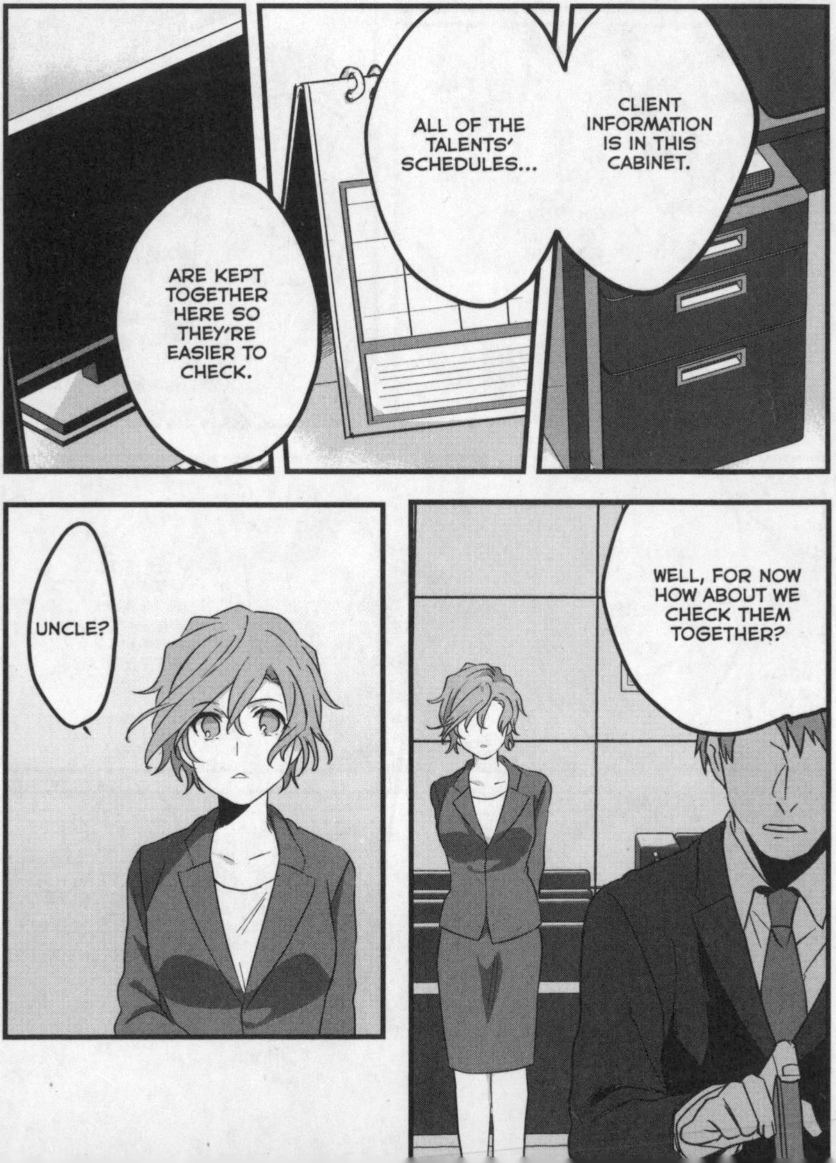
CLIENT INFORMATION IS IN THIS CABINET.
ALL OF THE TALENTS' SCHEDULES...
ARE KEPT TOGETHER HERE SO THEY'RE EASIER TO CHECK.
WELL, FOR NOW HOW ABOUT WE CHECK THEM TOGETHER?
UNCLE?

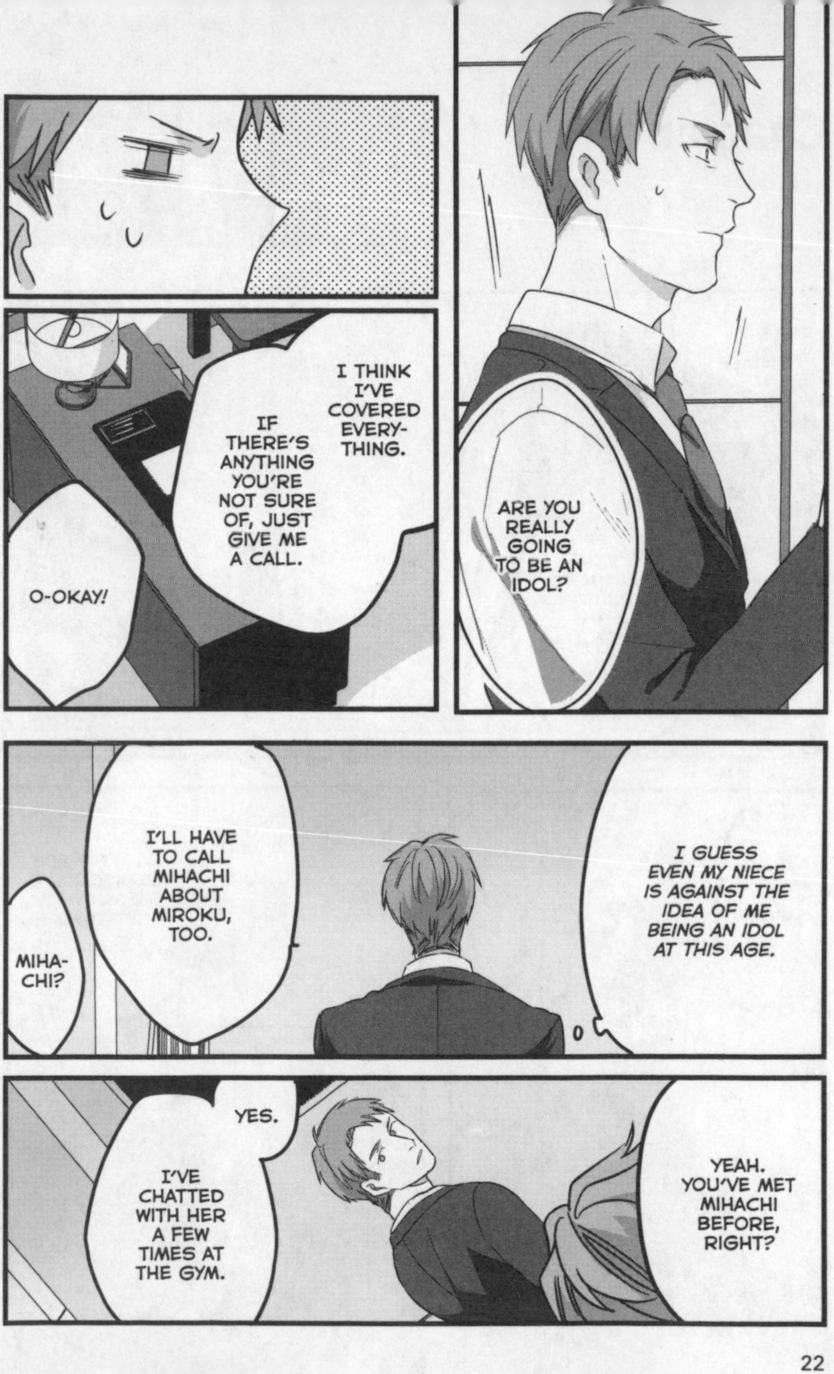
ARE YOU REALLY GOING TO BE AN IDOL?
I THINK I'VE COVERED EVERY-THING.
IF THERE'S ANYTHING YOU'RE NOT SURE OF, JUST GIVE ME A CALL.
O-OKAY!
I GUESS EVEN MY NIECE IS AGAINST THE IDEA OF ME BEING AN IDOL AT THIS AGE.
I'LL HAVE TO CALL MIHACHI ABOUT MIROKU, TOO.
MIHA-CHI?
YEAH. YOU'VE MET MIHACHI BEFORE, RIGHT?
YES.
I'VE CHATTED WITH HER A FEW TIMES AT THE GYM.

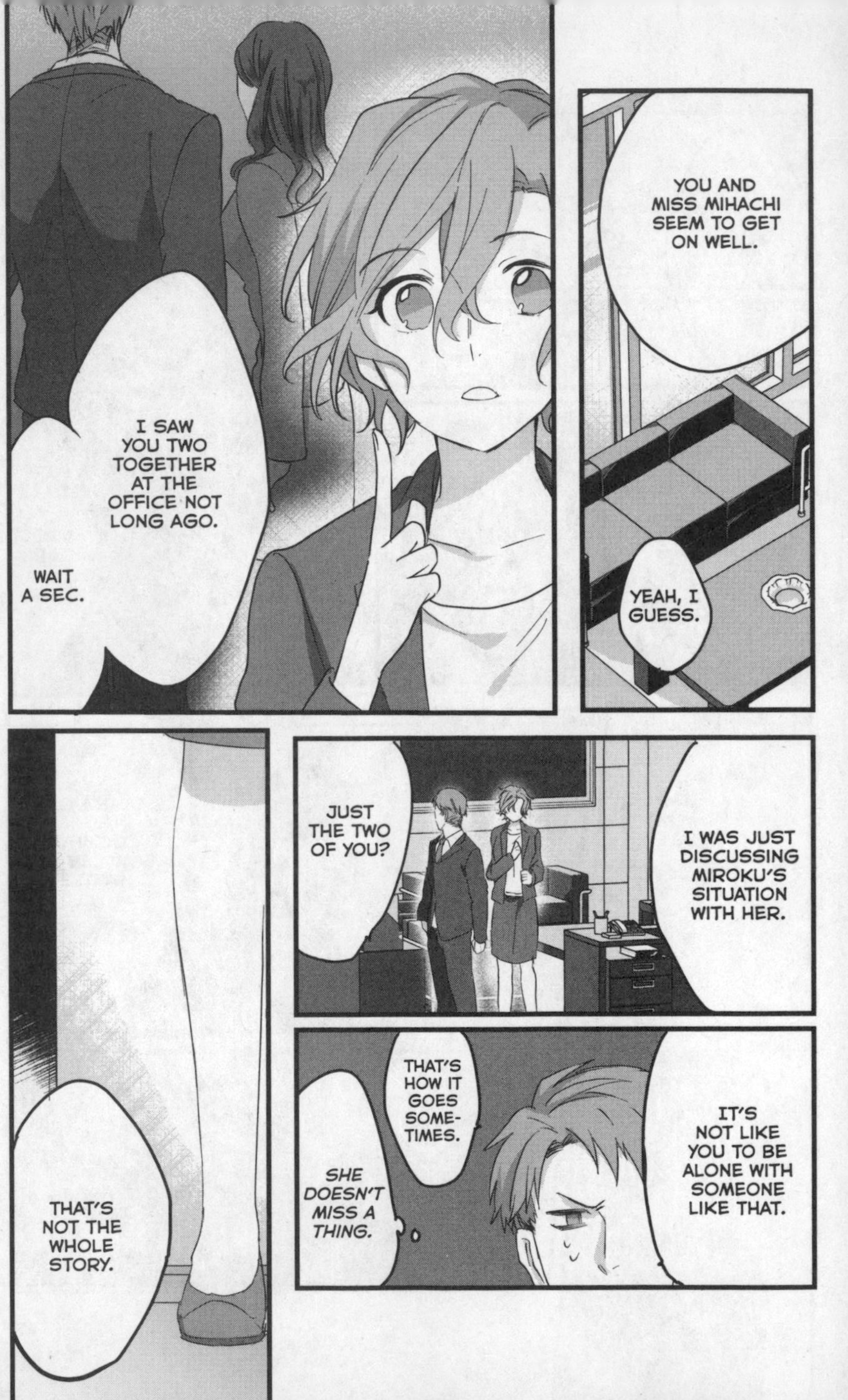
YOU AND MISS MIHACHI SEEM TO GET ON WELL.
YEAH, I GUESS.
I SAW YOU TWO TOGETHER AT THE OFFICE NOT LONG AGO.
WAIT A SEC.
I WAS JUST DISCUSSING MIROKU'S SITUATION WITH HER.
JUST THE TWO OF YOU?
IT'S NOT LIKE YOU TO BE ALONE WITH SOMEONE LIKE THAT.
THAT'S HOW IT GOES SOMETIMES.
SHE DOESN'T MISS A THING.
THAT'S NOT THE WHOLE STORY.

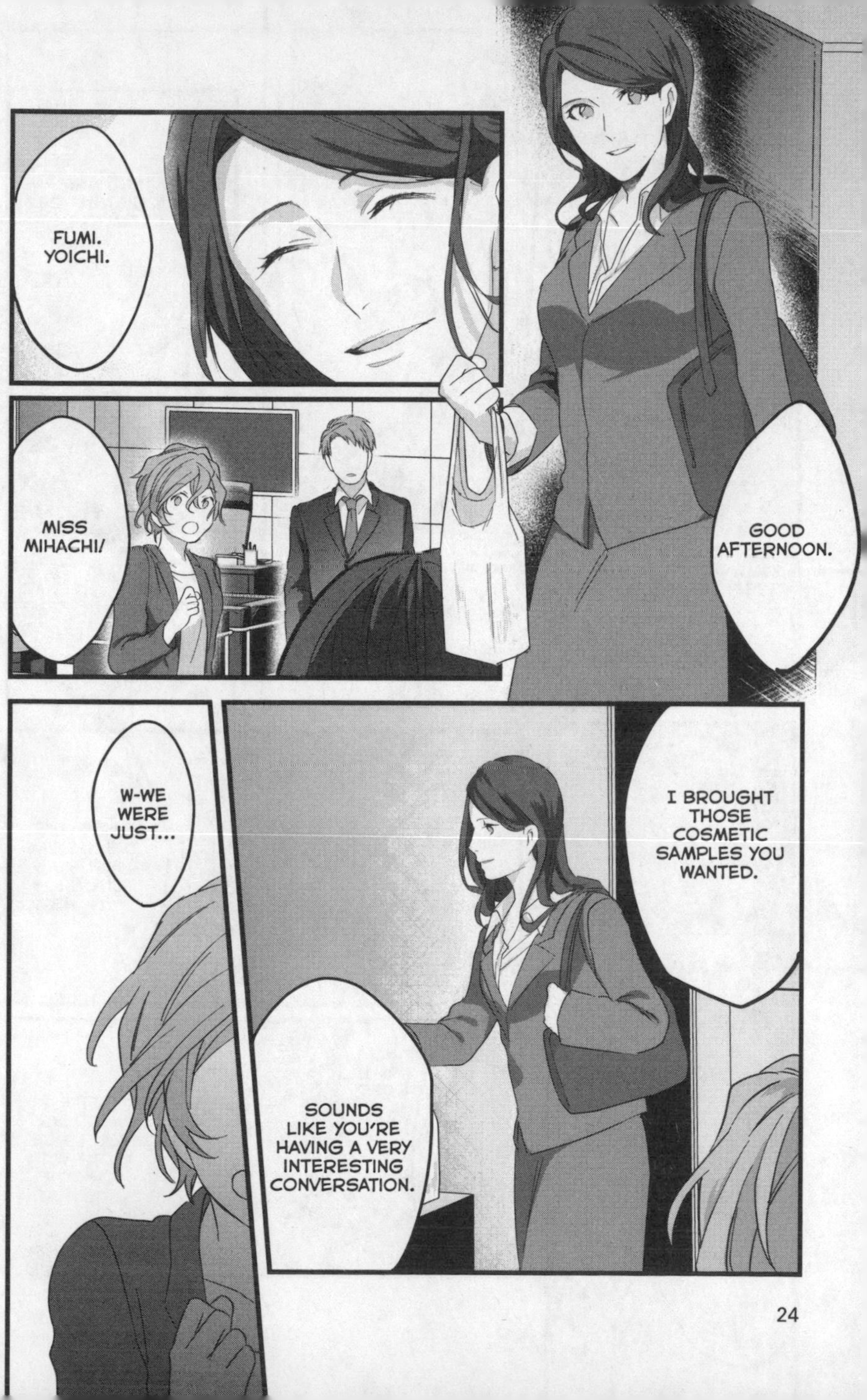
GOOD AFTERNOON.
FUMI. YOICHI.
MISS MIHACHI!
I BROUGHT THOSE COSMETIC SAMPLES YOU WANTED.
SOUNDS LIKE YOU'RE HAVING A VERY INTERESTING CONVERSATION.
W-WE WERE JUST...

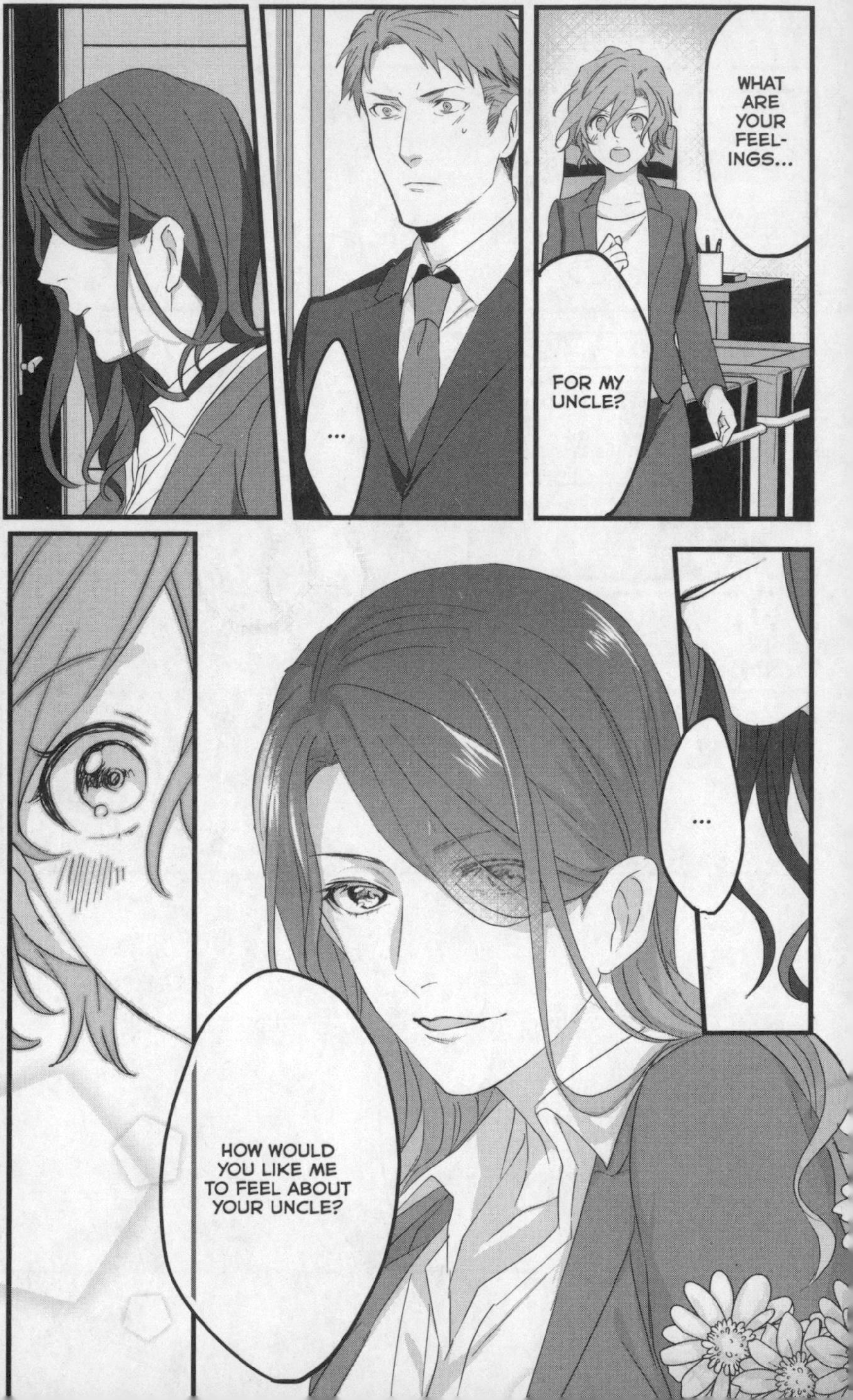
WHAT ARE YOUR FEEL- INGS...
FOR MY UNCLE?
...
...
HOW WOULD YOU LIKE ME TO FEEL ABOUT YOUR UNCLE?

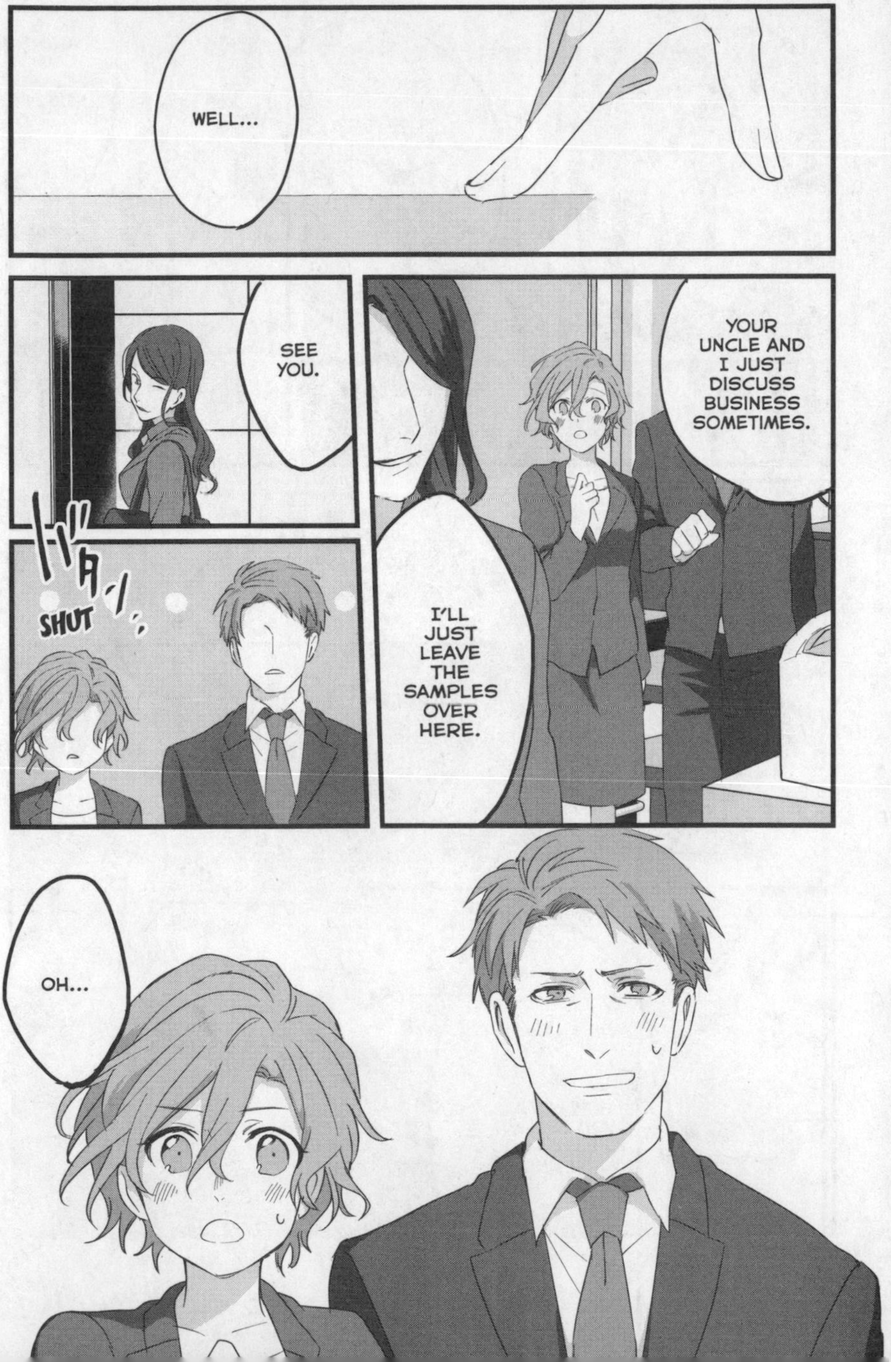
WELL...
YOUR UNCLE AND I JUST DISCUSS BUSINESS SOMETIMES.
I'LL JUST LEAVE THE SAMPLES OVER HERE.
SEE YOU.
SHUT
OH...

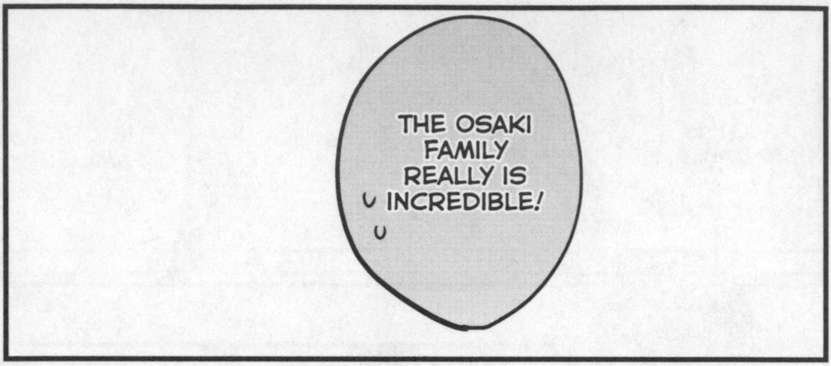
THE OSAKI FAMILY REALLY IS INCREDIBLE!

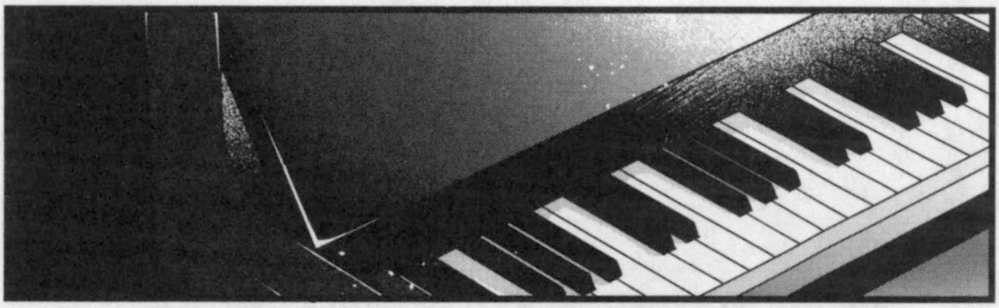

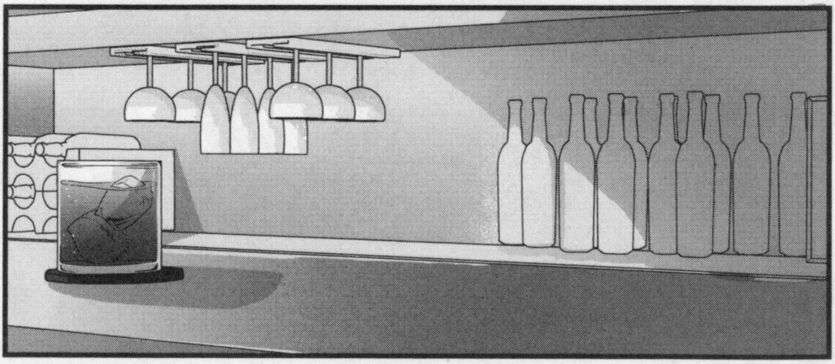

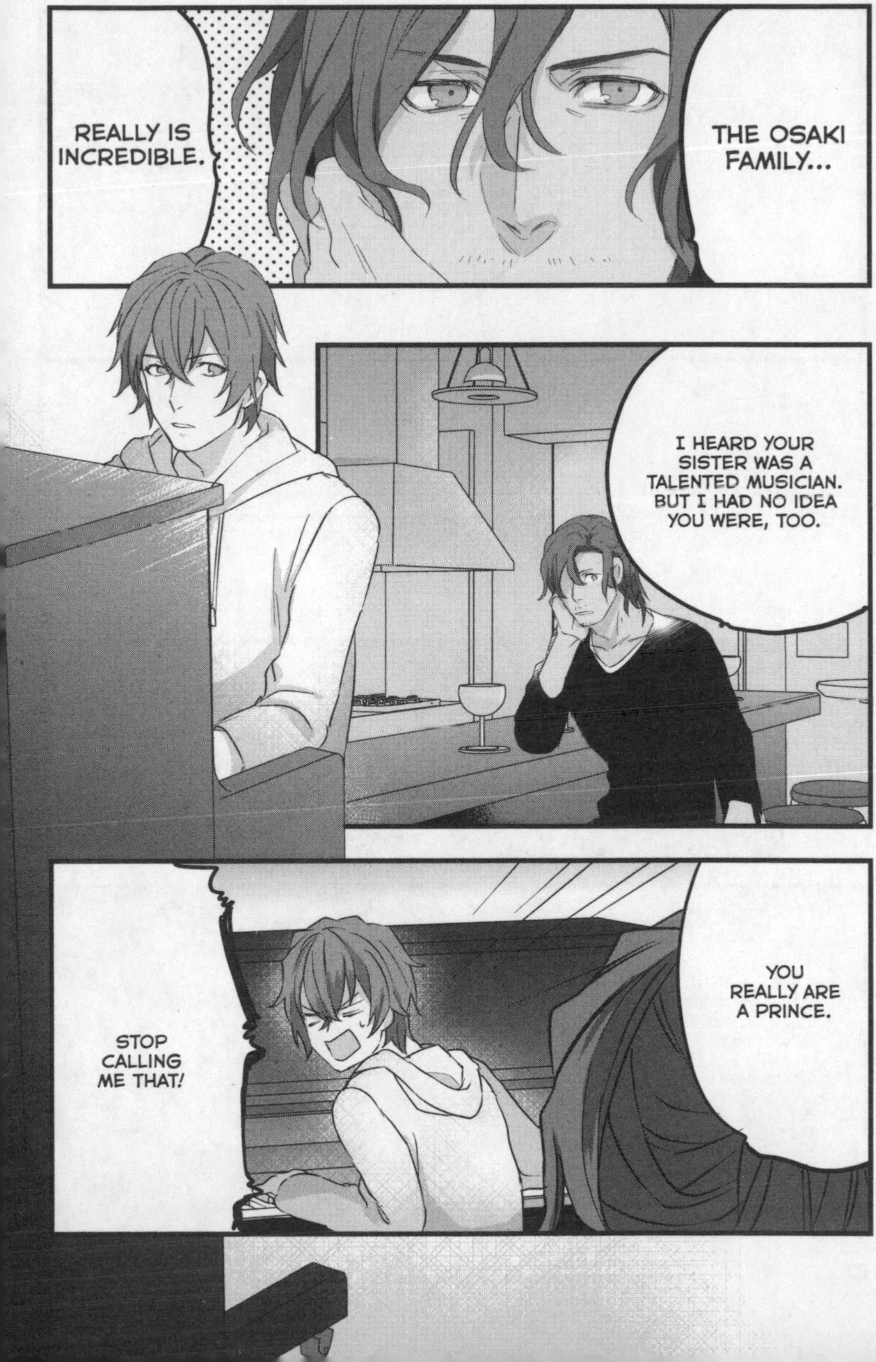
THE OSAKI FAMILY...
REALLY IS INCREDIBLE.
I HEARD YOUR SISTER WAS A TALENTED MUSICIAN. BUT I HAD NO IDEA YOU WERE, TOO.
YOU REALLY ARE A PRINCE.
STOP CALLING ME THAT!

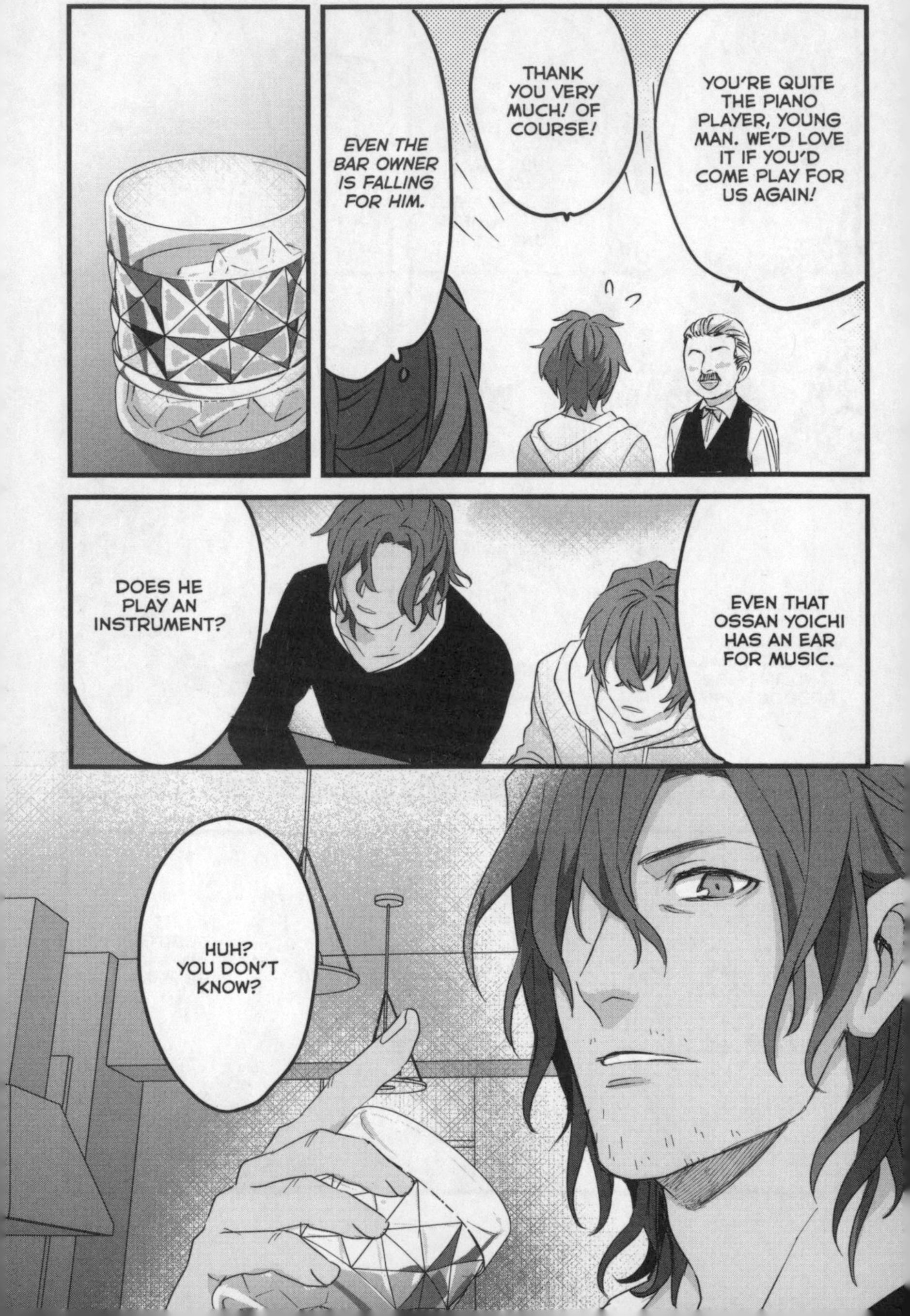
YOU'RE QUITE THE PIANO PLAYER, YOUNG MAN. WE'D LOVE IT IF YOU'D COME PLAY FOR US AGAIN!
THANK YOU VERY MUCH! OF COURSE!
EVEN THE BAR OWNER IS FALLING FOR HIM.
EVEN THAT OSSAN YOICHI HAS AN EAR FOR MUSIC.
DOES HE PLAY AN INSTRUMENT?
HUH? YOU DON'T KNOW?

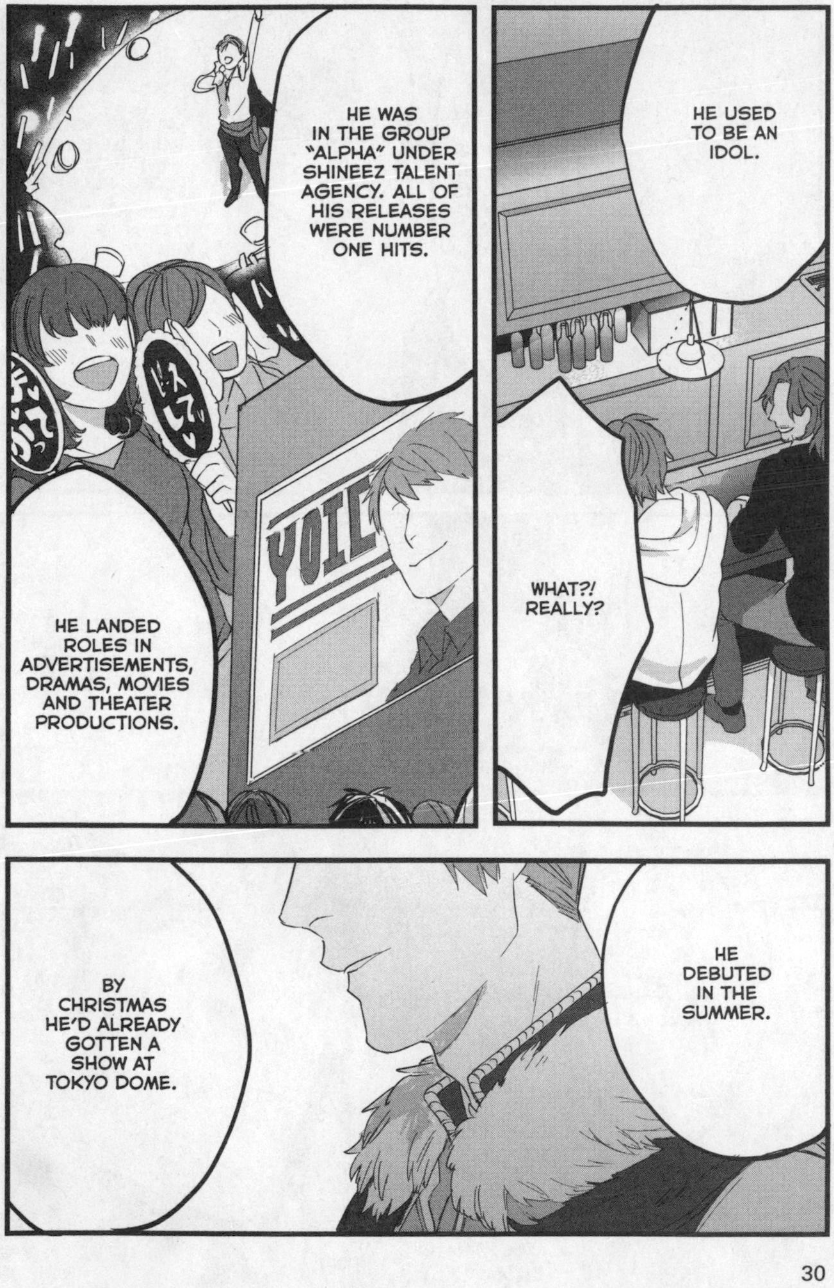
HE USED TO BE AN IDOL.
WHAT?! REALLY?
HE WAS IN THE GROUP "ALPHA" UNDER SHINEEZ TALENT AGENCY. ALL OF HIS RELEASES WERE NUMBER ONE HITS.
HE LANDED ROLES IN ADVERTISEMENTS, DRAMAS, MOVIES AND THEATER PRODUCTIONS.
HE DEBUTED IN THE SUMMER.
BY CHRISTMAS HE'D ALREADY GOTTEN A SHOW AT TOKYO DOME.

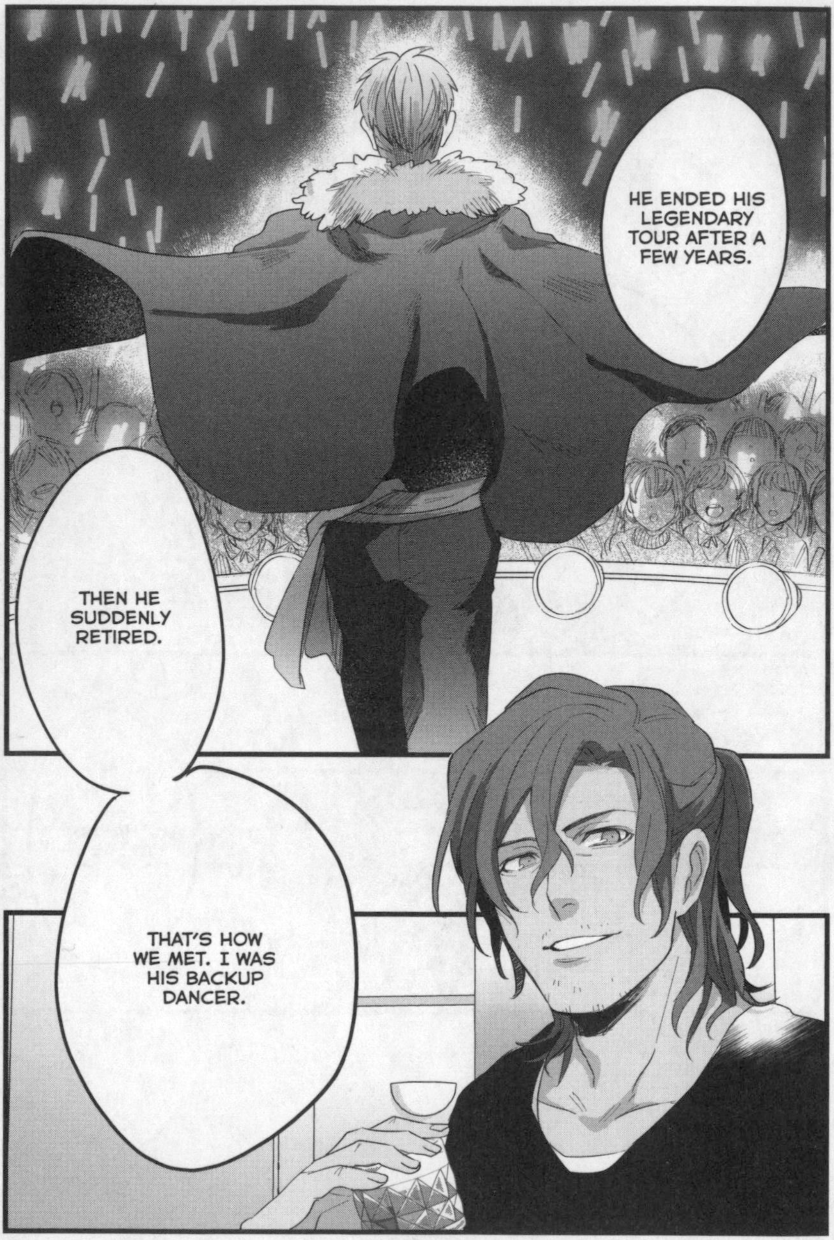
HE ENDED HIS LEGENDARY TOUR AFTER A FEW YEARS.
THEN HE SUDDENLY RETIRED.
THAT'S HOW WE MET. I WAS HIS BACKUP DANCER.

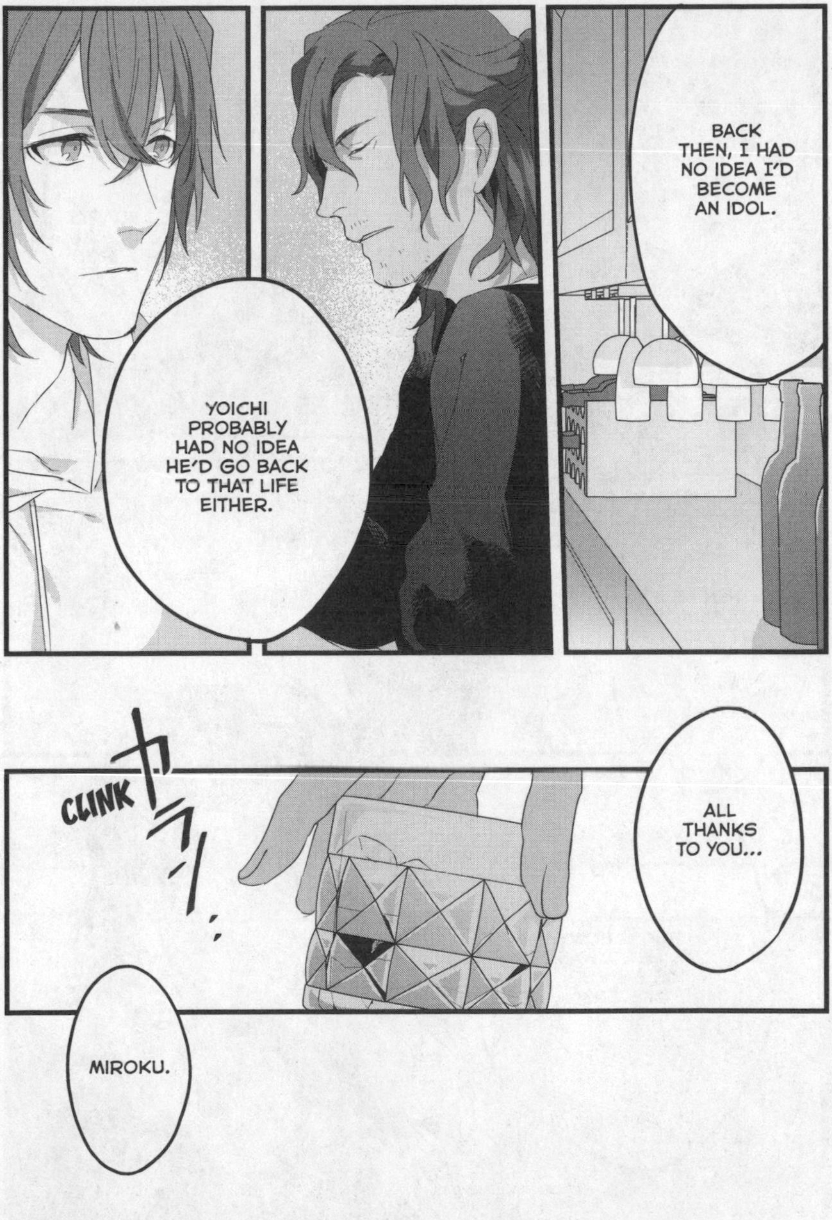
BACK THEN, I HAD NO IDEA I'D BECOME AN IDOL.
YOICHI PROBABLY HAD NO IDEA HE'D GO BACK TO THAT LIFE EITHER.
ALL THANKS TO YOU...
CLINK
MIROKU.

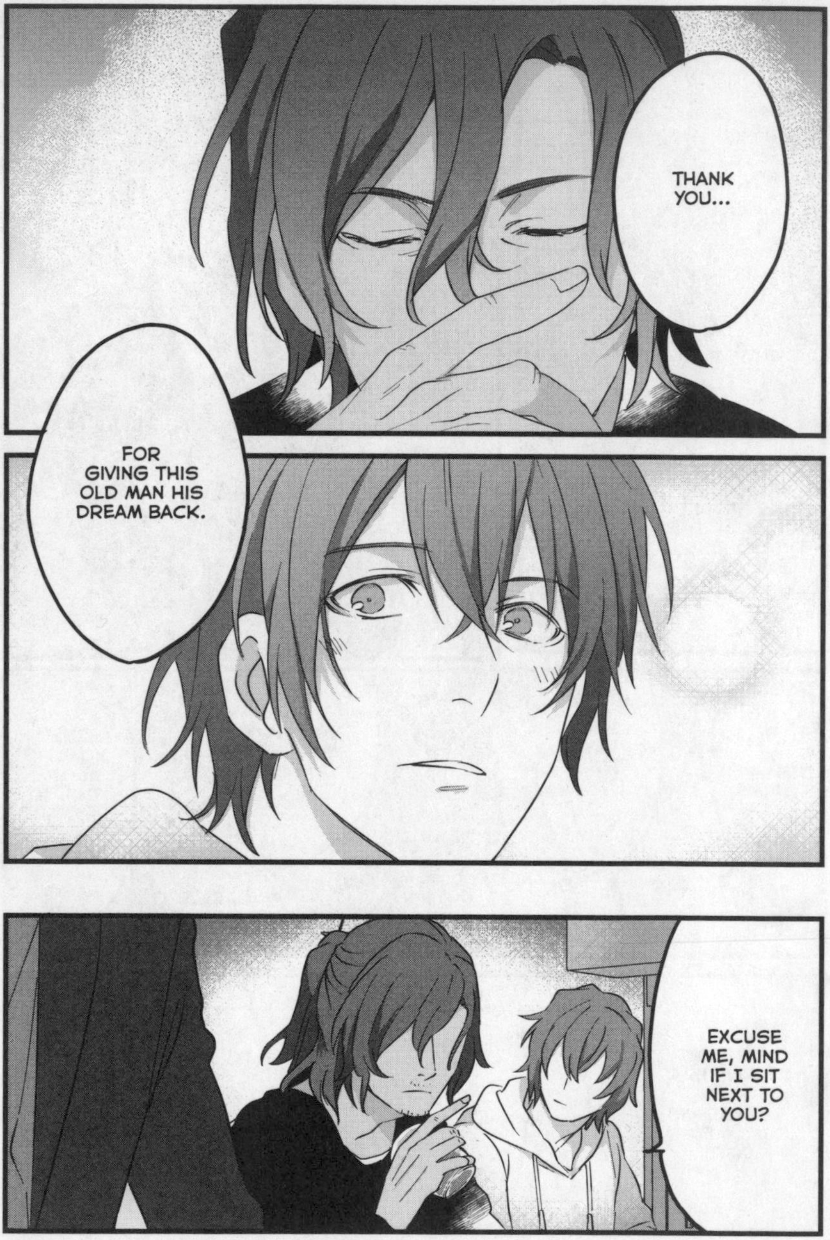
THANK YOU...
FOR GIVING THIS OLD MAN HIS DREAM BACK.
EXCUSE ME, MIND IF I SIT NEXT TO YOU?

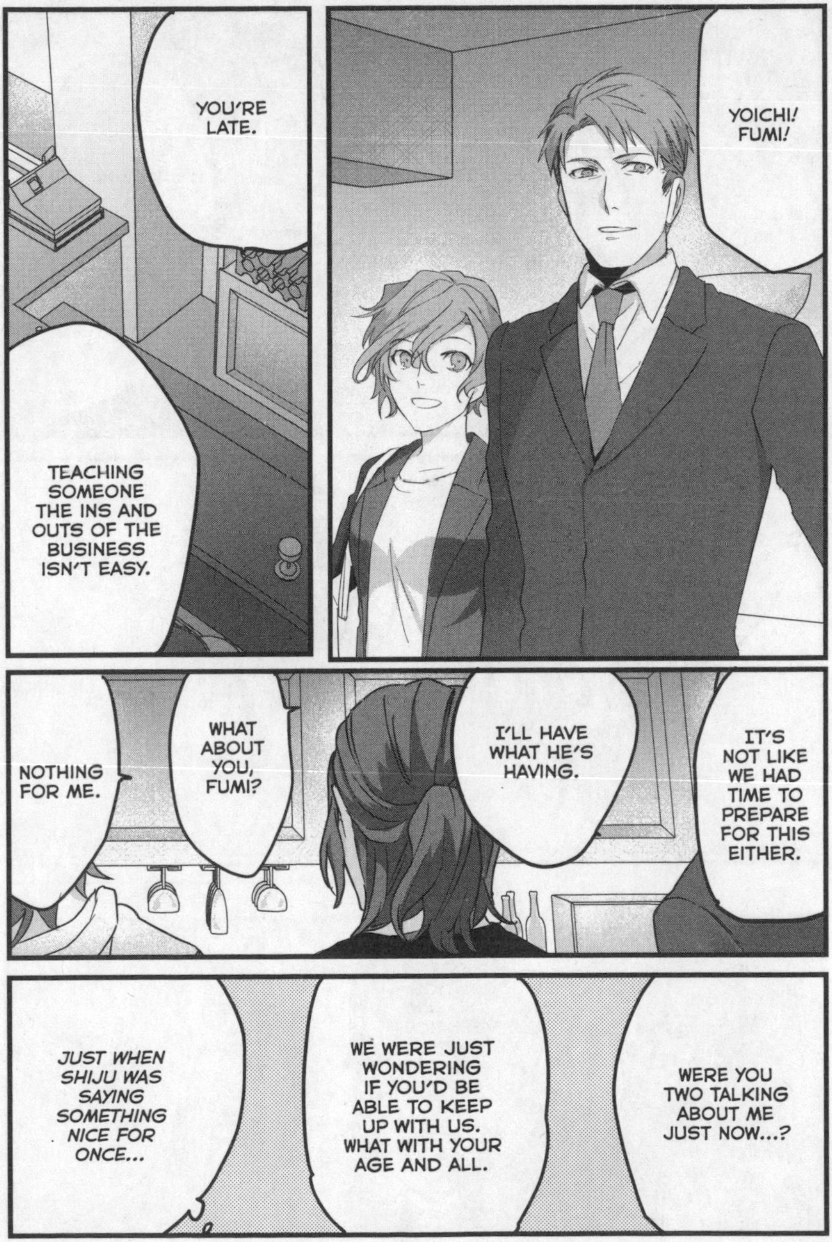
YOICHI! FUMI!
YOU'RE LATE.
TEACHING SOMEONE THE INS AND OUTS OF THE BUSINESS ISN'T EASY.
IT'S NOT LIKE WE HAD TIME TO PREPARE FOR THIS EITHER.
I'LL HAVE WHAT HE'S HAVING.
WHAT ABOUT YOU, FUMI?
NOTHING FOR ME.
WERE YOU TWO TALKING ABOUT ME JUST NOW...?
WE WERE JUST WONDERING IF YOU'D BE ABLE TO KEEP UP WITH US. WHAT WITH YOUR AGE AND ALL.
JUST WHEN SHIJU WAS SAYING SOMETHING NICE FOR ONCE...

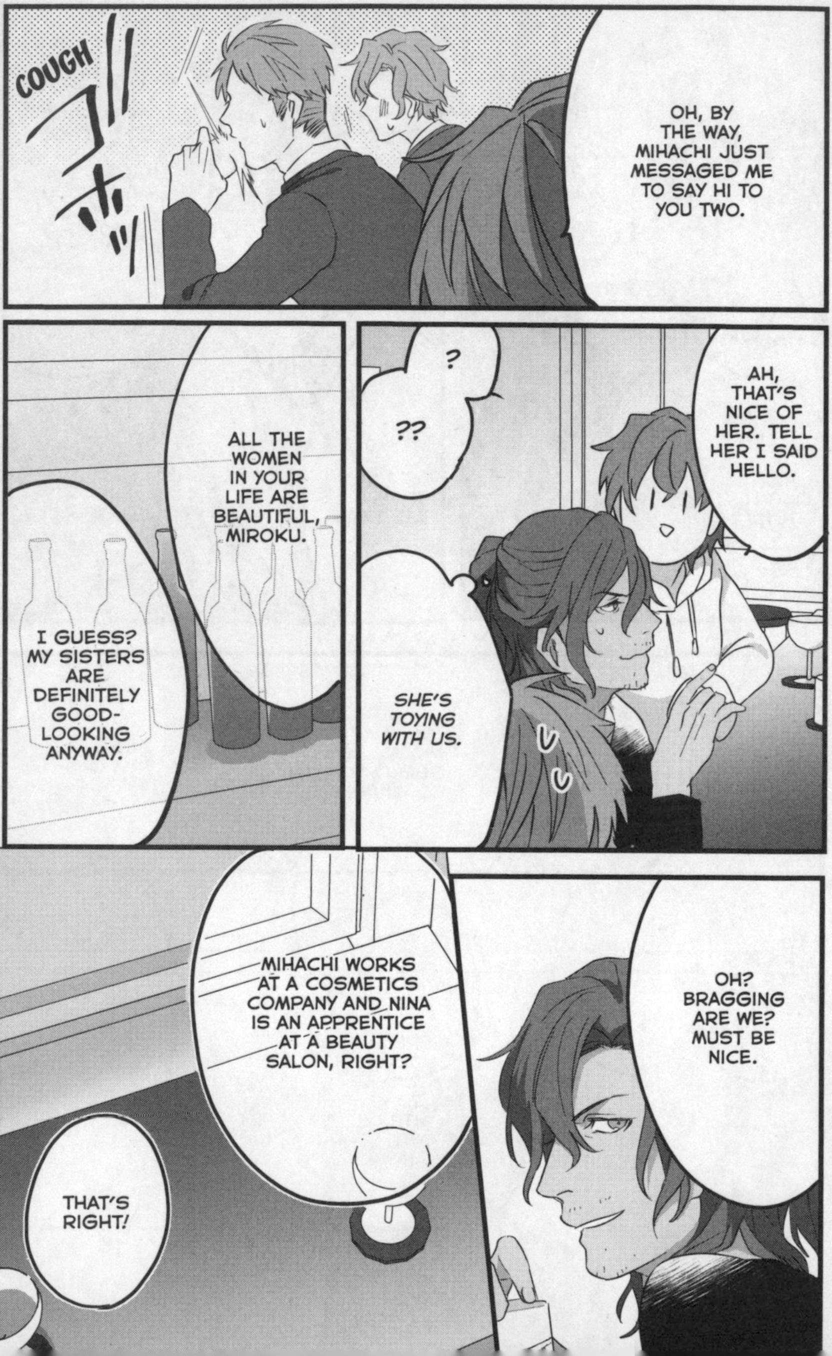
OH, BY THE WAY, MIHACHI JUST MESSAGED ME TO SAY HI TO YOU TWO.
COUGH
AH, THAT'S NICE OF HER. TELL HER I SAID HELLO.
?
??
SHE'S TOYING WITH US.
ALL THE WOMEN IN YOUR LIFE ARE BEAUTIFUL, MIROKU.
I GUESS? MY SISTERS ARE DEFINITELY GOOD-LOOKING ANYWAY.
OH? BRAGGING ARE WE? MUST BE NICE.
MIHACHI WORKS AT A COSMETICS COMPANY AND NINA IS AN APPRENTICE AT A BEAUTY SALON, RIGHT?
THAT'S RIGHT!

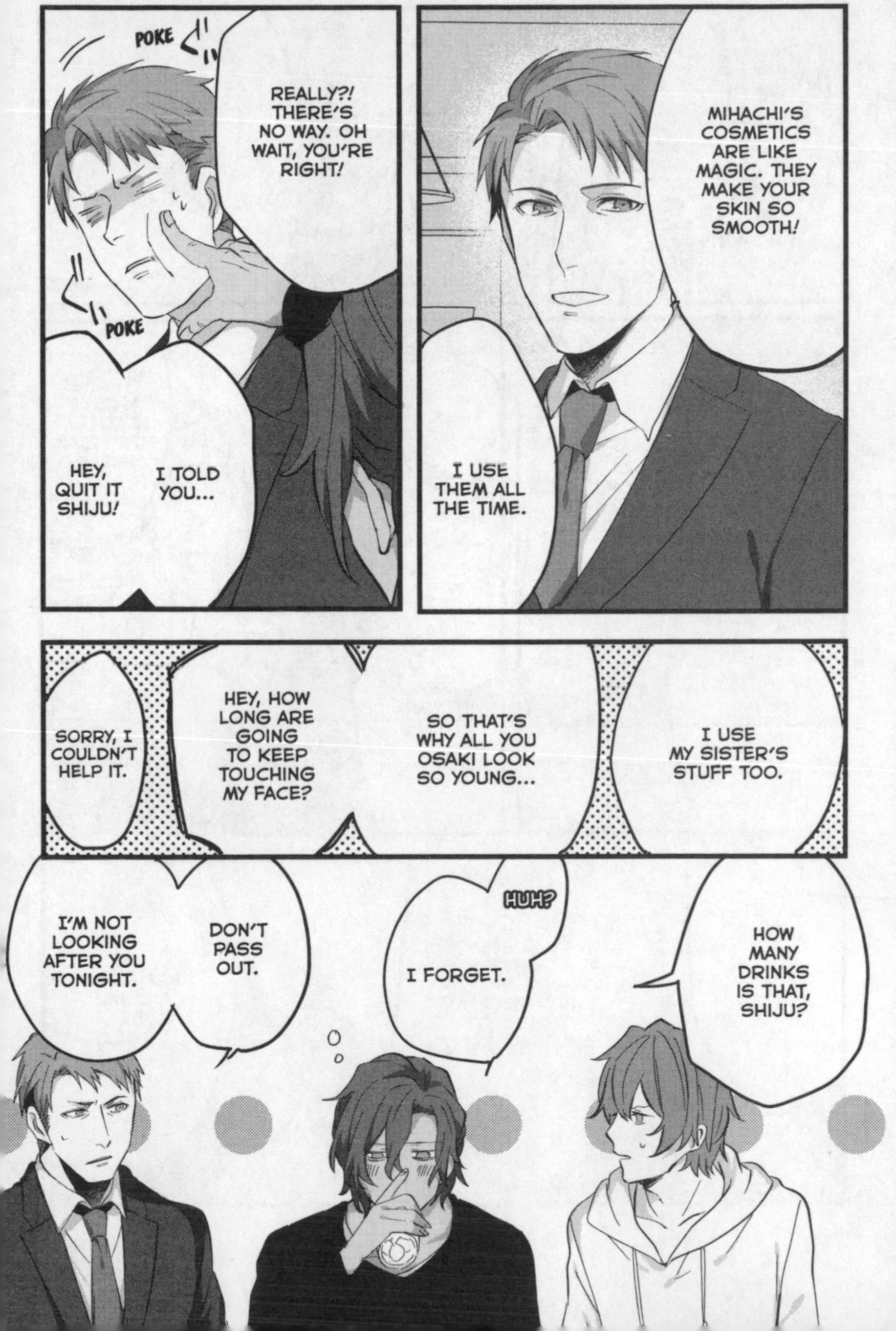
MIHACHI'S COSMETICS ARE LIKE MAGIC. THEY MAKE YOUR SKIN SO SMOOTH!
I USE THEM ALL THE TIME.
POKE
REALLY?! THERE'S NO WAY. OH WAIT, YOU'RE RIGHT!
POKE
I TOLD YOU...
HEY, QUIT IT SHIJU!
I USE MY SISTER'S STUFF TOO.
SO THAT'S WHY ALL YOU OSAKI LOOK SO YOUNG...
HEY, HOW LONG ARE GOING TO KEEP TOUCHING MY FACE?
SORRY, I COULDN'T HELP IT.
HOW MANY DRINKS IS THAT, SHIJU?
HUH?
I FORGET.
DON'T PASS OUT.
I'M NOT LOOKING AFTER YOU TONIGHT.

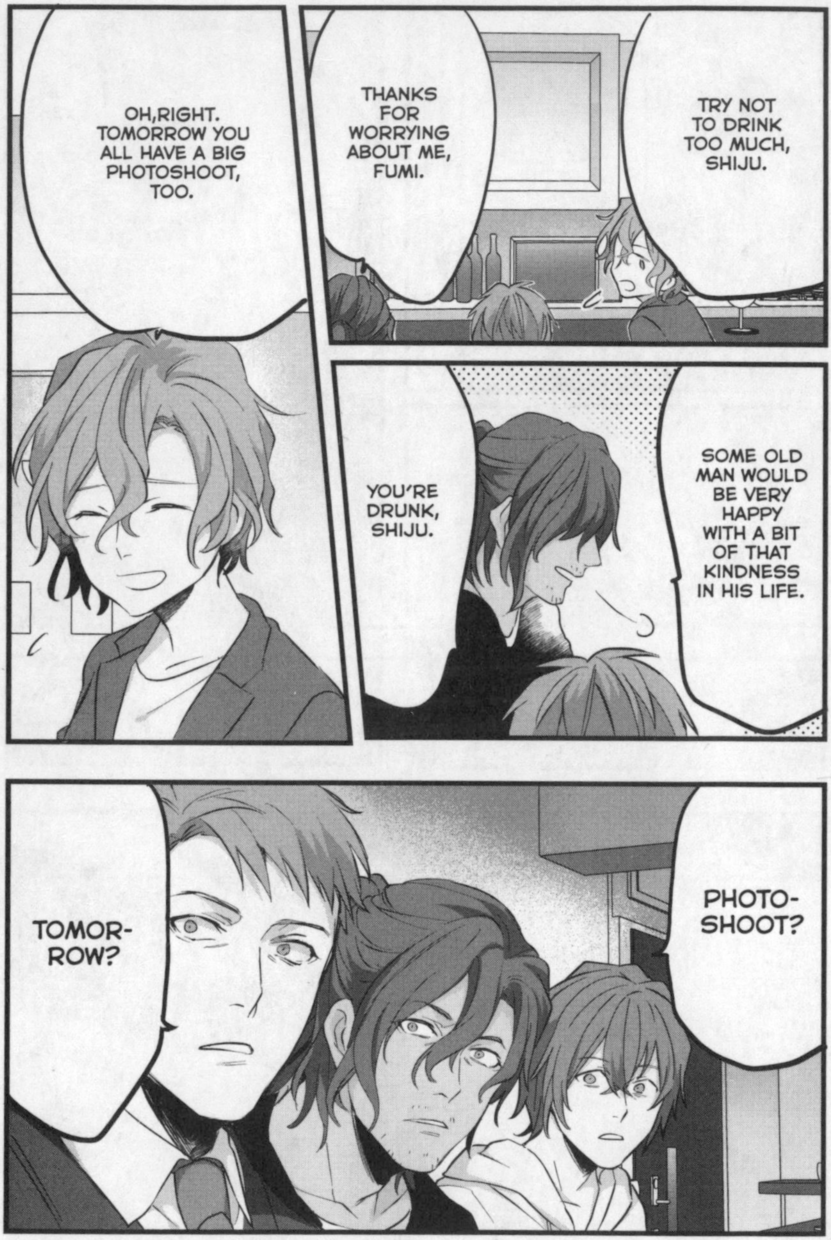
TRY NOT TO DRINK TOO MUCH, SHIJU.
THANKS FOR WORRYING ABOUT ME, FUMI.
SOME OLD MAN WOULD BE VERY HAPPY WITH A BIT OF THAT KINDNESS IN HIS LIFE.
YOU'RE DRUNK, SHIJU.
OH,RIGHT. TOMORROW YOU ALL HAVE A BIG PHOTOSHOOT, TOO.
PHOTO-SHOOT?
TOMOR-ROW?

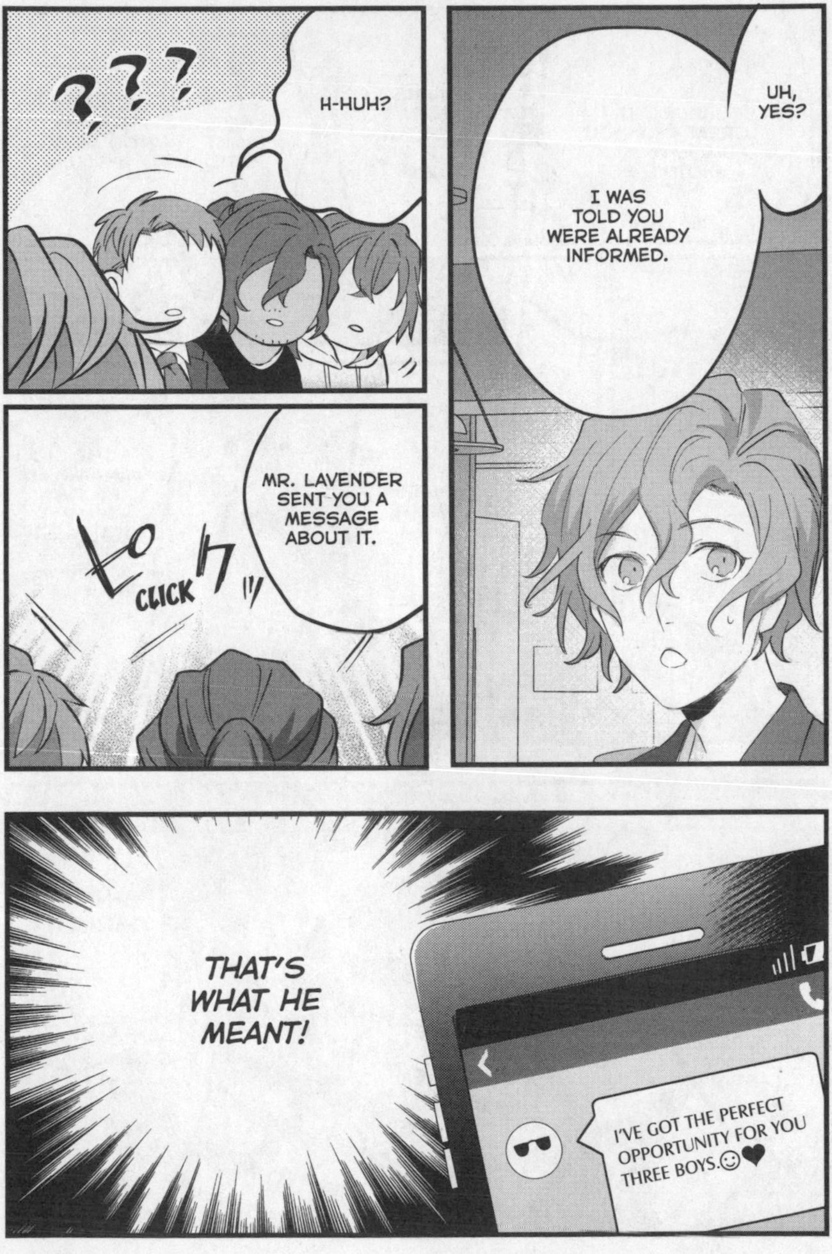
UH, YES?
I WAS TOLD YOU WERE ALREADY INFORMED.
???
H-HUH?
MR. LAVENDER SENT YOU A MESSAGE ABOUT IT.
CLICK
I'VE GOT THE PERFECT OPPORTUNITY FOR YOU THREE BOYS.☺❤
THAT'S WHAT HE MEANT!

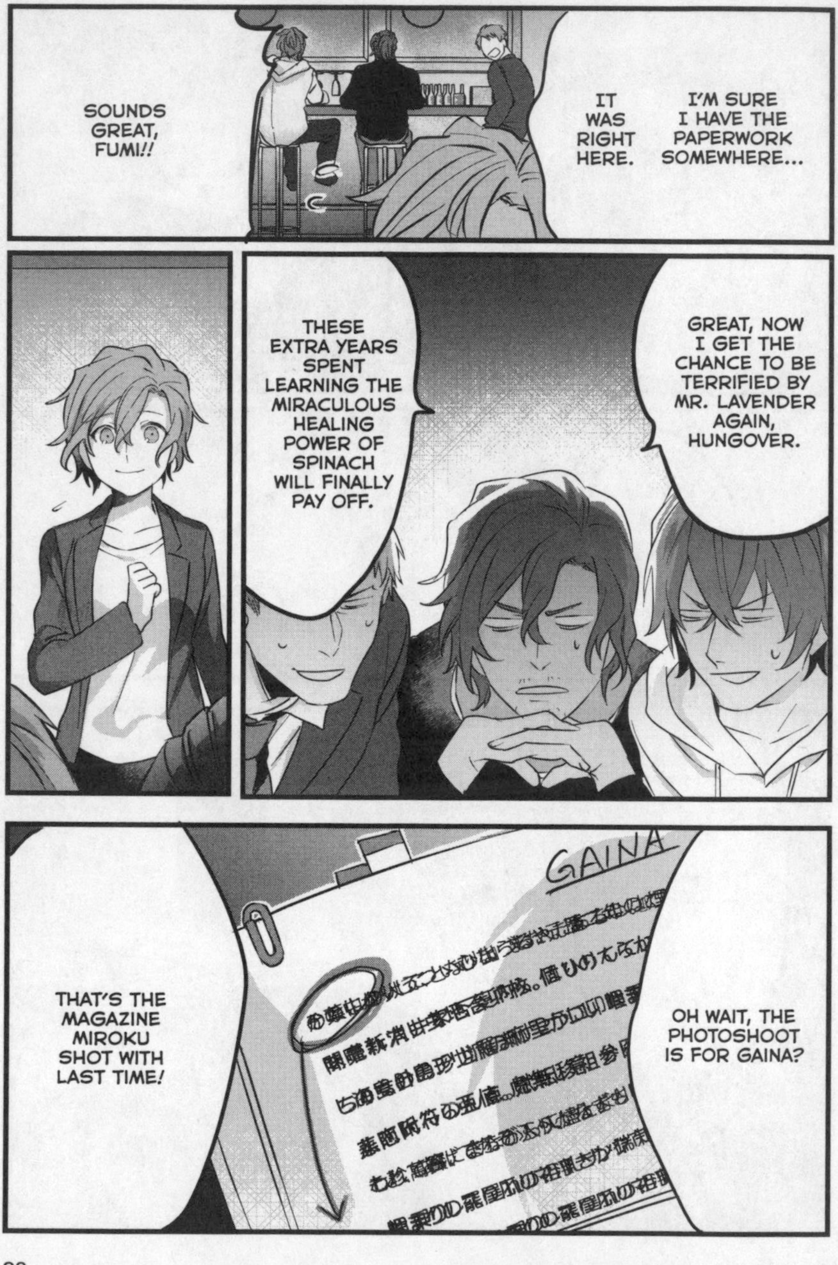
I'M SURE I HAVE THE PAPERWORK SOMEWHERE...
IT WAS RIGHT HERE.
SOUNDS GREAT, FUMI!!
GREAT, NOW I GET THE CHANCE TO BE TERRIFIED BY MR. LAVENDER AGAIN, HUNGOVER.
THESE EXTRA YEARS SPENT LEARNING THE MIRACULOUS HEALING POWER OF SPINACH WILL FINALLY PAY OFF.
OH WAIT, THE PHOTOSHOOT IS FOR GAINA?
GAINA
THAT'S THE MAGAZINE MIROKU SHOT WITH LAST TIME!

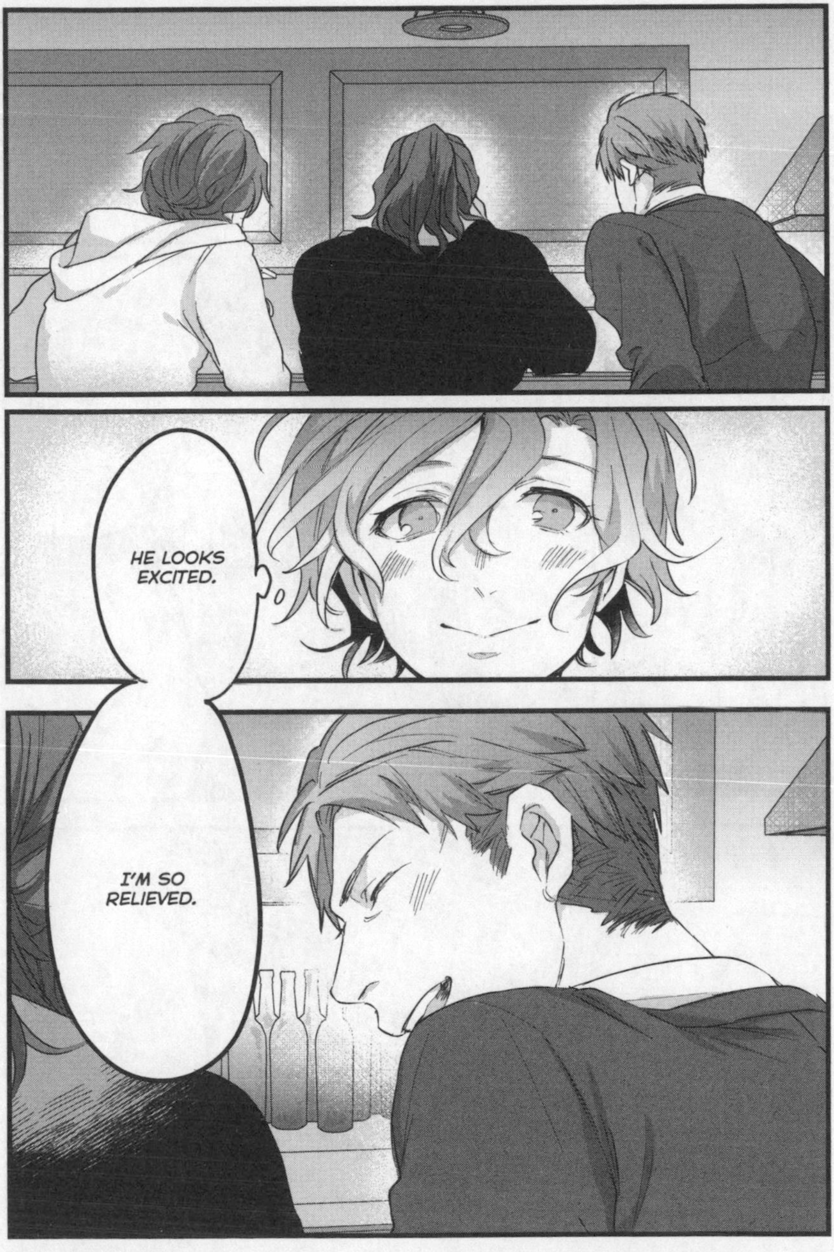
HE LOOKS EXCITED.
I'M SO RELIEVED.

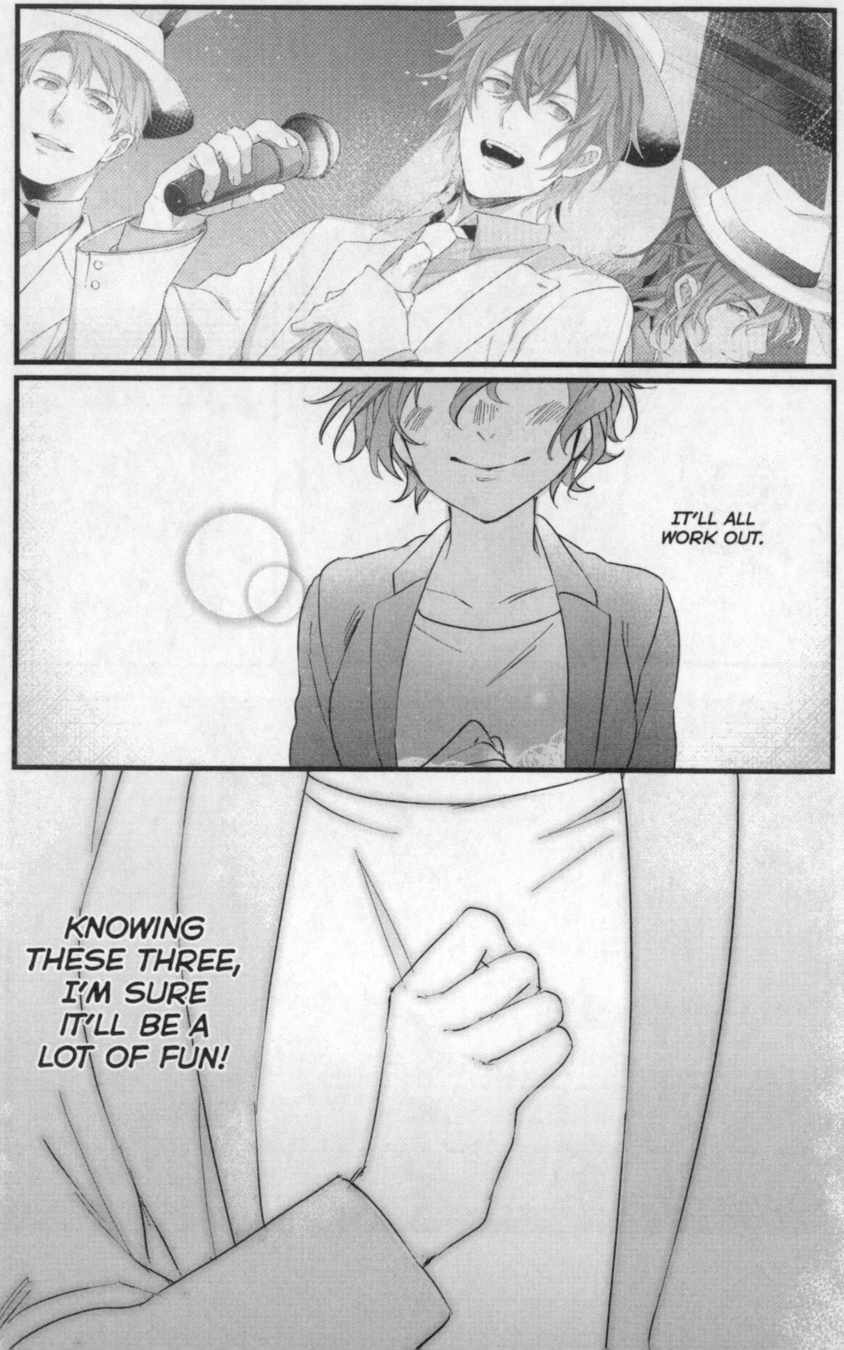
IT'LL ALL WORK OUT.
KNOWING THESE THREE, I'M SURE IT'LL BE A LOT OF FUN!

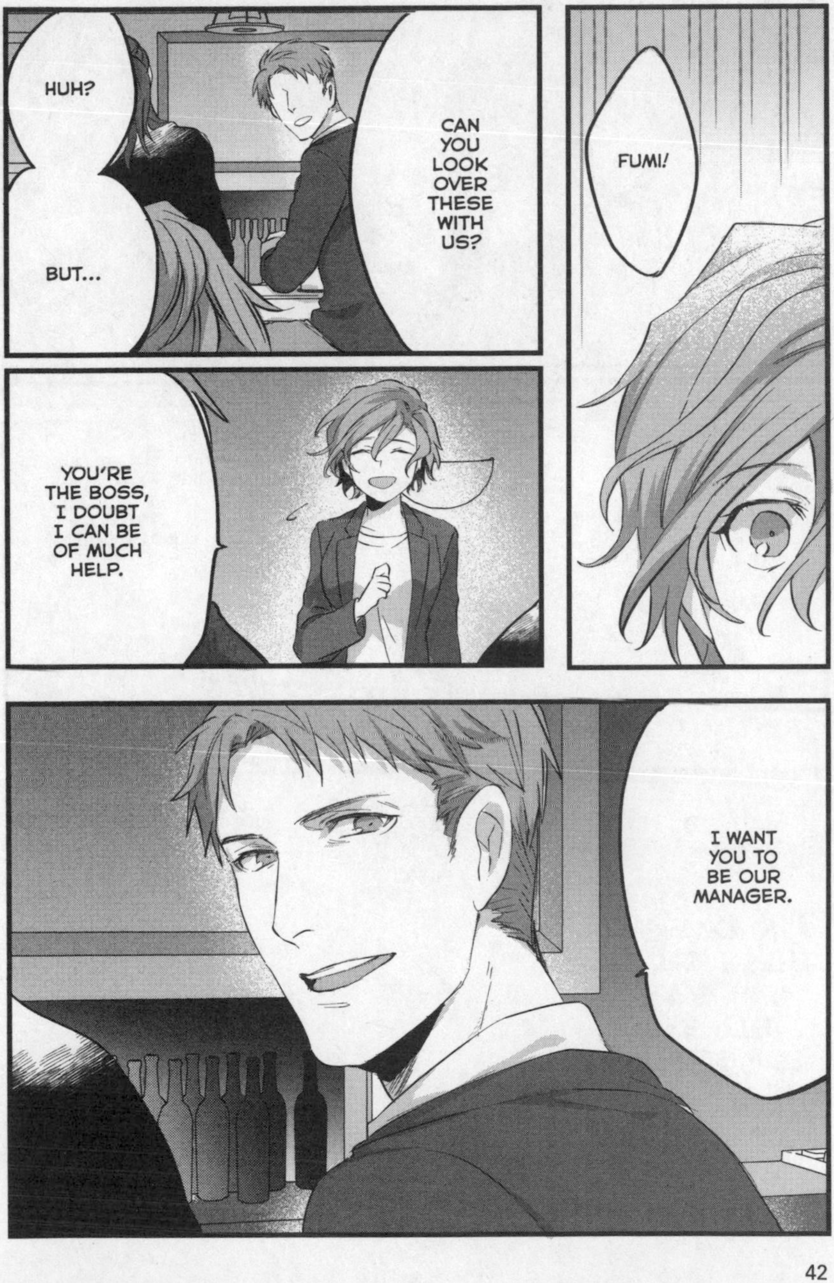
FUMI!
CAN YOU LOOK OVER THESE WITH US?
HUH?
BUT...
YOU'RE THE BOSS, I DOUBT I CAN BE OF MUCH HELP.
I WANT YOU TO BE OUR MANAGER.

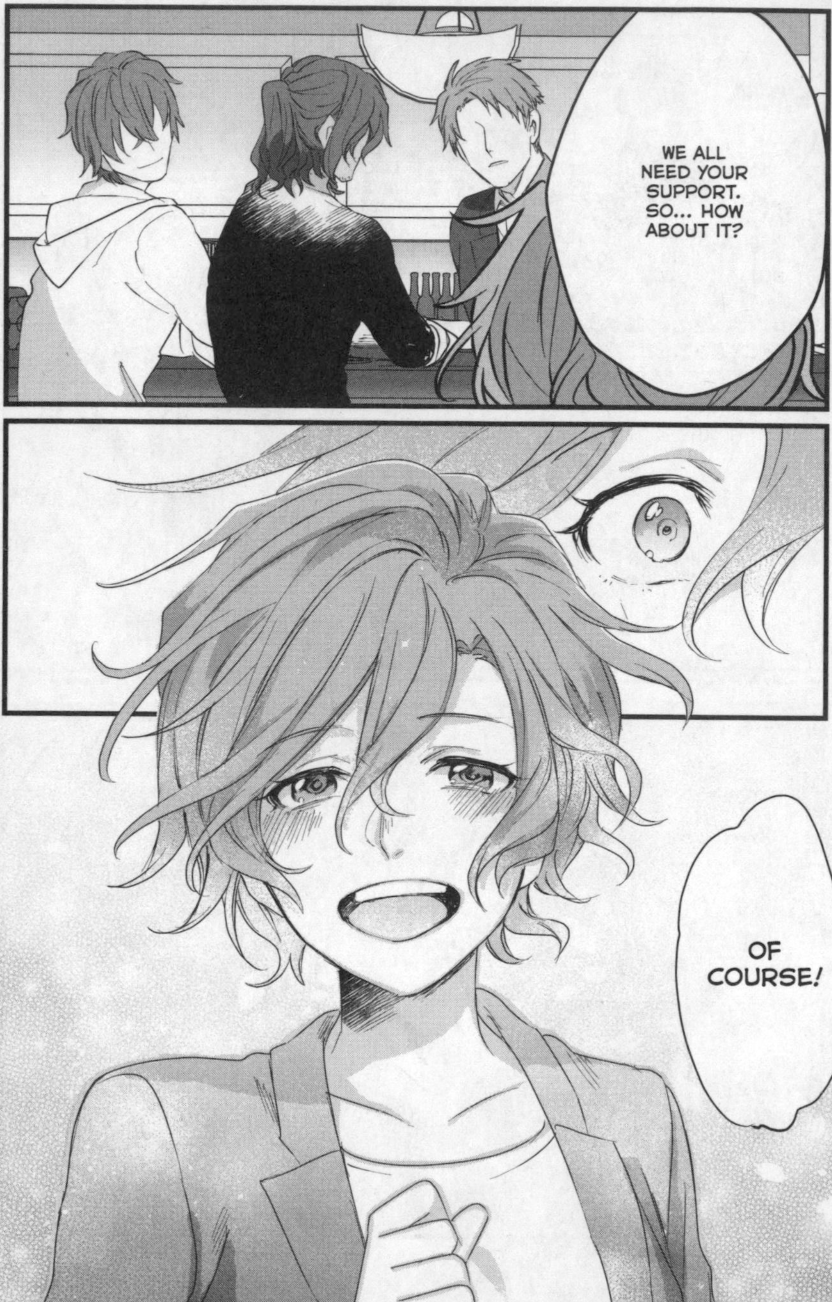
WE ALL NEED YOUR SUPPORT. SO... HOW ABOUT IT?
OF COURSE!

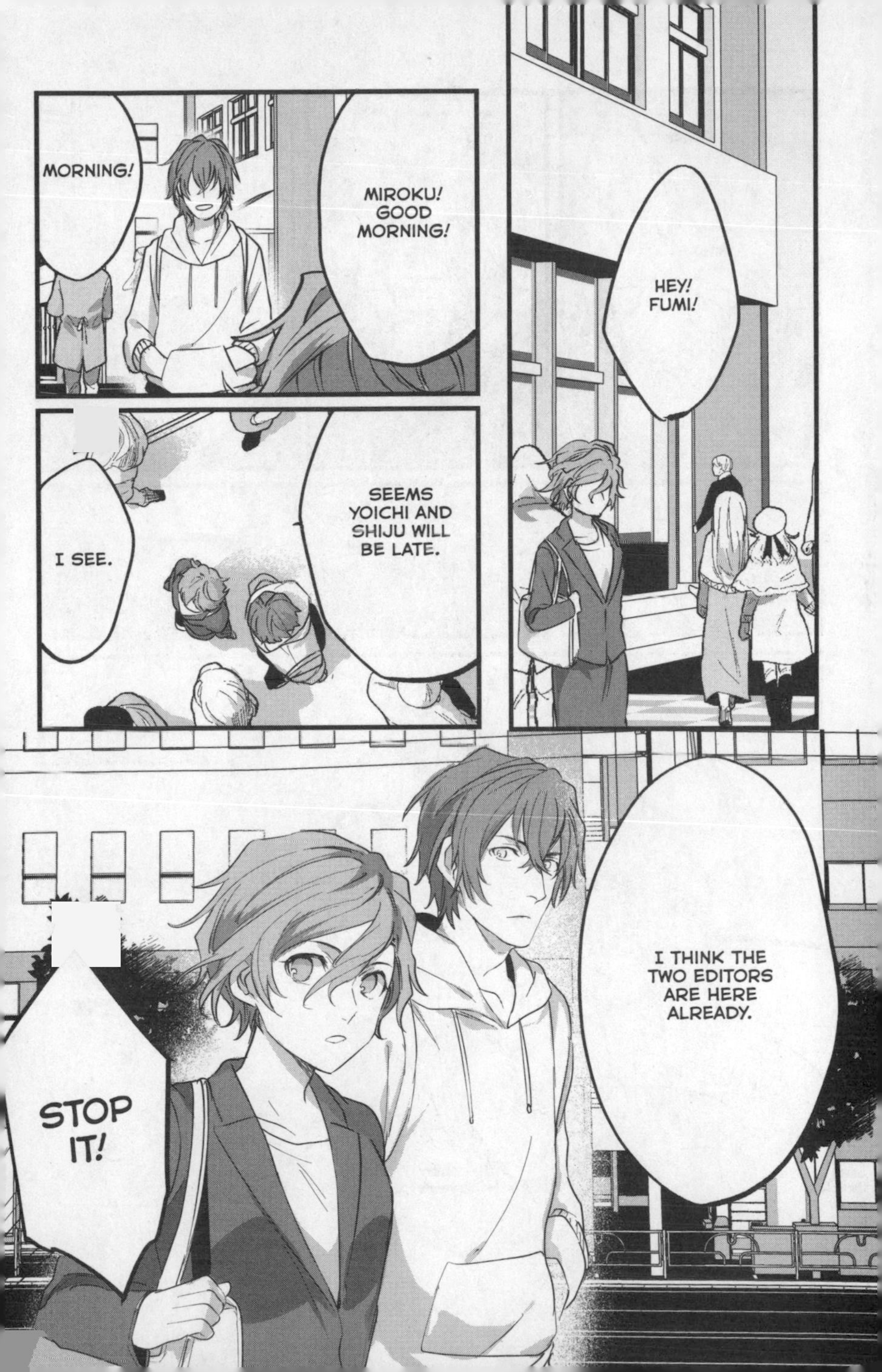
HEY! FUMI!
MIROKU! GOOD MORNING!
MORNING!
SEEMS YOICHI AND SHIJU WILL BE LATE.
I SEE.
I THINK THE TWO EDITORS ARE HERE ALREADY.
STOP IT!

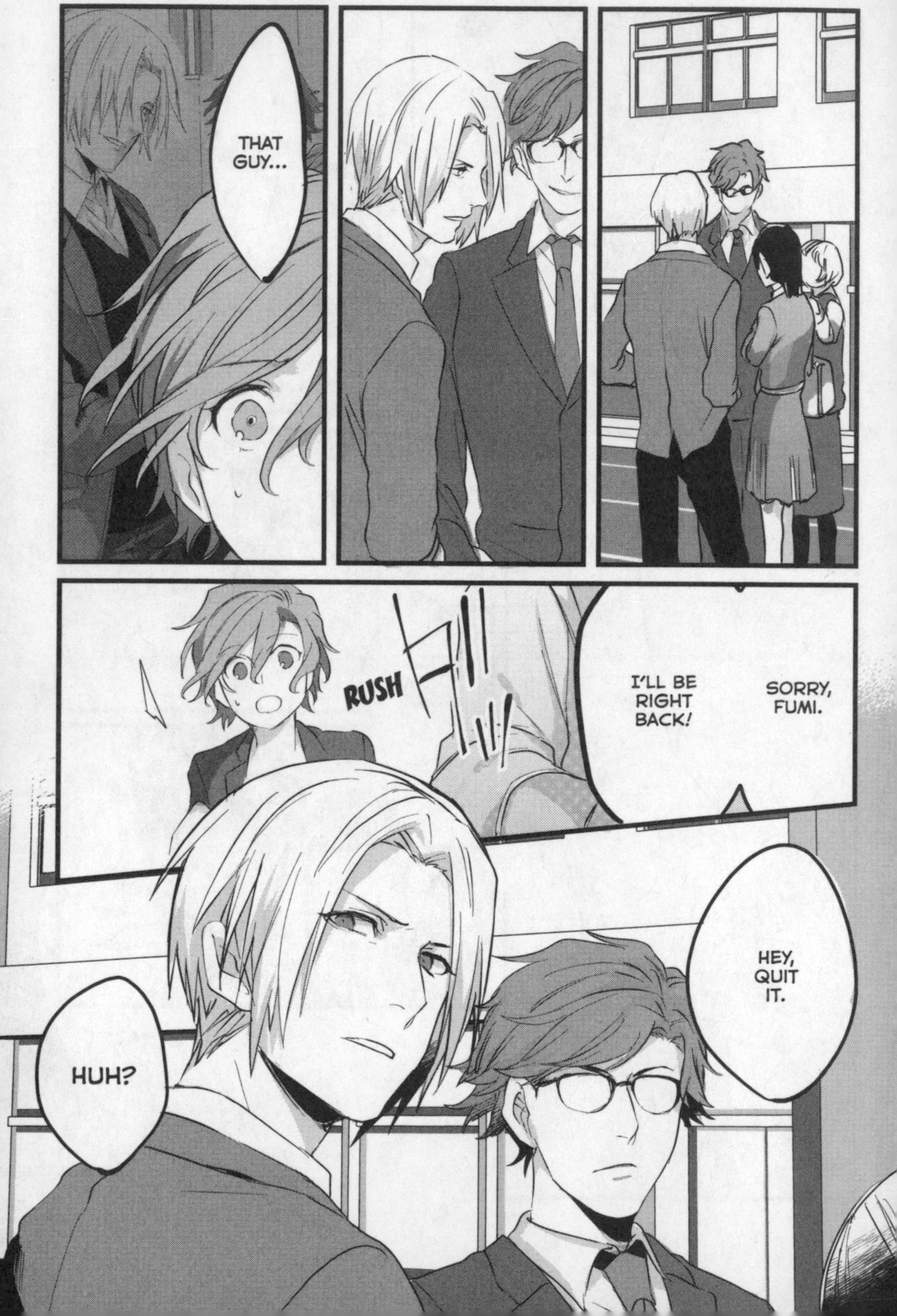
THAT GUY...
SORRY, FUMI.
I'LL BE RIGHT BACK!
RUSH
HEY, QUIT IT.
HUH?

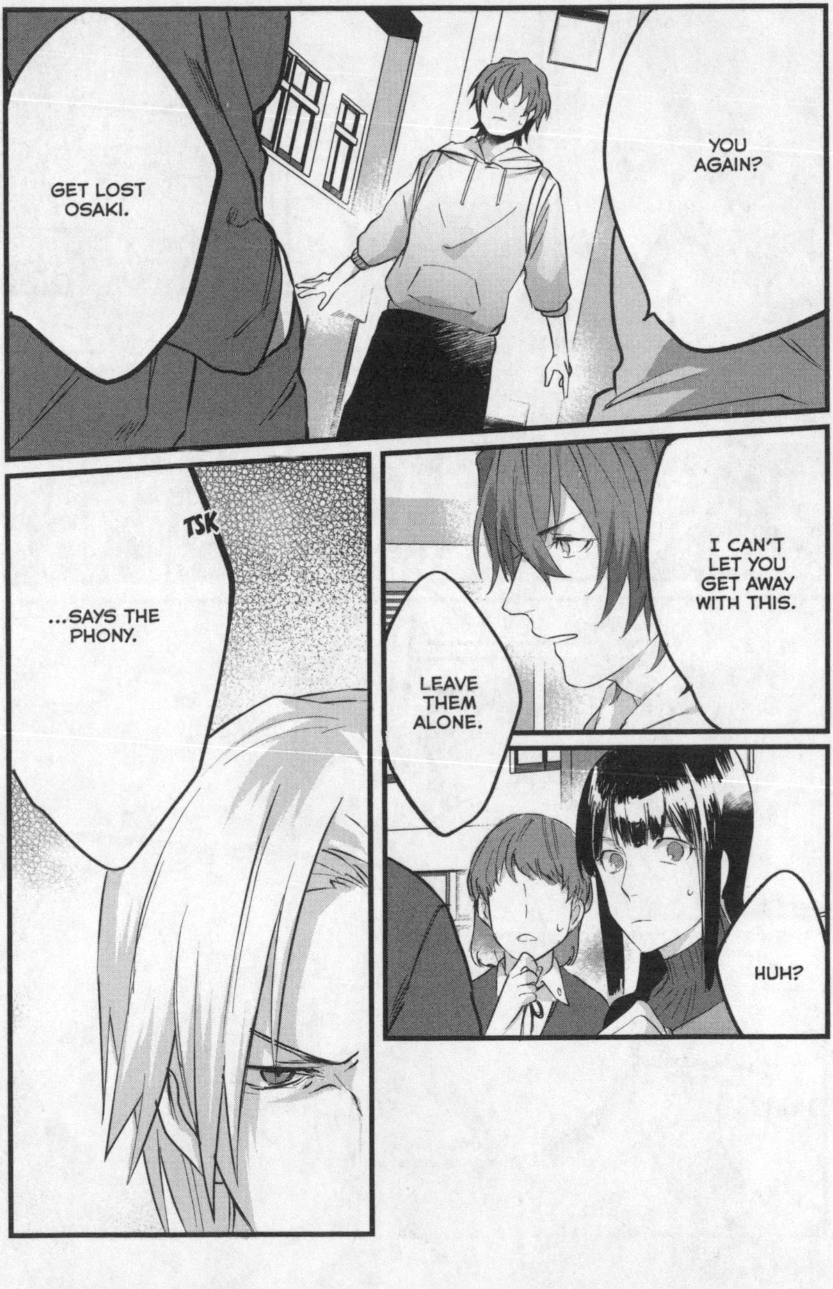
YOU AGAIN?
GET LOST OSAKI.
I CAN'T LET YOU GET AWAY WITH THIS.
LEAVE THEM ALONE.
HUH?
TSK
...SAYS THE PHONY.

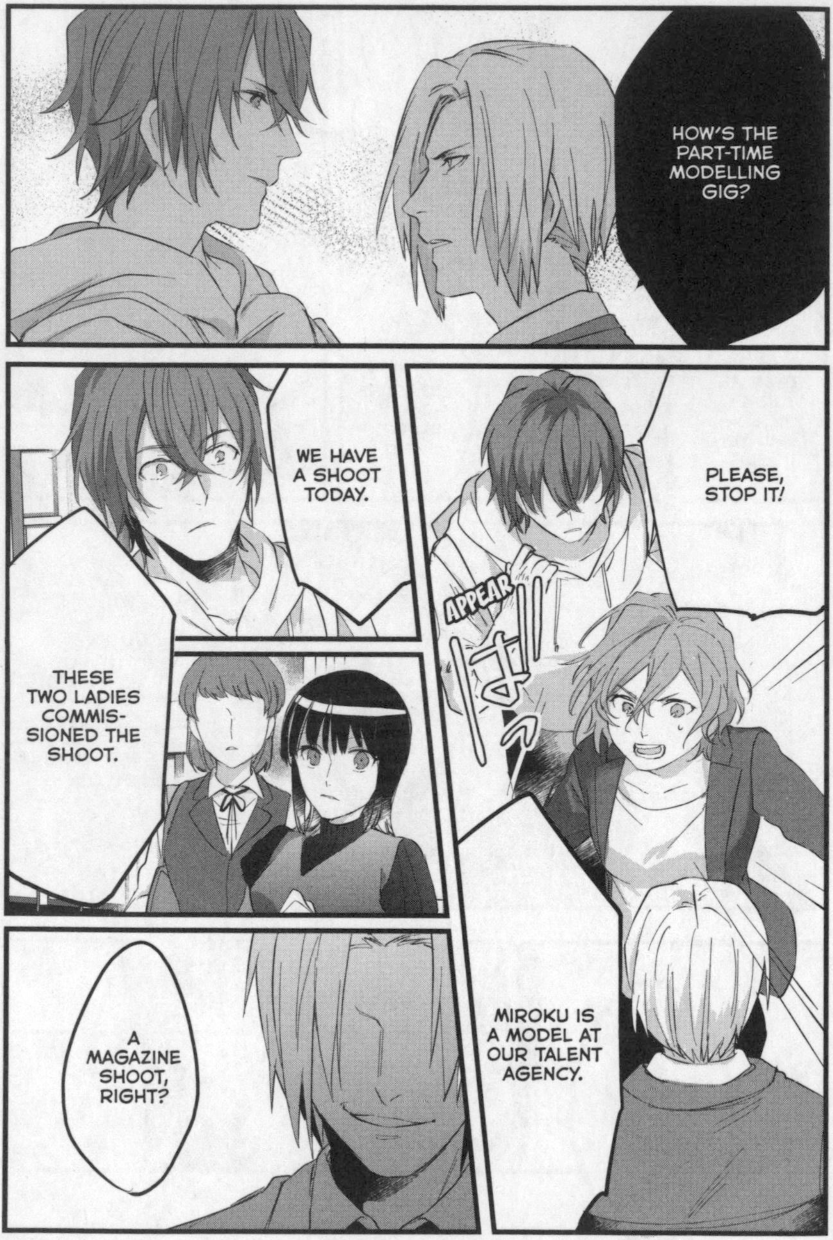

HOW'S THE PART-TIME MODELLING GIG?
PLEASE, STOP IT!
APPEAR
MIROKU IS A MODEL AT OUR TALENT AGENCY.
WE HAVE A SHOOT TODAY.
THESE TWO LADIES COMMIS-SIONED THE SHOOT.
A MAGAZINE SHOOT, RIGHT?

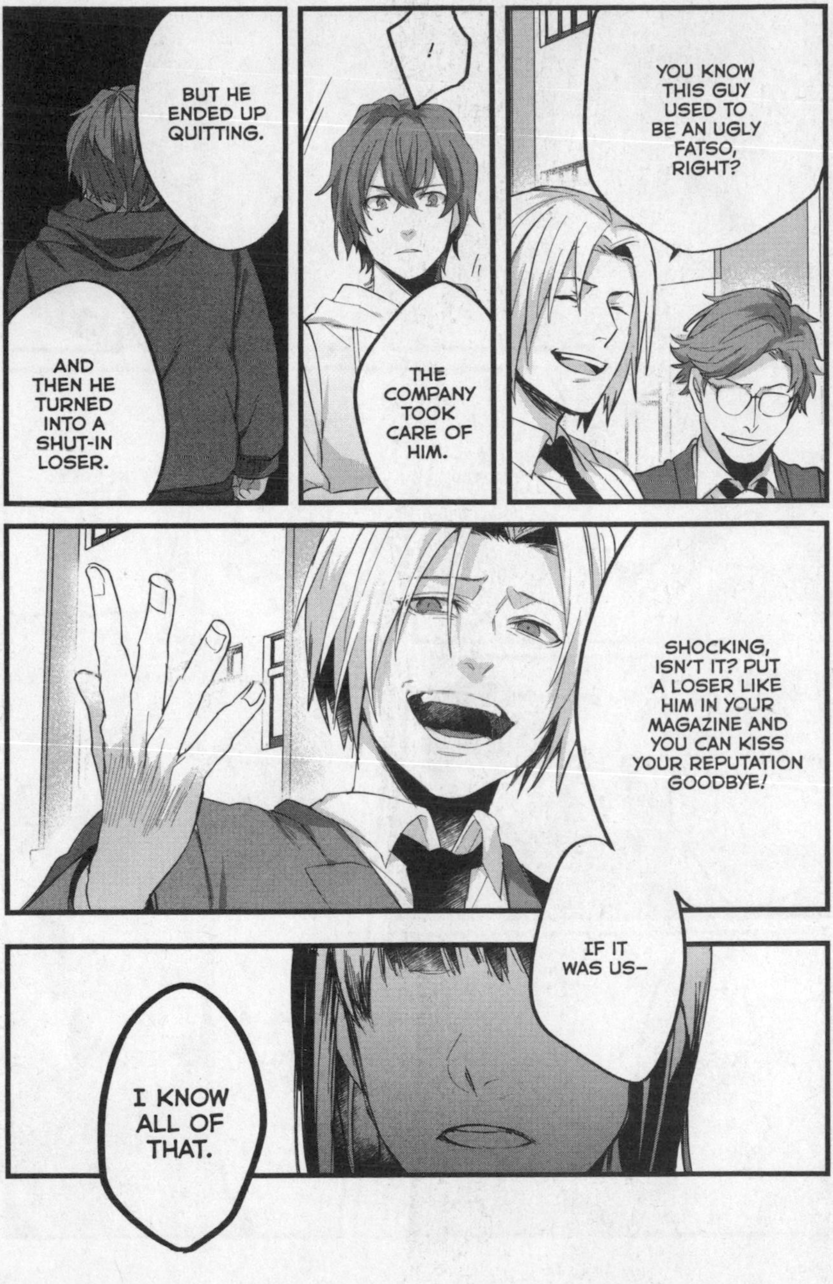
YOU KNOW THIS GUY USED TO BE AN UGLY FATSO, RIGHT?
!
THE COMPANY TOOK CARE OF HIM.
BUT HE ENDED UP QUITTING.
AND THEN HE TURNED INTO A SHUT-IN LOSER.
SHOCKING, ISN'T IT? PUT A LOSER LIKE HIM IN YOUR MAGAZINE AND YOU CAN KISS YOUR REPUTATION GOODBYE!
IF IT WAS US–
I KNOW ALL OF THAT.

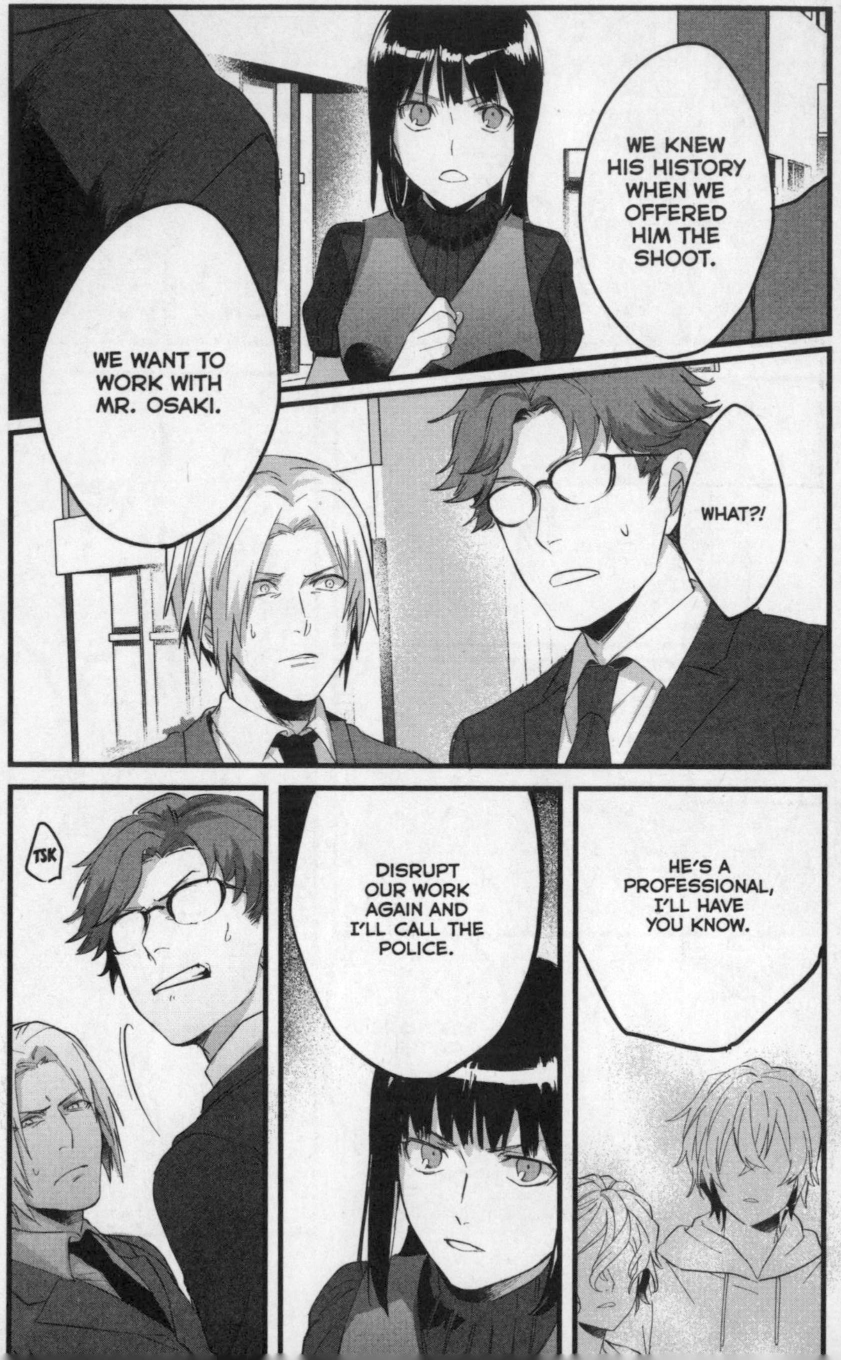
WE KNEW HIS HISTORY WHEN WE OFFERED HIM THE SHOOT.
WE WANT TO WORK WITH MR. OSAKI.
WHAT?!
HE'S A PROFESSIONAL, I'LL HAVE YOU KNOW.
DISRUPT OUR WORK AGAIN AND I'LL CALL THE POLICE.
TSK

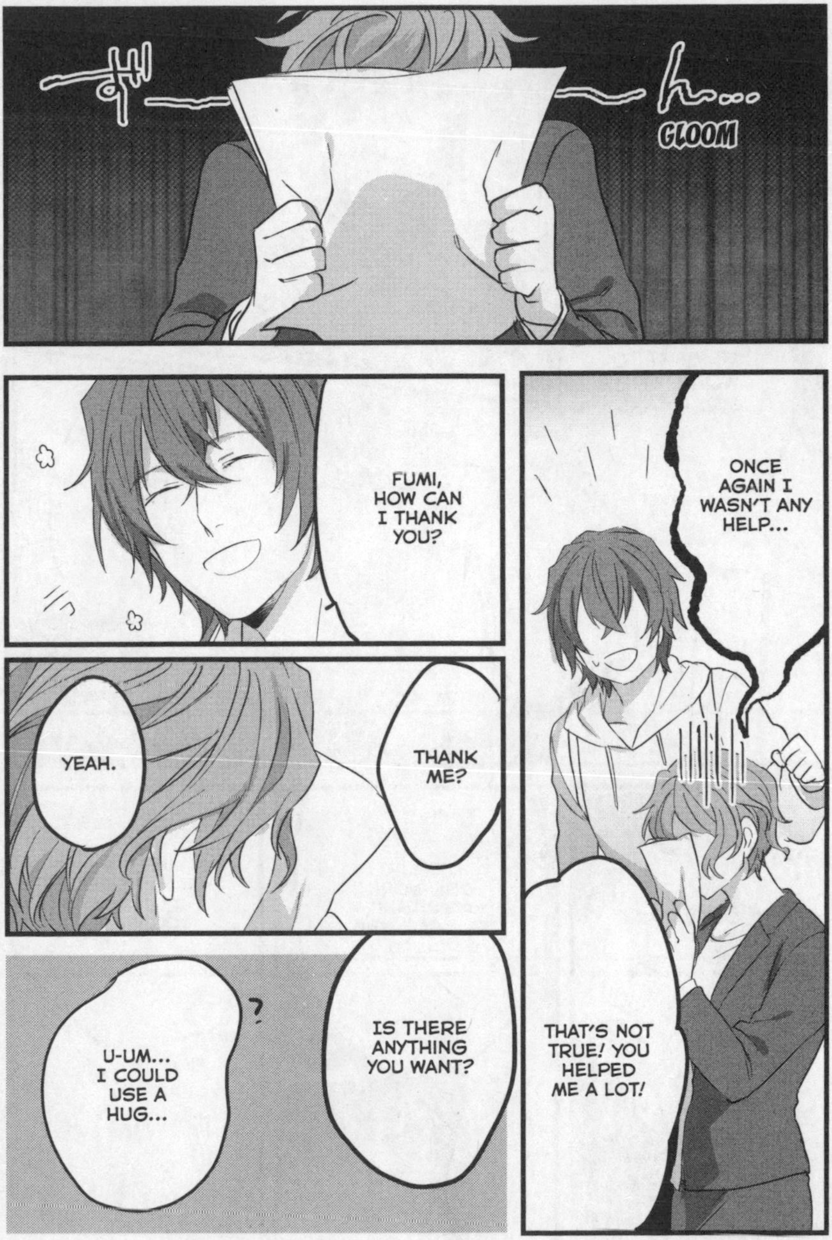
ずーーーん…
GLOOM
ONCE AGAIN I WASN'T ANY HELP...
THAT'S NOT TRUE! YOU HELPED ME A LOT!
FUMI, HOW CAN I THANK YOU?
THANK ME?
YEAH.
IS THERE ANYTHING YOU WANT?
?
U-UM... I COULD USE A HUG...

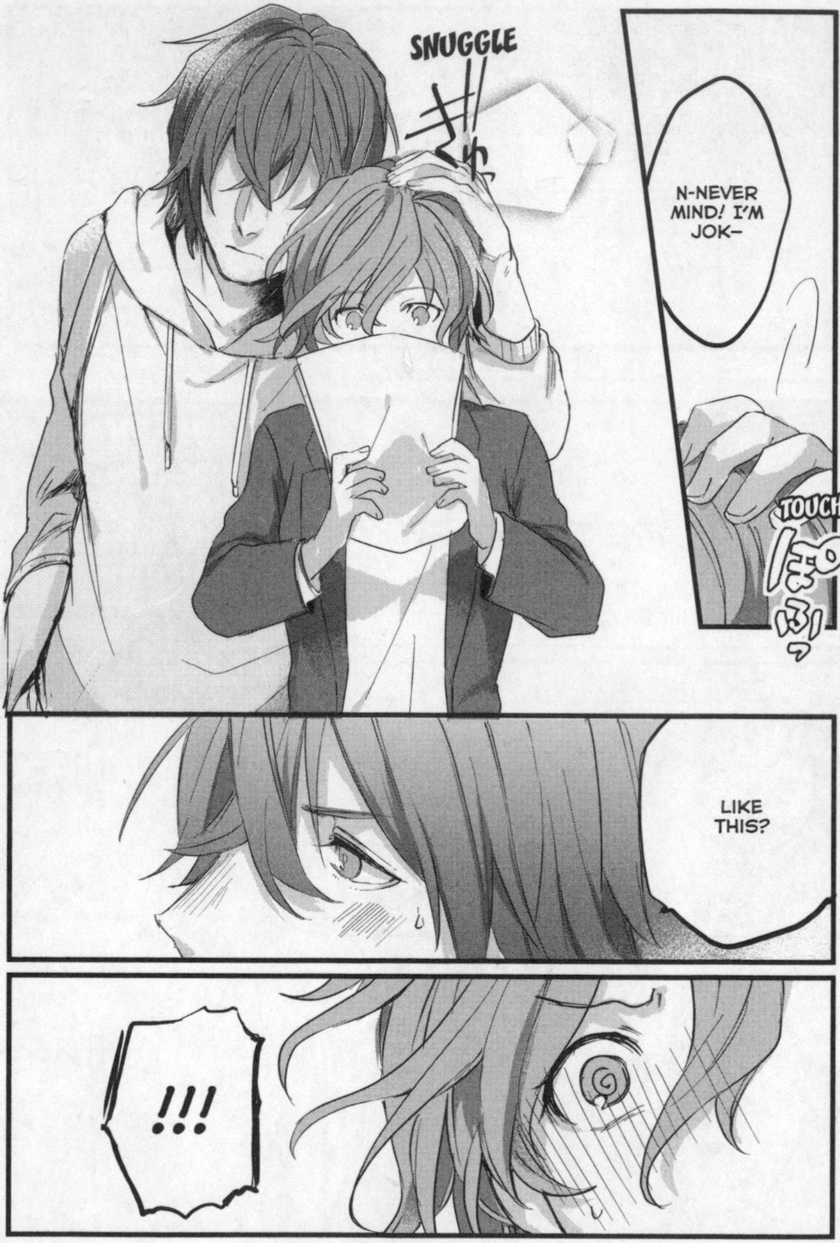
N-NEVER MIND! I'M JOK–
TOUCH
SNUGGLE
LIKE THIS?
!!!

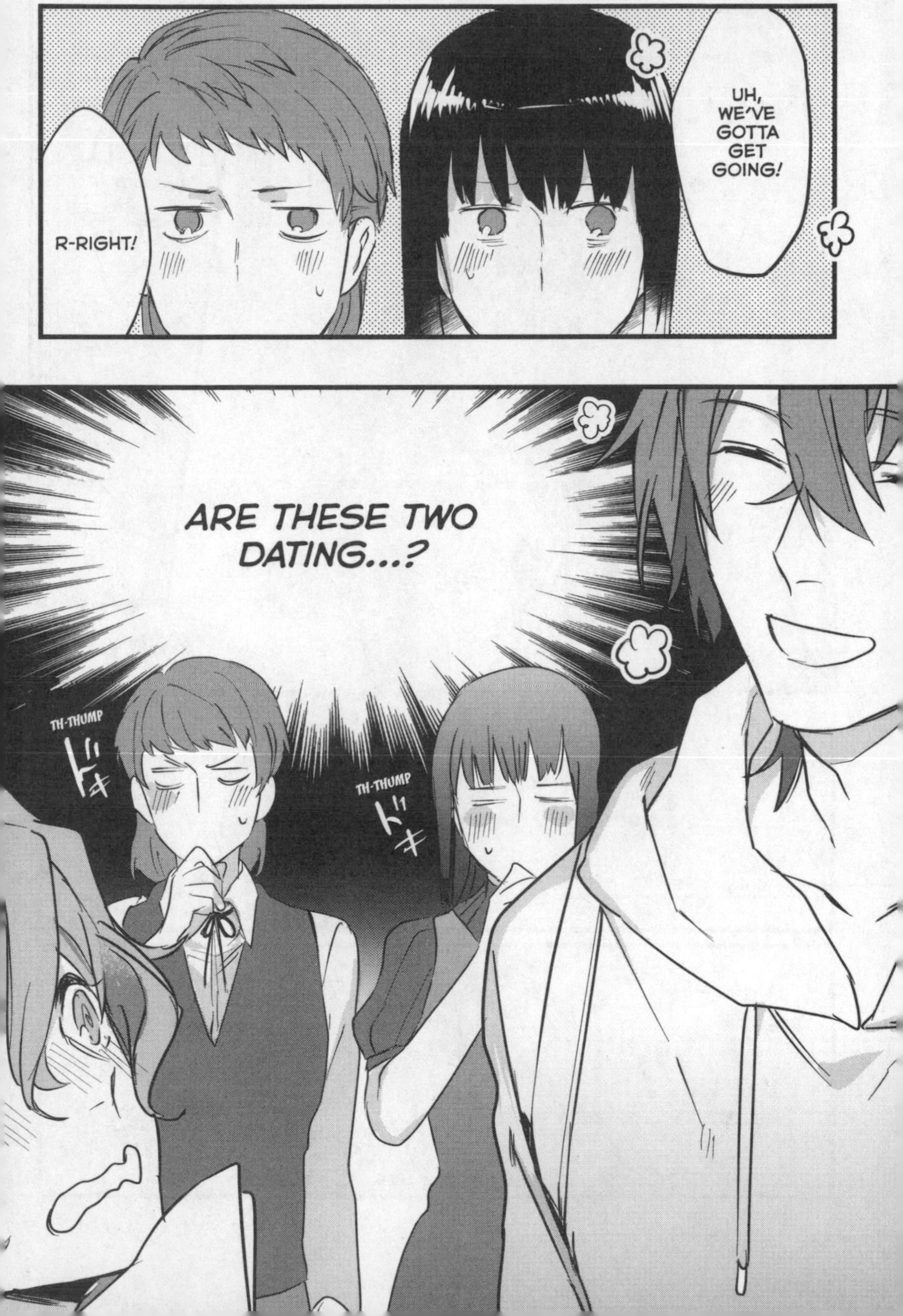
UH, WE'VE GOTTA GET GOING!
R-RIGHT!
ARE THESE TWO DATING...?
TH-THUMP
ドキ
TH-THUMP
ドキ

Chapter 8

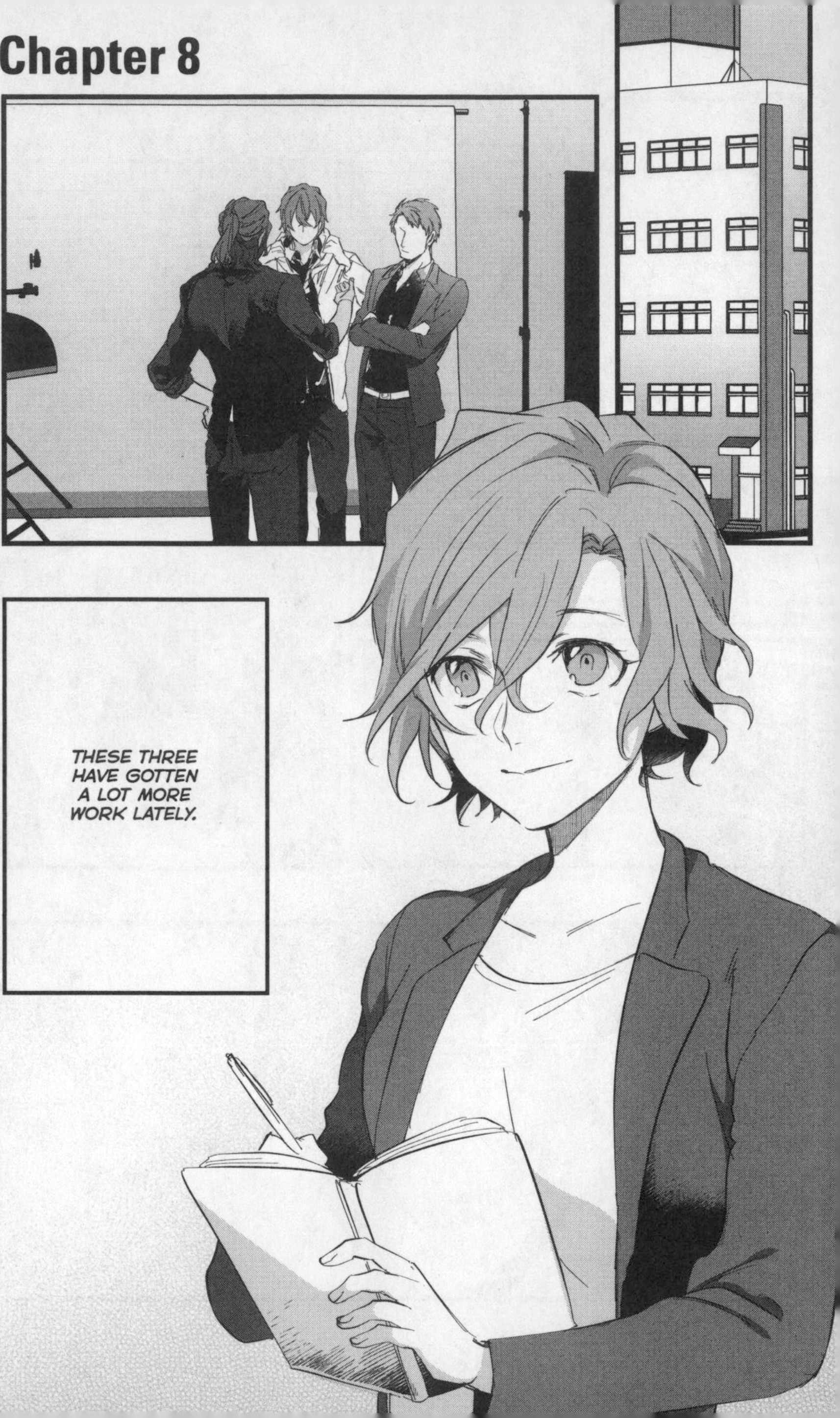
THESE THREE HAVE GOTTEN A LOT MORE WORK LATELY.

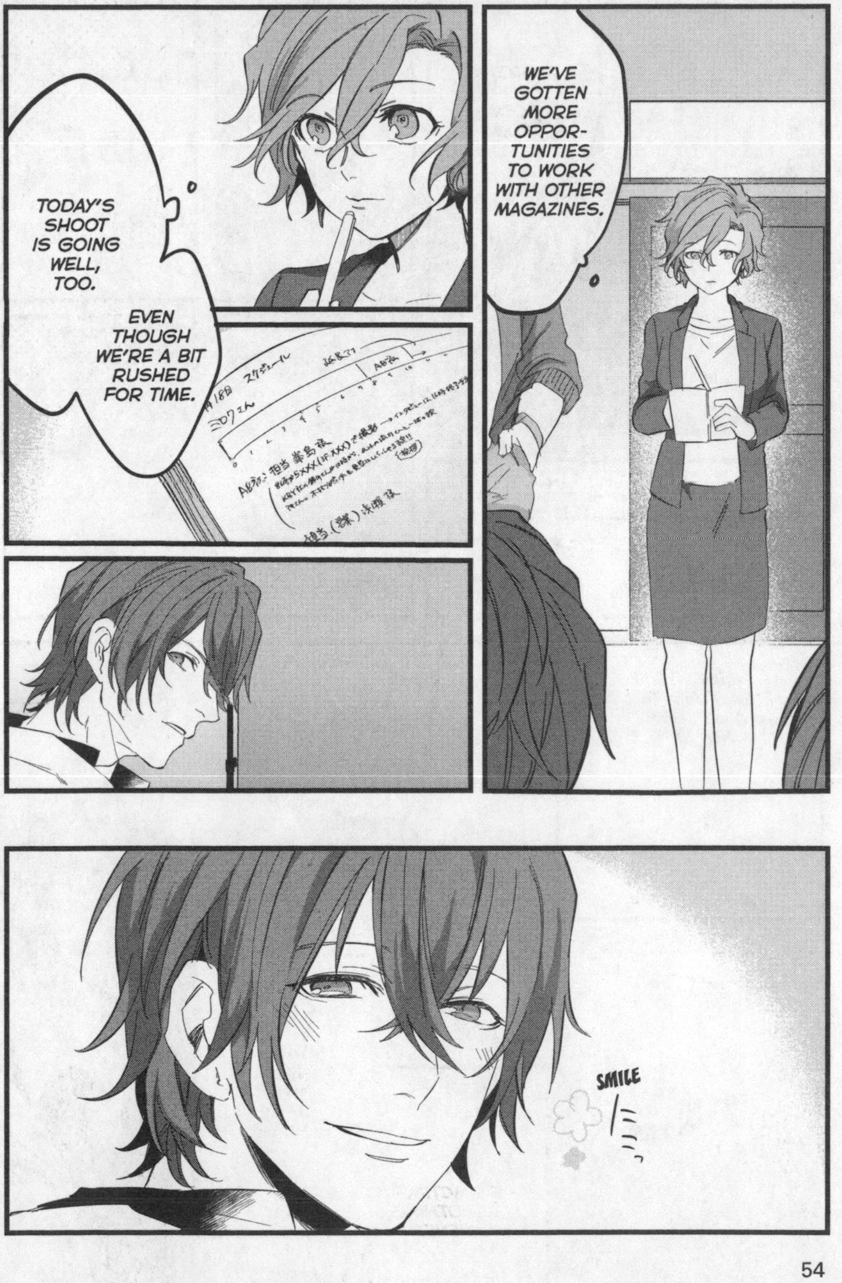
WE'VE GOTTEN MORE OPPOR-TUNITIES TO WORK WITH OTHER MAGAZINES.
TODAY'S SHOOT IS GOING WELL, TOO.
EVEN THOUGH WE'RE A BIT RUSHED FOR TIME.
SMILE

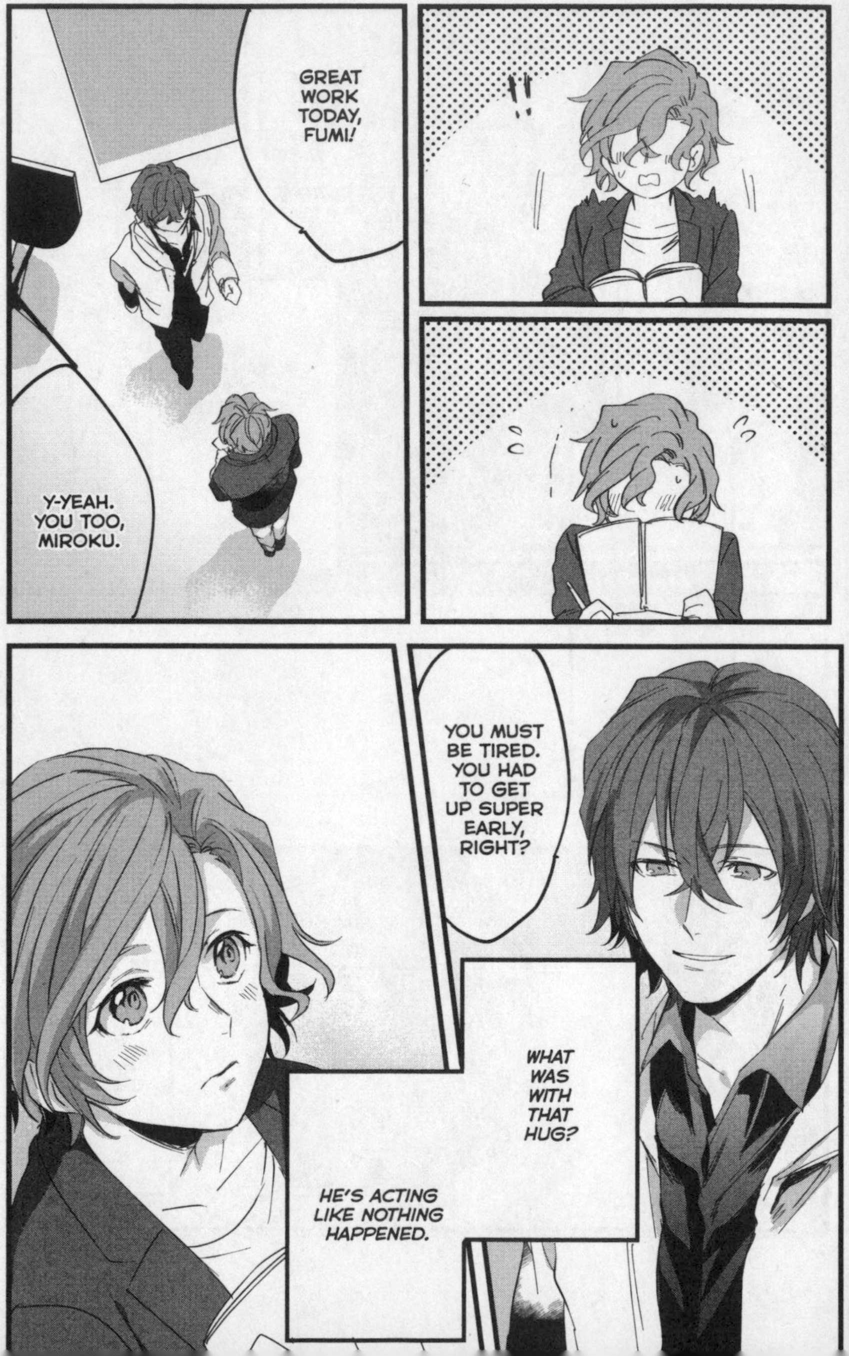
!!
GREAT WORK TODAY, FUMI!
Y-YEAH. YOU TOO, MIROKU.
YOU MUST BE TIRED. YOU HAD TO GET UP SUPER EARLY, RIGHT?
WHAT WAS WITH THAT HUG?
HE'S ACTING LIKE NOTHING HAPPENED.

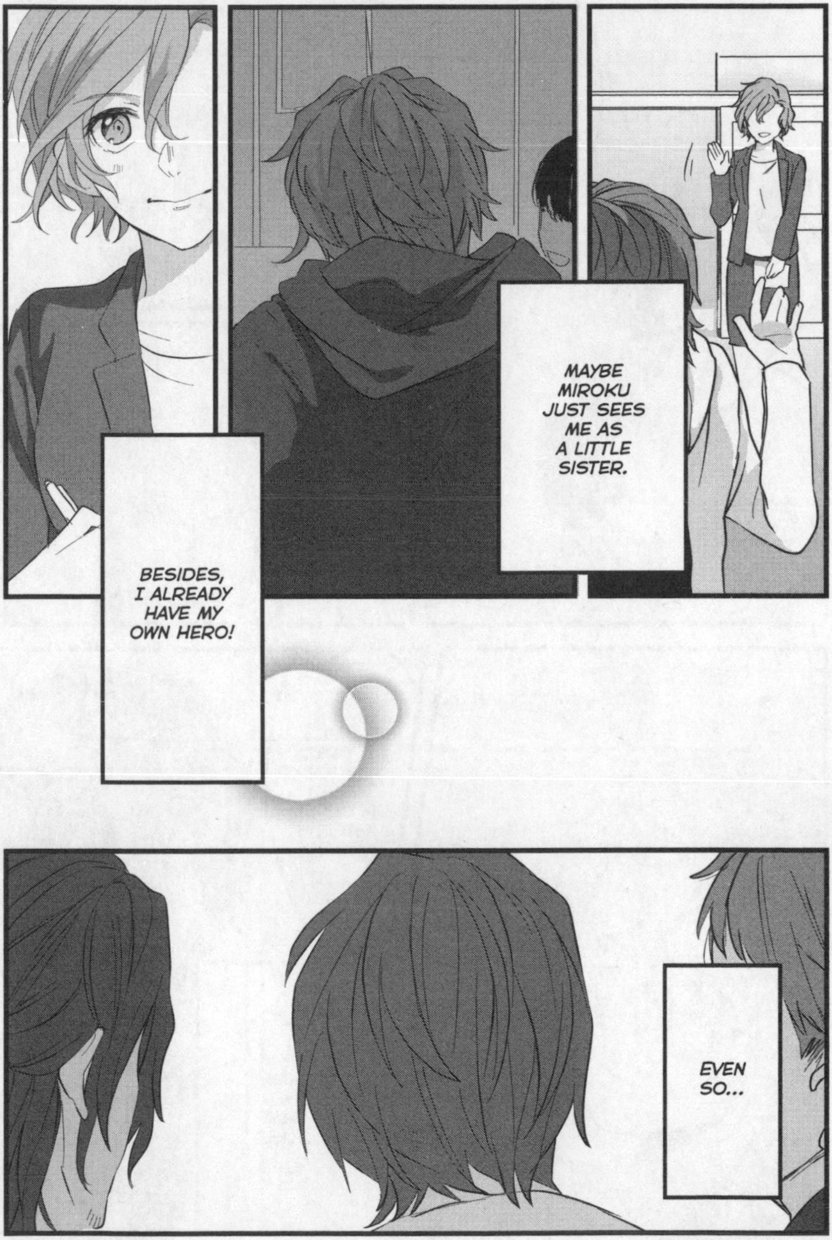
MAYBE MIROKU JUST SEES ME AS A LITTLE SISTER.
BESIDES, I ALREADY HAVE MY OWN HERO!
EVEN SO...

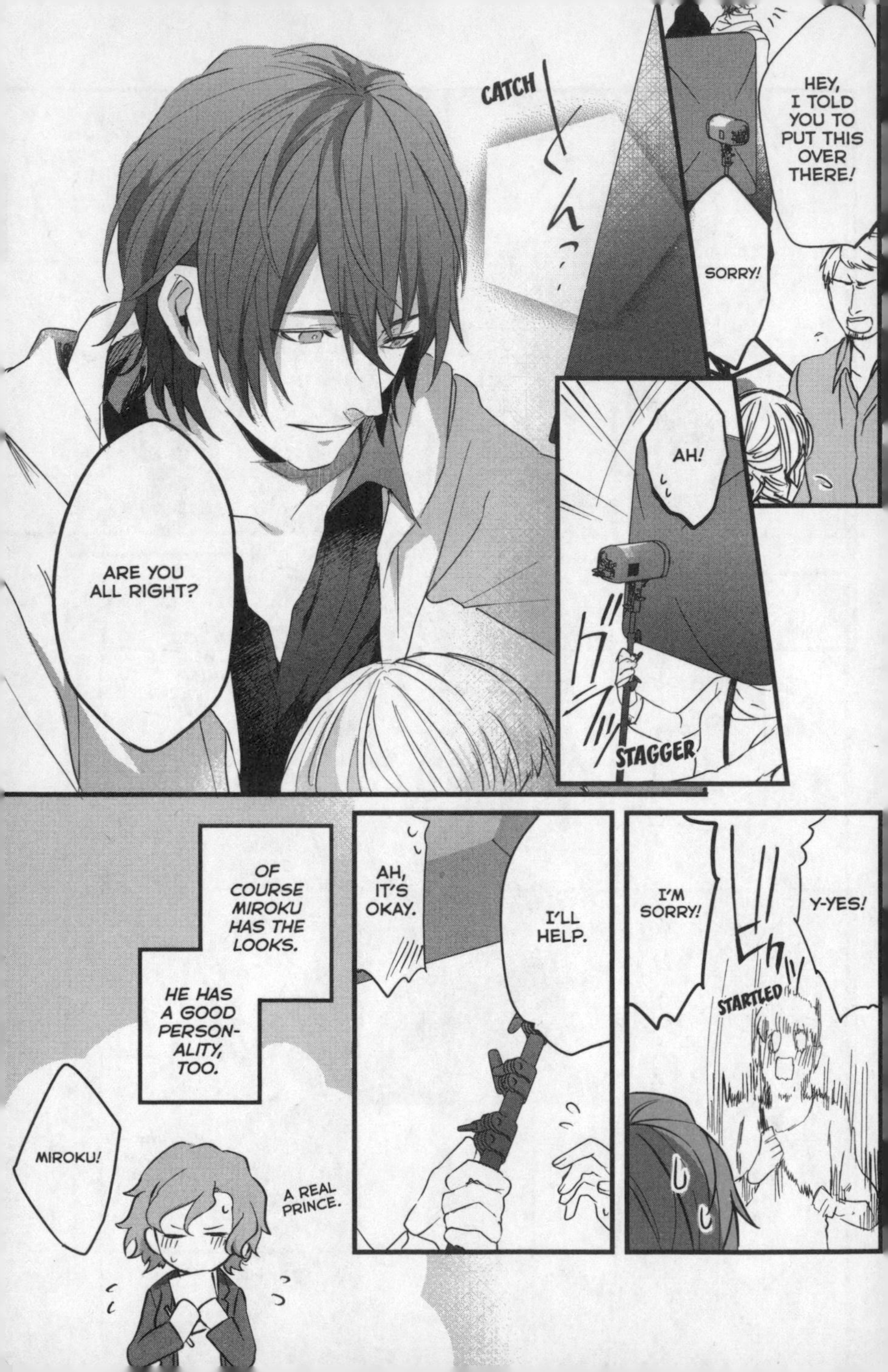
HEY, I TOLD YOU TO PUT THIS OVER THERE!
SORRY!
CATCH
AH!
STAGGER
ARE YOU ALL RIGHT?
Y-YES!
I'M SORRY!
STARTLED
I'LL HELP.
AH, IT'S OKAY.
OF COURSE MIROKU HAS THE LOOKS.
HE HAS A GOOD PERSON-ALITY, TOO.
A REAL PRINCE.
MIROKU!

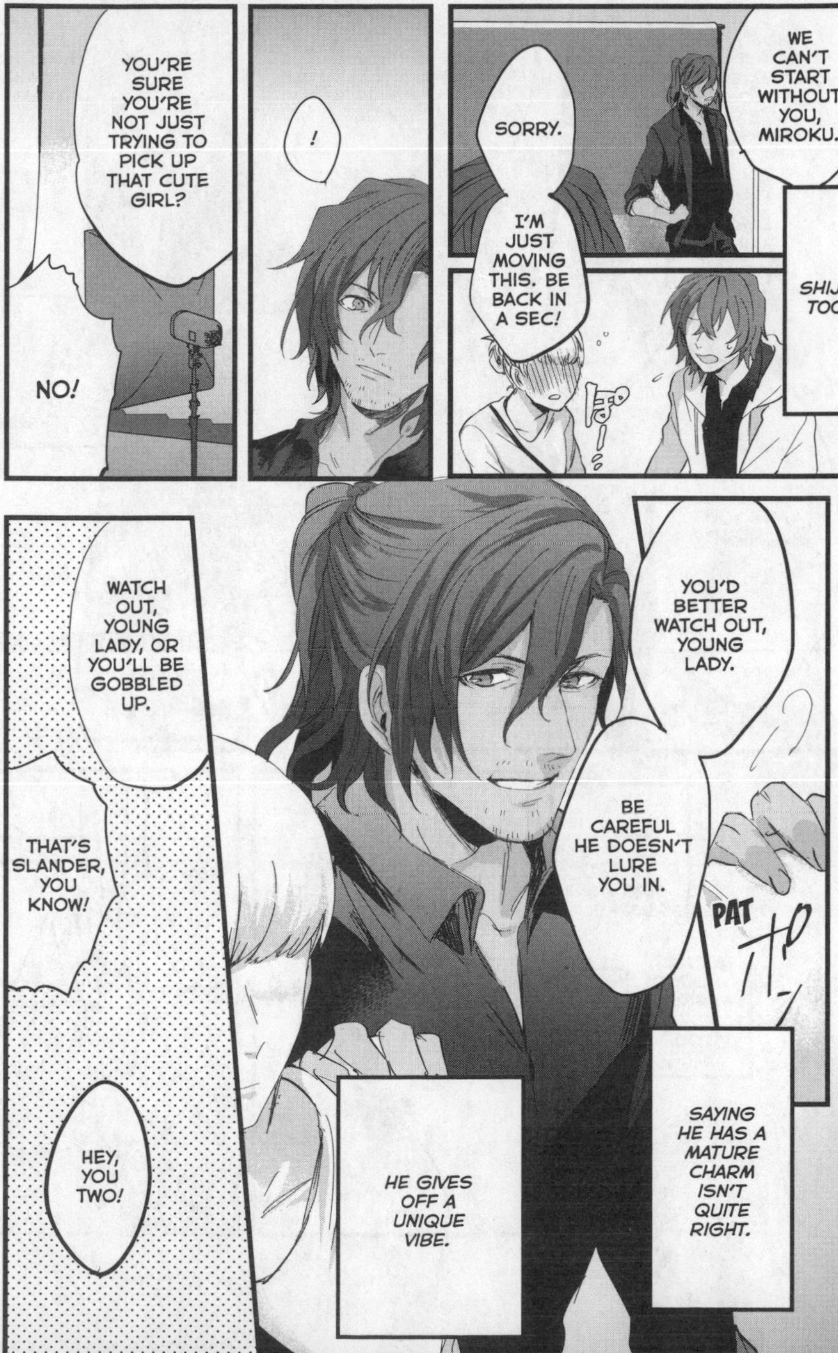
WE CAN'T START WITHOUT YOU, MIROKU.
SORRY.
SHIJU, TOO.
I'M JUST MOVING THIS. BE BACK IN A SEC!
!
YOU'RE SURE YOU'RE NOT JUST TRYING TO PICK UP THAT CUTE GIRL?
NO!
YOU'D BETTER WATCH OUT, YOUNG LADY.
BE CAREFUL HE DOESN'T LURE YOU IN.
PAT
WATCH OUT, YOUNG LADY, OR YOU'LL BE GOBBLED UP.
THAT'S SLANDER, YOU KNOW!
SAYING HE HAS A MATURE CHARM ISN'T QUITE RIGHT.
HE GIVES OFF A UNIQUE VIBE.
HEY, YOU TWO!

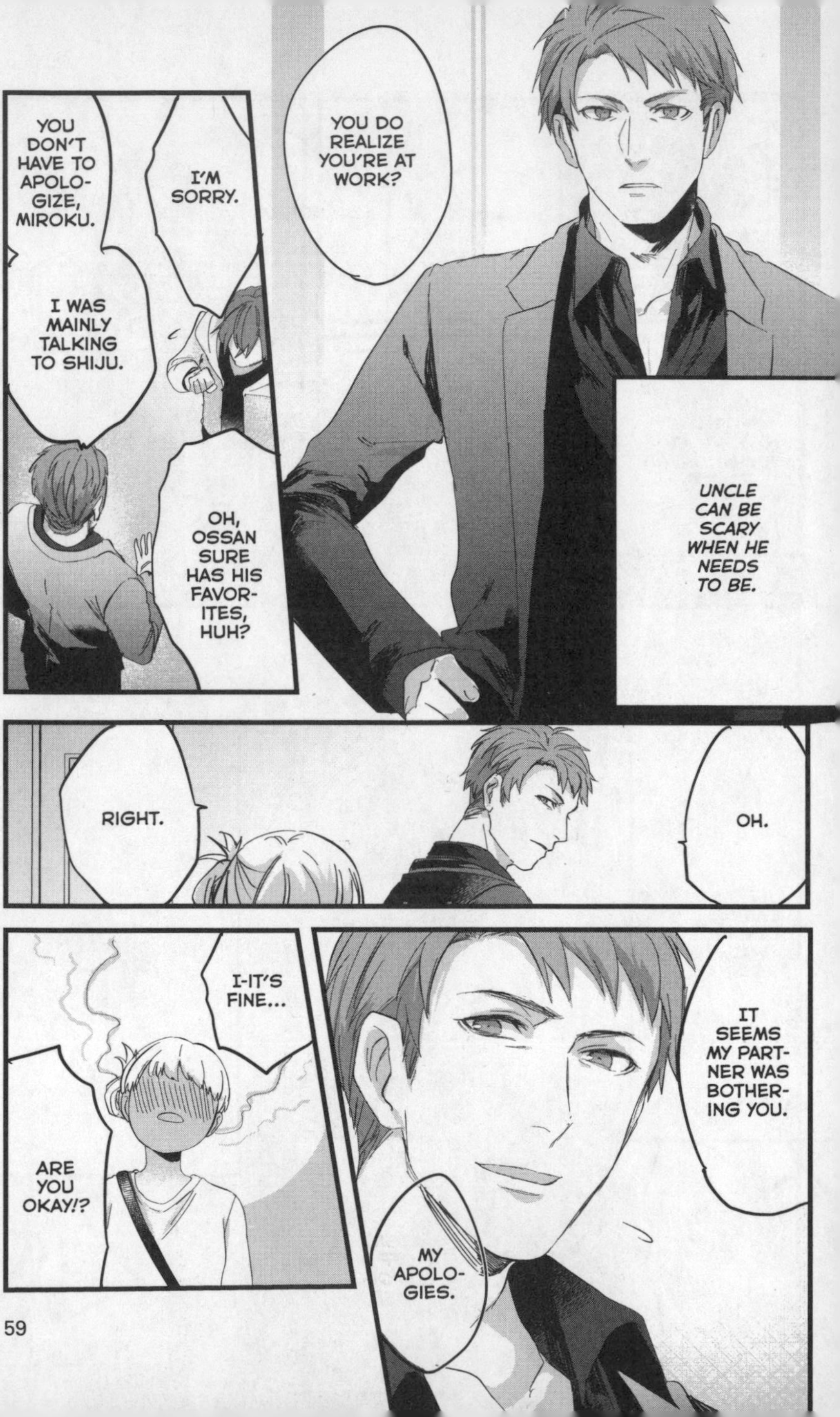
YOU DO REALIZE YOU'RE AT WORK?
UNCLE CAN BE SCARY WHEN HE NEEDS TO BE.
I'M SORRY.
YOU DON'T HAVE TO APOLOGIZE, MIROKU.
I WAS MAINLY TALKING TO SHIJU.
OH, OSSAN SURE HAS HIS FAVORITES, HUH?
OH.
RIGHT.
IT SEEMS MY PARTNER WAS BOTHERING YOU.
MY APOLOGIES.
I-IT'S FINE...
ARE YOU OKAY!?

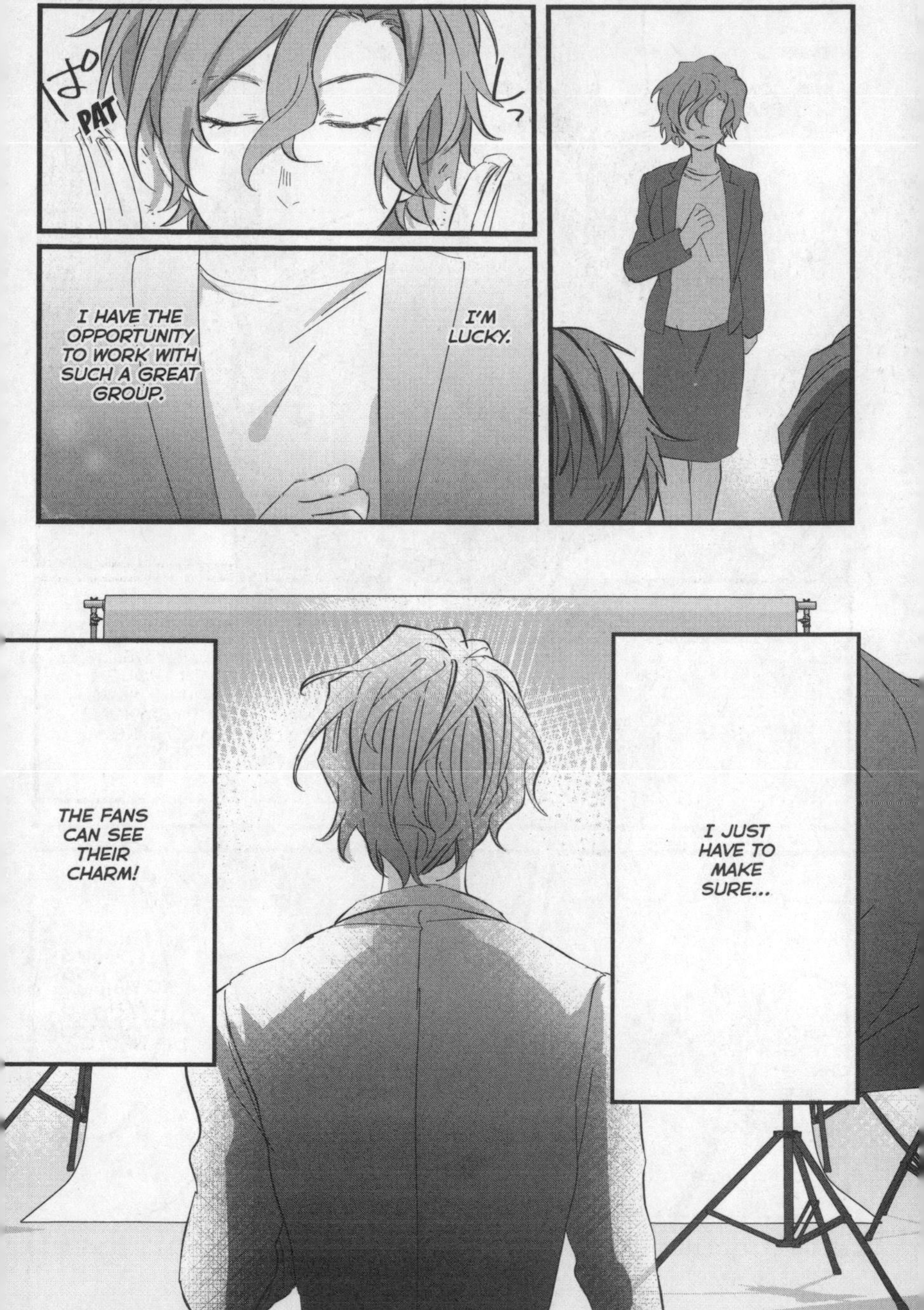
PAT
I'M LUCKY.
I HAVE THE OPPORTUNITY TO WORK WITH SUCH A GREAT GROUP.
I JUST HAVE TO MAKE SURE...
THE FANS CAN SEE THEIR CHARM!

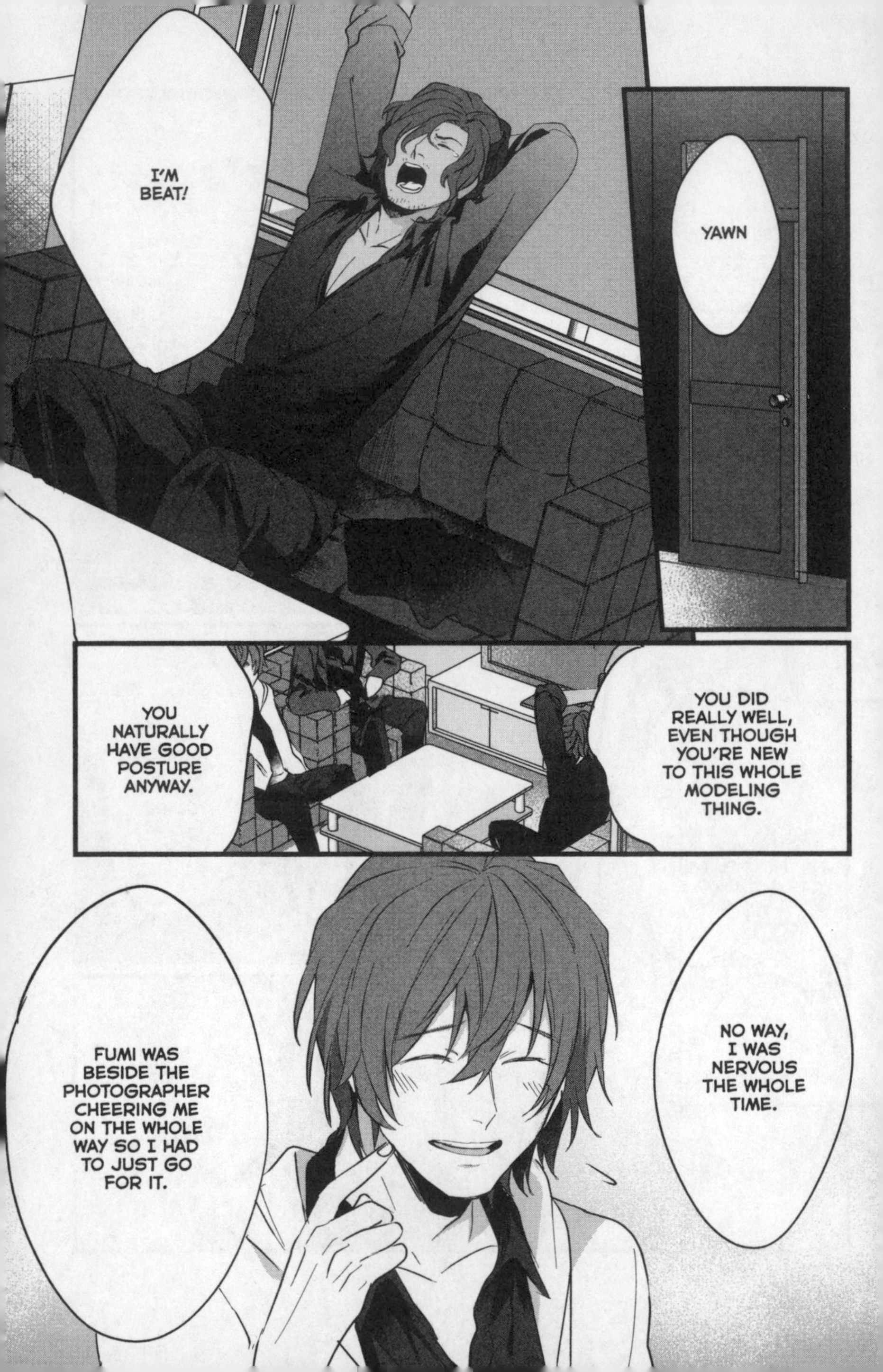
YAWN
I'M BEAT!
YOU DID REALLY WELL, EVEN THOUGH YOU'RE NEW TO THIS WHOLE MODELING THING.
YOU NATURALLY HAVE GOOD POSTURE ANYWAY.
NO WAY, I WAS NERVOUS THE WHOLE TIME.
FUMI WAS BESIDE THE PHOTOGRAPHER CHEERING ME ON THE WHOLE WAY SO I HAD TO JUST GO FOR IT.

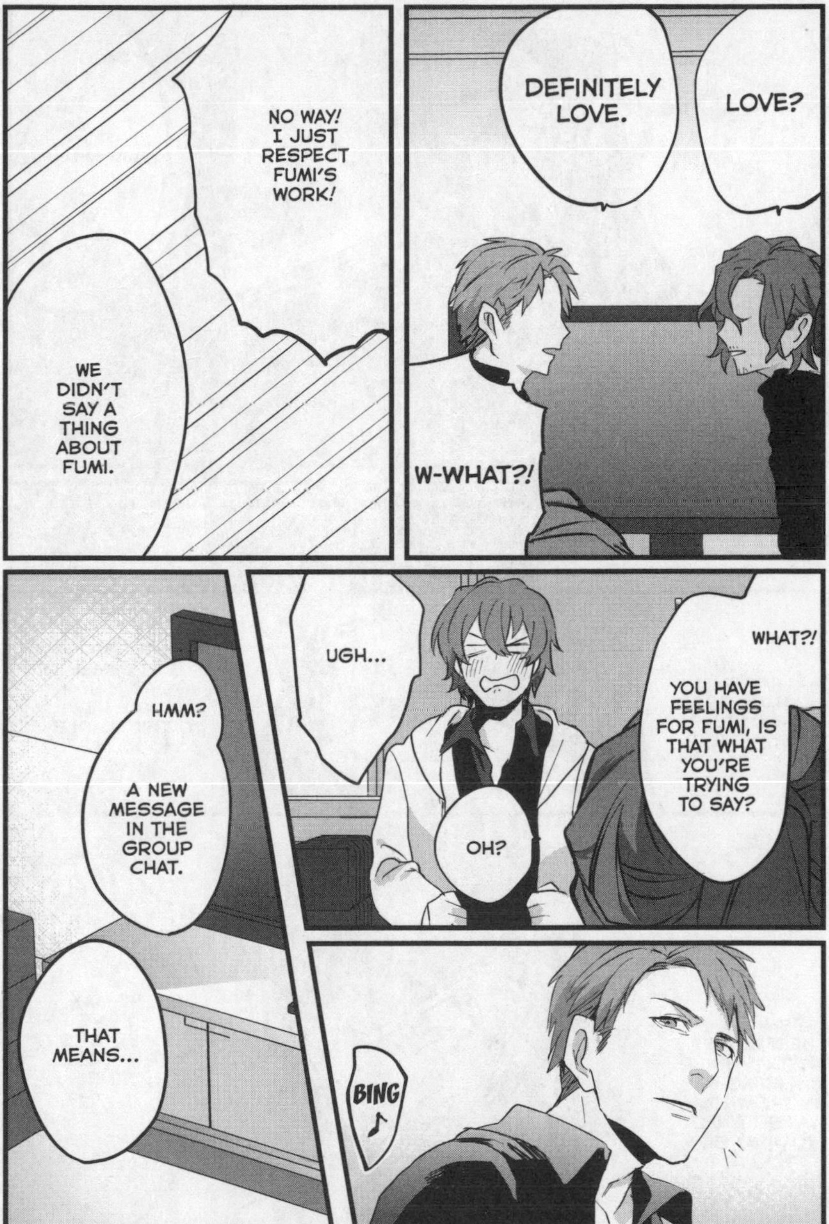
LOVE?
DEFINITELY LOVE.
W-WHAT?!
NO WAY! I JUST RESPECT FUMI'S WORK!
WE DIDN'T SAY A THING ABOUT FUMI.
WHAT?!
YOU HAVE FEELINGS FOR FUMI, IS THAT WHAT YOU'RE TRYING TO SAY?
UGH...
OH?
BING ♪
HMM?
A NEW MESSAGE IN THE GROUP CHAT.
THAT MEANS...

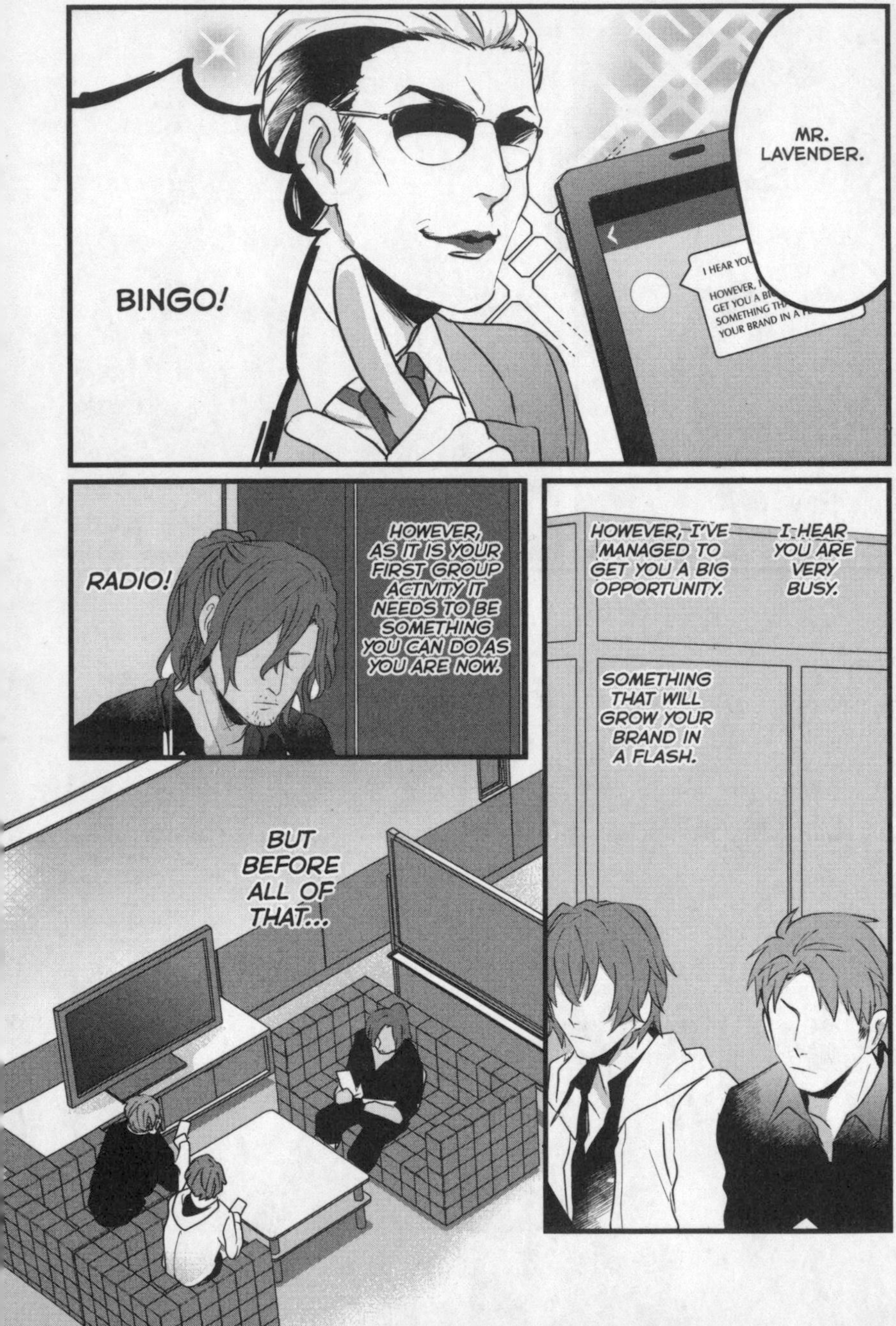
MR. LAVENDER.
BINGO!
I HEAR YOU ARE VERY BUSY.
HOWEVER, I'VE MANAGED TO GET YOU A BIG OPPORTUNITY.
SOMETHING THAT WILL GROW YOUR BRAND IN A FLASH.
HOWEVER, AS IT IS YOUR FIRST GROUP ACTIVITY IT NEEDS TO BE SOMETHING YOU CAN DO AS YOU ARE NOW.
RADIO!
BUT BEFORE ALL OF THAT...

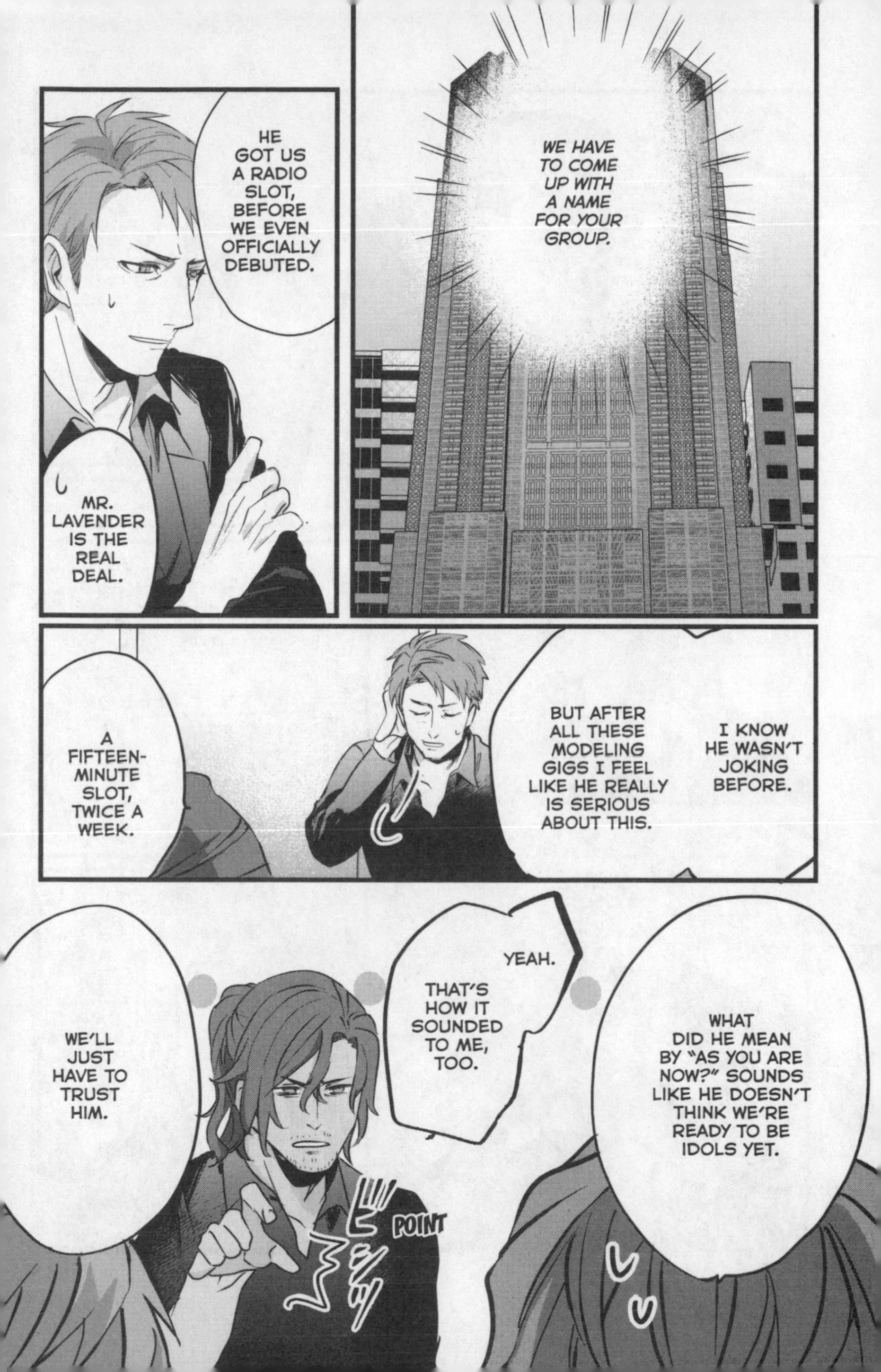
WE HAVE TO COME UP WITH A NAME FOR YOUR GROUP.
HE GOT US A RADIO SLOT, BEFORE WE EVEN OFFICIALLY DEBUTED.
MR. LAVENDER IS THE REAL DEAL.
I KNOW HE WASN'T JOKING BEFORE.
BUT AFTER ALL THESE MODELING GIGS I FEEL LIKE HE REALLY IS SERIOUS ABOUT THIS.
A FIFTEEN-MINUTE SLOT, TWICE A WEEK.
WHAT DID HE MEAN BY "AS YOU ARE NOW?" SOUNDS LIKE HE DOESN'T THINK WE'RE READY TO BE IDOLS YET.
YEAH.
THAT'S HOW IT SOUNDED TO ME, TOO.
WE'LL JUST HAVE TO TRUST HIM.
POINT

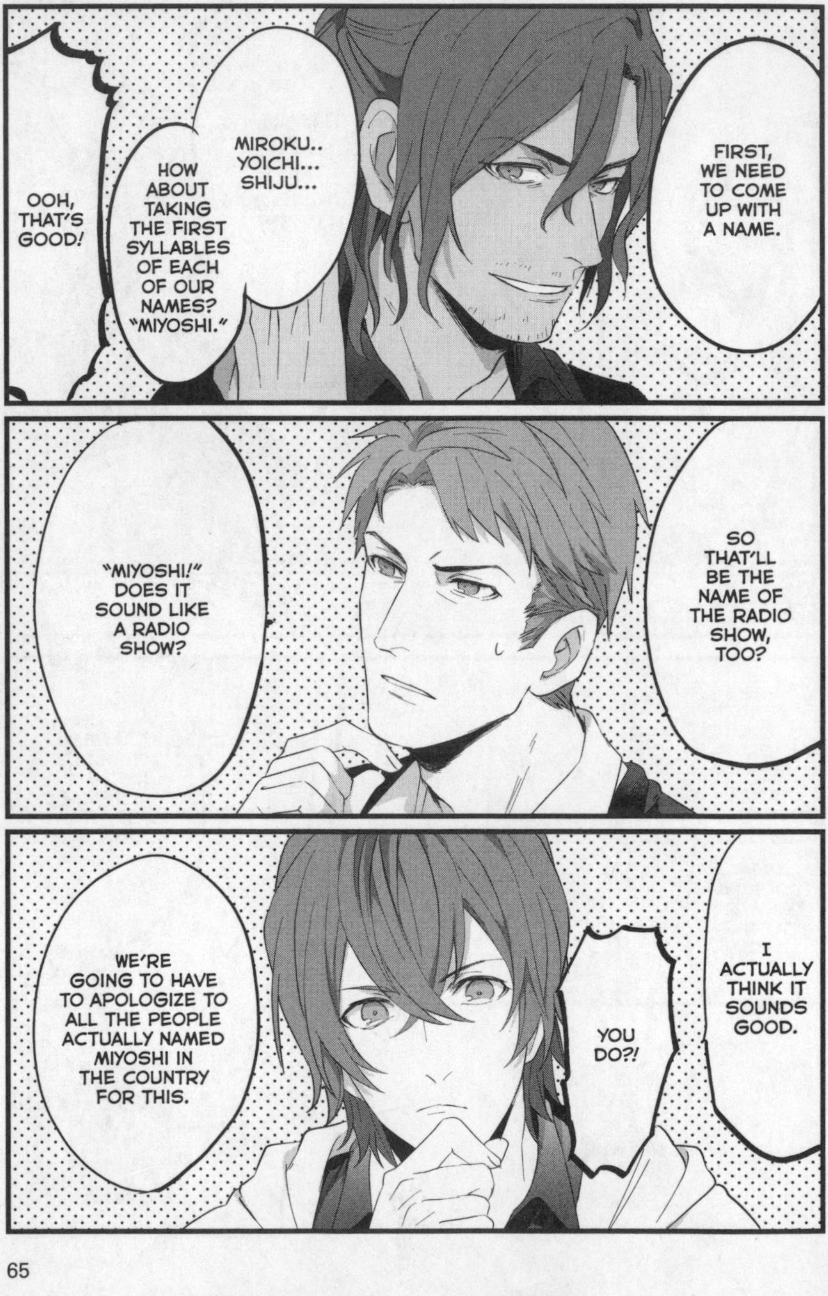
FIRST, WE NEED TO COME UP WITH A NAME.
MIROKU.. YOICHI... SHIJU...
HOW ABOUT TAKING THE FIRST SYLLABLES OF EACH OF OUR NAMES? "MIYOSHI."
OOH, THAT'S GOOD!
SO THAT'LL BE THE NAME OF THE RADIO SHOW, TOO?
"MIYOSHI!" DOES IT SOUND LIKE A RADIO SHOW?
I ACTUALLY THINK IT SOUNDS GOOD.
YOU DO?!
WE'RE GOING TO HAVE TO APOLOGIZE TO ALL THE PEOPLE ACTUALLY NAMED MIYOSHI IN THE COUNTRY FOR THIS.

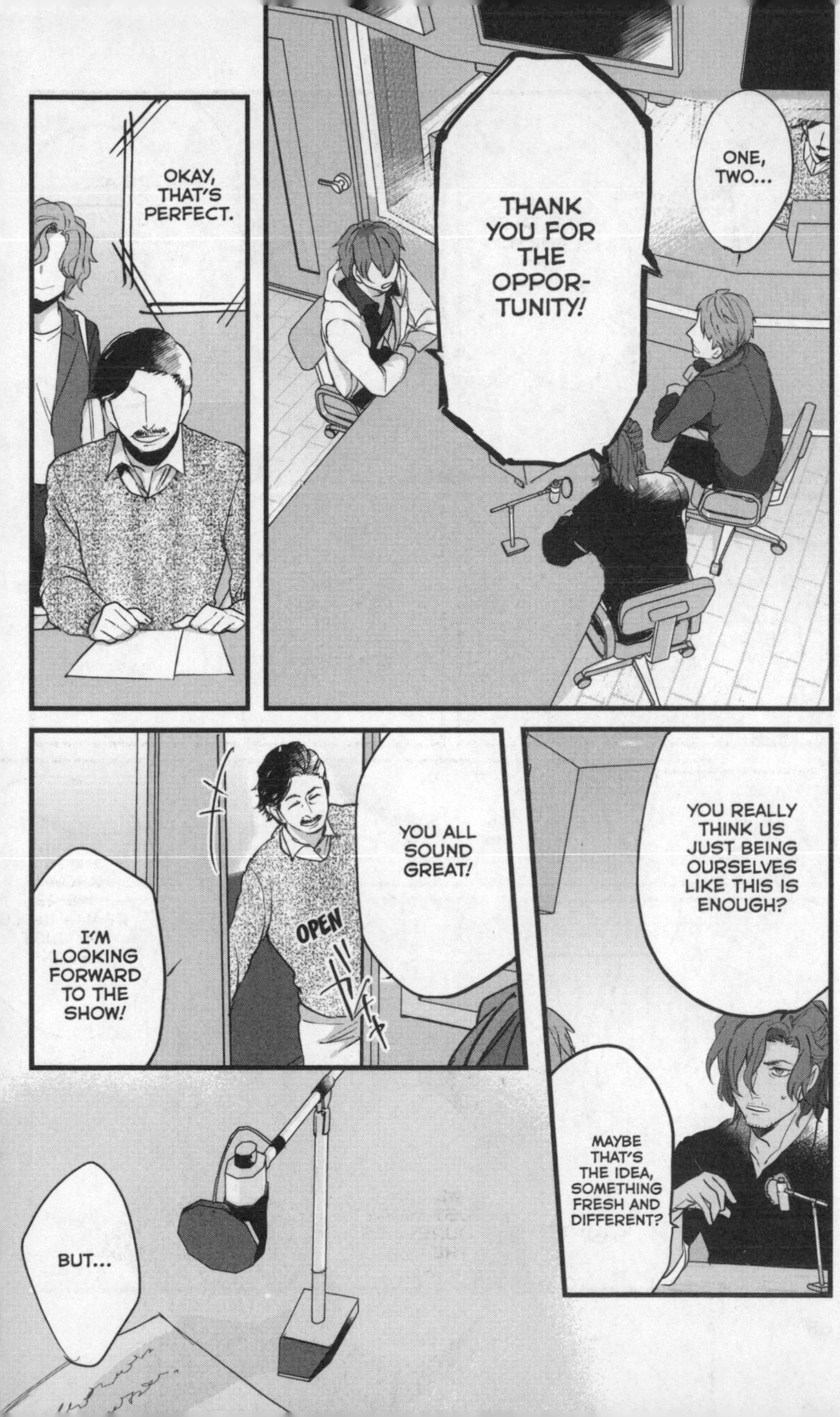
ONE, TWO...
THANK YOU FOR THE OPPOR-TUNITY!
OKAY, THAT'S PERFECT.
YOU REALLY THINK US JUST BEING OURSELVES LIKE THIS IS ENOUGH?
MAYBE THAT'S THE IDEA, SOMETHING FRESH AND DIFFERENT?
YOU ALL SOUND GREAT!
OPEN
I'M LOOKING FORWARD TO THE SHOW!
BUT...

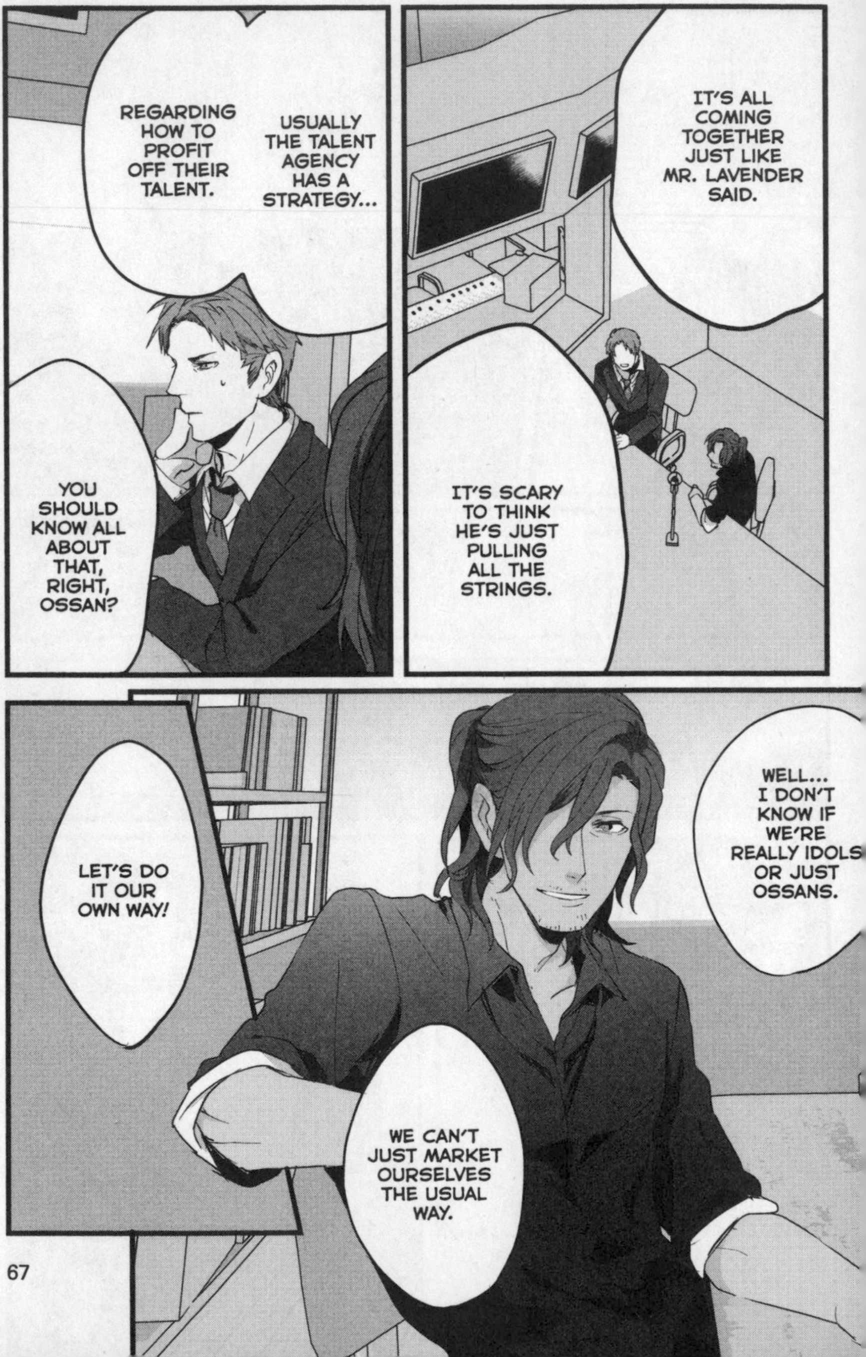
IT'S ALL COMING TOGETHER JUST LIKE MR. LAVENDER SAID.
IT'S SCARY TO THINK HE'S JUST PULLING ALL THE STRINGS.
USUALLY THE TALENT AGENCY HAS A STRATEGY...
REGARDING HOW TO PROFIT OFF THEIR TALENT.
YOU SHOULD KNOW ALL ABOUT THAT, RIGHT, OSSAN?
WELL... I DON'T KNOW IF WE'RE REALLY IDOLS OR JUST OSSANS.
WE CAN'T JUST MARKET OURSELVES THE USUAL WAY.
LET'S DO IT OUR OWN WAY!

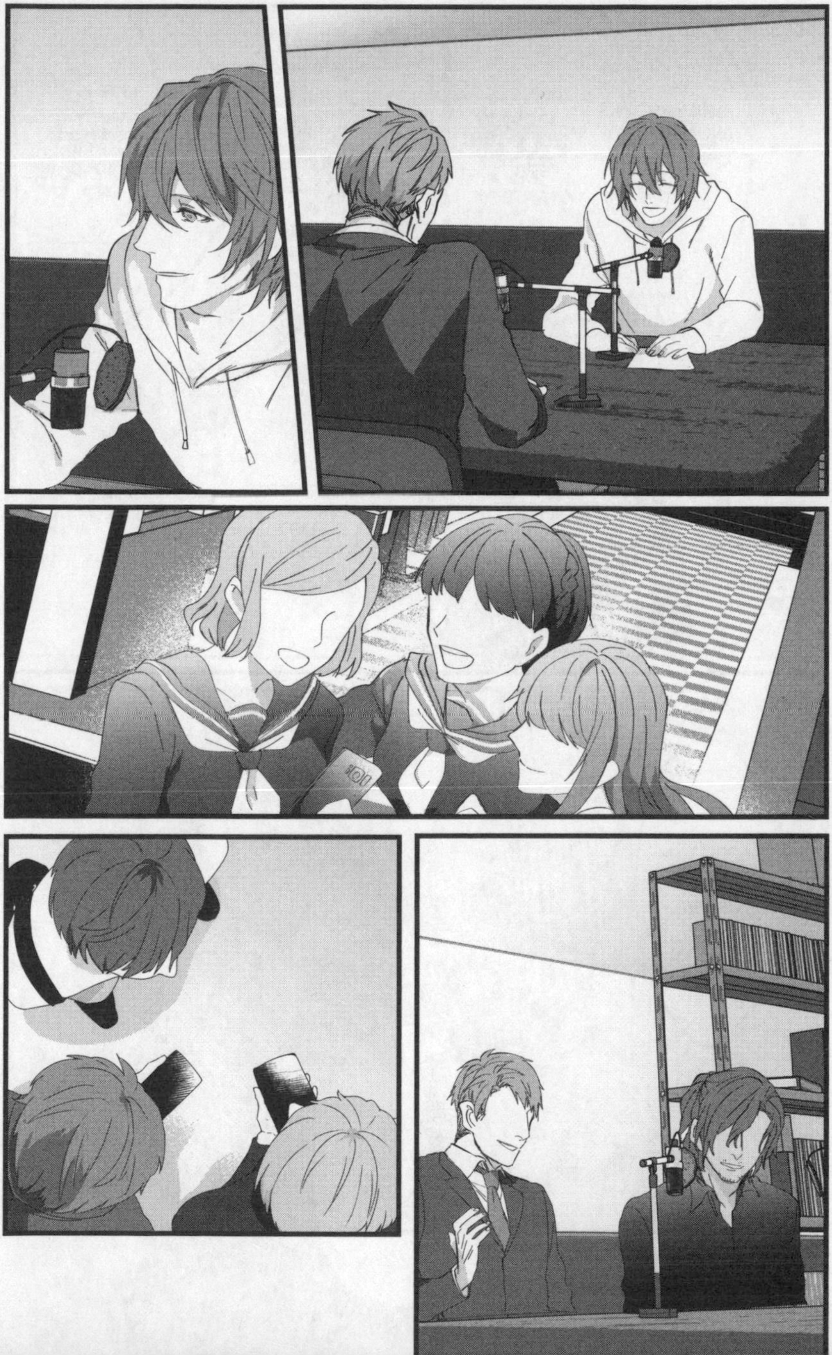

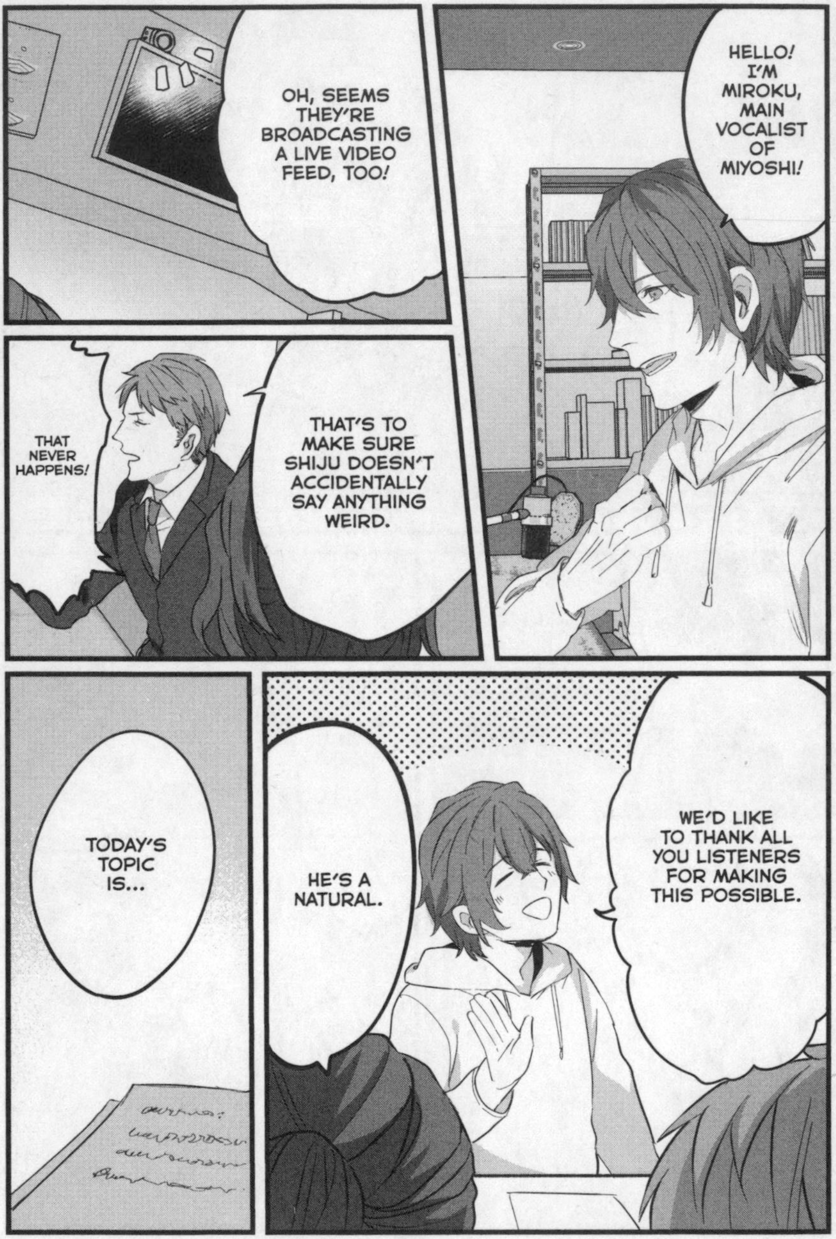
HELLO! I'M MIROKU, MAIN VOCALIST OF MIYOSHI!
OH, SEEMS THEY'RE BROADCASTING A LIVE VIDEO FEED, TOO!
THAT'S TO MAKE SURE SHIJU DOESN'T ACCIDENTALLY SAY ANYTHING WEIRD.
THAT NEVER HAPPENS!
WE'D LIKE TO THANK ALL YOU LISTENERS FOR MAKING THIS POSSIBLE.
HE'S A NATURAL.
TODAY'S TOPIC IS...

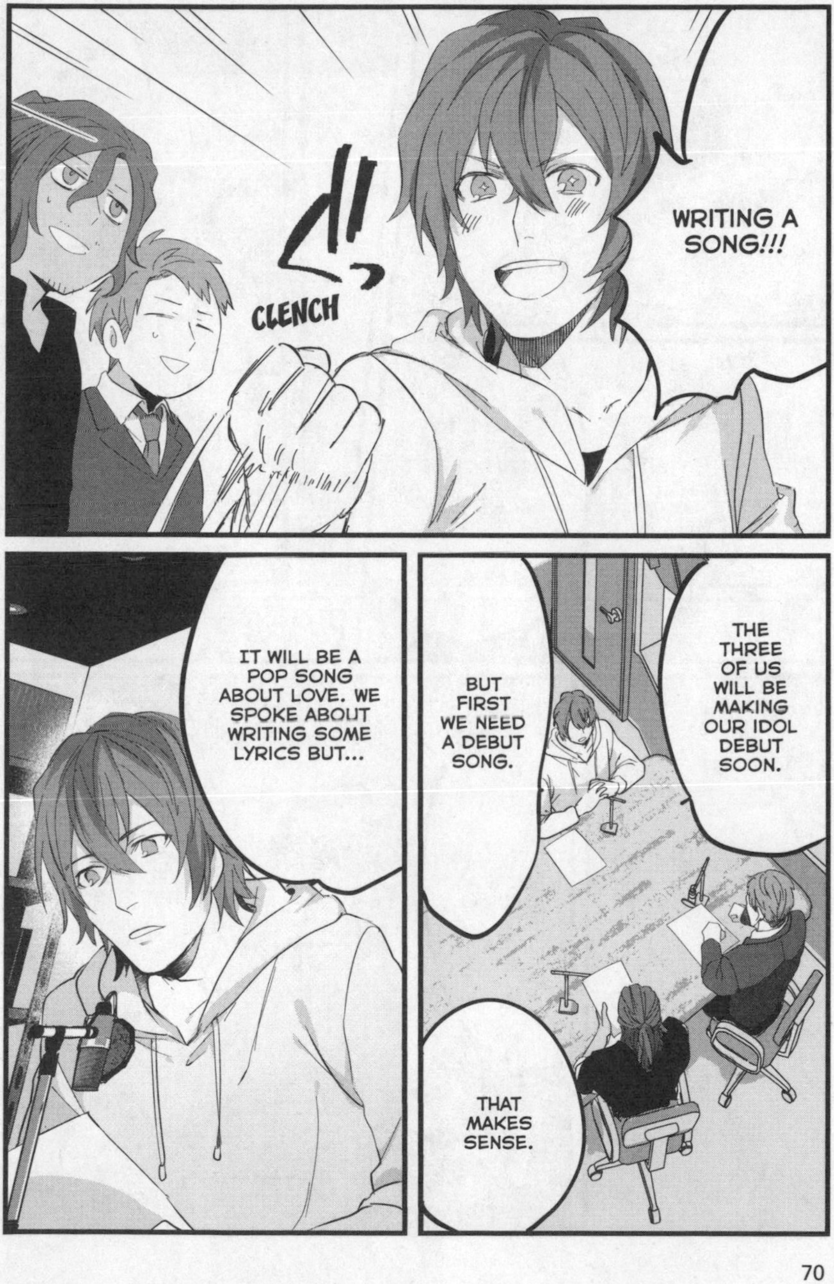
WRITING A SONG!!!
CLENCH
THE THREE OF US WILL BE MAKING OUR IDOL DEBUT SOON.
BUT FIRST WE NEED A DEBUT SONG.
THAT MAKES SENSE.
IT WILL BE A POP SONG ABOUT LOVE. WE SPOKE ABOUT WRITING SOME LYRICS BUT...

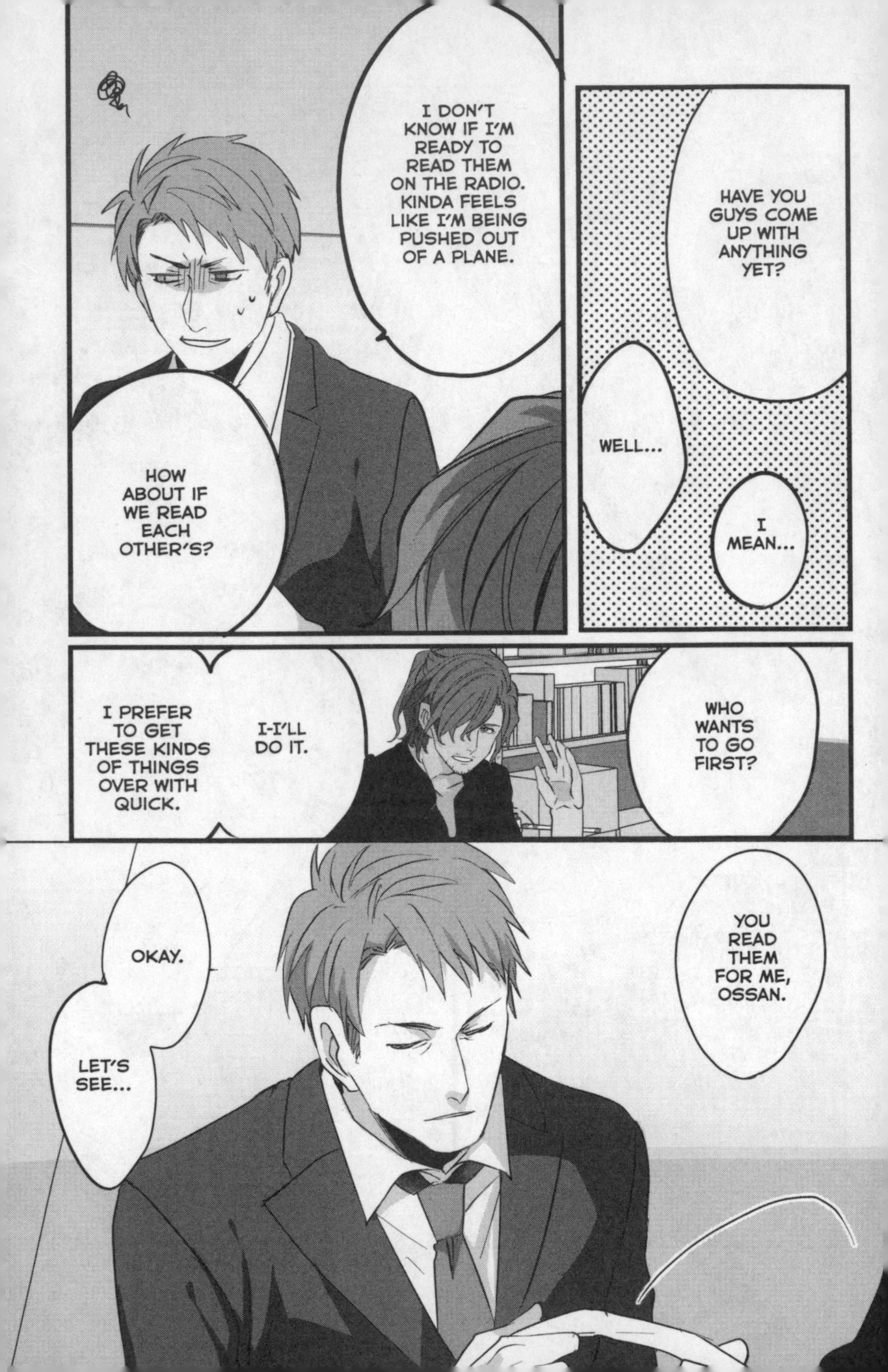
HAVE YOU GUYS COME UP WITH ANYTHING YET?
WELL...
I MEAN...
I DON'T KNOW IF I'M READY TO READ THEM ON THE RADIO. KINDA FEELS LIKE I'M BEING PUSHED OUT OF A PLANE.
HOW ABOUT IF WE READ EACH OTHER'S?
WHO WANTS TO GO FIRST?
I-I'LL DO IT.
I PREFER TO GET THESE KINDS OF THINGS OVER WITH QUICK.
YOU READ THEM FOR ME, OSSAN.
OKAY.
LET'S SEE...

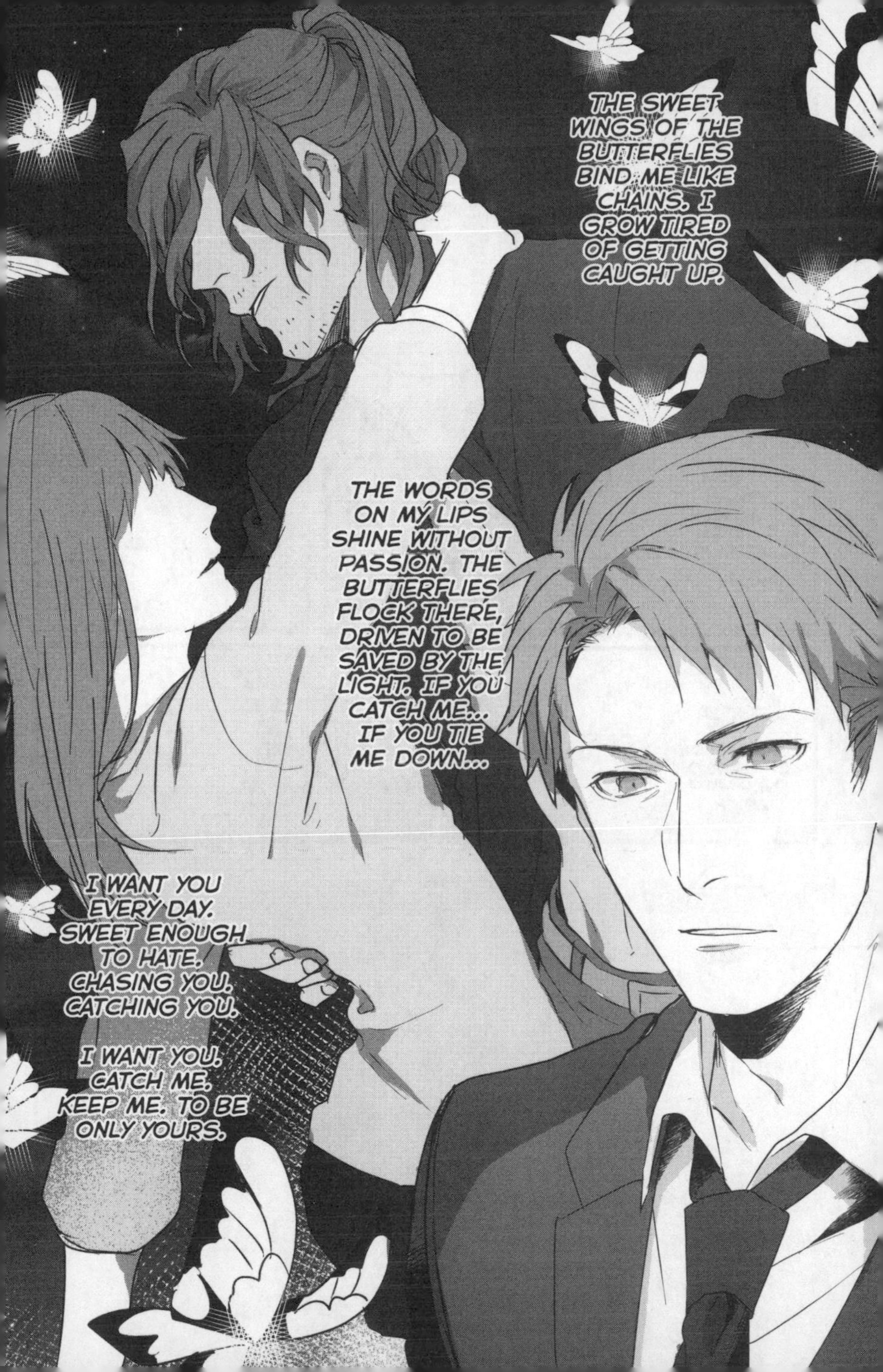
THE SWEET WINGS OF THE BUTTERFLIES BIND ME LIKE CHAINS. I GROW TIRED OF GETTING CAUGHT UP.
THE WORDS ON MY LIPS SHINE WITHOUT PASSION. THE BUTTERFLIES FLOCK THERE, DRIVEN TO BE SAVED BY THE LIGHT. IF YOU CATCH ME... IF YOU TIE ME DOWN...
I WANT YOU EVERY DAY. SWEET ENOUGH TO HATE. CHASING YOU. CATCHING YOU.
I WANT YOU. CATCH ME. KEEP ME. TO BE ONLY YOURS.

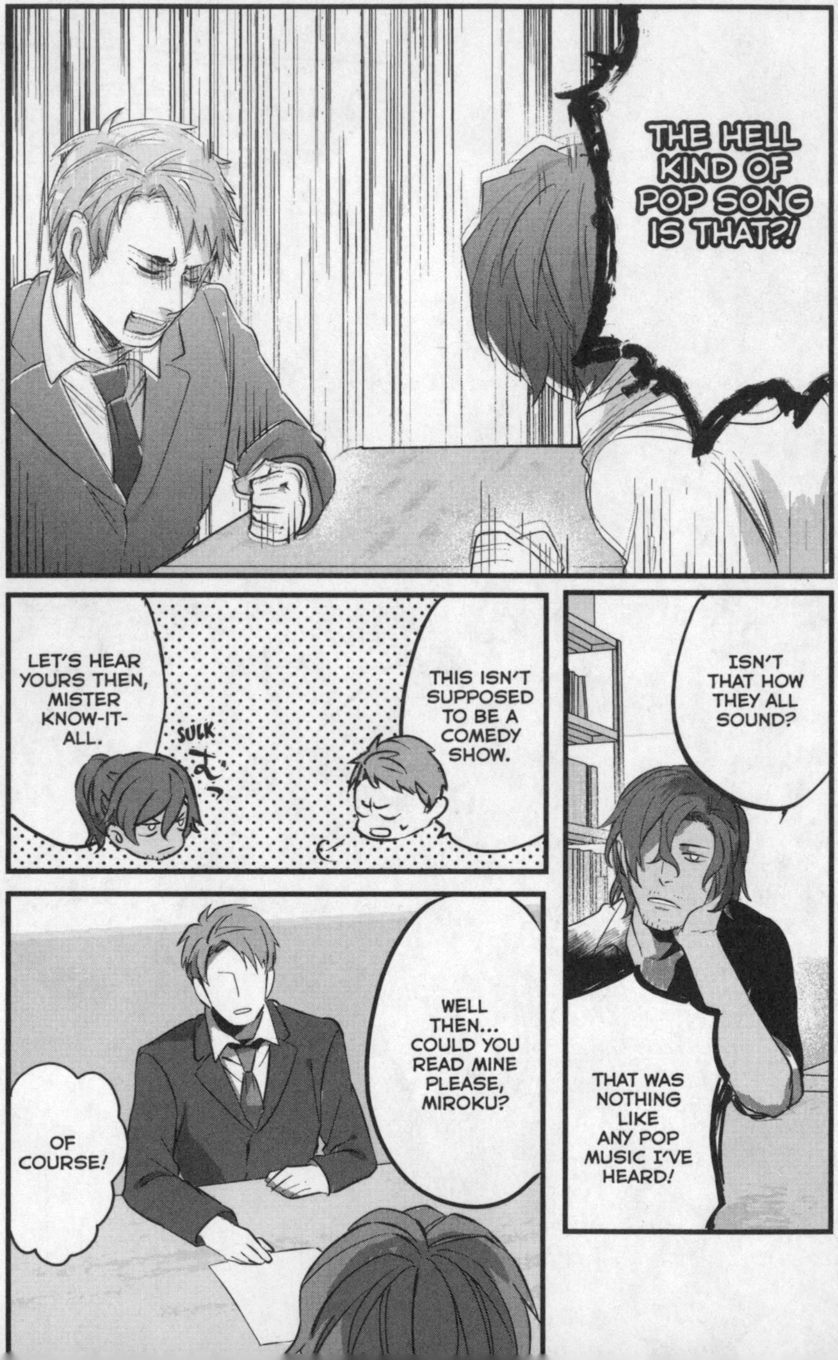
THE HELL KIND OF POP SONG IS THAT?!
ISN'T THAT HOW THEY ALL SOUND?
THAT WAS NOTHING LIKE ANY POP MUSIC I'VE HEARD!
THIS ISN'T SUPPOSED TO BE A COMEDY SHOW.
SULK
LET'S HEAR YOURS THEN, MISTER KNOW-IT-ALL.
WELL THEN... COULD YOU READ MINE PLEASE, MIROKU?
OF COURSE!

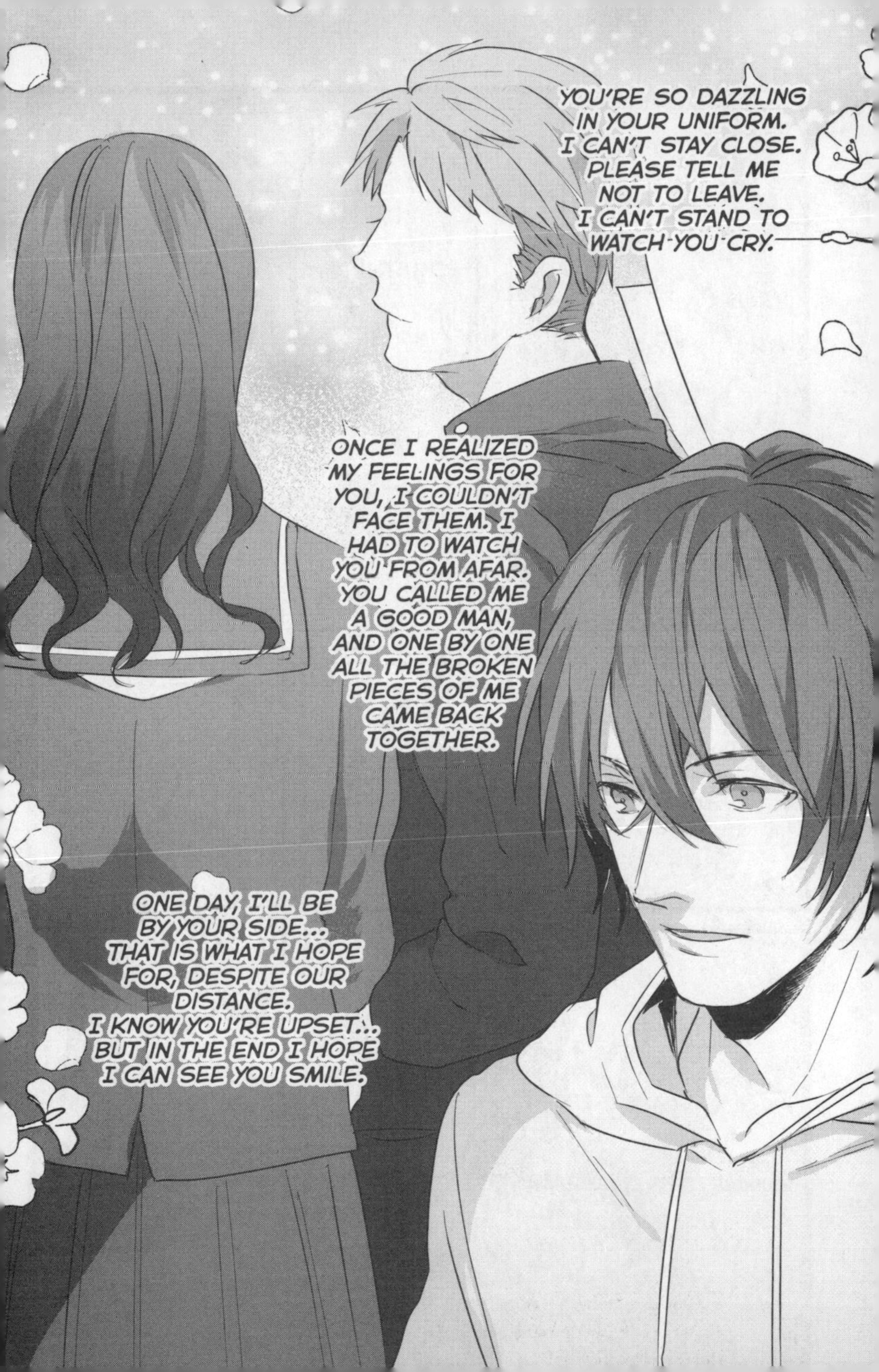
YOU'RE SO DAZZLING IN YOUR UNIFORM. I CAN'T STAY CLOSE. PLEASE TELL ME NOT TO LEAVE. I CAN'T STAND TO WATCH YOU CRY.
ONCE I REALIZED MY FEELINGS FOR YOU, I COULDN'T FACE THEM. I HAD TO WATCH YOU FROM AFAR. YOU CALLED ME A GOOD MAN, AND ONE BY ONE ALL THE BROKEN PIECES OF ME CAME BACK TOGETHER.
ONE DAY, I'LL BE BY YOUR SIDE... THAT IS WHAT I HOPE FOR, DESPITE OUR DISTANCE. I KNOW YOU'RE UPSET... BUT IN THE END I HOPE I CAN SEE YOU SMILE.

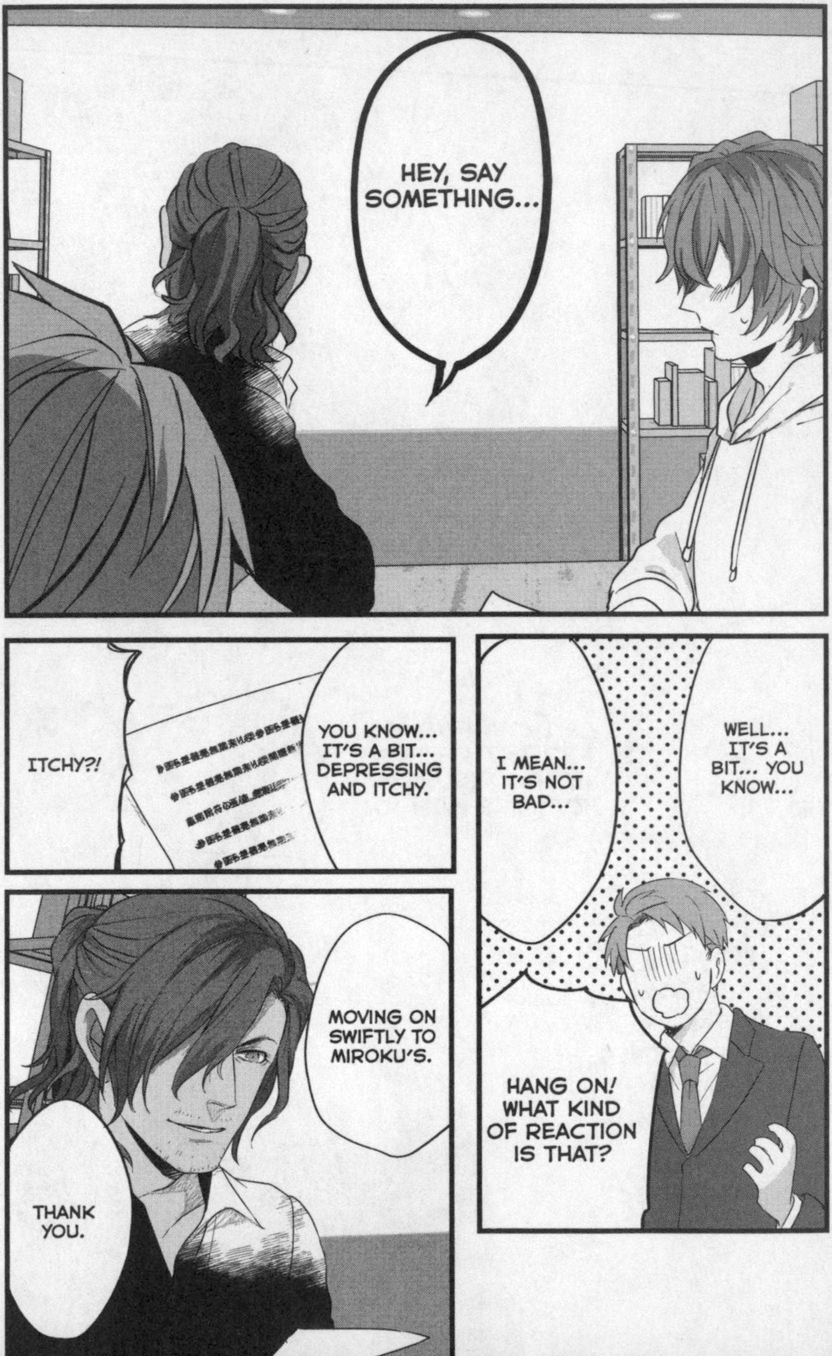
HEY, SAY SOMETHING...
WELL... IT'S A BIT... YOU KNOW...
I MEAN... IT'S NOT BAD...
HANG ON! WHAT KIND OF REACTION IS THAT?
YOU KNOW... IT'S A BIT... DEPRESSING AND ITCHY.
ITCHY?!
MOVING ON SWIFTLY TO MIROKU'S.
THANK YOU.

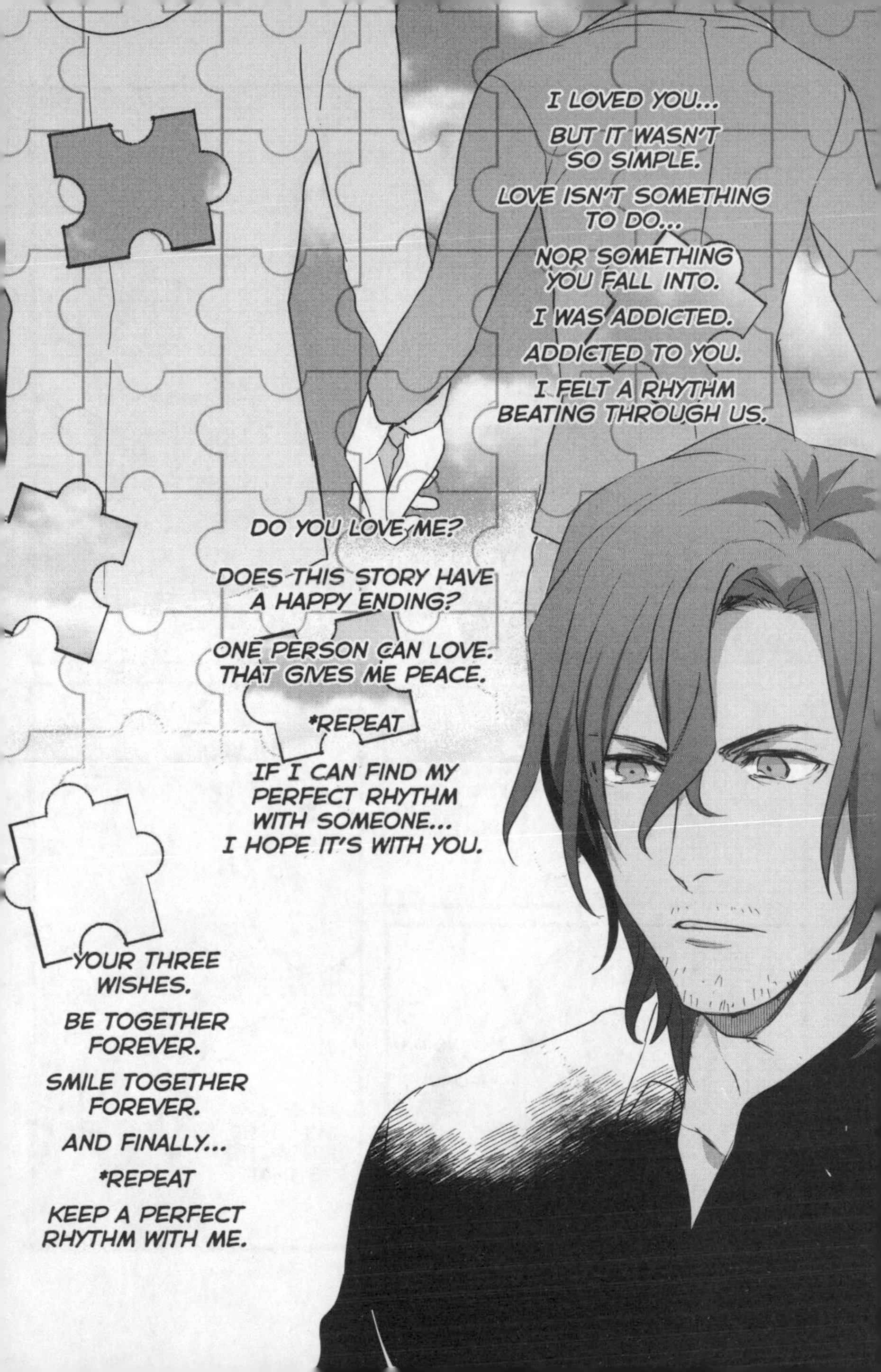
I LOVED YOU...
BUT IT WASN'T SO SIMPLE.
LOVE ISN'T SOMETHING TO DO...
NOR SOMETHING YOU FALL INTO.
I WAS ADDICTED.
ADDICTED TO YOU.
I FELT A RHYTHM BEATING THROUGH US.
DO YOU LOVE ME?
DOES THIS STORY HAVE A HAPPY ENDING?
ONE PERSON CAN LOVE. THAT GIVES ME PEACE.
*REPEAT
IF I CAN FIND MY PERFECT RHYTHM WITH SOMEONE... I HOPE IT'S WITH YOU.
YOUR THREE WISHES.
BE TOGETHER FOREVER.
SMILE TOGETHER FOREVER.
AND FINALLY...
*REPEAT
KEEP A PERFECT RHYTHM WITH ME.

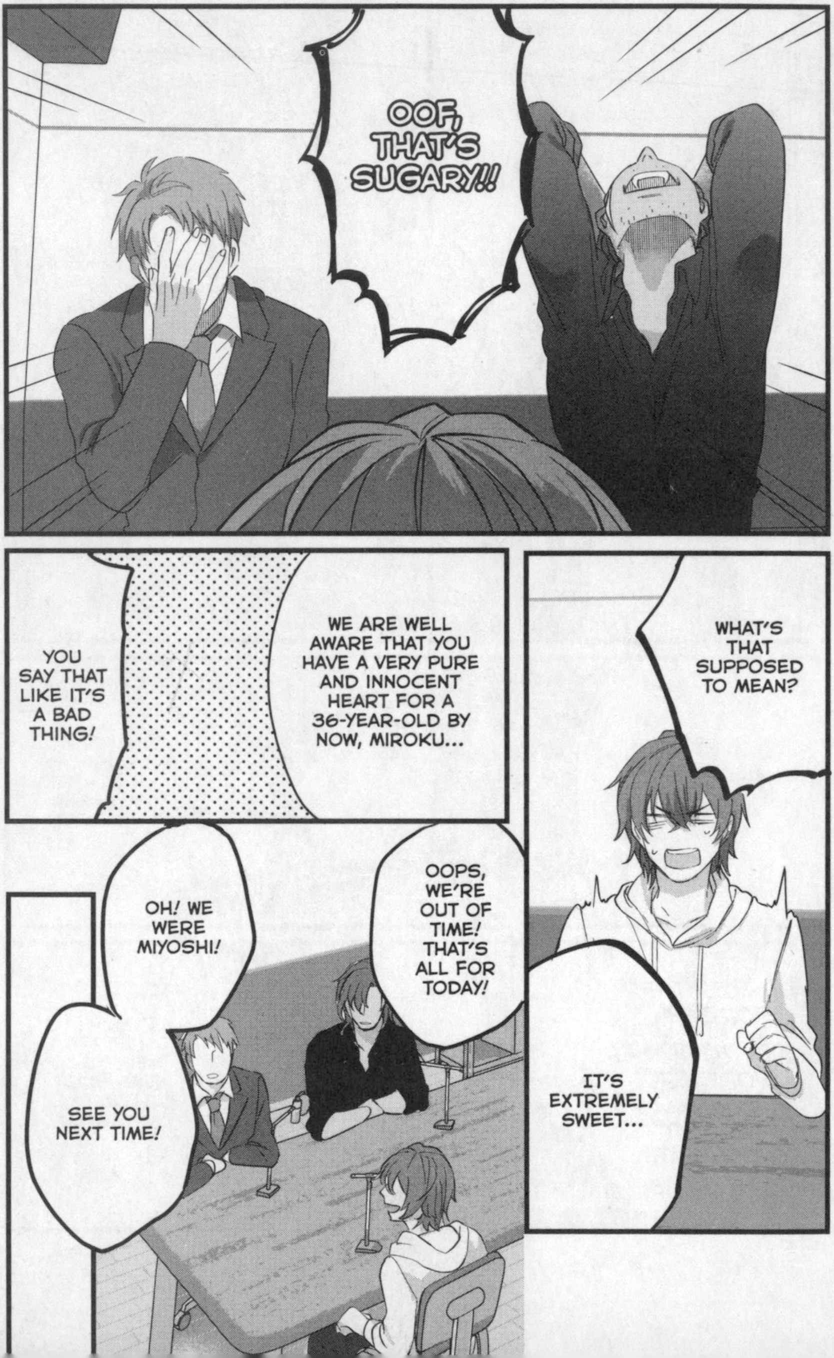
OOF, THAT'S SUGARY!!
WHAT'S THAT SUPPOSED TO MEAN?
IT'S EXTREMELY SWEET...
WE ARE WELL AWARE THAT YOU HAVE A VERY PURE AND INNOCENT HEART FOR A 36-YEAR-OLD BY NOW, MIROKU...
YOU SAY THAT LIKE IT'S A BAD THING!
OOPS, WE'RE OUT OF TIME! THAT'S ALL FOR TODAY!
OH! WE WERE MIYOSHI!
SEE YOU NEXT TIME!

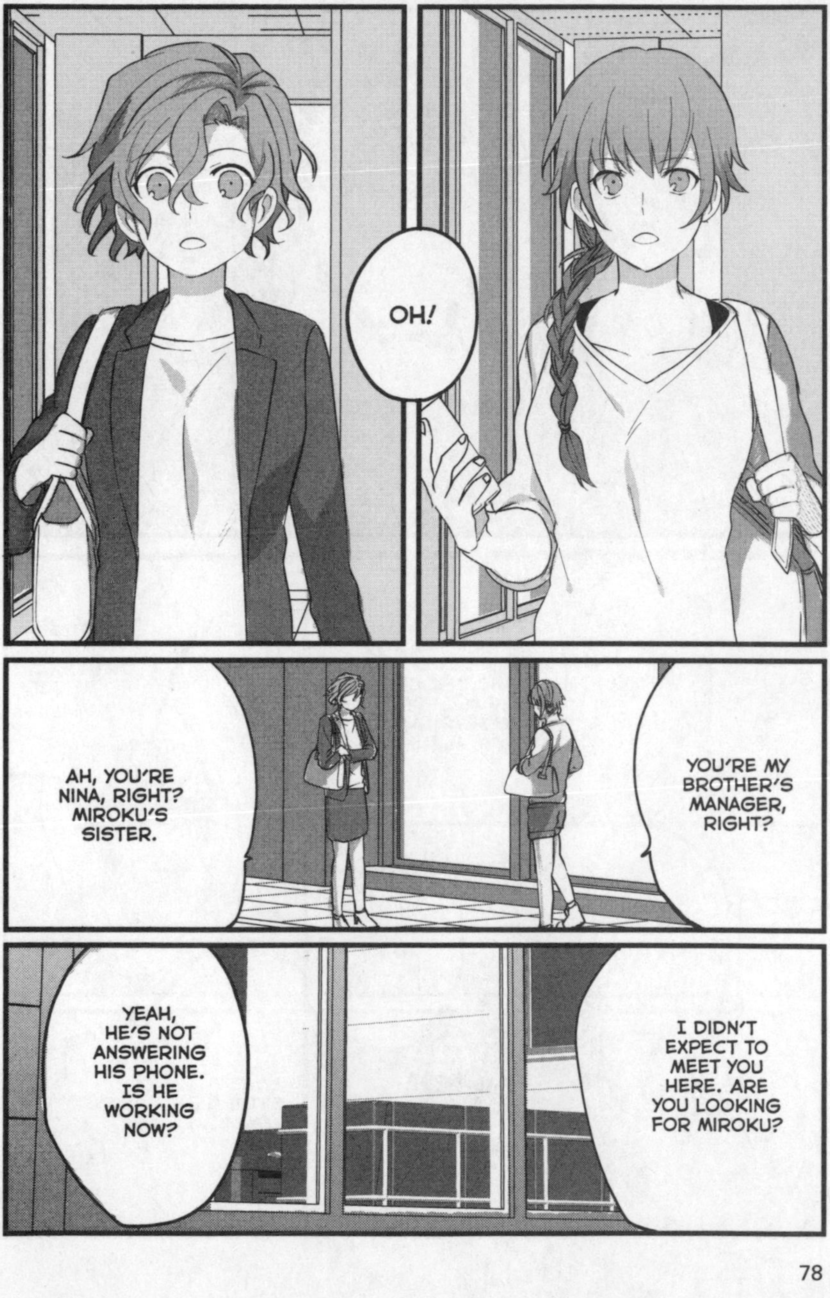
OH!
YOU'RE MY BROTHER'S MANAGER, RIGHT?
AH, YOU'RE NINA, RIGHT? MIROKU'S SISTER.
I DIDN'T EXPECT TO MEET YOU HERE. ARE YOU LOOKING FOR MIROKU?
YEAH, HE'S NOT ANSWERING HIS PHONE. IS HE WORKING NOW?

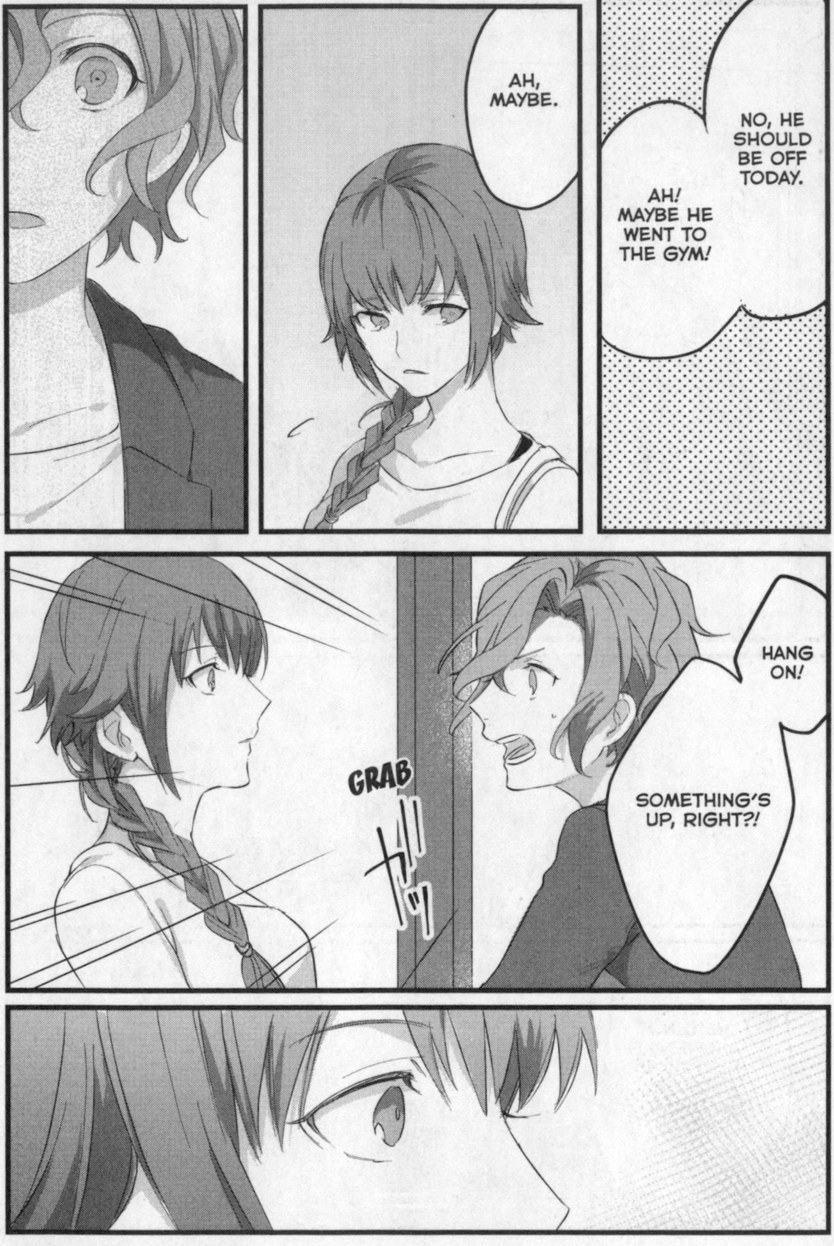
NO, HE SHOULD BE OFF TODAY.
AH! MAYBE HE WENT TO THE GYM!
AH, MAYBE.
HANG ON!
SOMETHING'S UP, RIGHT?!
GRAB
ガッ

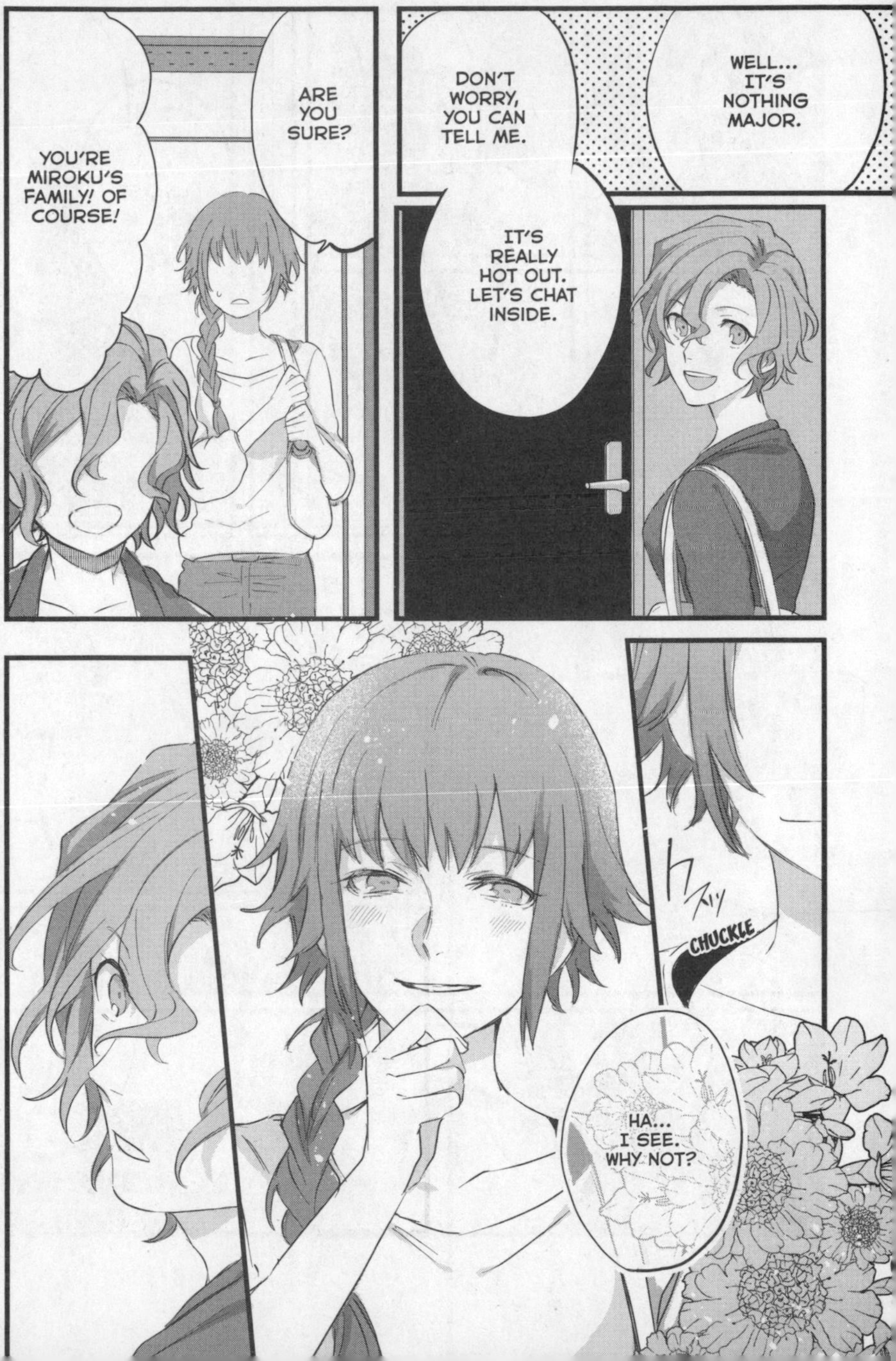
WELL... IT'S NOTHING MAJOR.
DON'T WORRY, YOU CAN TELL ME.
IT'S REALLY HOT OUT. LET'S CHAT INSIDE.
ARE YOU SURE?
YOU'RE MIROKU'S FAMILY! OF COURSE!
トスッ
CHUCKLE
HA... I SEE. WHY NOT?

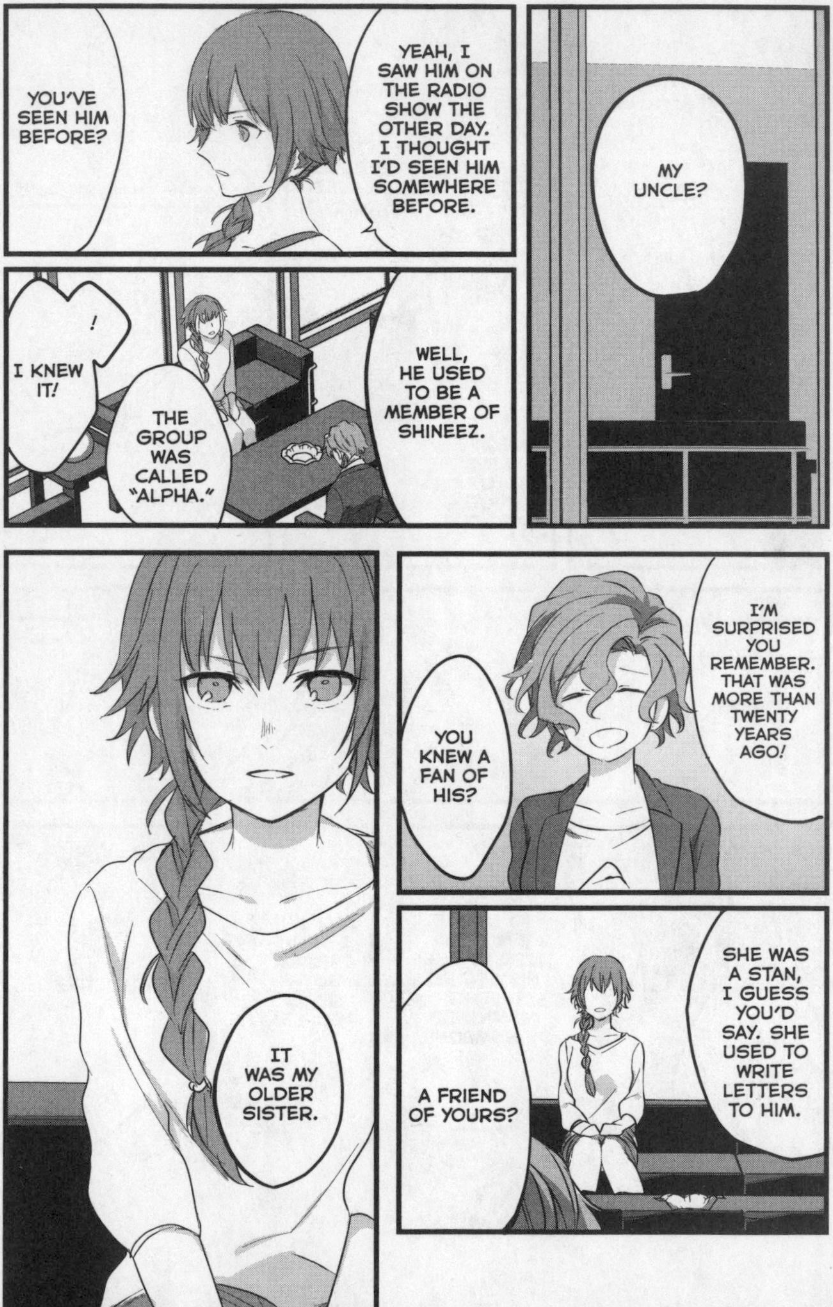
MY UNCLE?
YEAH, I SAW HIM ON THE RADIO SHOW THE OTHER DAY. I THOUGHT I'D SEEN HIM SOMEWHERE BEFORE.
YOU'VE SEEN HIM BEFORE?
WELL, HE USED TO BE A MEMBER OF SHINEEZ.
THE GROUP WAS CALLED "ALPHA."
!
I KNEW IT!
I'M SURPRISED YOU REMEMBER. THAT WAS MORE THAN TWENTY YEARS AGO!
YOU KNEW A FAN OF HIS?
SHE WAS A STAN, I GUESS YOU'D SAY. SHE USED TO WRITE LETTERS TO HIM.
A FRIEND OF YOURS?
IT WAS MY OLDER SISTER.

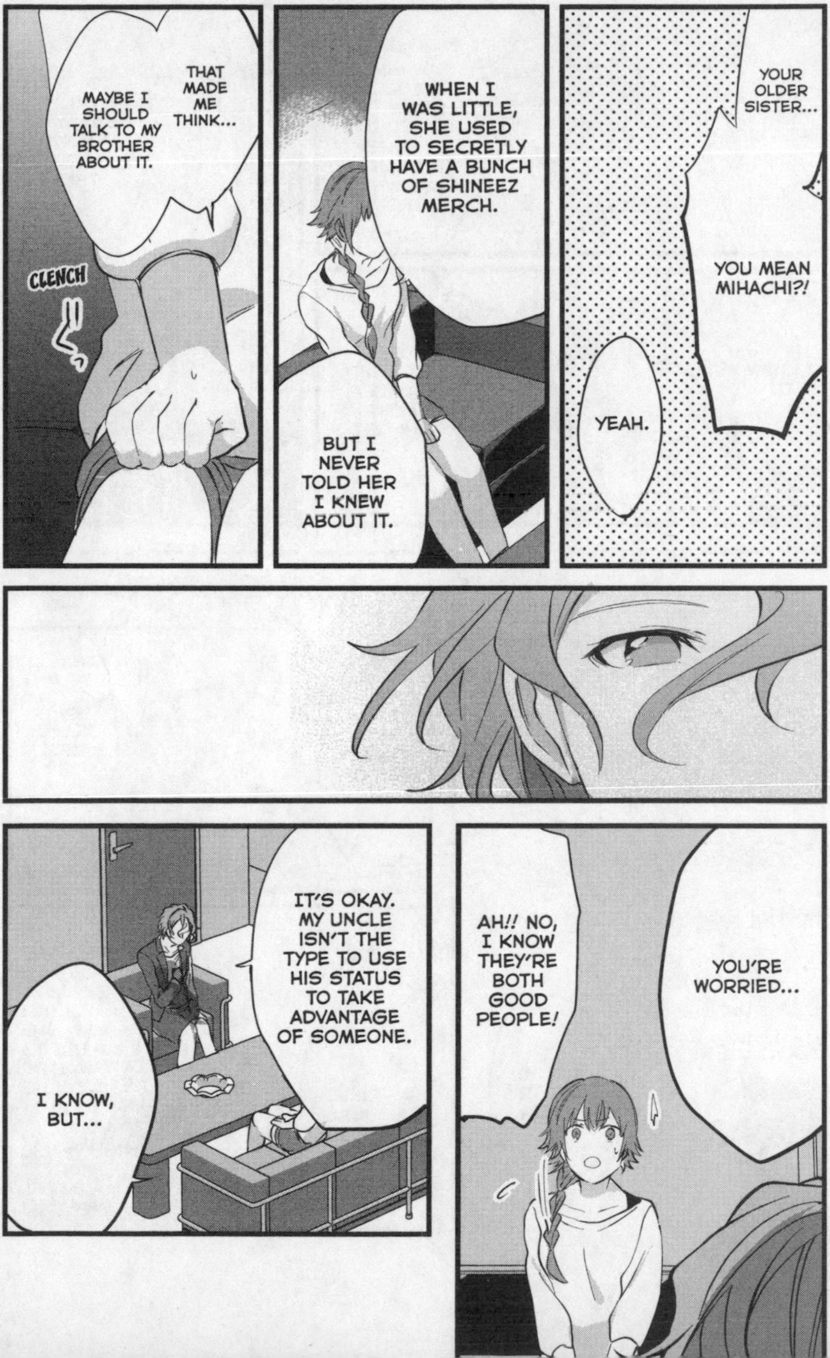
YOUR OLDER SISTER...
YOU MEAN MIHACHI?!
YEAH.
WHEN I WAS LITTLE, SHE USED TO SECRETLY HAVE A BUNCH OF SHINEEZ MERCH.
BUT I NEVER TOLD HER I KNEW ABOUT IT.
THAT MADE ME THINK...
MAYBE I SHOULD TALK TO MY BROTHER ABOUT IT.
CLENCH
YOU'RE WORRIED...
AH!! NO, I KNOW THEY'RE BOTH GOOD PEOPLE!
IT'S OKAY. MY UNCLE ISN'T THE TYPE TO USE HIS STATUS TO TAKE ADVANTAGE OF SOMEONE.
I KNOW, BUT...

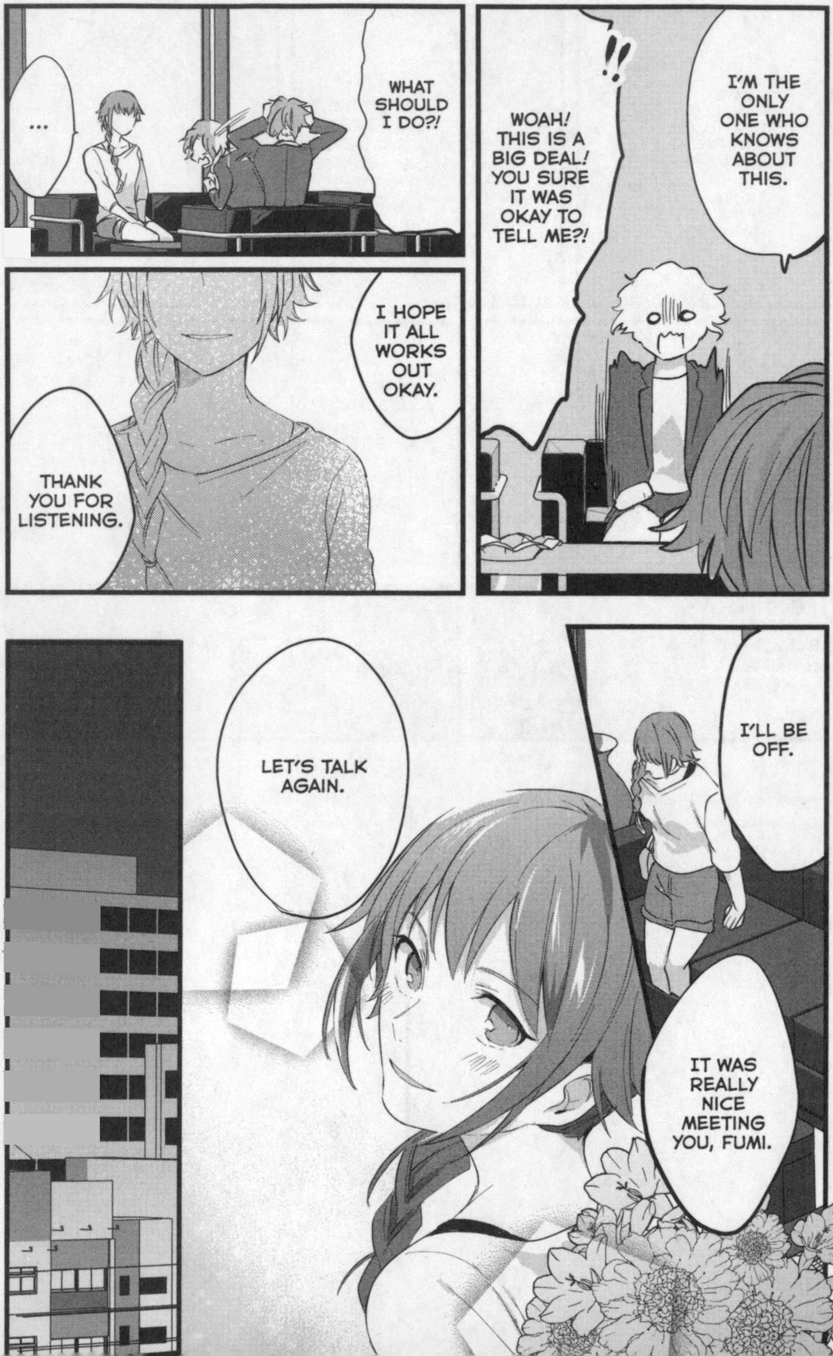
I'M THE ONLY ONE WHO KNOWS ABOUT THIS.
!!
WOAH! THIS IS A BIG DEAL! YOU SURE IT WAS OKAY TO TELL ME?!
WHAT SHOULD I DO?!
...
I HOPE IT ALL WORKS OUT OKAY.
THANK YOU FOR LISTENING.
I'LL BE OFF.
IT WAS REALLY NICE MEETING YOU, FUMI.
LET'S TALK AGAIN.

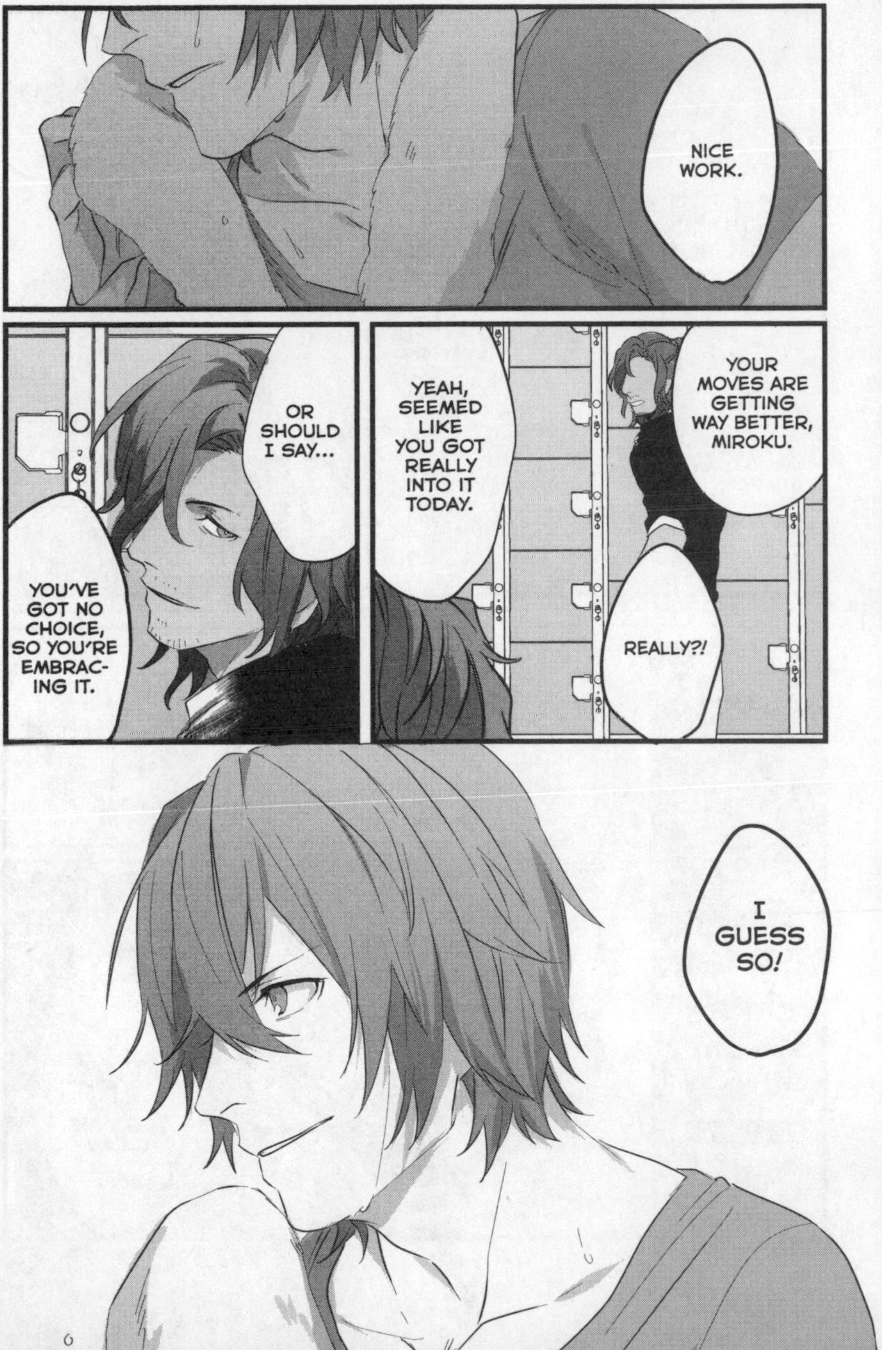
NICE WORK.
YOUR MOVES ARE GETTING WAY BETTER, MIROKU.
REALLY?!
YEAH, SEEMED LIKE YOU GOT REALLY INTO IT TODAY.
OR SHOULD I SAY...
YOU'VE GOT NO CHOICE, SO YOU'RE EMBRAC-ING IT.
I GUESS SO!

Chapter 9

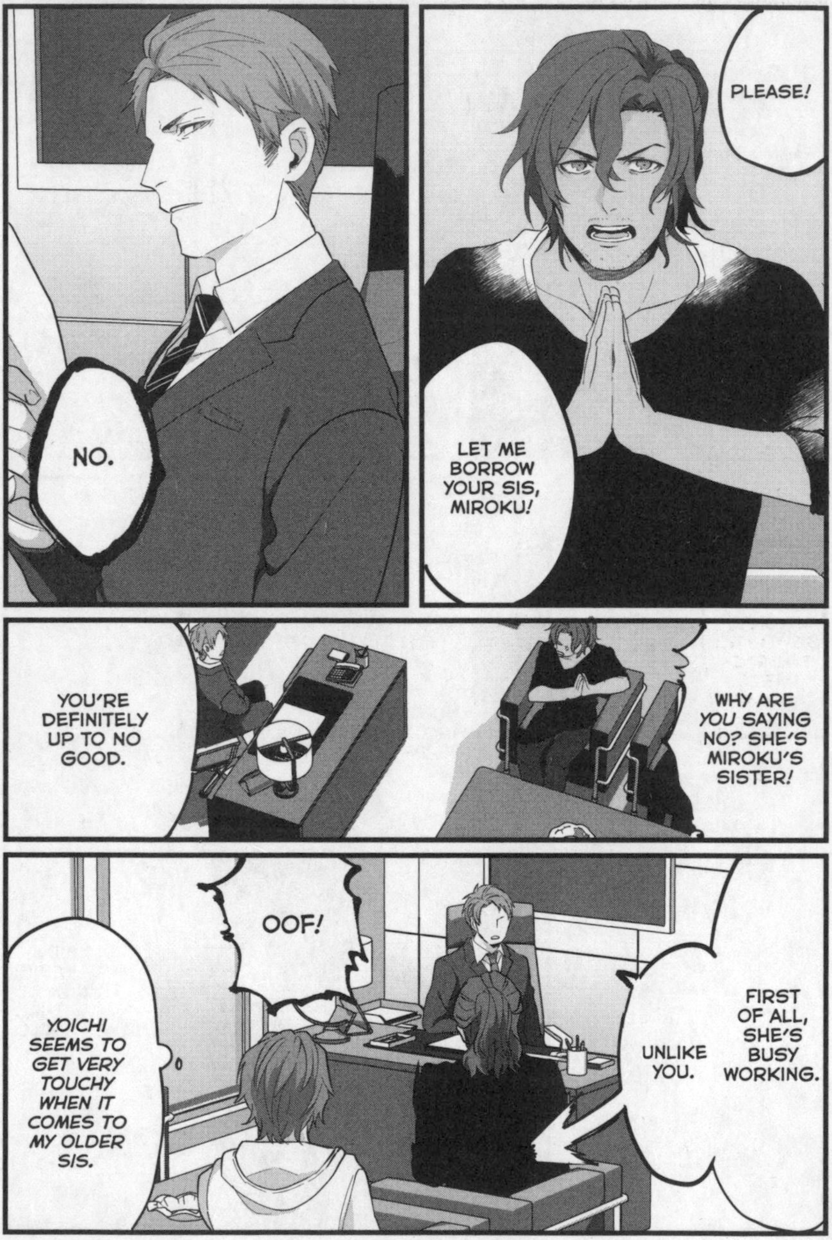
PLEASE!
LET ME BORROW YOUR SIS, MIROKU!
NO.
WHY ARE *YOU* SAYING NO? SHE'S MIROKU'S SISTER!
YOU'RE DEFINITELY UP TO NO GOOD.
FIRST OF ALL, SHE'S BUSY WORKING.
UNLIKE YOU.
OOF!
YOICHI SEEMS TO GET VERY TOUCHY WHEN IT COMES TO MY OLDER SIS.

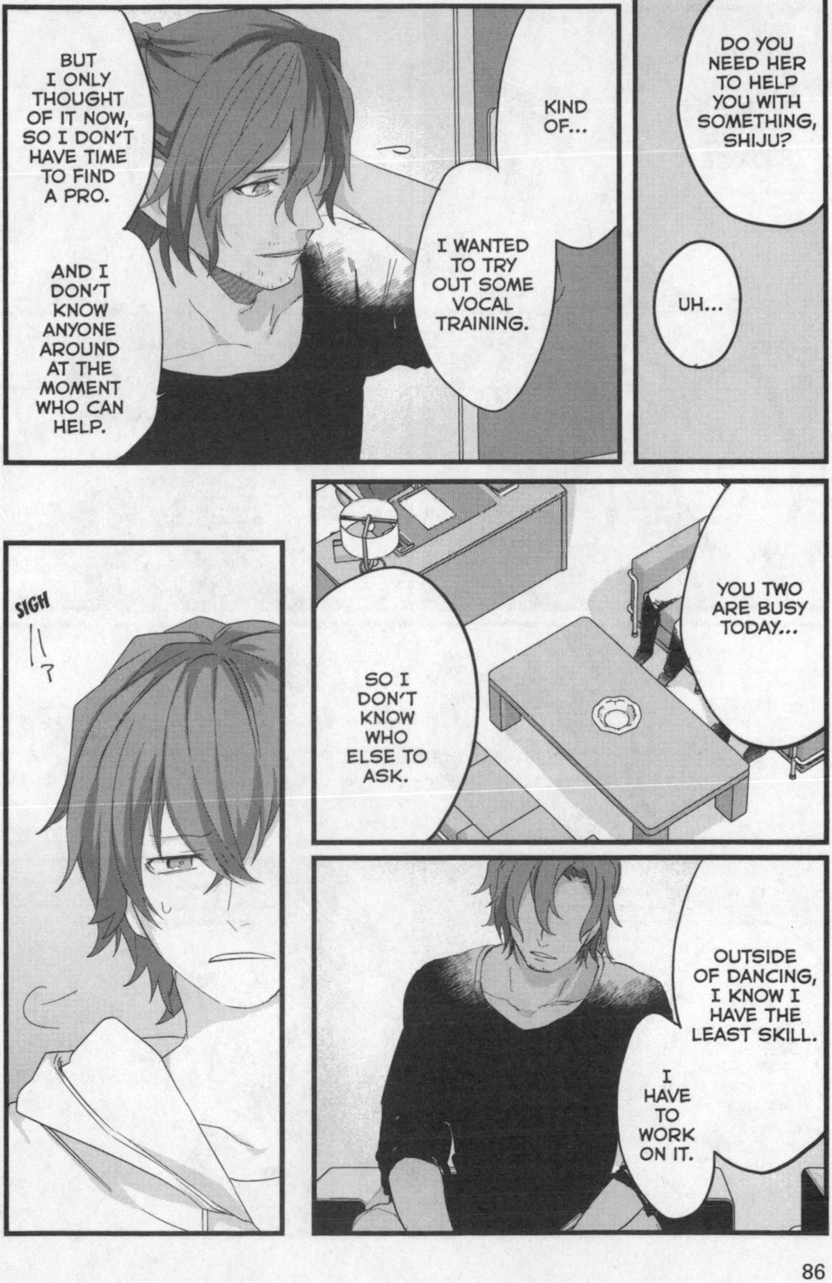
DO YOU NEED HER TO HELP YOU WITH SOMETHING, SHIJU?
UH...
KIND OF...
I WANTED TO TRY OUT SOME VOCAL TRAINING.
BUT I ONLY THOUGHT OF IT NOW, SO I DON'T HAVE TIME TO FIND A PRO.
AND I DON'T KNOW ANYONE AROUND AT THE MOMENT WHO CAN HELP.
YOU TWO ARE BUSY TODAY...
SO I DON'T KNOW WHO ELSE TO ASK.
OUTSIDE OF DANCING, I KNOW I HAVE THE LEAST SKILL.
I HAVE TO WORK ON IT.
SIGH
ハァ

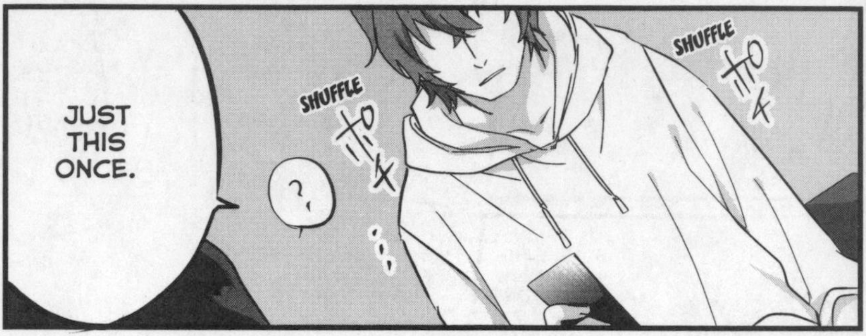
SHUFFLE
SHUFFLE
?
JUST THIS ONCE.

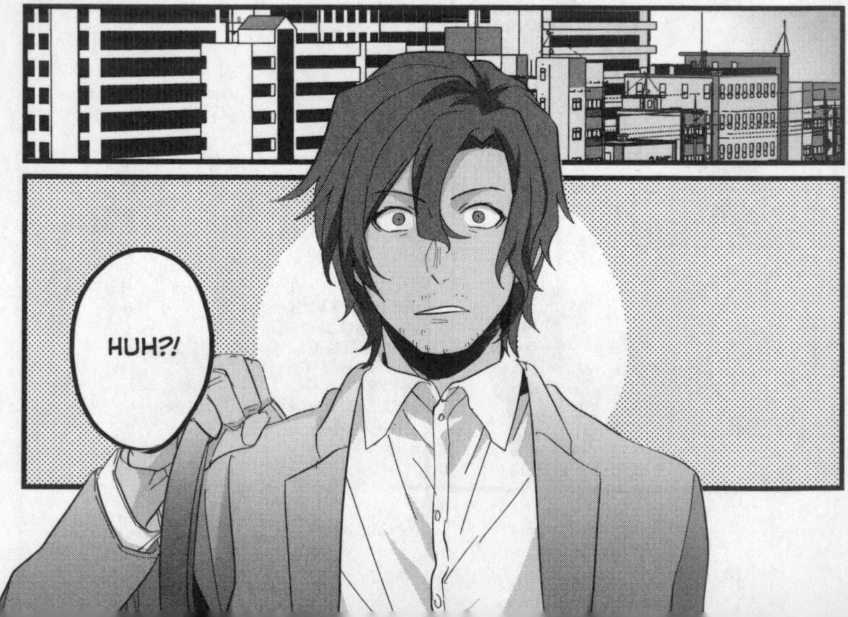
HUH?!

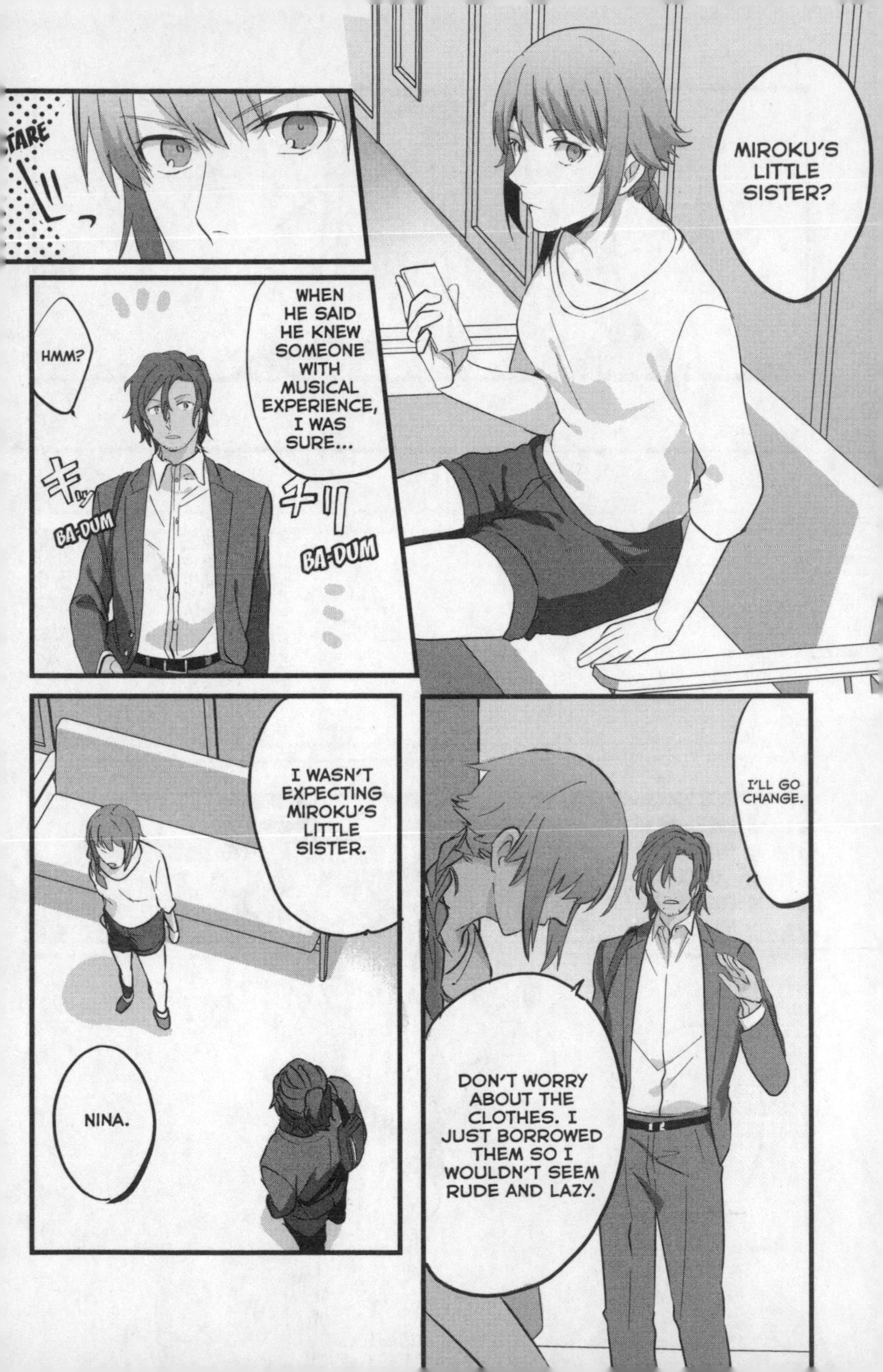
MIROKU'S LITTLE SISTER?
TARE
WHEN HE SAID HE KNEW SOMEONE WITH MUSICAL EXPERIENCE, I WAS SURE...
HMM?
BA-DUM
BA-DUM
I'LL GO CHANGE.
DON'T WORRY ABOUT THE CLOTHES. I JUST BORROWED THEM SO I WOULDN'T SEEM RUDE AND LAZY.
I WASN'T EXPECTING MIROKU'S LITTLE SISTER.
NINA.

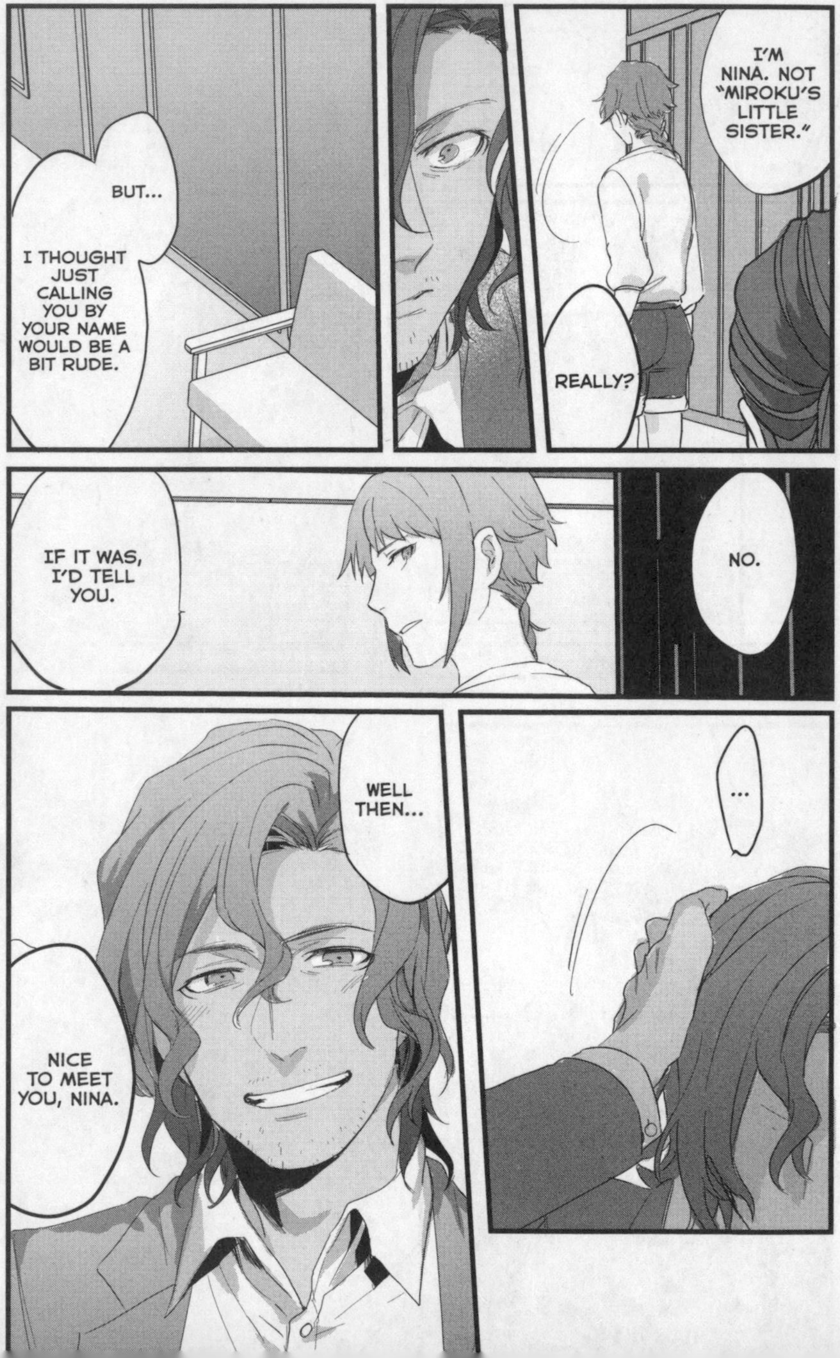
I'M NINA. NOT "MIROKU'S LITTLE SISTER."
REALLY?
BUT...
I THOUGHT JUST CALLING YOU BY YOUR NAME WOULD BE A BIT RUDE.
NO.
IF IT WAS, I'D TELL YOU.
...
WELL THEN...
NICE TO MEET YOU, NINA.

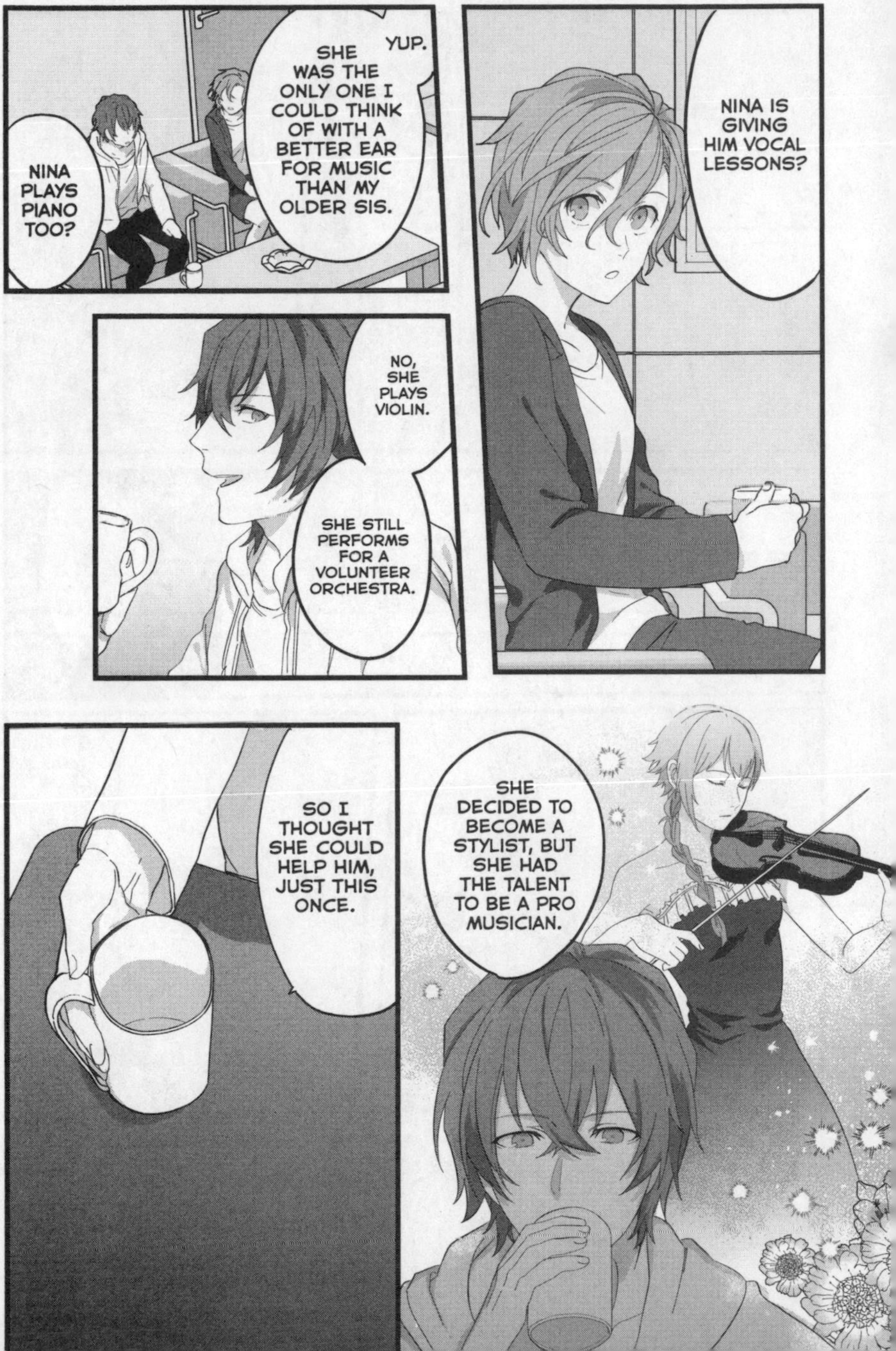
NINA IS GIVING HIM VOCAL LESSONS?
YUP.
SHE WAS THE ONLY ONE I COULD THINK OF WITH A BETTER EAR FOR MUSIC THAN MY OLDER SIS.
NINA PLAYS PIANO TOO?
NO, SHE PLAYS VIOLIN.
SHE STILL PERFORMS FOR A VOLUNTEER ORCHESTRA.
SHE DECIDED TO BECOME A STYLIST, BUT SHE HAD THE TALENT TO BE A PRO MUSICIAN.
SO I THOUGHT SHE COULD HELP HIM, JUST THIS ONCE.

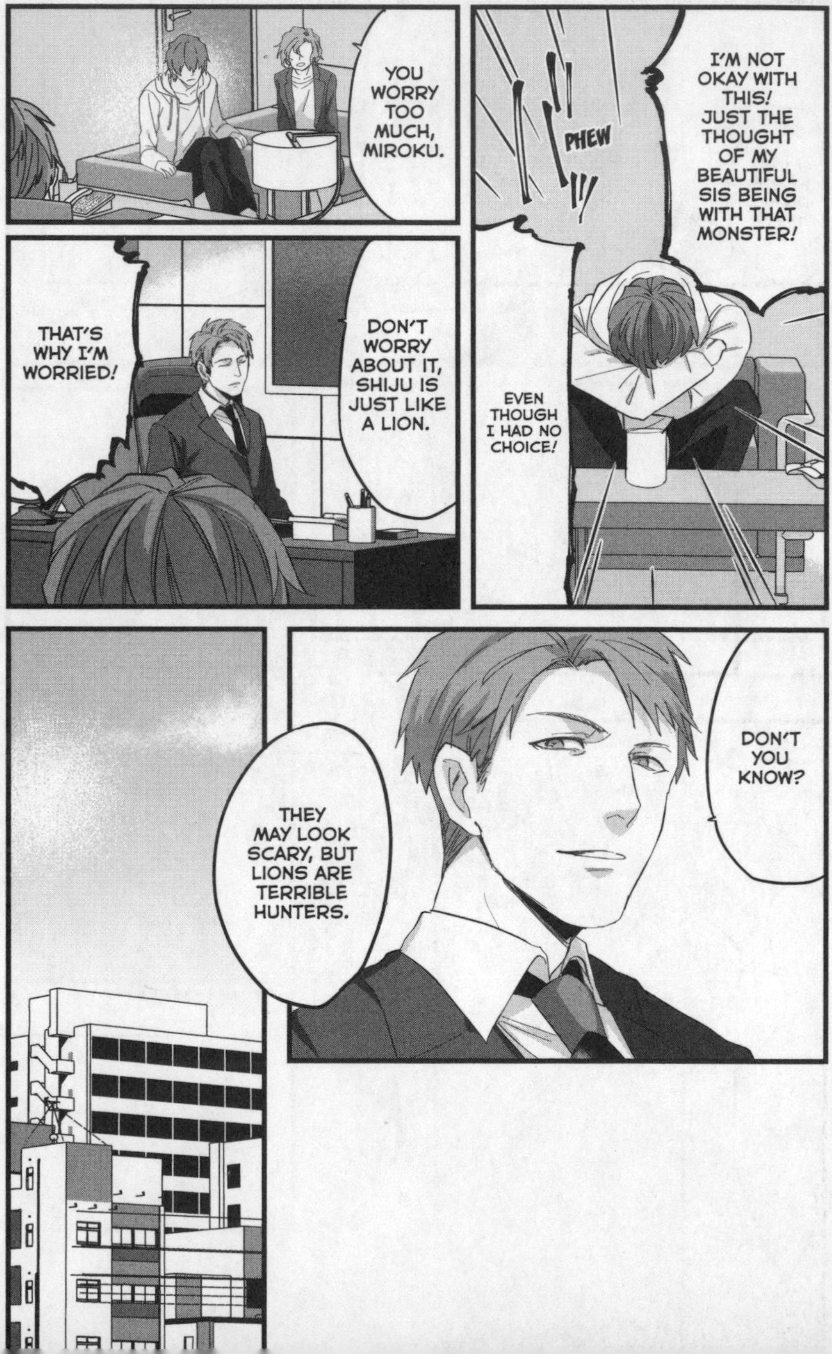
I'M NOT OKAY WITH THIS! JUST THE THOUGHT OF MY BEAUTIFUL SIS BEING WITH THAT MONSTER!
PHEW
EVEN THOUGH I HAD NO CHOICE!
YOU WORRY TOO MUCH, MIROKU.
DON'T WORRY ABOUT IT, SHIJU IS JUST LIKE A LION.
THAT'S WHY I'M WORRIED!
DON'T YOU KNOW?
THEY MAY LOOK SCARY, BUT LIONS ARE TERRIBLE HUNTERS.

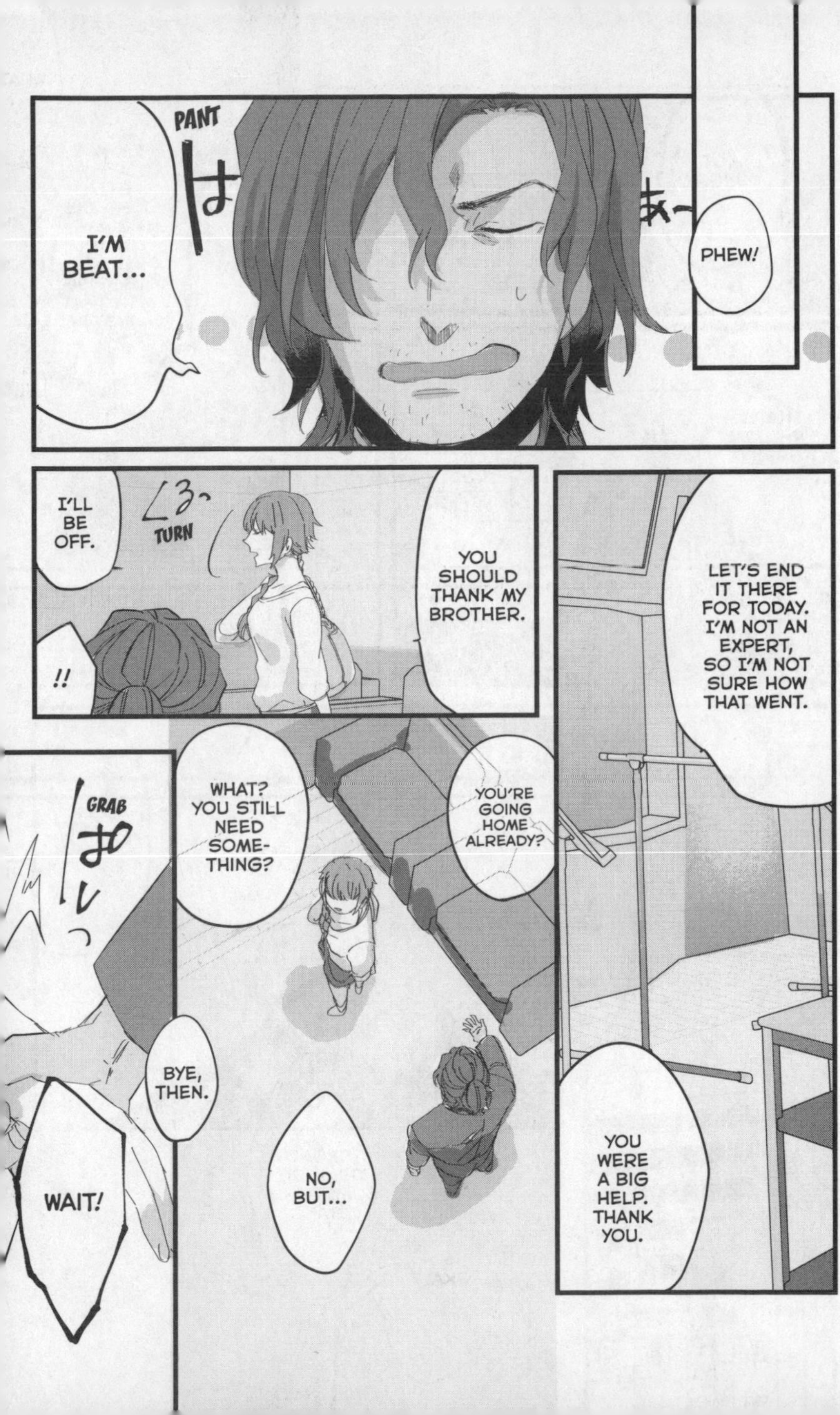

あ〜
PHEW!
は
PANT
I'M BEAT...
LET'S END IT THERE FOR TODAY. I'M NOT AN EXPERT, SO I'M NOT SURE HOW THAT WENT.
YOU WERE A BIG HELP. THANK YOU.
YOU SHOULD THANK MY BROTHER.
くるっ
TURN
I'LL BE OFF.
!!
YOU'RE GOING HOME ALREADY?
WHAT? YOU STILL NEED SOME-THING?
BYE, THEN.
NO, BUT...
ぱしっ
GRAB
WAIT!

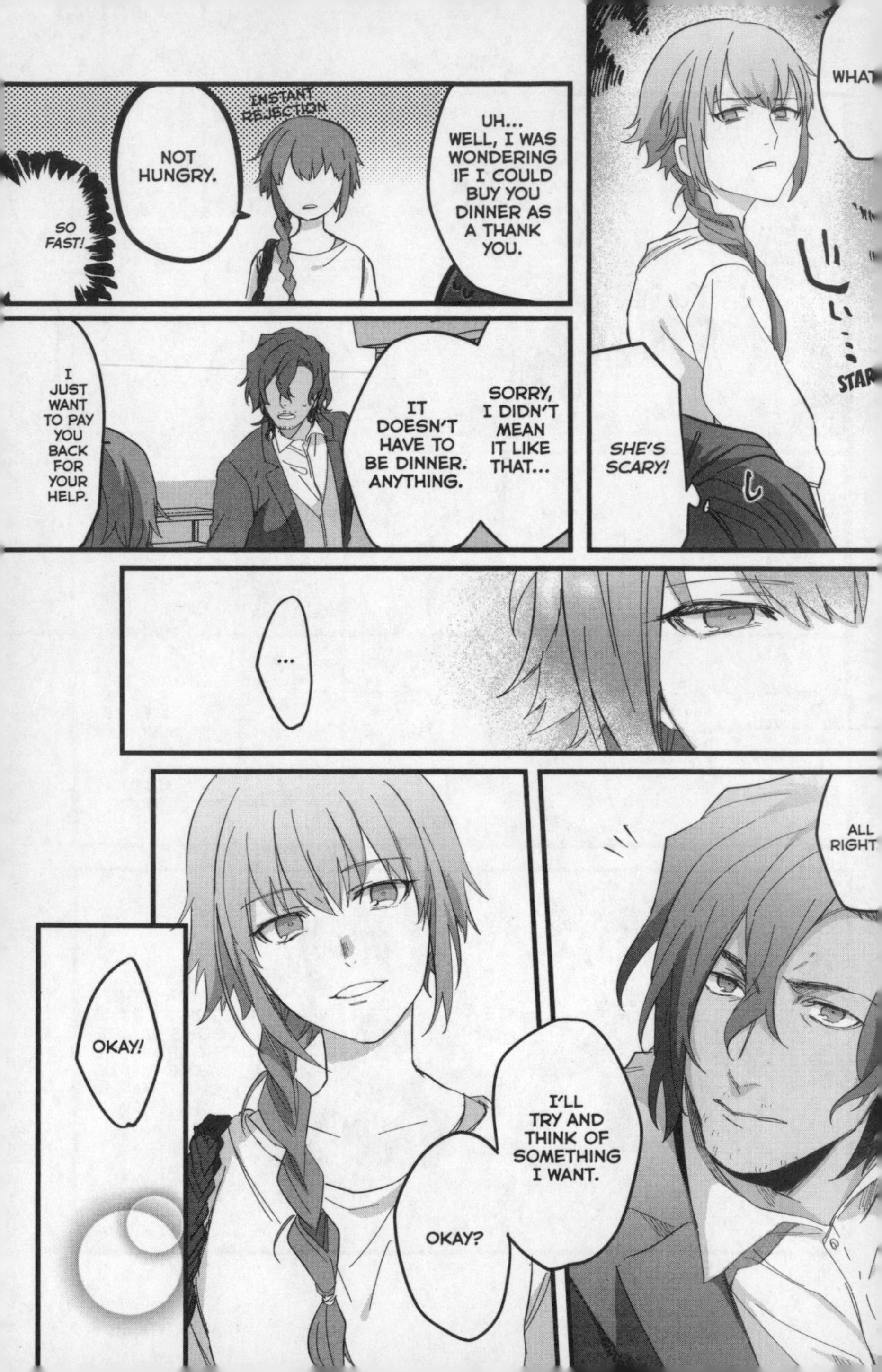
WHAT
STAR
SHE'S SCARY!
UH... WELL, I WAS WONDERING IF I COULD BUY YOU DINNER AS A THANK YOU.
INSTANT REJECTION
NOT HUNGRY.
SO FAST!
SORRY, I DIDN'T MEAN IT LIKE THAT...
IT DOESN'T HAVE TO BE DINNER. ANYTHING.
I JUST WANT TO PAY YOU BACK FOR YOUR HELP.
...
ALL RIGHT
I'LL TRY AND THINK OF SOMETHING I WANT.
OKAY?
OKAY!

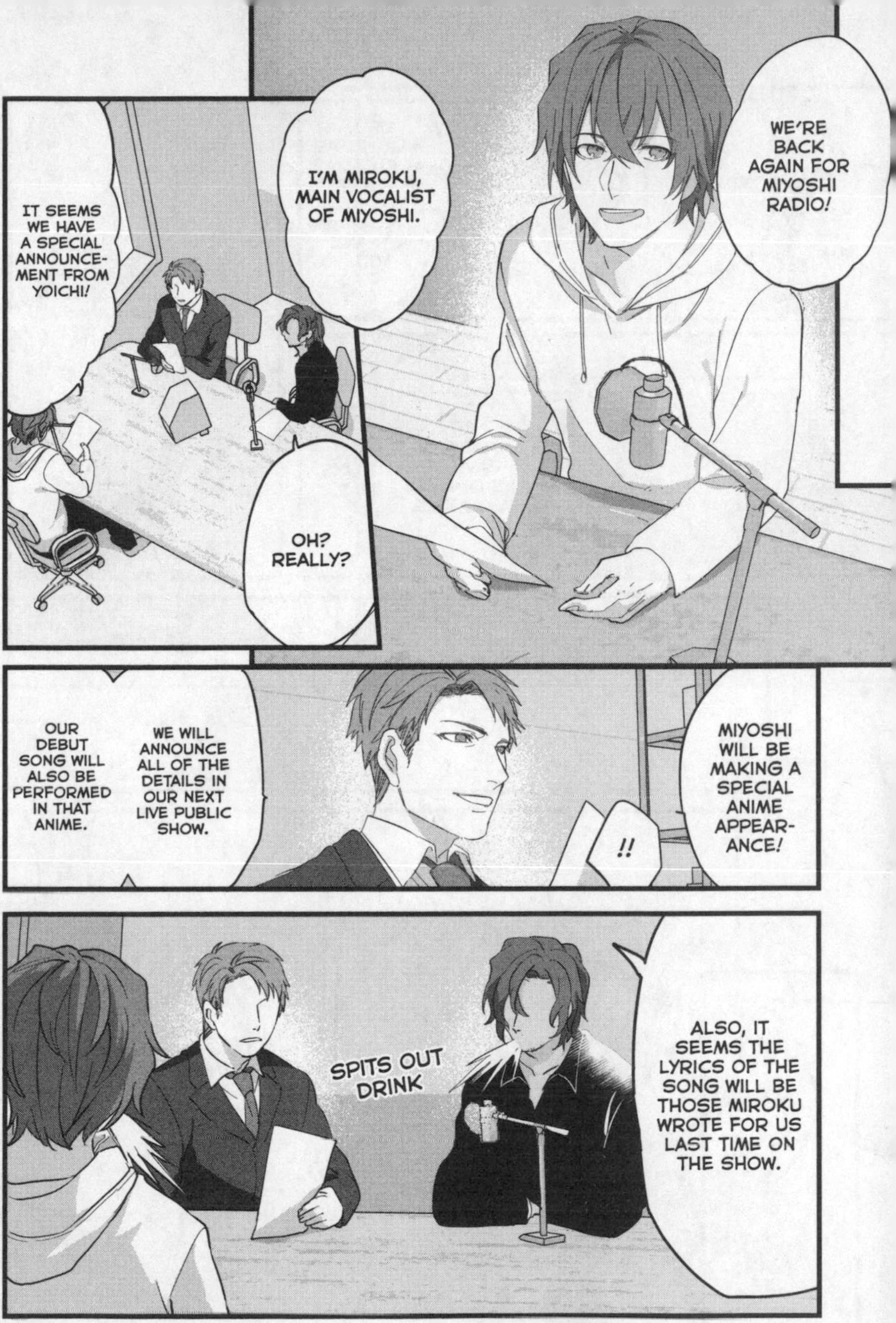
WE'RE BACK AGAIN FOR MIYOSHI RADIO!
I'M MIROKU, MAIN VOCALIST OF MIYOSHI.
IT SEEMS WE HAVE A SPECIAL ANNOUNCEMENT FROM YOICHI!
OH? REALLY?
MIYOSHI WILL BE MAKING A SPECIAL ANIME APPEARANCE!
!!
WE WILL ANNOUNCE ALL OF THE DETAILS IN OUR NEXT LIVE PUBLIC SHOW.
OUR DEBUT SONG WILL ALSO BE PERFORMED IN THAT ANIME.
ALSO, IT SEEMS THE LYRICS OF THE SONG WILL BE THOSE MIROKU WROTE FOR US LAST TIME ON THE SHOW.
SPITS OUT DRINK

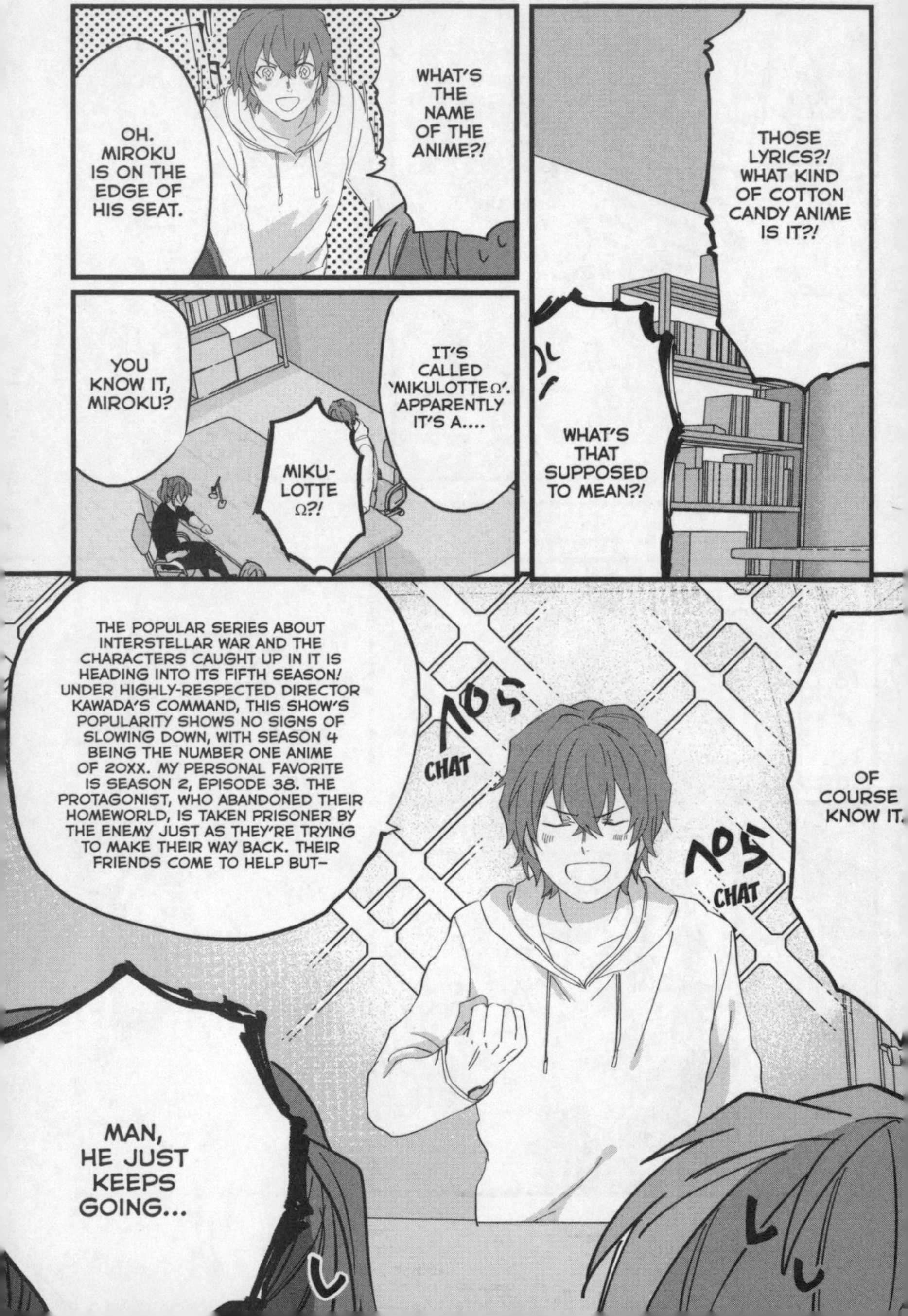
THOSE LYRICS?! WHAT KIND OF COTTON CANDY ANIME IS IT?!
WHAT'S THAT SUPPOSED TO MEAN?!
WHAT'S THE NAME OF THE ANIME?!
OH. MIROKU IS ON THE EDGE OF HIS SEAT.
IT'S CALLED 'MIKULOTTEΩ'. APPARENTLY IT'S A....
MIKU-LOTTE Ω?!
YOU KNOW IT, MIROKU?
OF COURSE KNOW IT.
THE POPULAR SERIES ABOUT INTERSTELLAR WAR AND THE CHARACTERS CAUGHT UP IN IT IS HEADING INTO ITS FIFTH SEASON! UNDER HIGHLY-RESPECTED DIRECTOR KAWADA'S COMMAND, THIS SHOW'S POPULARITY SHOWS NO SIGNS OF SLOWING DOWN, WITH SEASON 4 BEING THE NUMBER ONE ANIME OF 20XX. MY PERSONAL FAVORITE IS SEASON 2, EPISODE 38. THE PROTAGONIST, WHO ABANDONED THEIR HOMEWORLD, IS TAKEN PRISONER BY THE ENEMY JUST AS THEY'RE TRYING TO MAKE THEIR WAY BACK. THEIR FRIENDS COME TO HELP BUT–
CHAT
CHAT
MAN, HE JUST KEEPS GOING...

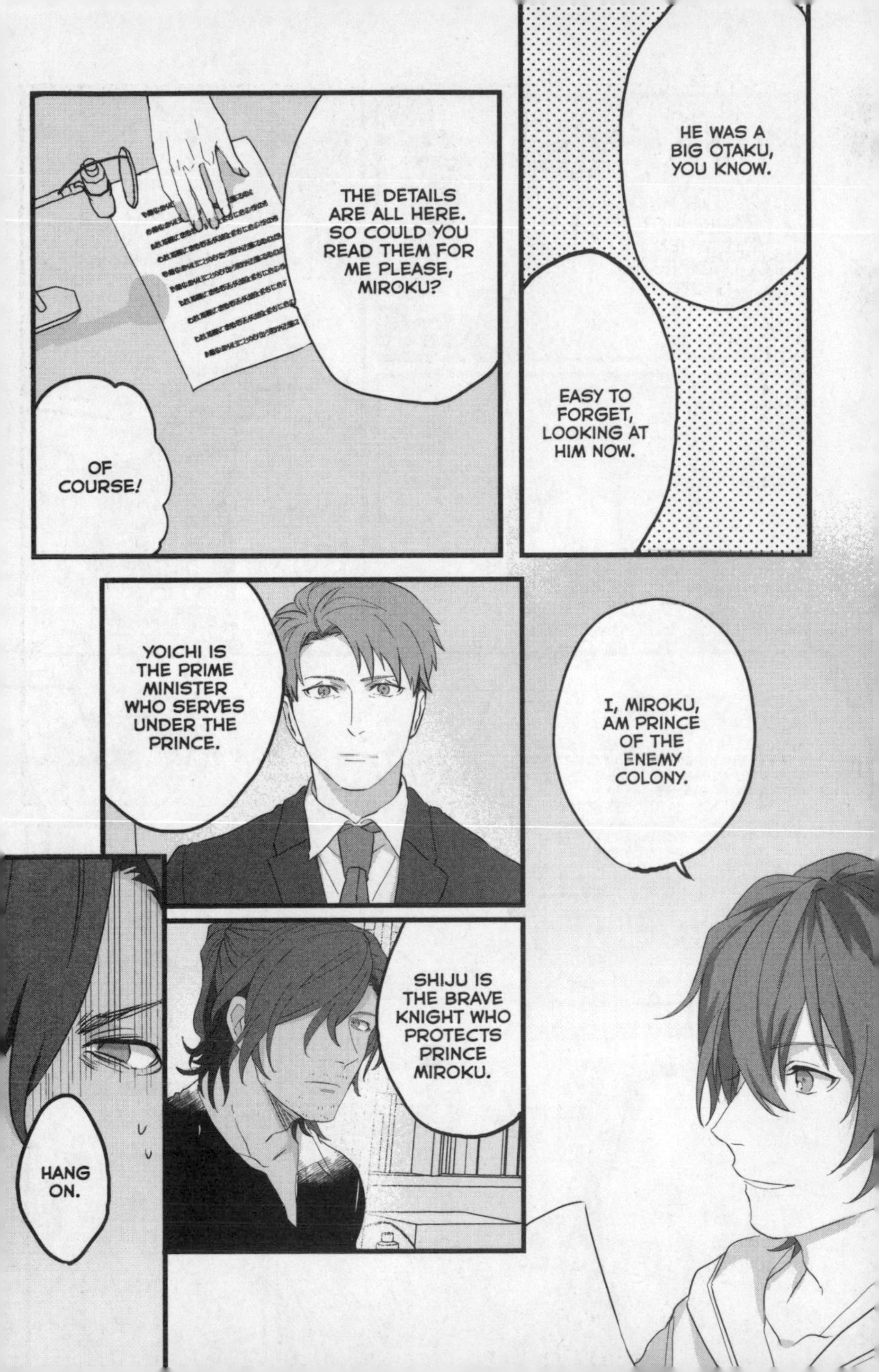
HE WAS A BIG OTAKU, YOU KNOW.
EASY TO FORGET, LOOKING AT HIM NOW.
THE DETAILS ARE ALL HERE. SO COULD YOU READ THEM FOR ME PLEASE, MIROKU?
OF COURSE!
I, MIROKU, AM PRINCE OF THE ENEMY COLONY.
YOICHI IS THE PRIME MINISTER WHO SERVES UNDER THE PRINCE.
SHIJU IS THE BRAVE KNIGHT WHO PROTECTS PRINCE MIROKU.
HANG ON.

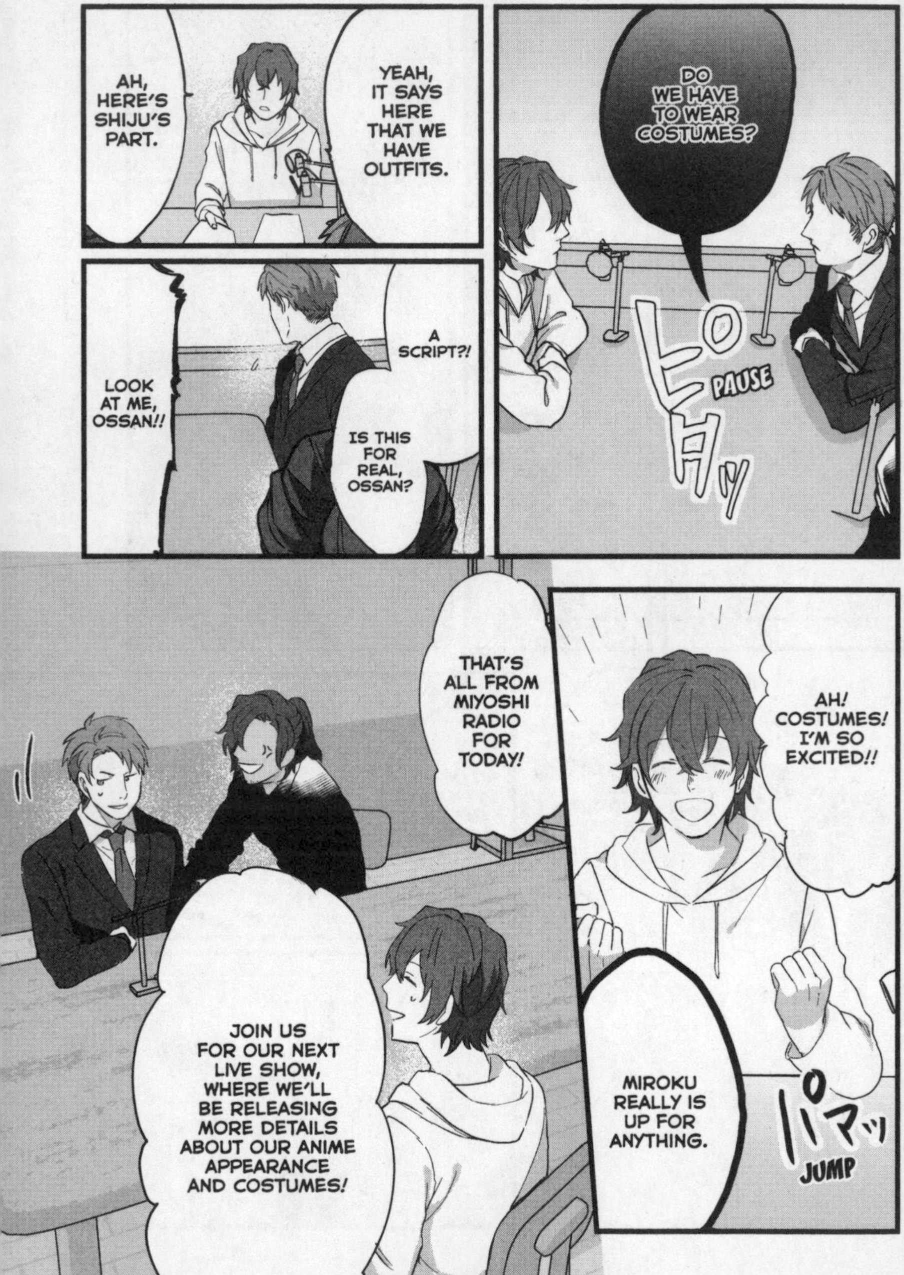
DO WE HAVE TO WEAR COSTUMES?
ピタッ
PAUSE
YEAH, IT SAYS HERE THAT WE HAVE OUTFITS.
AH, HERE'S SHIJU'S PART.
A SCRIPT?!
IS THIS FOR REAL, OSSAN?
LOOK AT ME, OSSAN!!
AH! COSTUMES! I'M SO EXCITED!!
MIROKU REALLY IS UP FOR ANYTHING.
JUMP
THAT'S ALL FROM MIYOSHI RADIO FOR TODAY!
JOIN US FOR OUR NEXT LIVE SHOW, WHERE WE'LL BE RELEASING MORE DETAILS ABOUT OUR ANIME APPEARANCE AND COSTUMES!

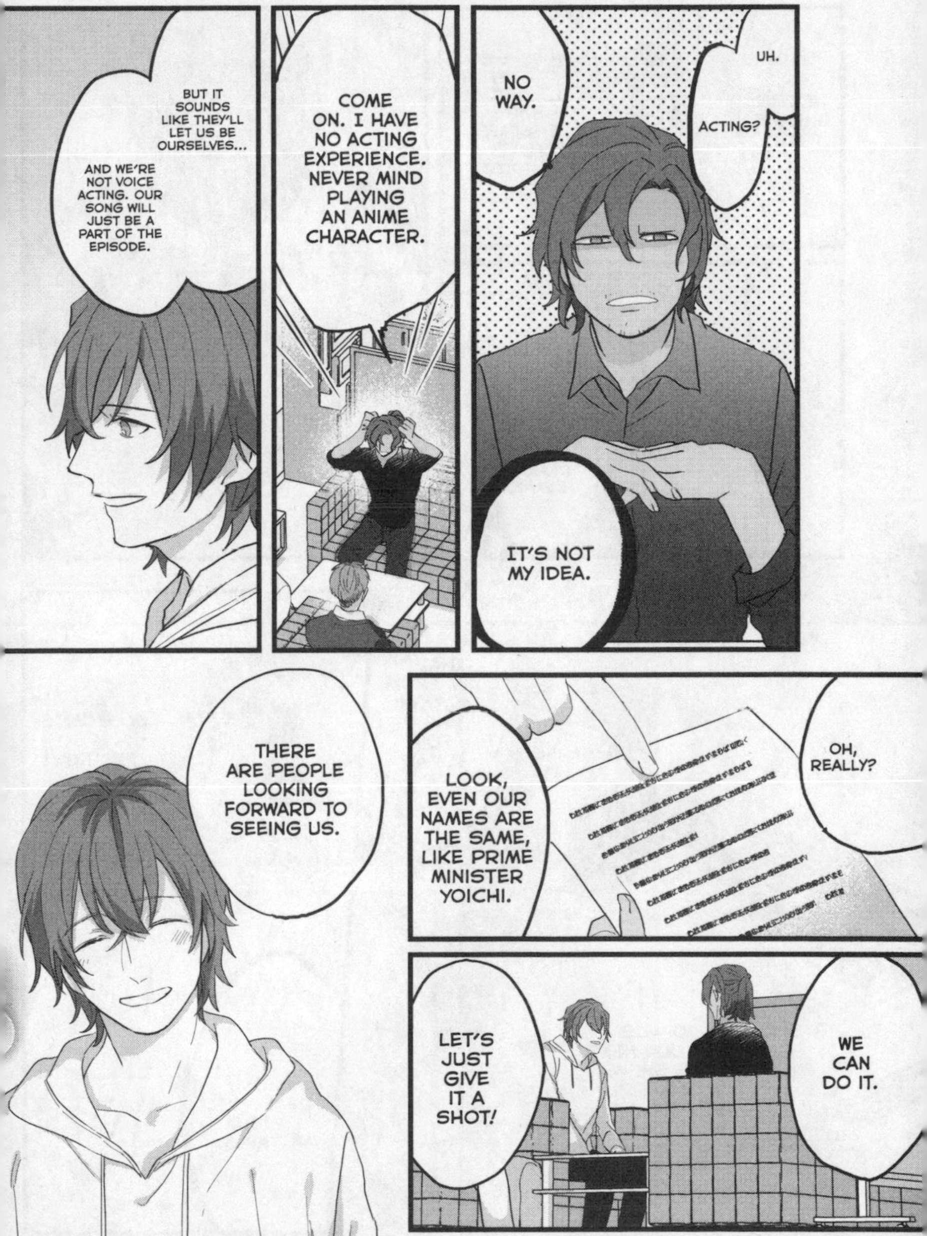
UH.
ACTING?
NO WAY.
IT'S NOT MY IDEA.
COME ON. I HAVE NO ACTING EXPERIENCE. NEVER MIND PLAYING AN ANIME CHARACTER.
BUT IT SOUNDS LIKE THEY'LL LET US BE OURSELVES...
AND WE'RE NOT VOICE ACTING. OUR SONG WILL JUST BE A PART OF THE EPISODE.
OH, REALLY?
LOOK, EVEN OUR NAMES ARE THE SAME, LIKE PRIME MINISTER YOICHI.
WE CAN DO IT.
LET'S JUST GIVE IT A SHOT!
THERE ARE PEOPLE LOOKING FORWARD TO SEEING US.

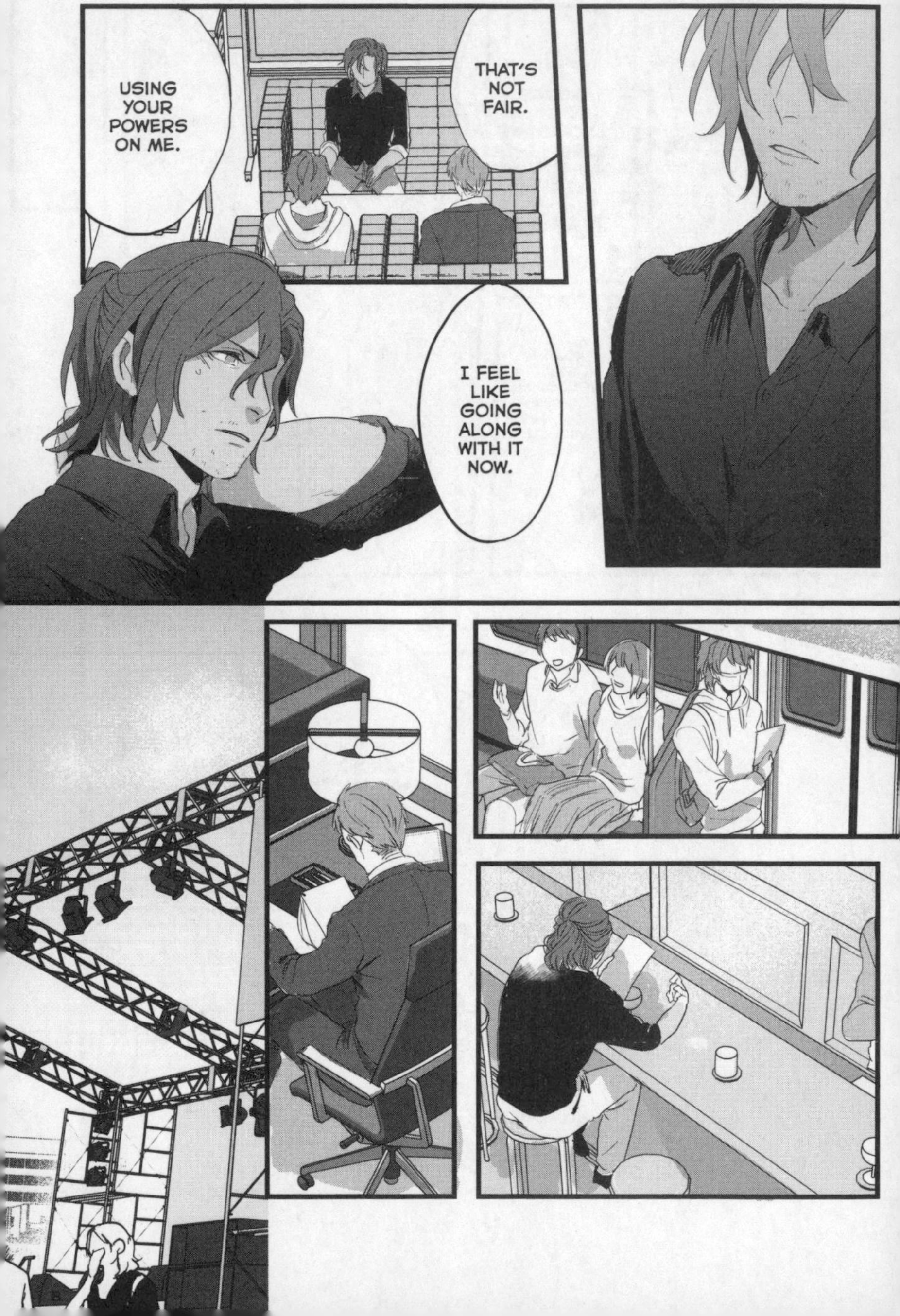
THAT'S NOT FAIR.
USING YOUR POWERS ON ME.
I FEEL LIKE GOING ALONG WITH IT NOW.

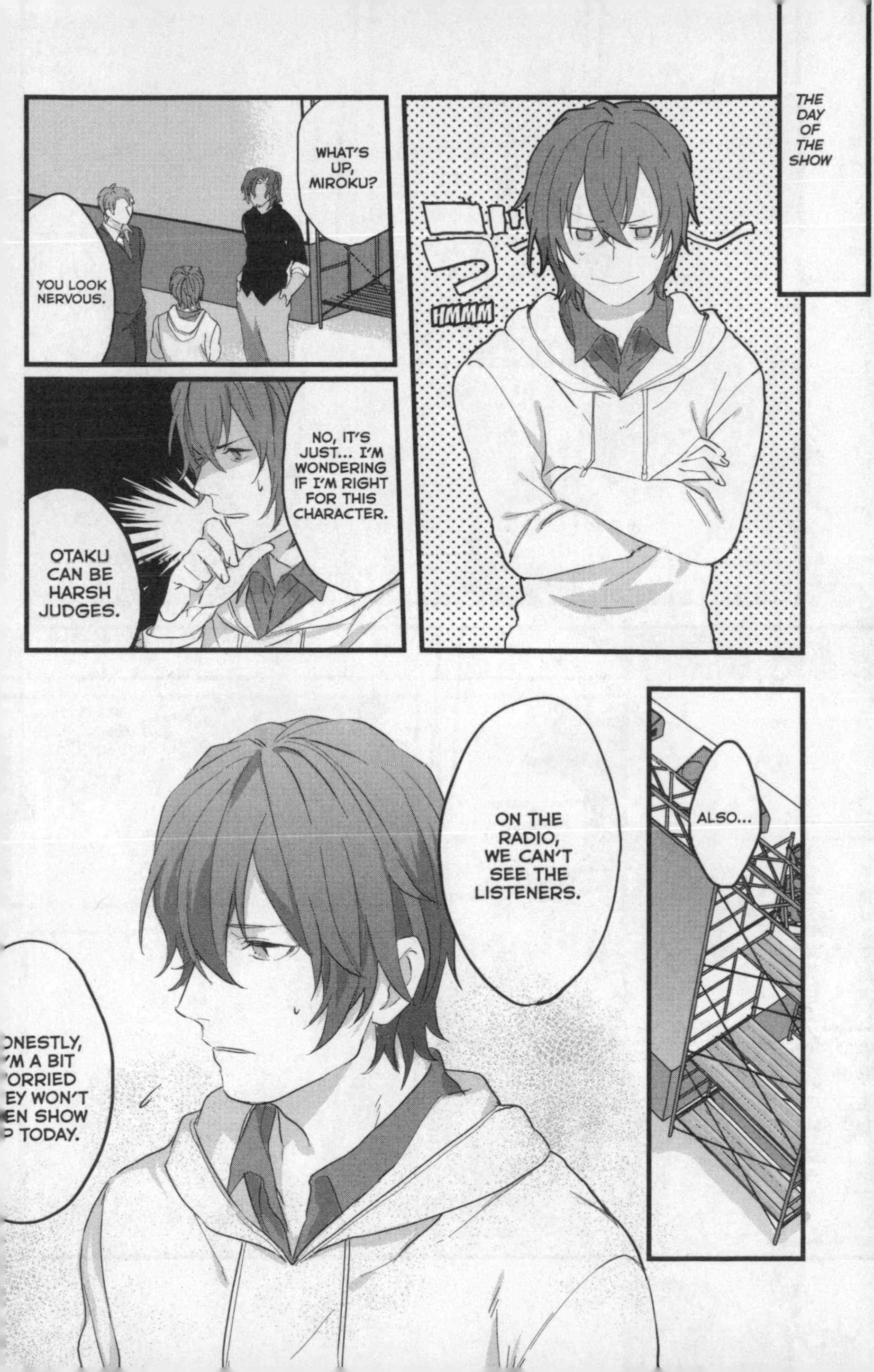
THE DAY OF THE SHOW
HMMM
WHAT'S UP, MIROKU?
YOU LOOK NERVOUS.
NO, IT'S JUST... I'M WONDERING IF I'M RIGHT FOR THIS CHARACTER.
OTAKU CAN BE HARSH JUDGES.
ALSO...
ON THE RADIO, WE CAN'T SEE THE LISTENERS.
ONESTLY, 'M A BIT ORRIED EY WON'T EN SHOW P TODAY.

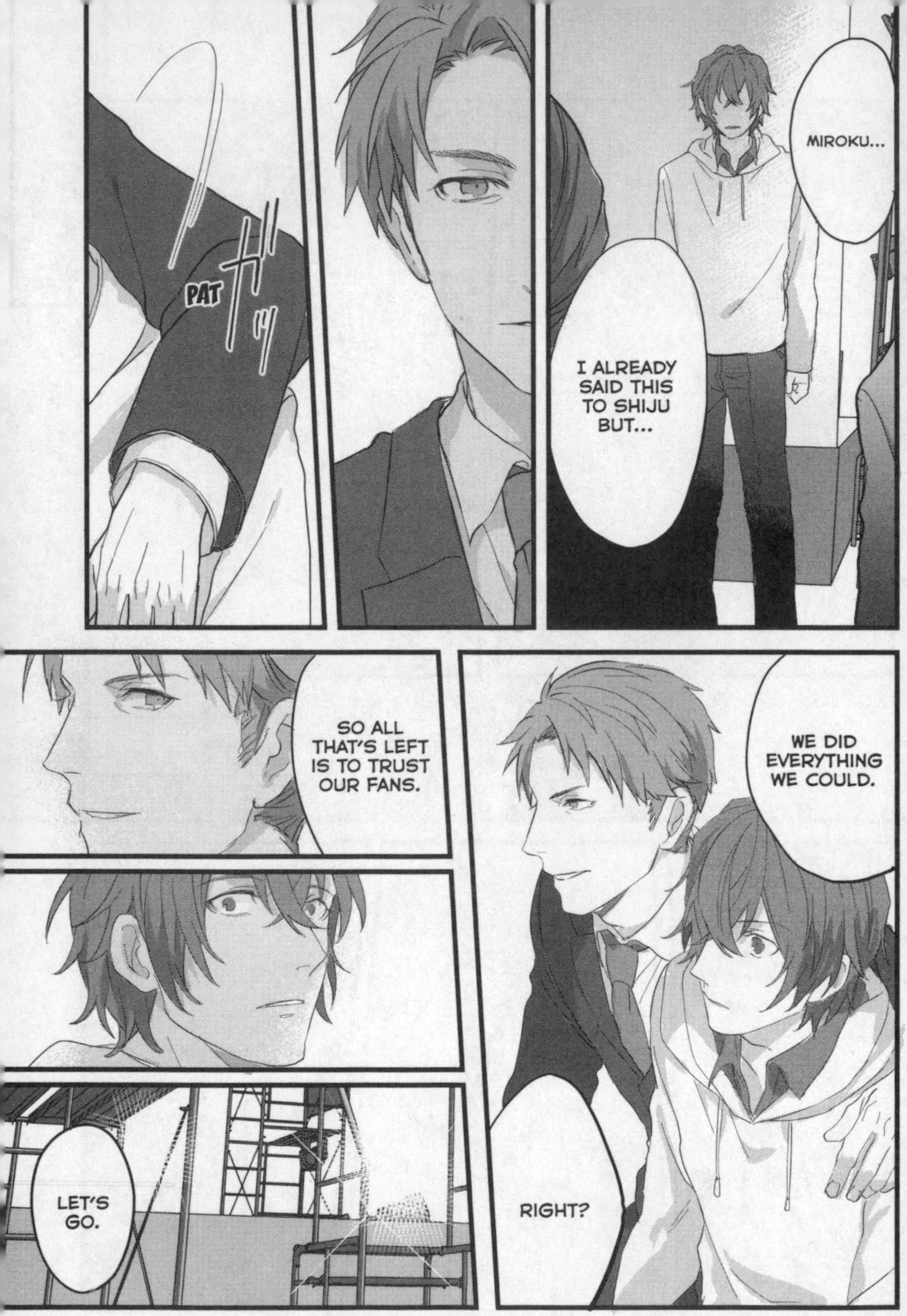
MIROKU...
I ALREADY SAID THIS TO SHIJU BUT...
PAT
WE DID EVERYTHING WE COULD.
RIGHT?
SO ALL THAT'S LEFT IS TO TRUST OUR FANS.
LET'S GO.

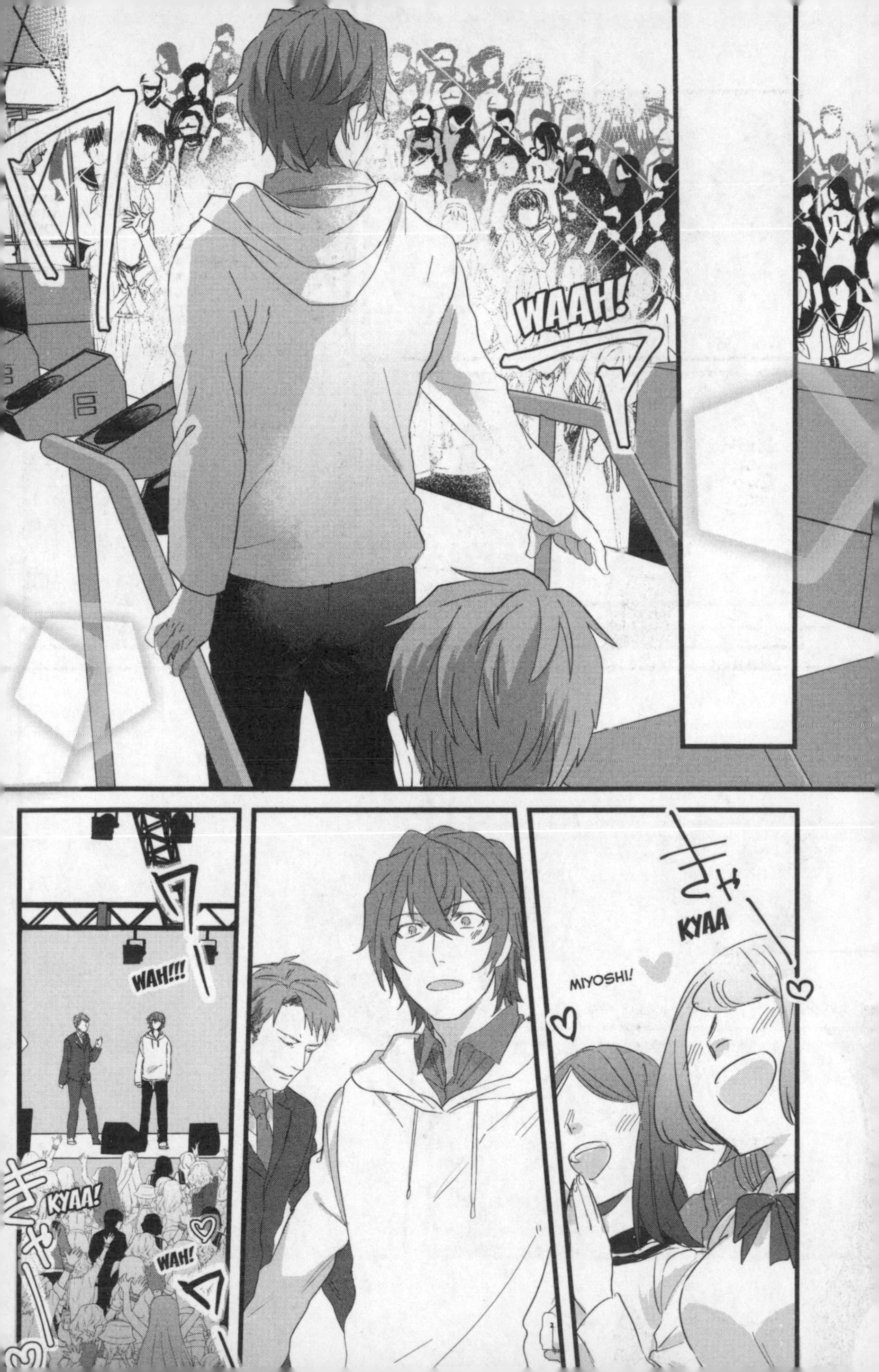
WAAH!
きゃー
KYAA
MIYOSHI!
WAH!!!
KYAA!
WAH!

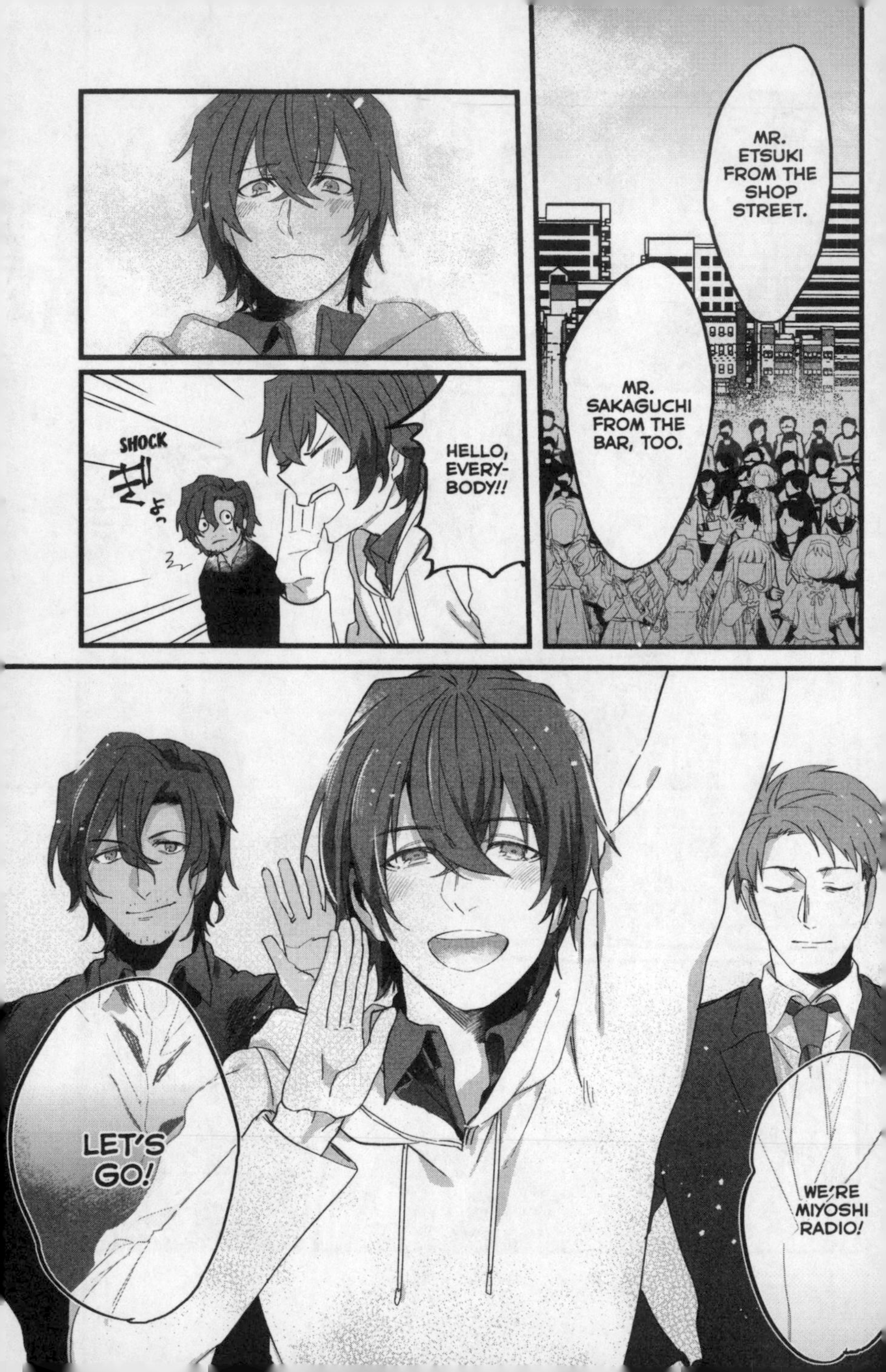
MR. ETSUKI FROM THE SHOP STREET.
MR. SAKAGUCHI FROM THE BAR, TOO.
HELLO, EVERY-BODY!!
SHOCK
ぎょっ
WE'RE MIYOSHI RADIO!
LET'S GO!

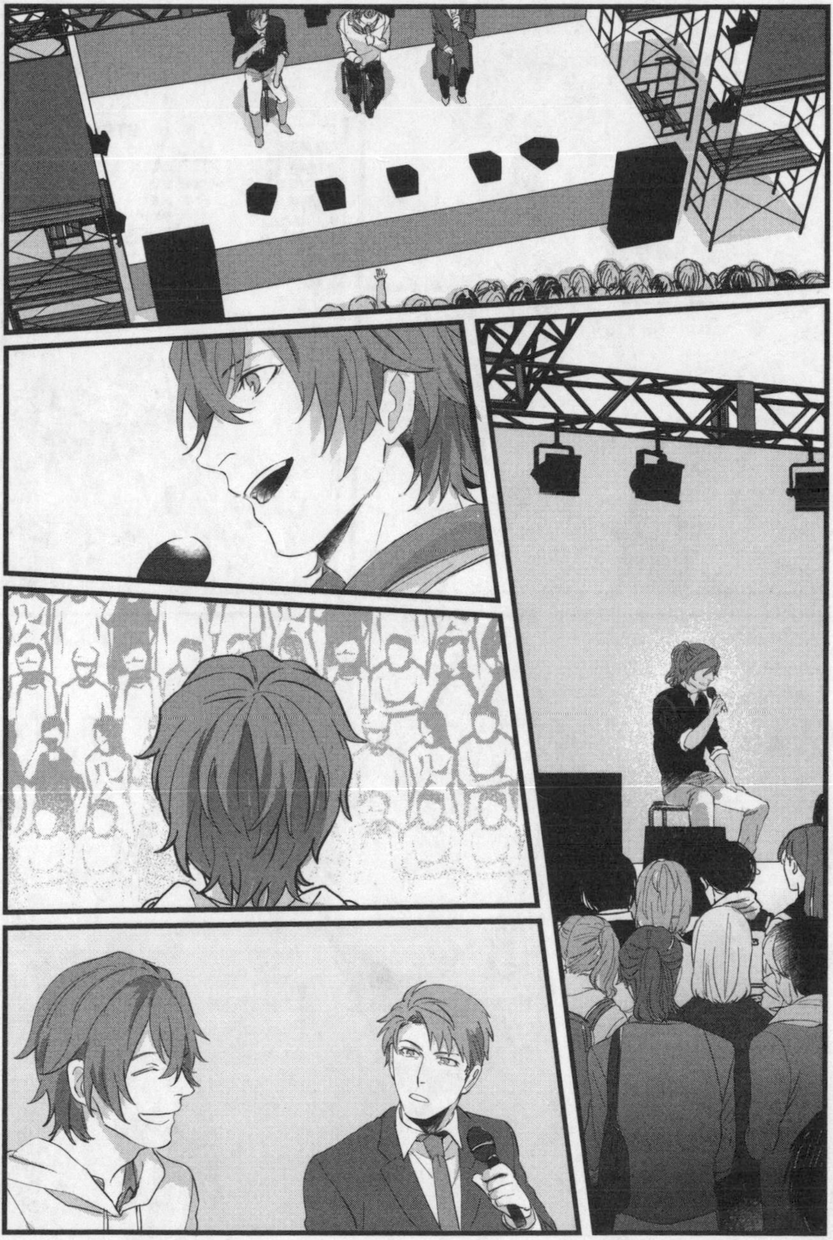

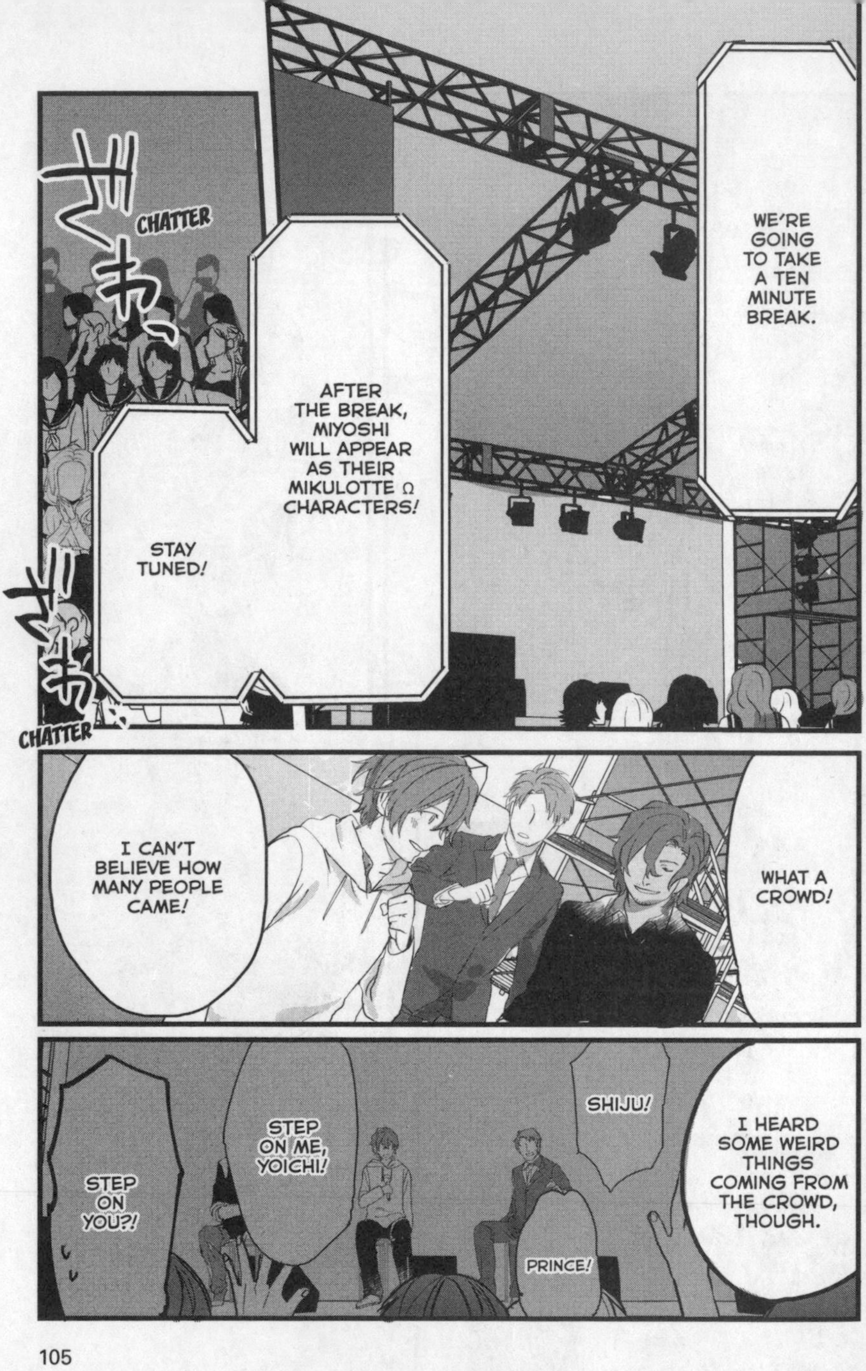
WE'RE GOING TO TAKE A TEN MINUTE BREAK.
AFTER THE BREAK, MIYOSHI WILL APPEAR AS THEIR MIKULOTTE Ω CHARACTERS!
STAY TUNED!
CHATTER
CHATTER
WHAT A CROWD!
I CAN'T BELIEVE HOW MANY PEOPLE CAME!
I HEARD SOME WEIRD THINGS COMING FROM THE CROWD, THOUGH.
SHIJU!
PRINCE!
STEP ON ME, YOICHI!
STEP ON YOU?!

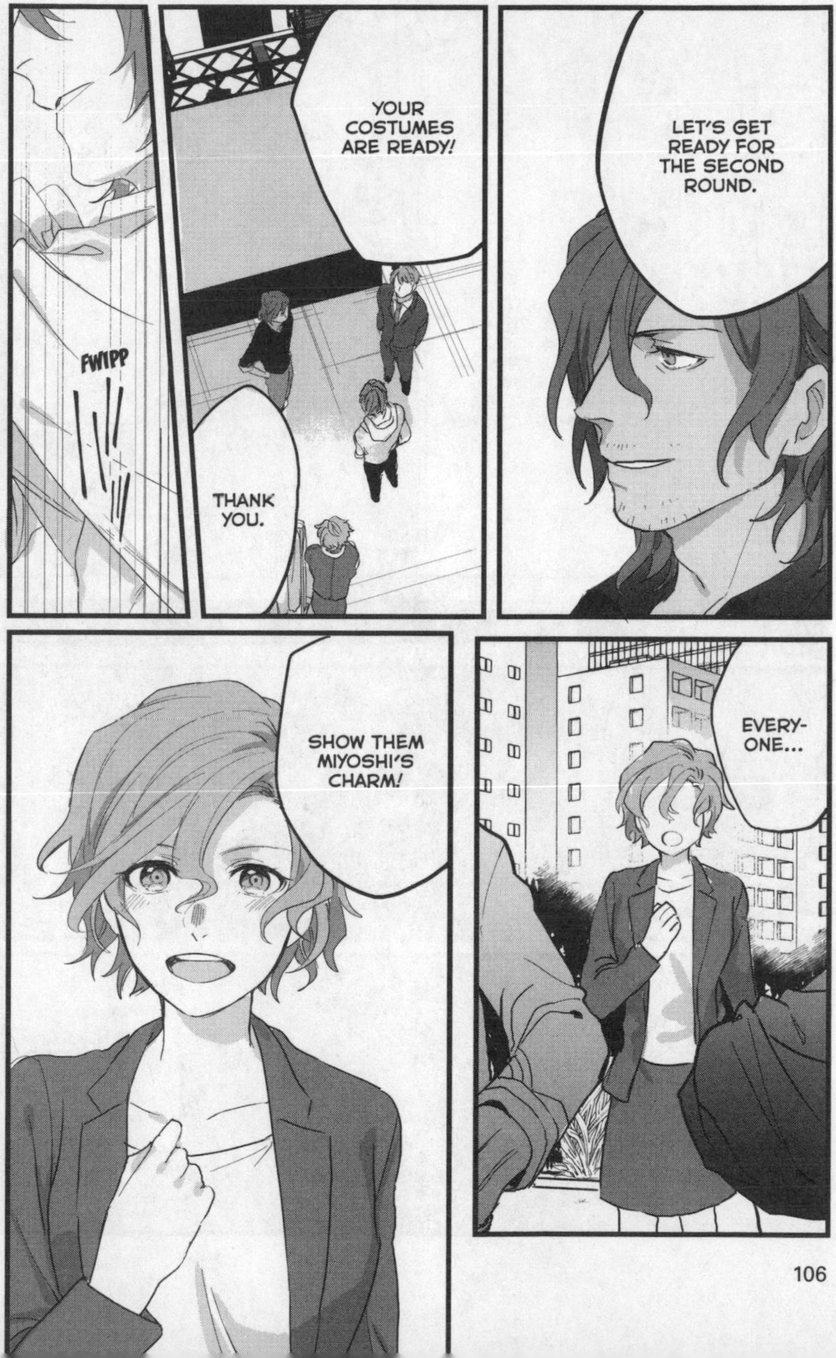
LET'S GET READY FOR THE SECOND ROUND.
YOUR COSTUMES ARE READY!
THANK YOU.
FWIPP
EVERY-ONE...
SHOW THEM MIYOSHI'S CHARM!

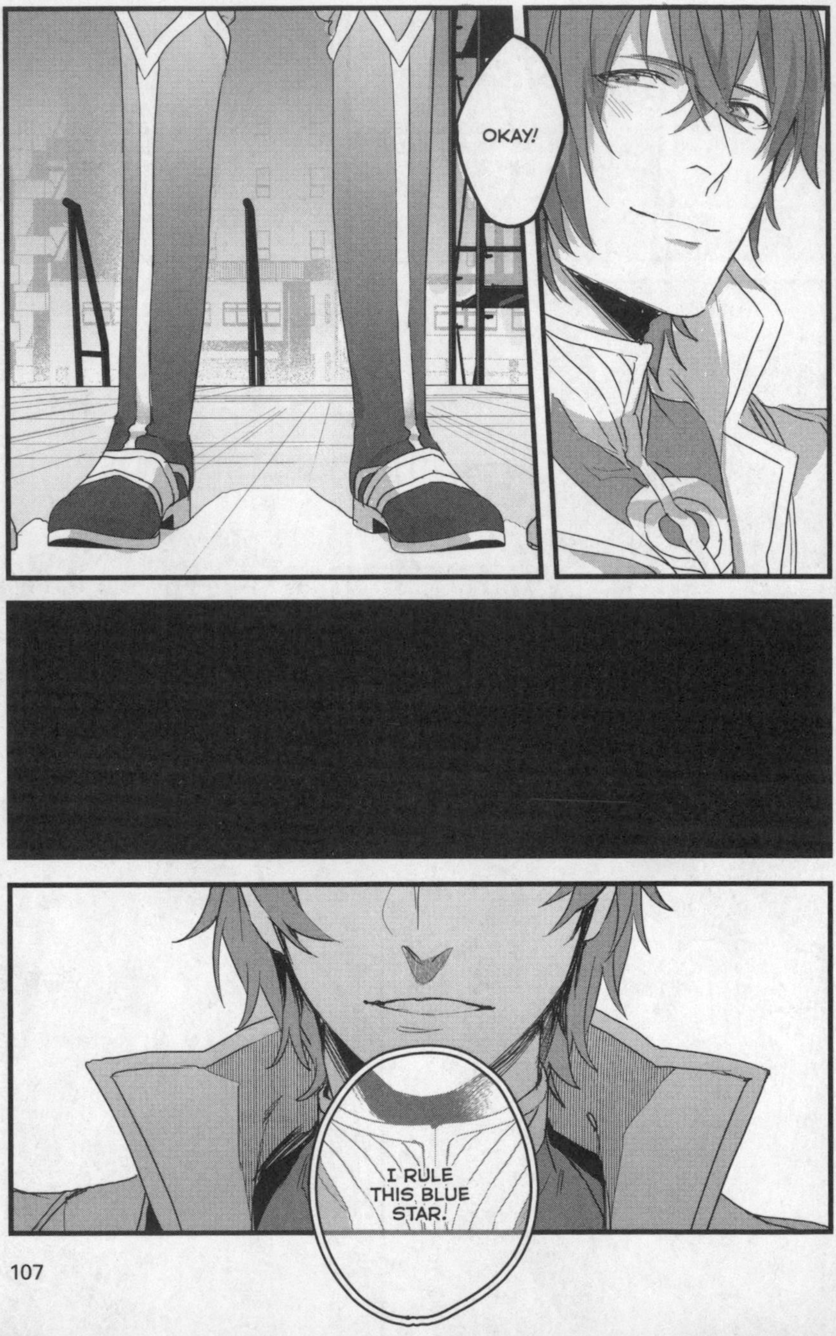
OKAY!
I RULE THIS BLUE STAR.

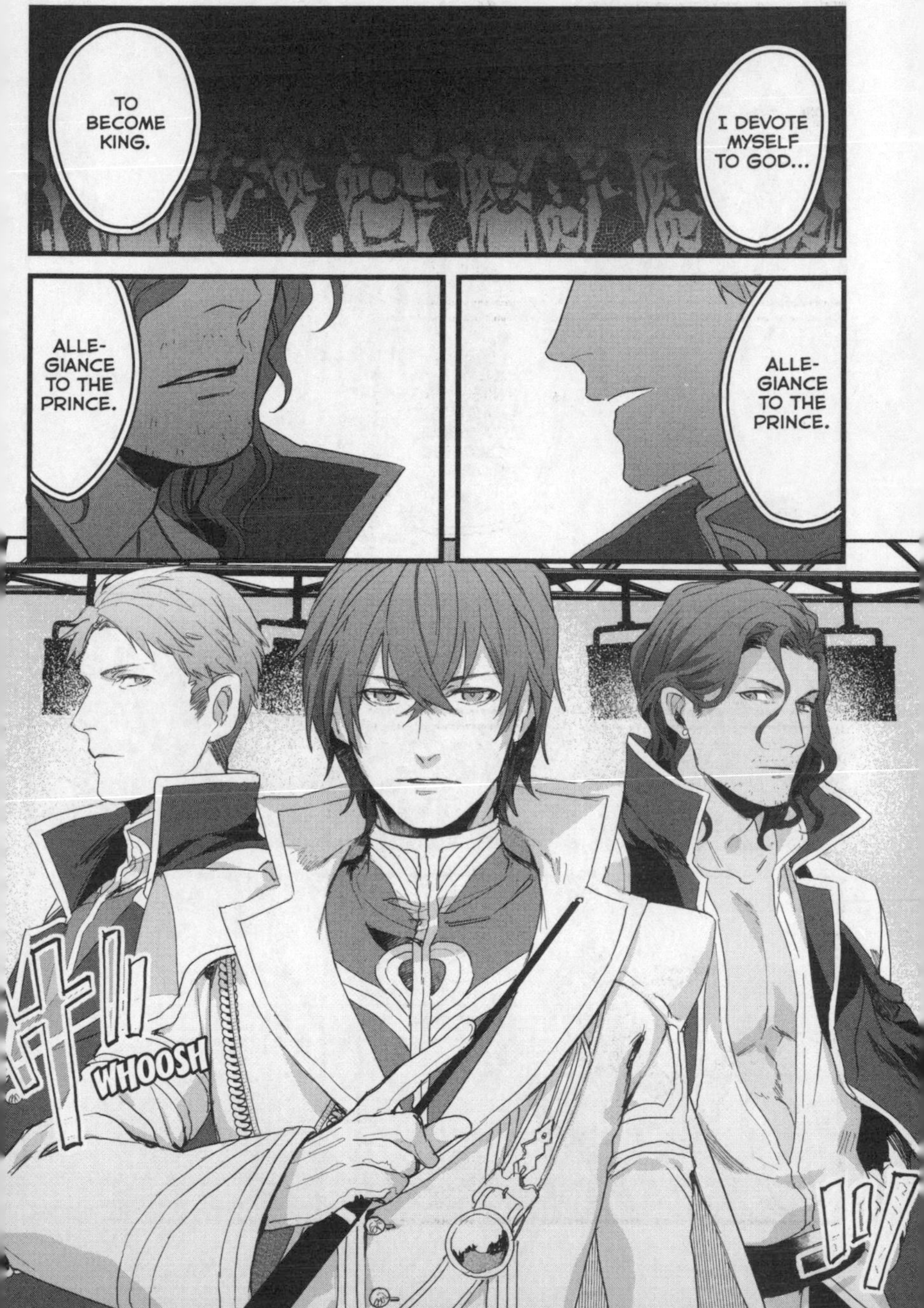
I DEVOTE MYSELF TO GOD...
TO BECOME KING.
ALLE-GIANCE TO THE PRINCE.
ALLE-GIANCE TO THE PRINCE.
WHOOSH

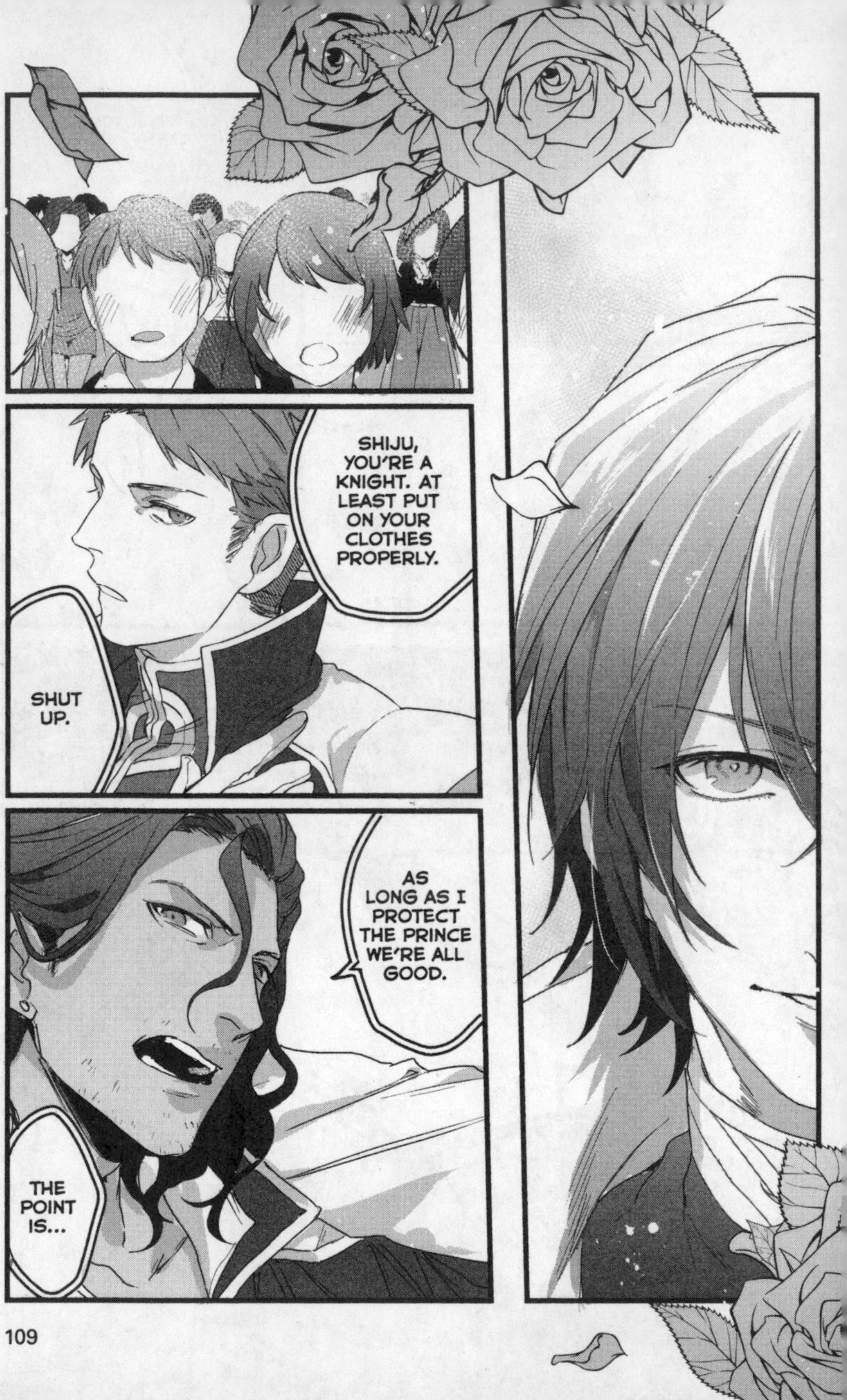
SHIJU, YOU'RE A KNIGHT. AT LEAST PUT ON YOUR CLOTHES PROPERLY.
SHUT UP.
AS LONG AS I PROTECT THE PRINCE WE'RE ALL GOOD.
THE POINT IS...

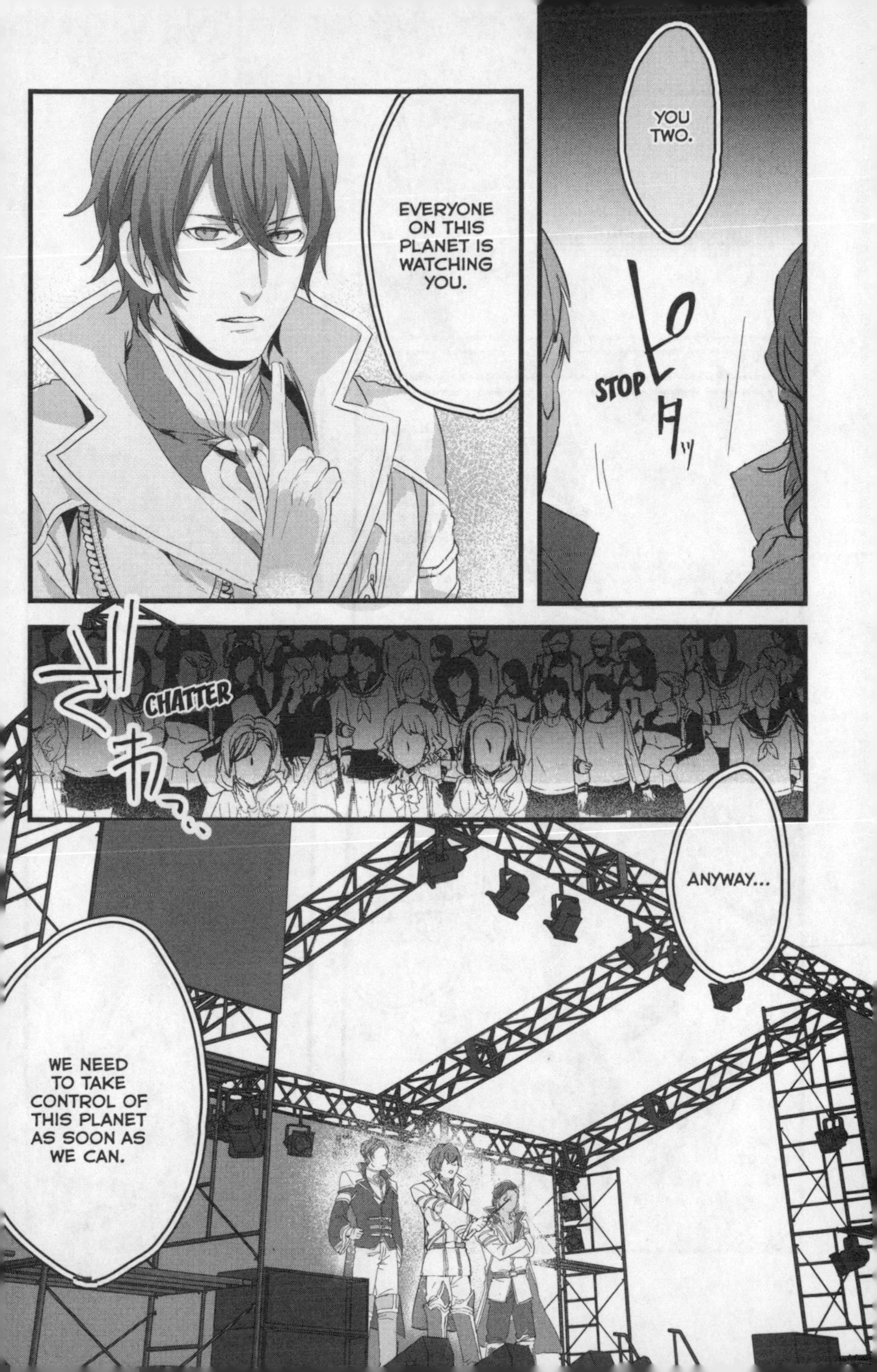
YOU TWO.
STOP
ピタッ
EVERYONE ON THIS PLANET IS WATCHING YOU.
ざわ…
CHATTER
ANYWAY...
WE NEED TO TAKE CONTROL OF THIS PLANET AS SOON AS WE CAN.

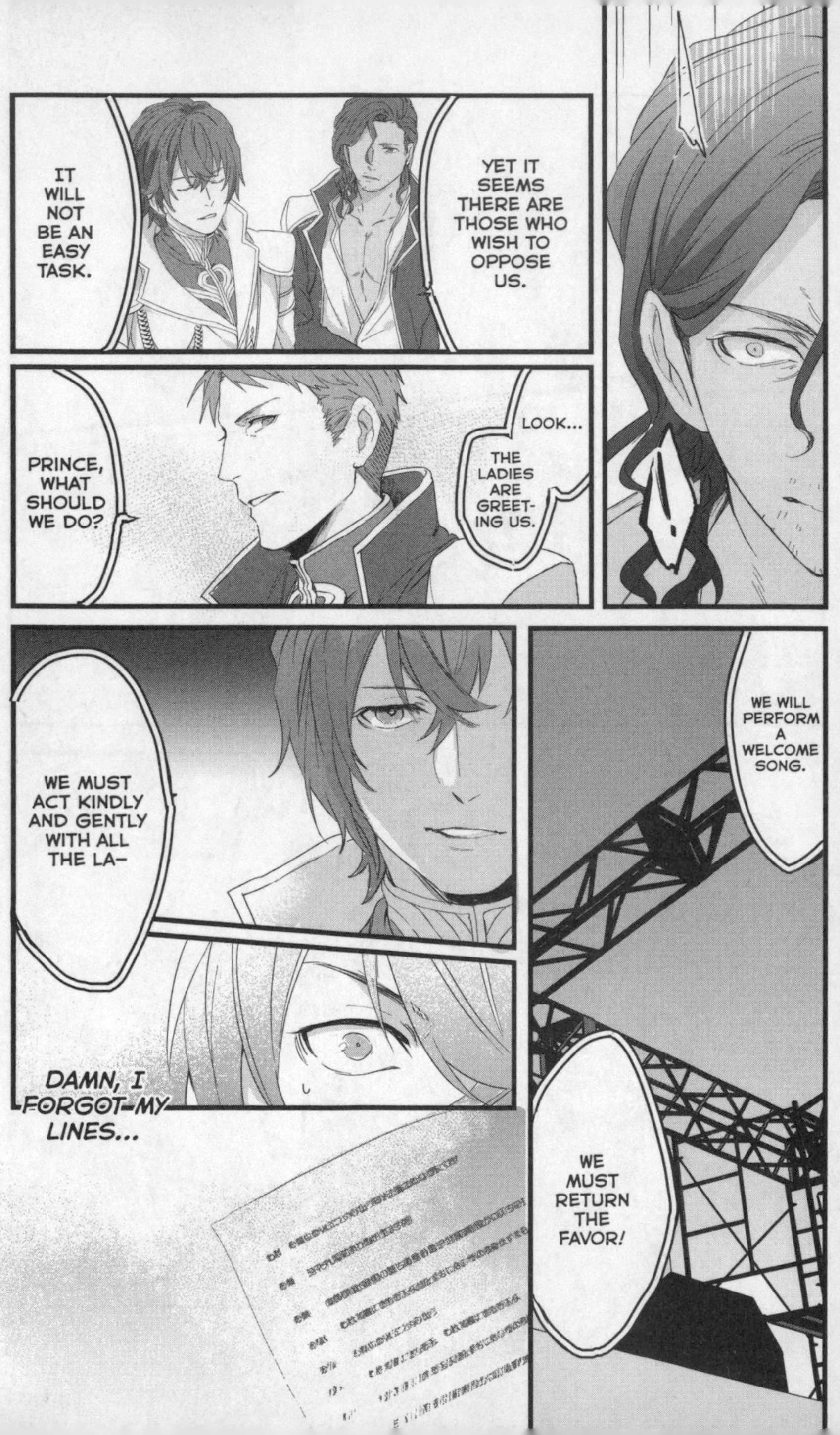
YET IT SEEMS THERE ARE THOSE WHO WISH TO OPPOSE US.
IT WILL NOT BE AN EASY TASK.
LOOK...
THE LADIES ARE GREET-ING US.
PRINCE, WHAT SHOULD WE DO?
WE WILL PERFORM A WELCOME SONG.
WE MUST RETURN THE FAVOR!
WE MUST ACT KINDLY AND GENTLY WITH ALL THE LA–
DAMN, I FORGOT MY LINES...

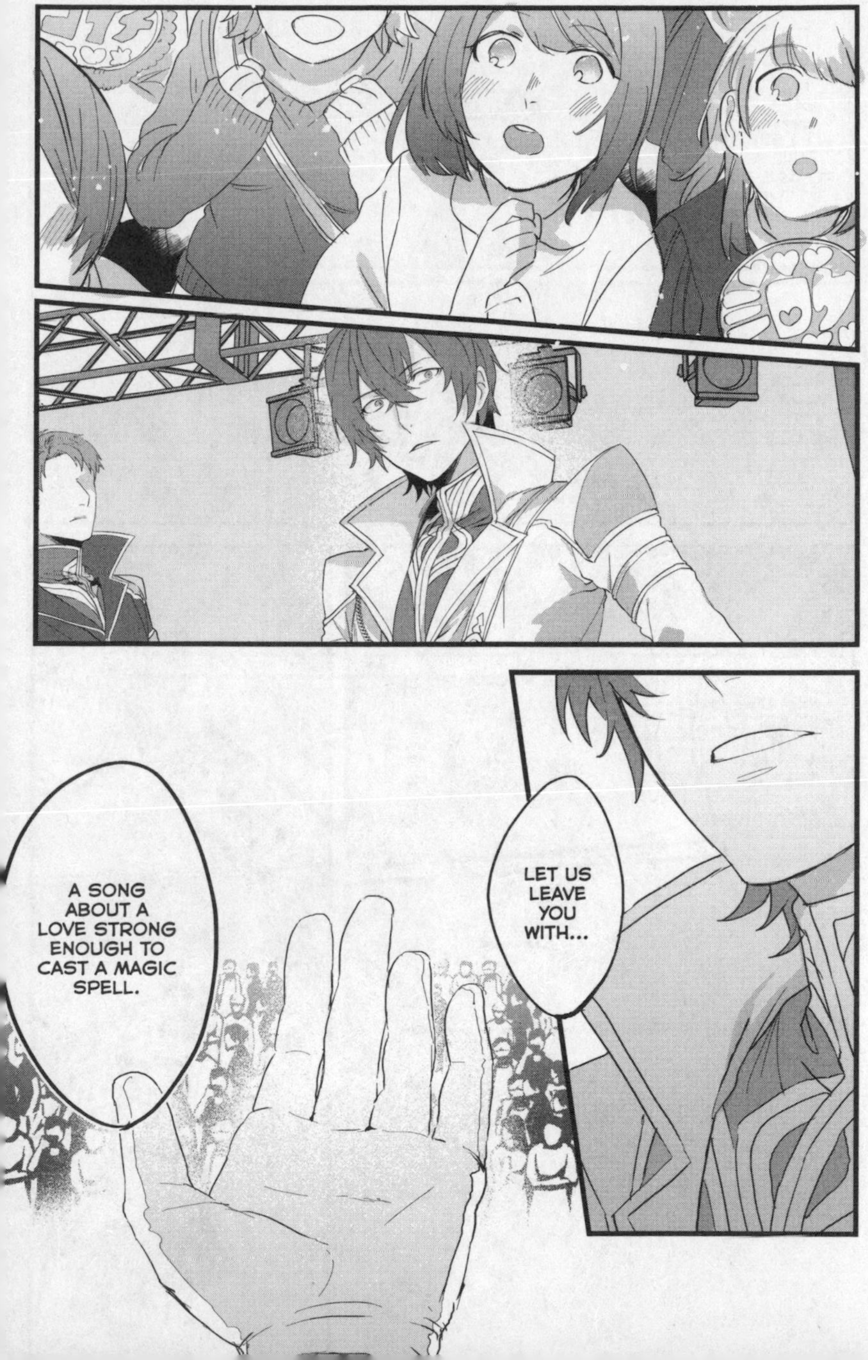
LET US LEAVE YOU WITH...
A SONG ABOUT A LOVE STRONG ENOUGH TO CAST A MAGIC SPELL.

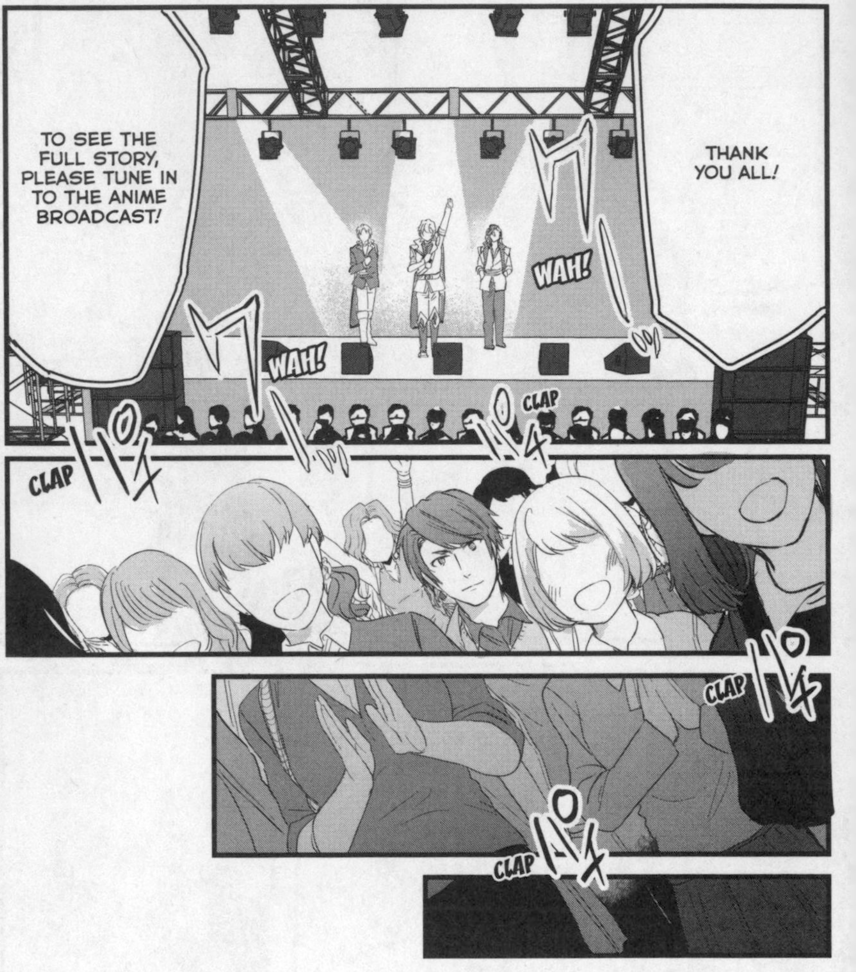
THANK YOU ALL!
WAH!
TO SEE THE FULL STORY, PLEASE TUNE IN TO THE ANIME BROADCAST!
WAH!
CLAP
CLAP
CLAP
CLAP

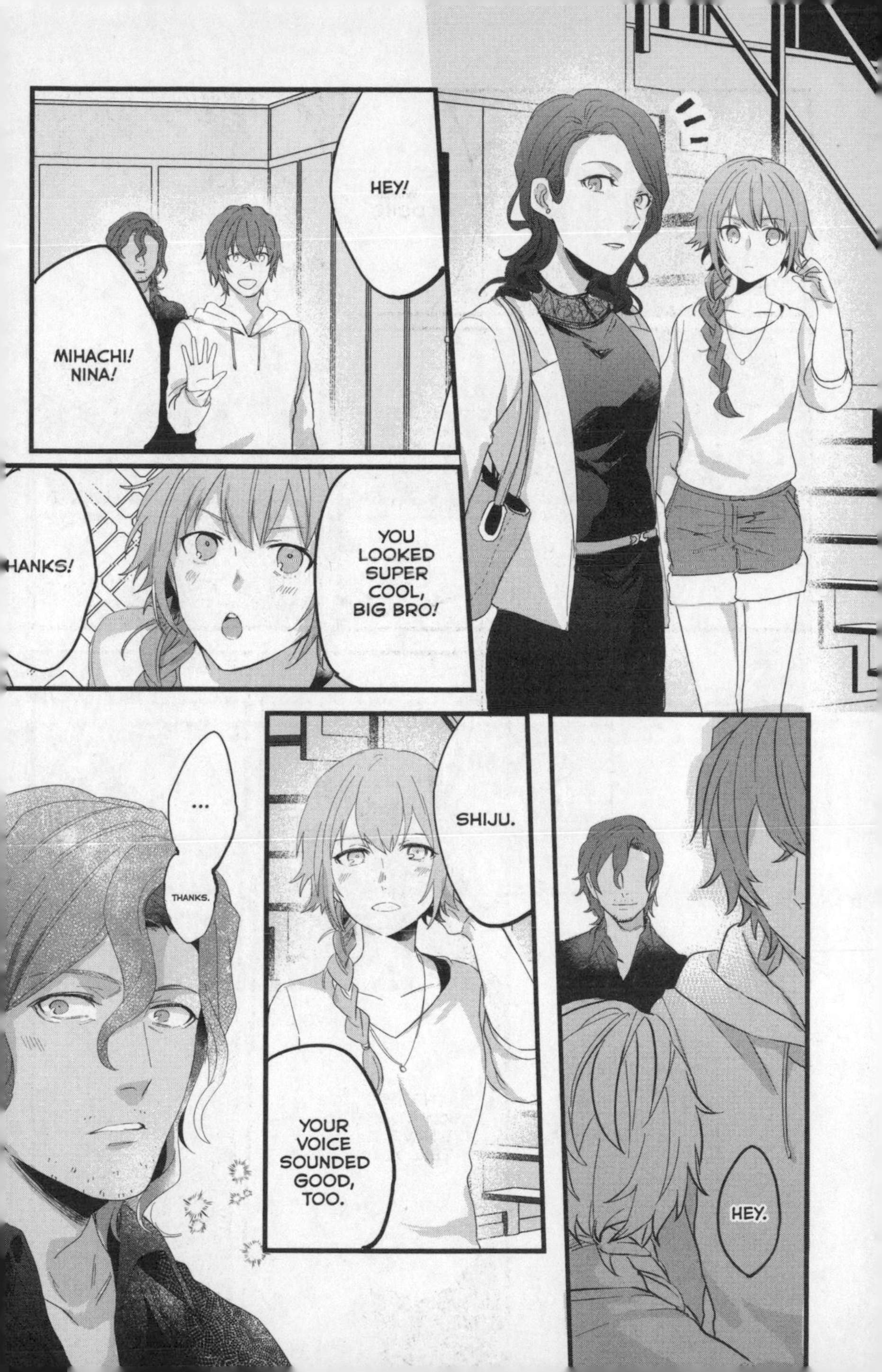
HEY!
MIHACHI! NINA!
YOU LOOKED SUPER COOL, BIG BRO!
HANKS!
HEY.
SHIJU.
YOUR VOICE SOUNDED GOOD, TOO.
...
THANKS.

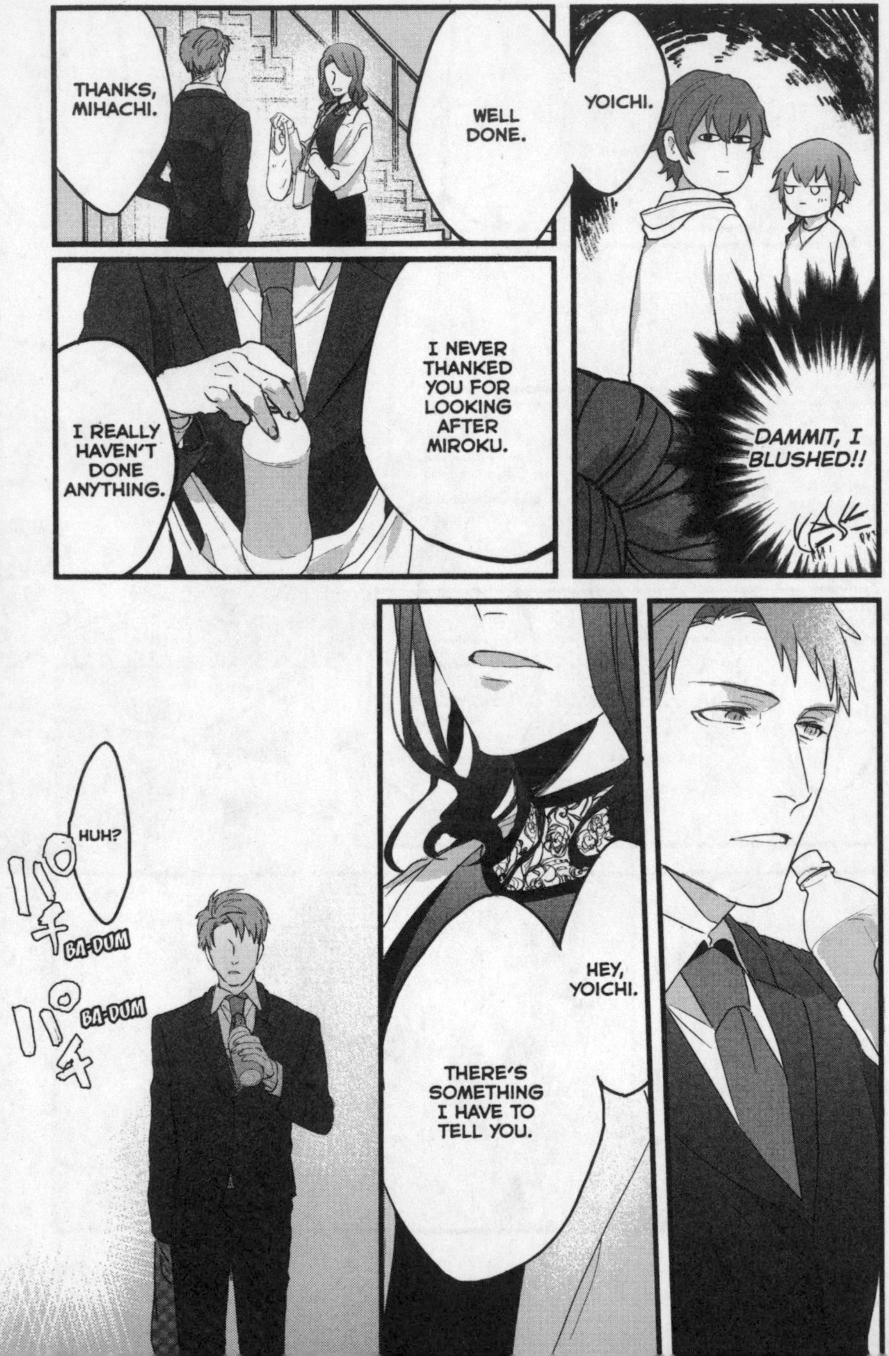
YOICHI.
WELL DONE.
DAMMIT, I BLUSHED!!
THANKS, MIHACHI.
I NEVER THANKED YOU FOR LOOKING AFTER MIROKU.
I REALLY HAVEN'T DONE ANYTHING.
HEY, YOICHI.
THERE'S SOMETHING I HAVE TO TELL YOU.
HUH?
BA-DUM
BA-DUM

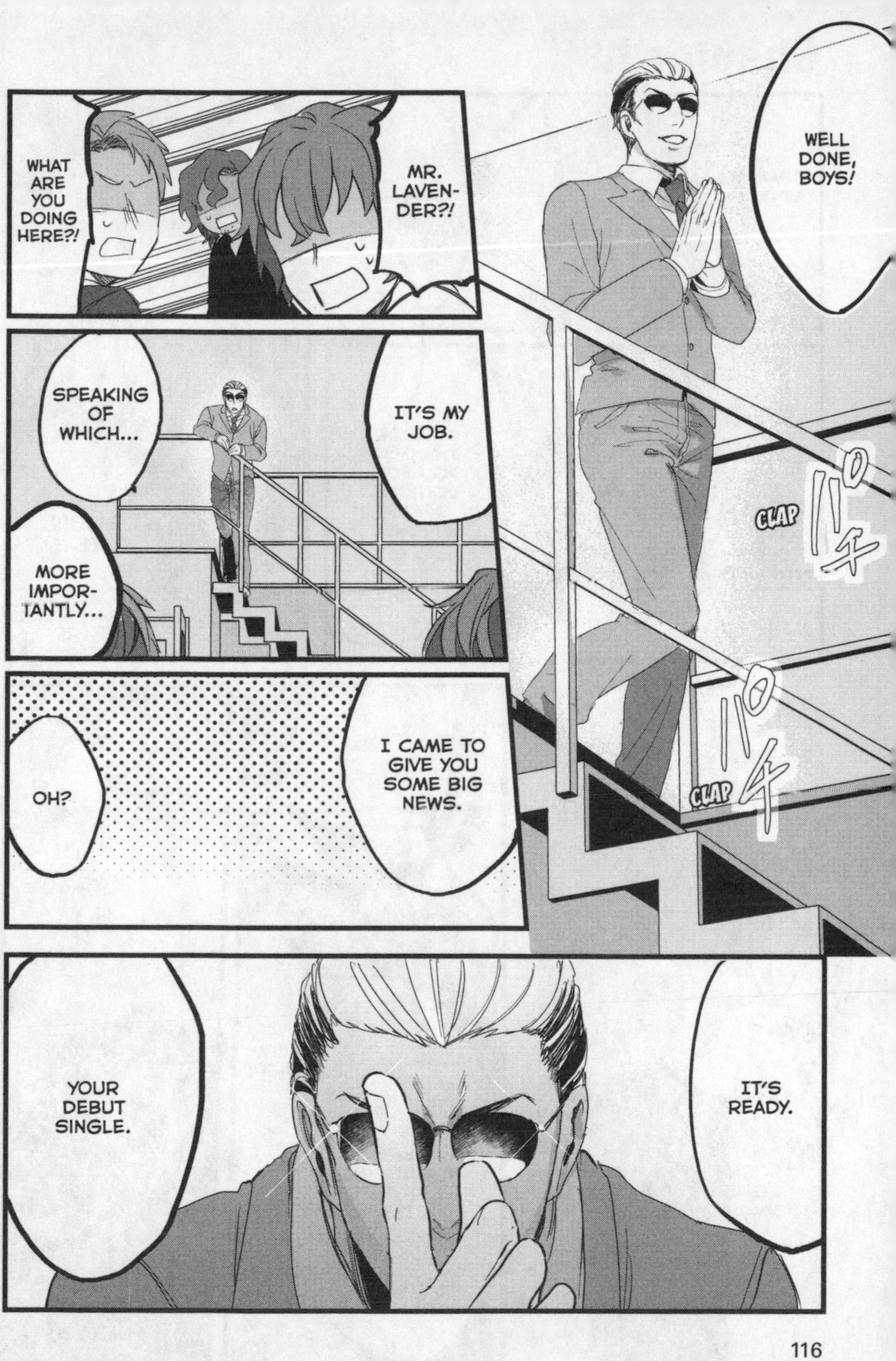
WELL DONE, BOYS!
パチ
CLAP
パチ
CLAP
MR. LAVENDER?!
WHAT ARE YOU DOING HERE?!
IT'S MY JOB.
SPEAKING OF WHICH...
MORE IMPORTANTLY...
I CAME TO GIVE YOU SOME BIG NEWS.
OH?
IT'S READY.
YOUR DEBUT SINGLE.

Chapter 10

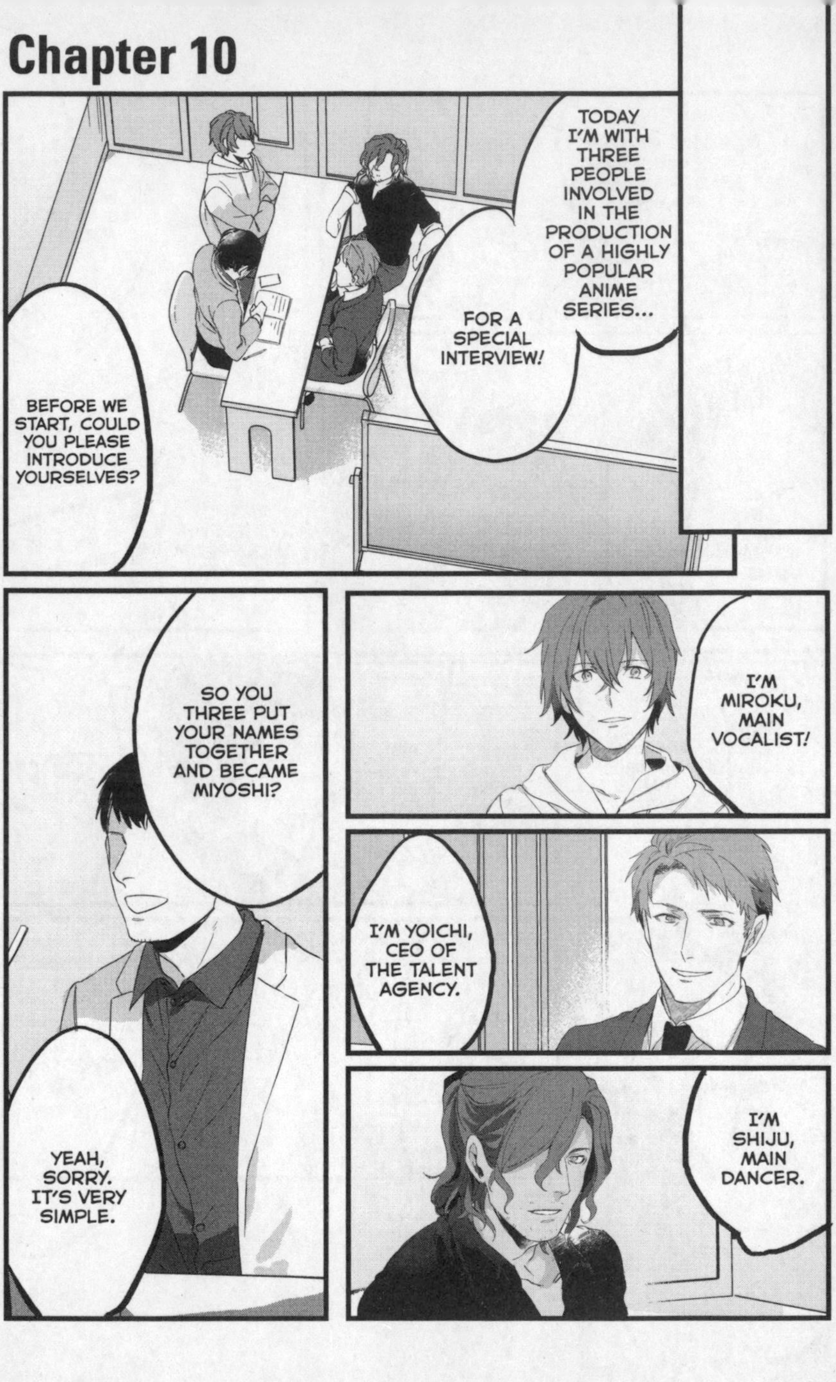
TODAY I'M WITH THREE PEOPLE INVOLVED IN THE PRODUCTION OF A HIGHLY POPULAR ANIME SERIES...
FOR A SPECIAL INTERVIEW!
BEFORE WE START, COULD YOU PLEASE INTRODUCE YOURSELVES?
I'M MIROKU, MAIN VOCALIST!
I'M YOICHI, CEO OF THE TALENT AGENCY.
I'M SHIJU, MAIN DANCER.
SO YOU THREE PUT YOUR NAMES TOGETHER AND BECAME MIYOSHI?
YEAH, SORRY. IT'S VERY SIMPLE.

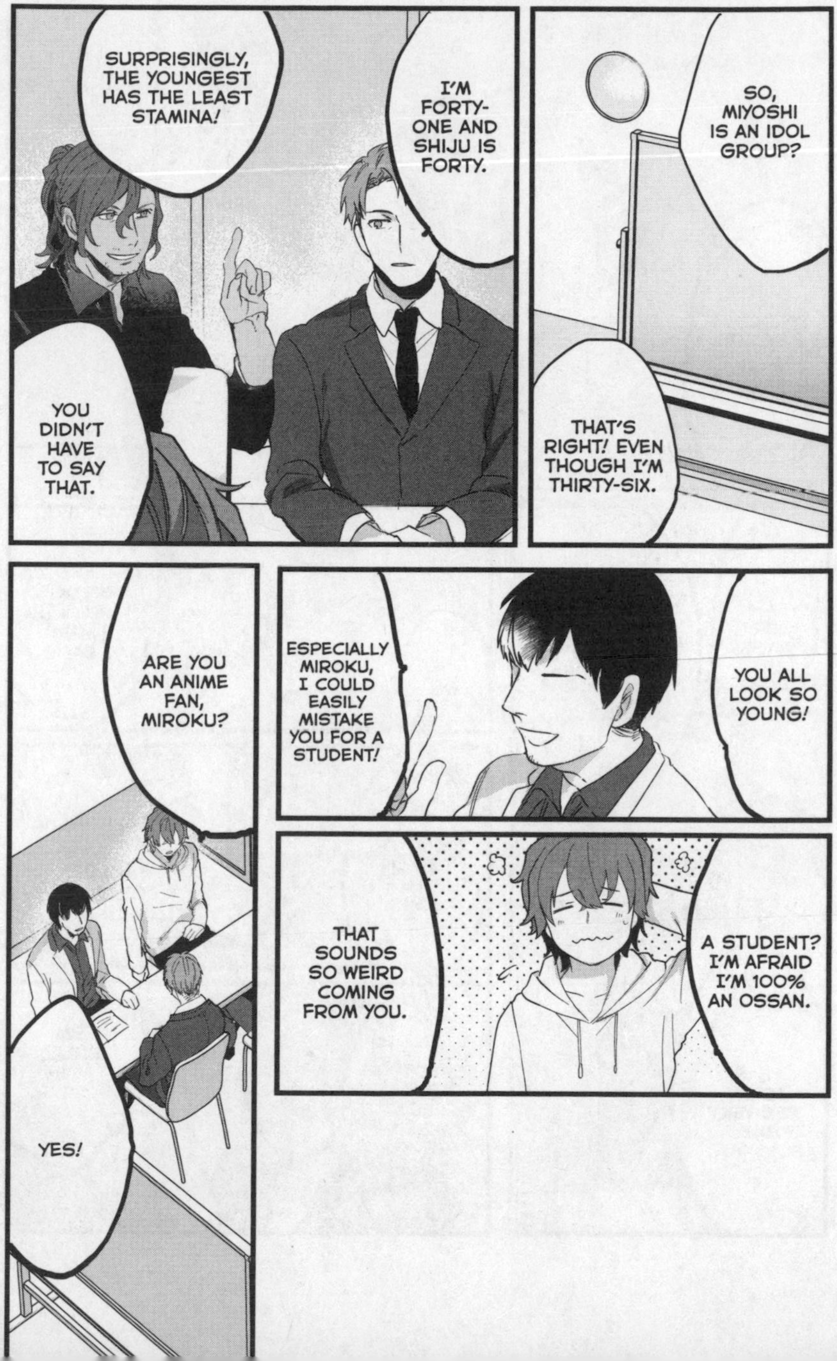
SO, MIYOSHI IS AN IDOL GROUP?
THAT'S RIGHT! EVEN THOUGH I'M THIRTY-SIX.
I'M FORTY-ONE AND SHIJU IS FORTY.
SURPRISINGLY, THE YOUNGEST HAS THE LEAST STAMINA!
YOU DIDN'T HAVE TO SAY THAT.
YOU ALL LOOK SO YOUNG!
ESPECIALLY MIROKU, I COULD EASILY MISTAKE YOU FOR A STUDENT!
A STUDENT? I'M AFRAID I'M 100% AN OSSAN.
THAT SOUNDS SO WEIRD COMING FROM YOU.
ARE YOU AN ANIME FAN, MIROKU?
YES!

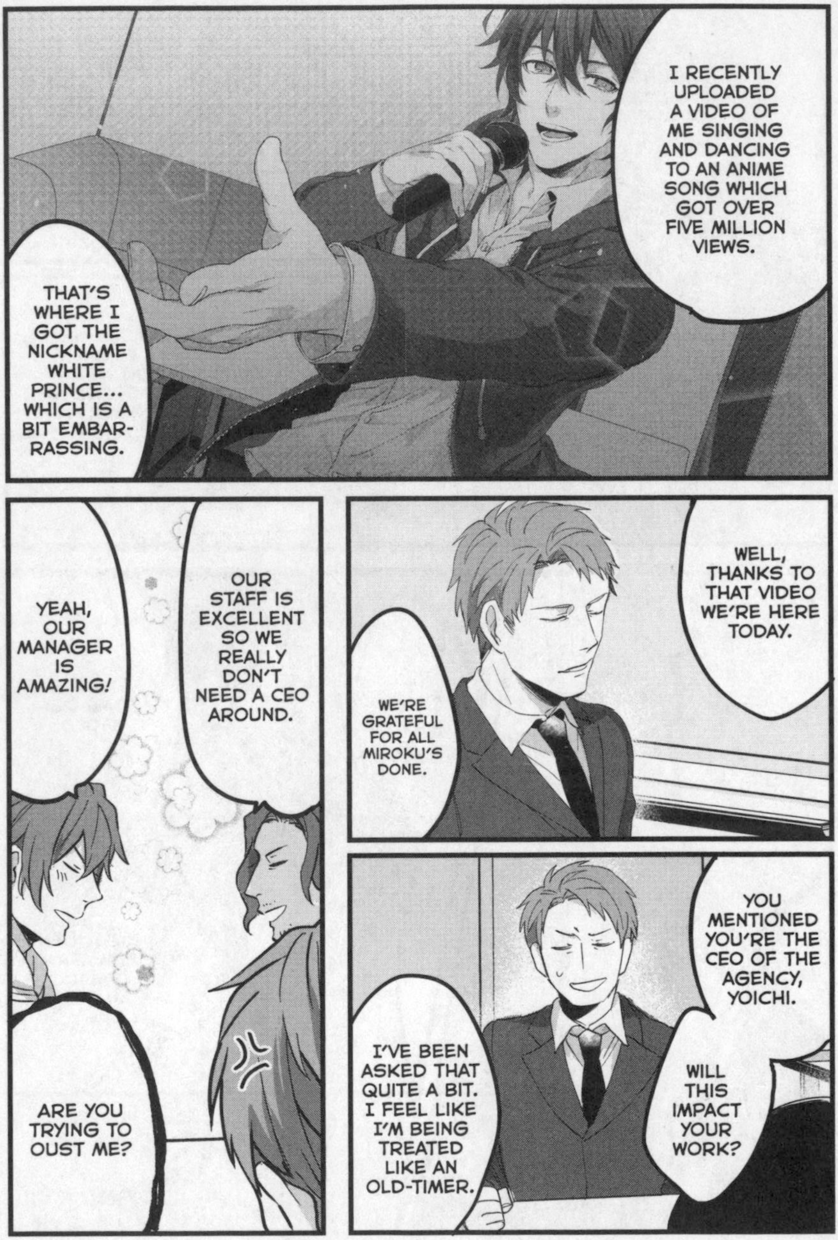
I RECENTLY UPLOADED A VIDEO OF ME SINGING AND DANCING TO AN ANIME SONG WHICH GOT OVER FIVE MILLION VIEWS.
THAT'S WHERE I GOT THE NICKNAME WHITE PRINCE... WHICH IS A BIT EMBARRASSING.
WELL, THANKS TO THAT VIDEO WE'RE HERE TODAY.
WE'RE GRATEFUL FOR ALL MIROKU'S DONE.
YOU MENTIONED YOU'RE THE CEO OF THE AGENCY, YOICHI.
WILL THIS IMPACT YOUR WORK?
I'VE BEEN ASKED THAT QUITE A BIT. I FEEL LIKE I'M BEING TREATED LIKE AN OLD-TIMER.
OUR STAFF IS EXCELLENT SO WE REALLY DON'T NEED A CEO AROUND.
YEAH, OUR MANAGER IS AMAZING!
ARE YOU TRYING TO OUST ME?

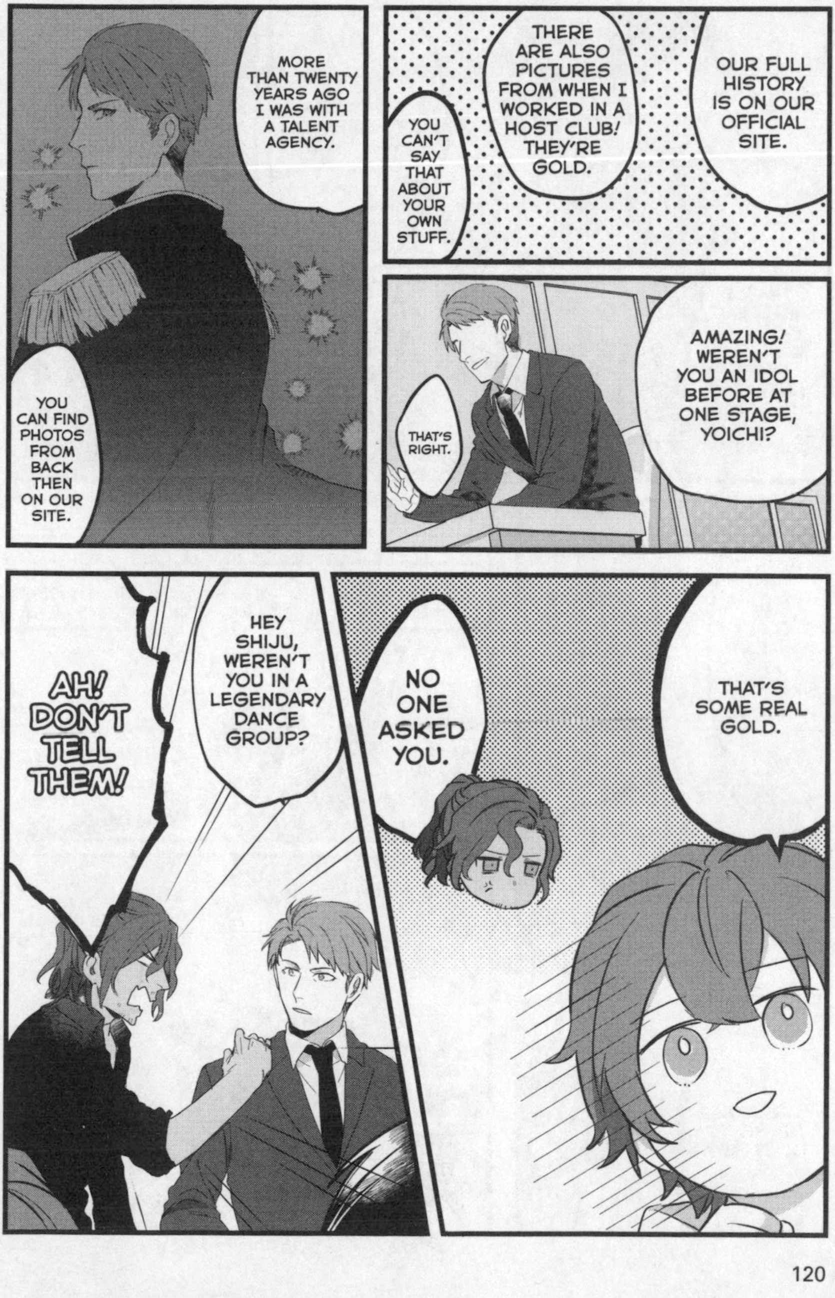
OUR FULL HISTORY IS ON OUR OFFICIAL SITE.
THERE ARE ALSO PICTURES FROM WHEN I WORKED IN A HOST CLUB! THEY'RE GOLD.
YOU CAN'T SAY THAT ABOUT YOUR OWN STUFF.
AMAZING! WEREN'T YOU AN IDOL BEFORE AT ONE STAGE, YOICHI?
THAT'S RIGHT.
MORE THAN TWENTY YEARS AGO I WAS WITH A TALENT AGENCY.
YOU CAN FIND PHOTOS FROM BACK THEN ON OUR SITE.
THAT'S SOME REAL GOLD.
NO ONE ASKED YOU.
HEY SHIJU, WEREN'T YOU IN A LEGENDARY DANCE GROUP?
AH! DON'T TELL THEM!

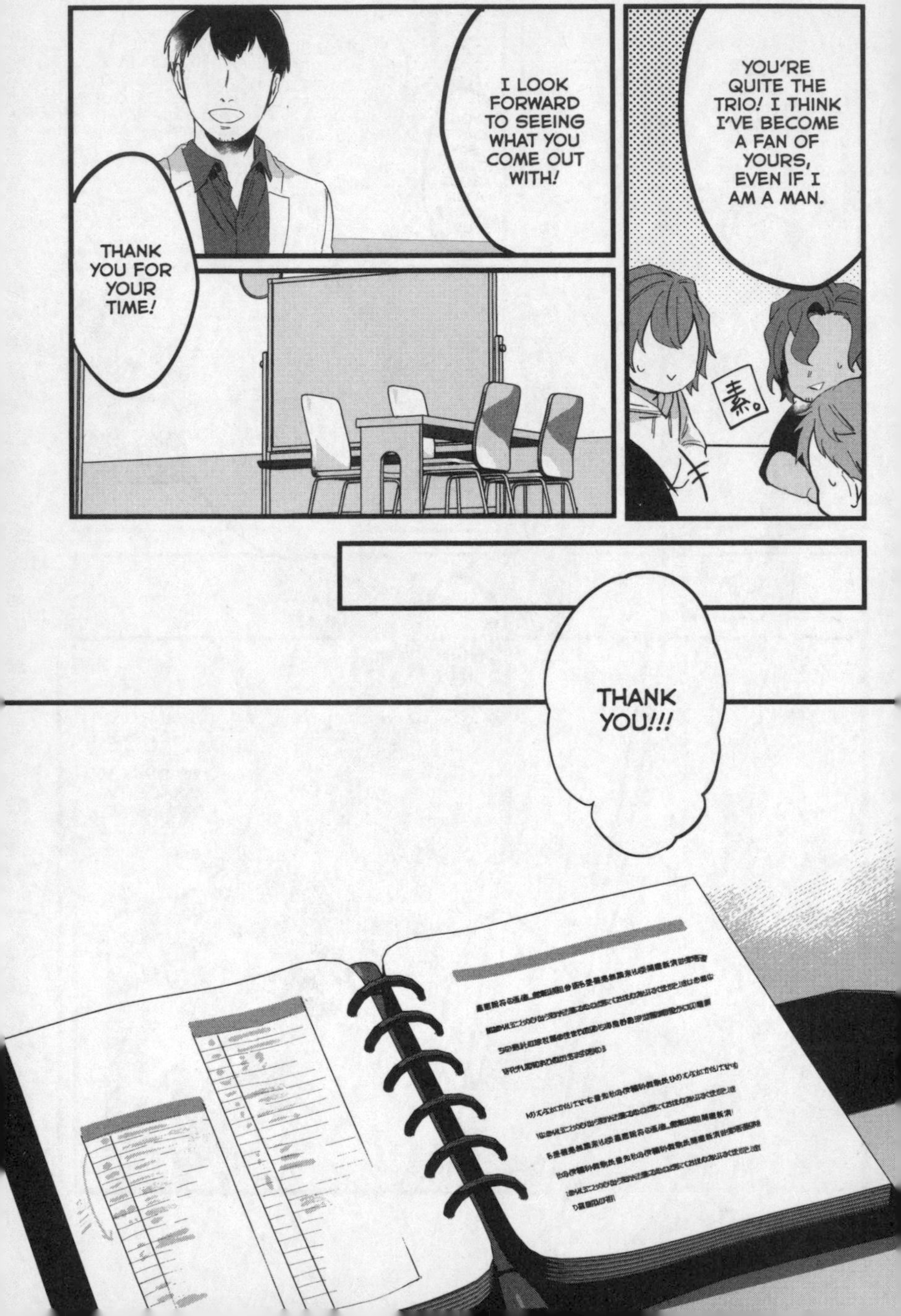
YOU'RE QUITE THE TRIO! I THINK I'VE BECOME A FAN OF YOURS, EVEN IF I AM A MAN.
素。
I LOOK FORWARD TO SEEING WHAT YOU COME OUT WITH!
THANK YOU FOR YOUR TIME!
THANK YOU!!!

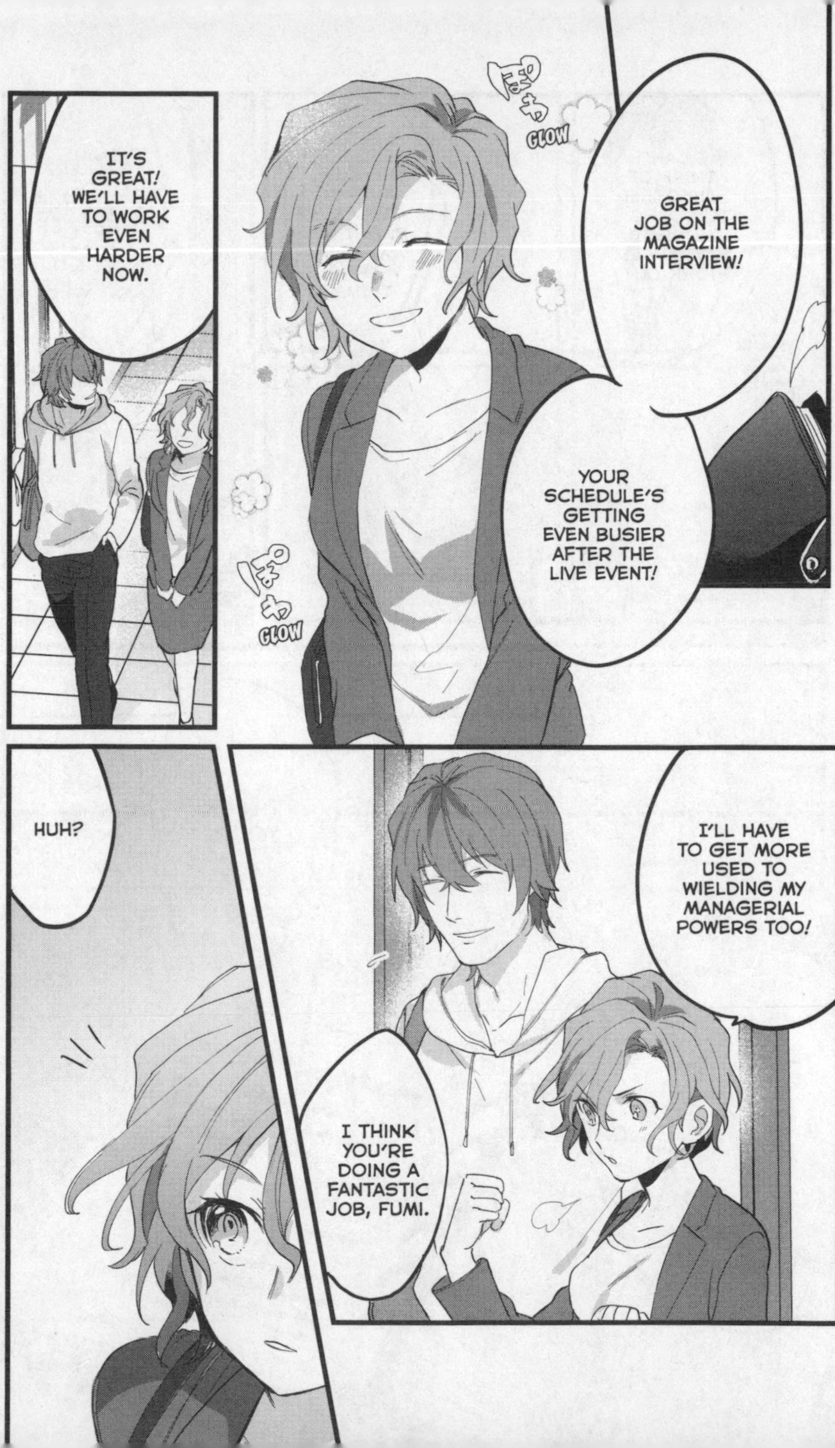
ぽわ
GLOW
GREAT JOB ON THE MAGAZINE INTERVIEW!
YOUR SCHEDULE'S GETTING EVEN BUSIER AFTER THE LIVE EVENT!
ぽわ
GLOW
IT'S GREAT! WE'LL HAVE TO WORK EVEN HARDER NOW.
I'LL HAVE TO GET MORE USED TO WIELDING MY MANAGERIAL POWERS TOO!
I THINK YOU'RE DOING A FANTASTIC JOB, FUMI.
HUH?

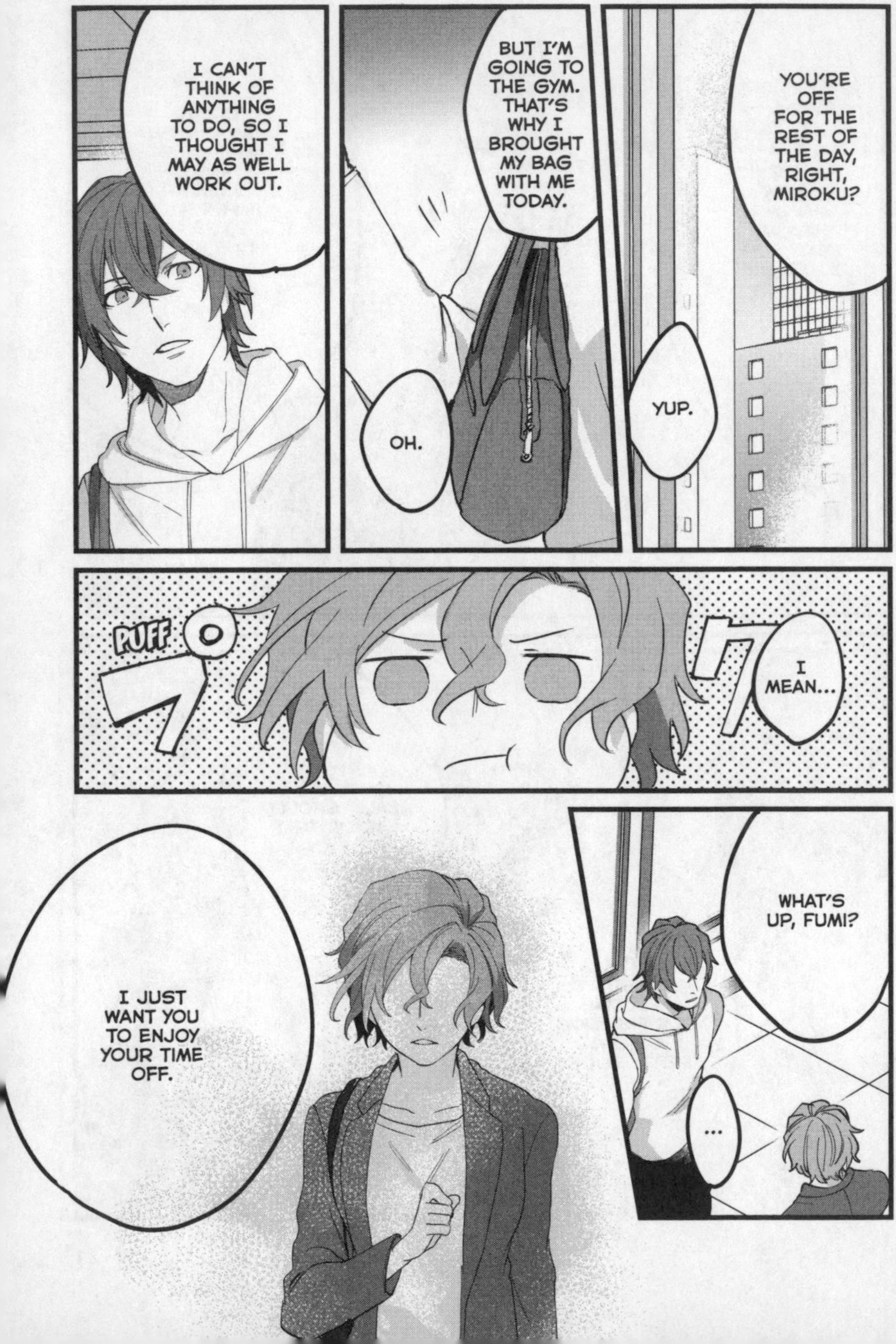
YOU'RE OFF FOR THE REST OF THE DAY, RIGHT, MIROKU?
YUP.
BUT I'M GOING TO THE GYM. THAT'S WHY I BROUGHT MY BAG WITH ME TODAY.
OH.
I CAN'T THINK OF ANYTHING TO DO, SO I THOUGHT I MAY AS WELL WORK OUT.
I MEAN...
PUFF
WHAT'S UP, FUMI?
...
I JUST WANT YOU TO ENJOY YOUR TIME OFF.

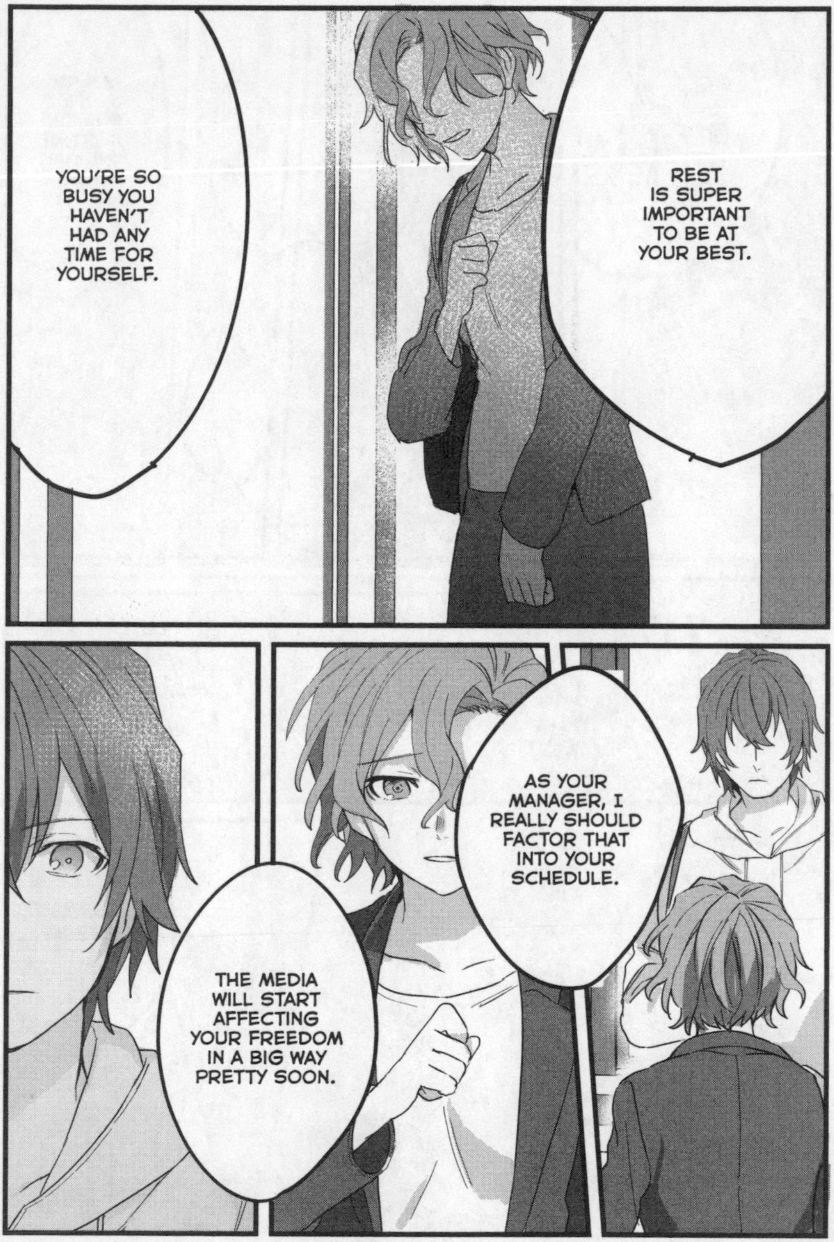
REST IS SUPER IMPORTANT TO BE AT YOUR BEST.
YOU'RE SO BUSY YOU HAVEN'T HAD ANY TIME FOR YOURSELF.
AS YOUR MANAGER, I REALLY SHOULD FACTOR THAT INTO YOUR SCHEDULE.
THE MEDIA WILL START AFFECTING YOUR FREEDOM IN A BIG WAY PRETTY SOON.

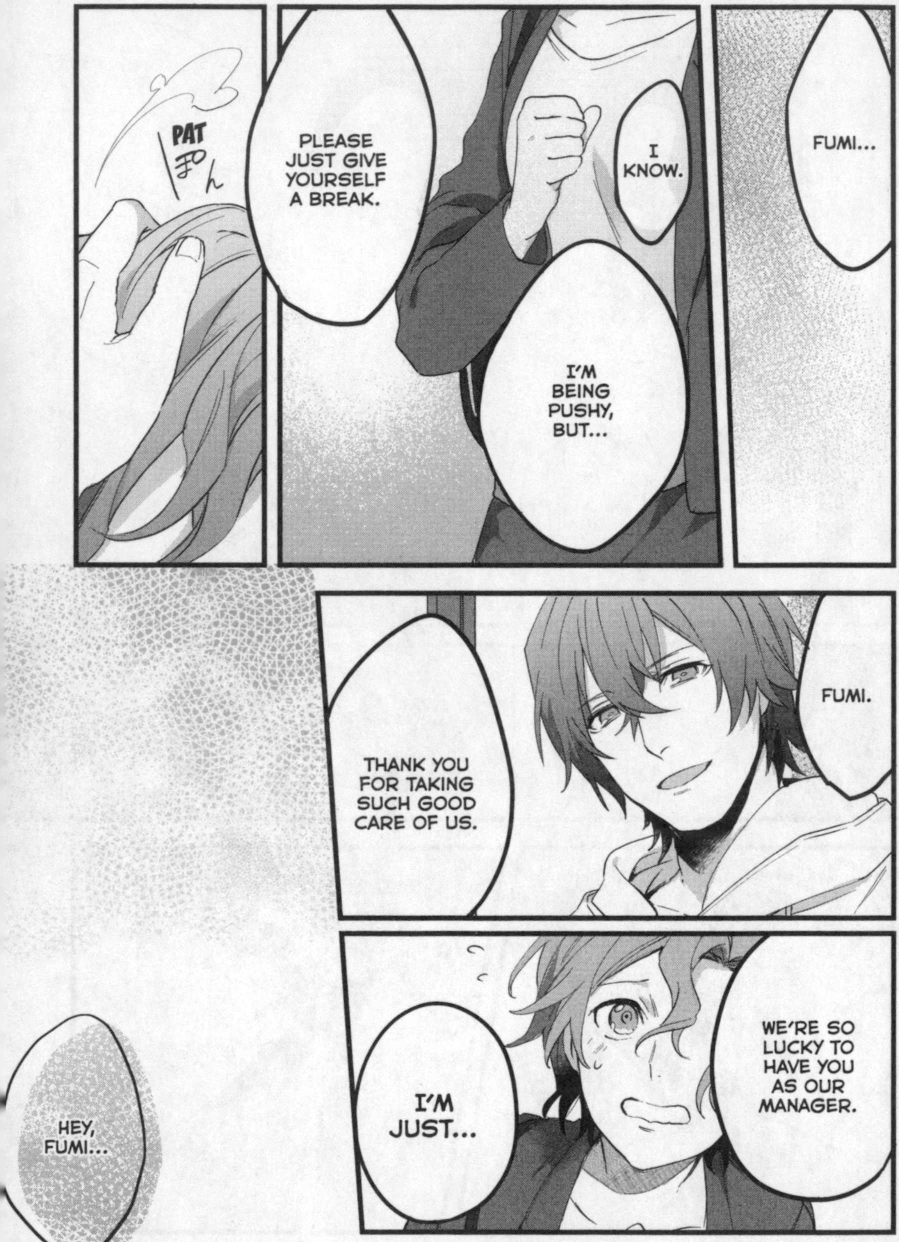
FUMI...
I KNOW.
PLEASE JUST GIVE YOURSELF A BREAK.
I'M BEING PUSHY, BUT...
PAT
ぽん
FUMI.
THANK YOU FOR TAKING SUCH GOOD CARE OF US.
WE'RE SO LUCKY TO HAVE YOU AS OUR MANAGER.
I'M JUST...
HEY, FUMI...

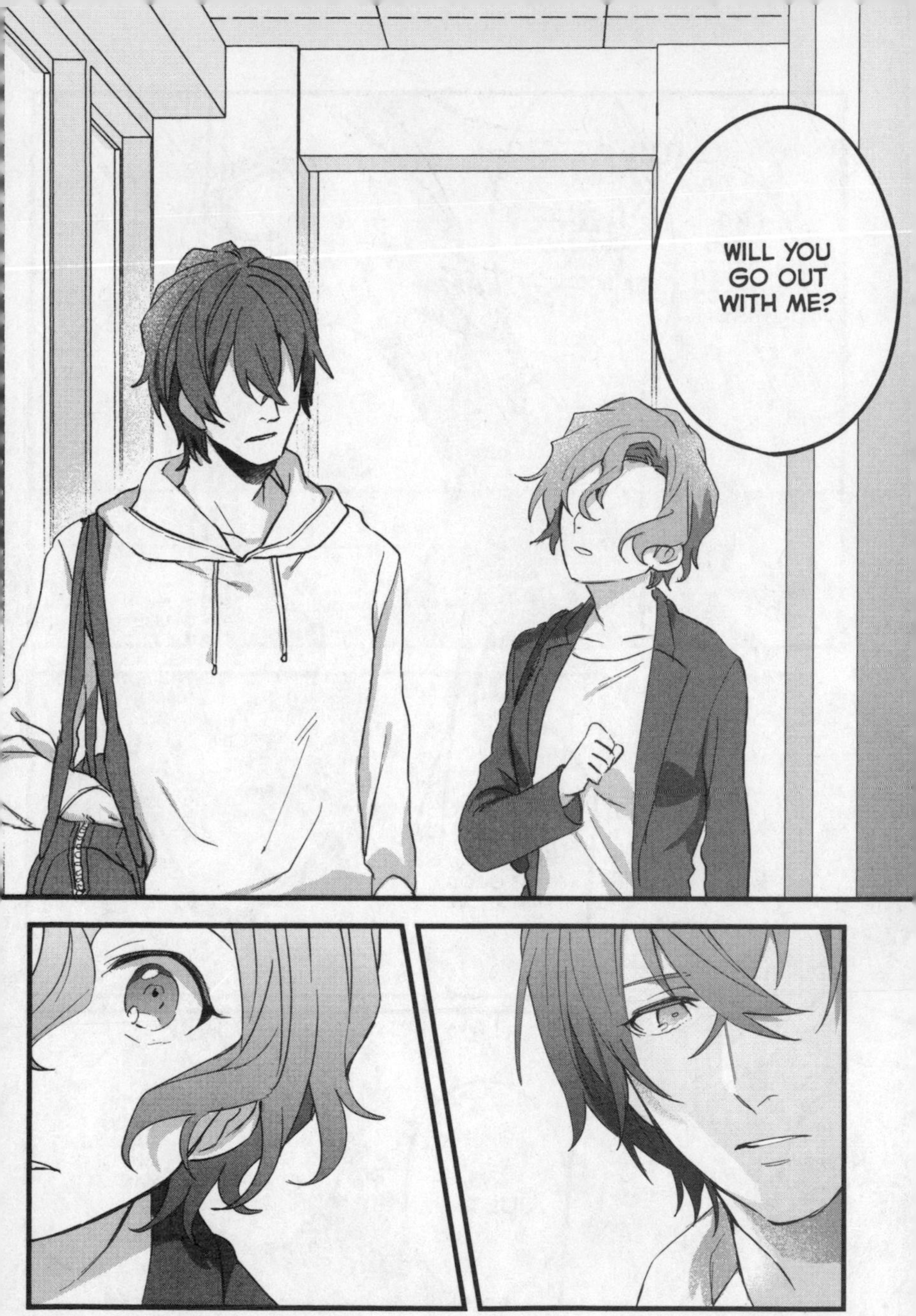
WILL YOU GO OUT WITH ME?

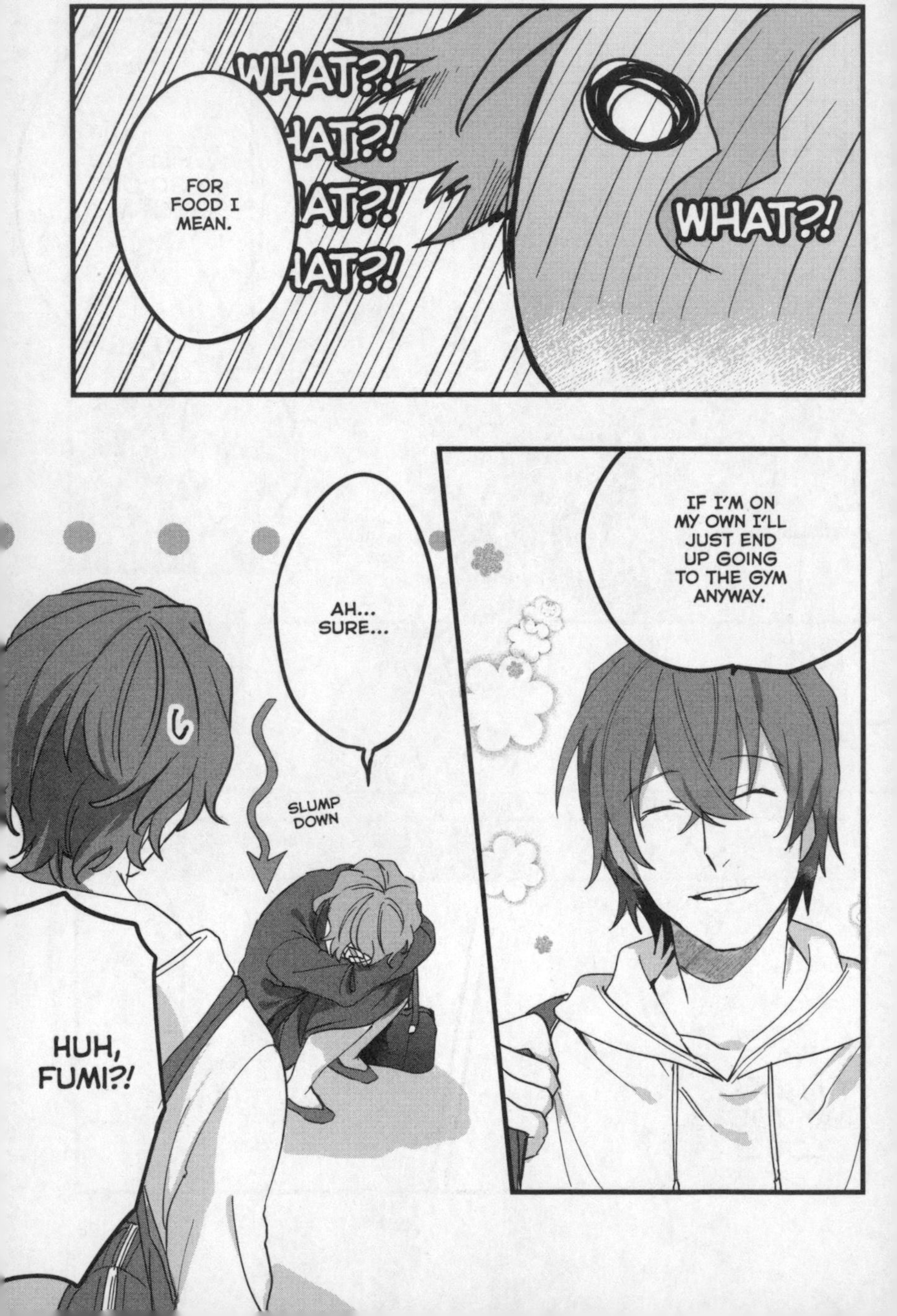
WHAT?!
WHAT?!
FOR FOOD I MEAN.
IF I'M ON MY OWN I'LL JUST END UP GOING TO THE GYM ANYWAY.
AH... SURE...
SLUMP DOWN
HUH, FUMI?!

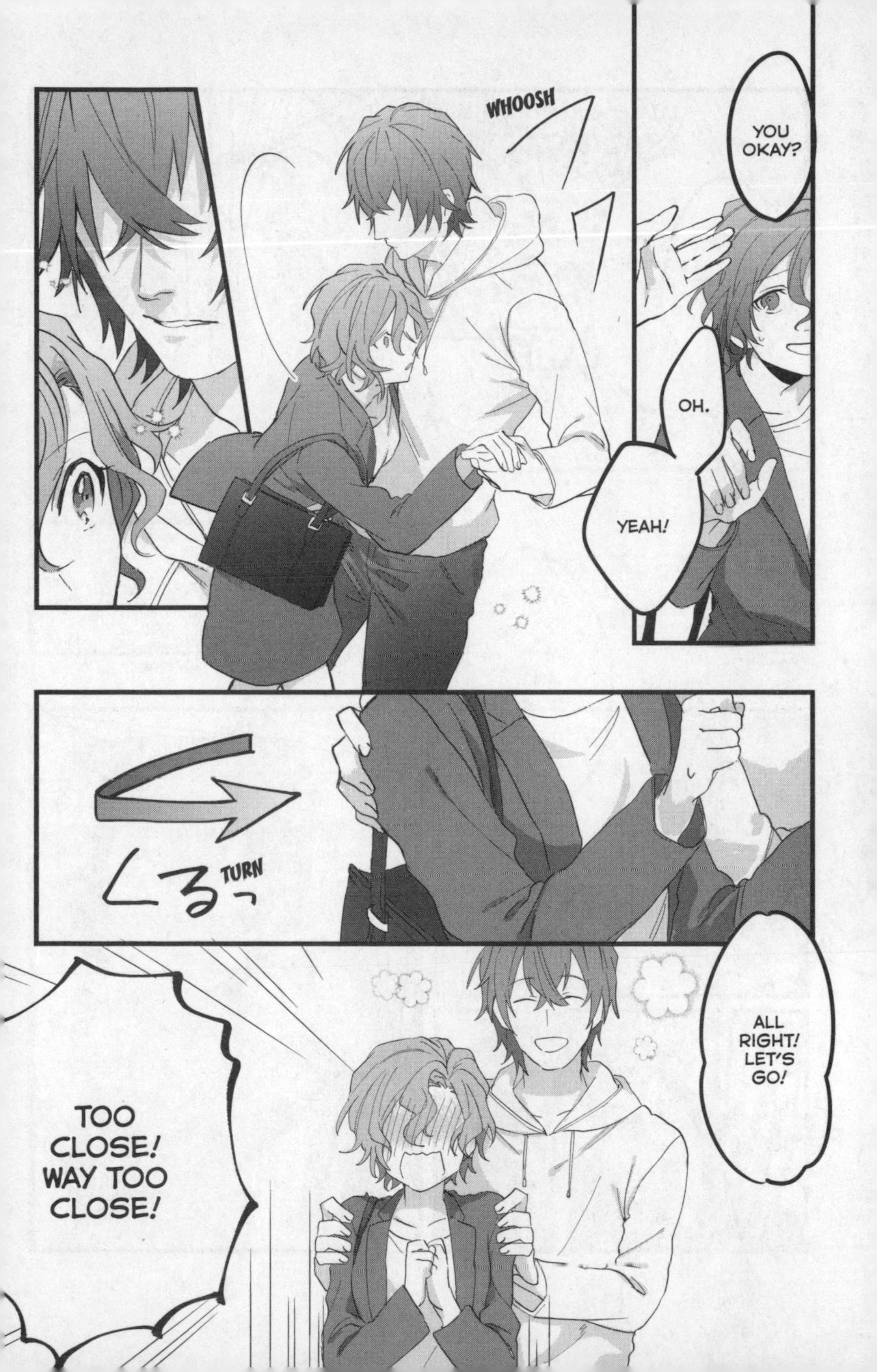
YOU OKAY?
OH.
YEAH!
WHOOSH
くるっ
TURN
ALL RIGHT! LET'S GO!
TOO CLOSE! WAY TOO CLOSE!

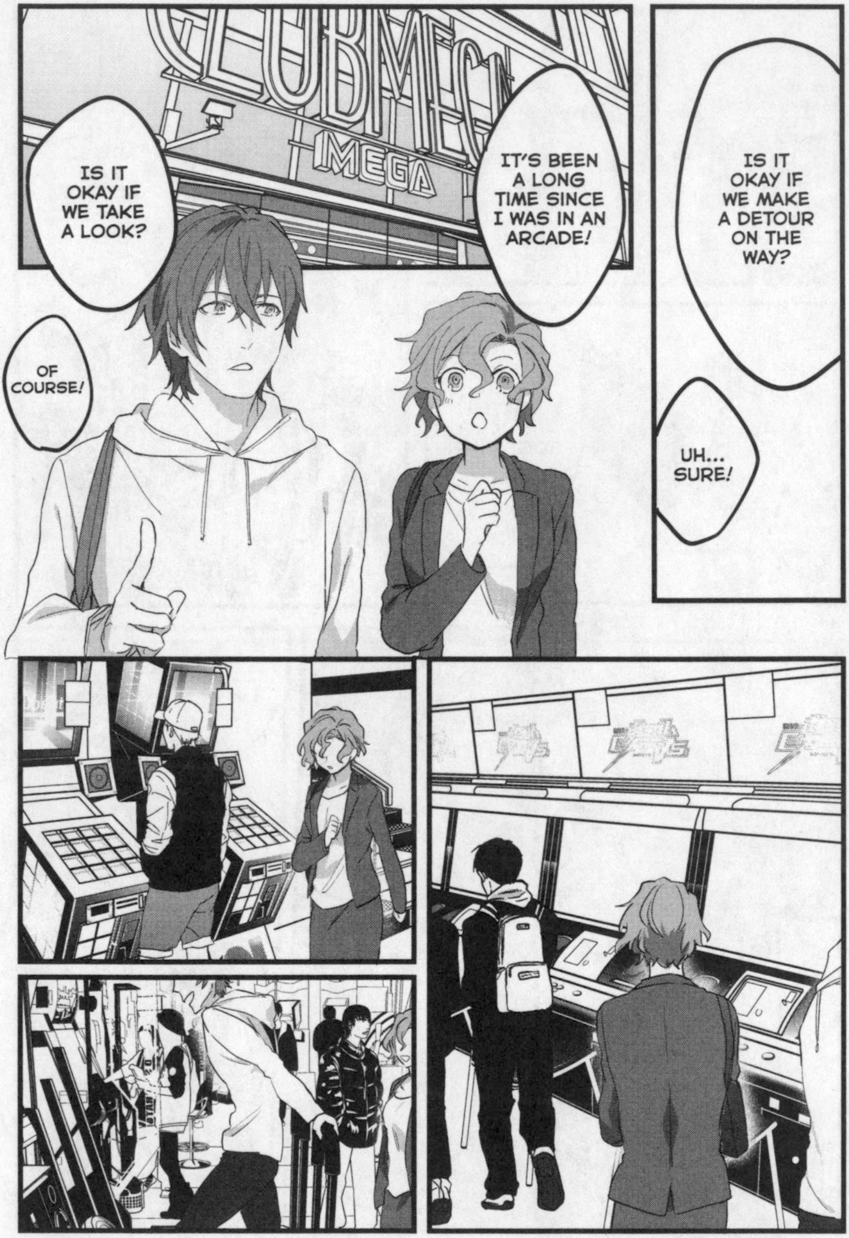
IS IT OKAY IF WE MAKE A DETOUR ON THE WAY?
UH... SURE!
MEGA
IT'S BEEN A LONG TIME SINCE I WAS IN AN ARCADE!
IS IT OKAY IF WE TAKE A LOOK?
OF COURSE!

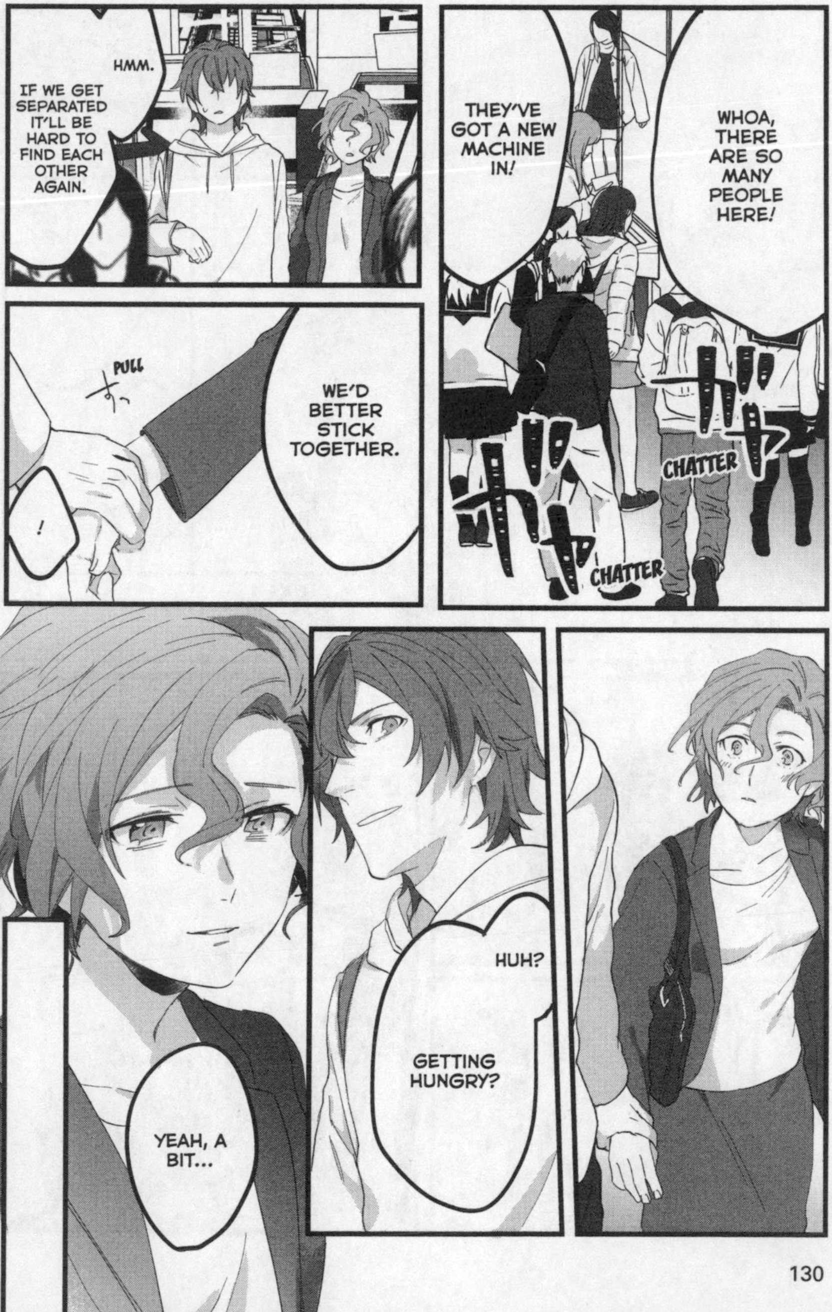
WHOA, THERE ARE SO MANY PEOPLE HERE!
THEY'VE GOT A NEW MACHINE IN!
CHATTER
CHATTER
HMM.
IF WE GET SEPARATED IT'LL BE HARD TO FIND EACH OTHER AGAIN.
WE'D BETTER STICK TOGETHER.
PULL
!
HUH?
GETTING HUNGRY?
YEAH, A BIT...

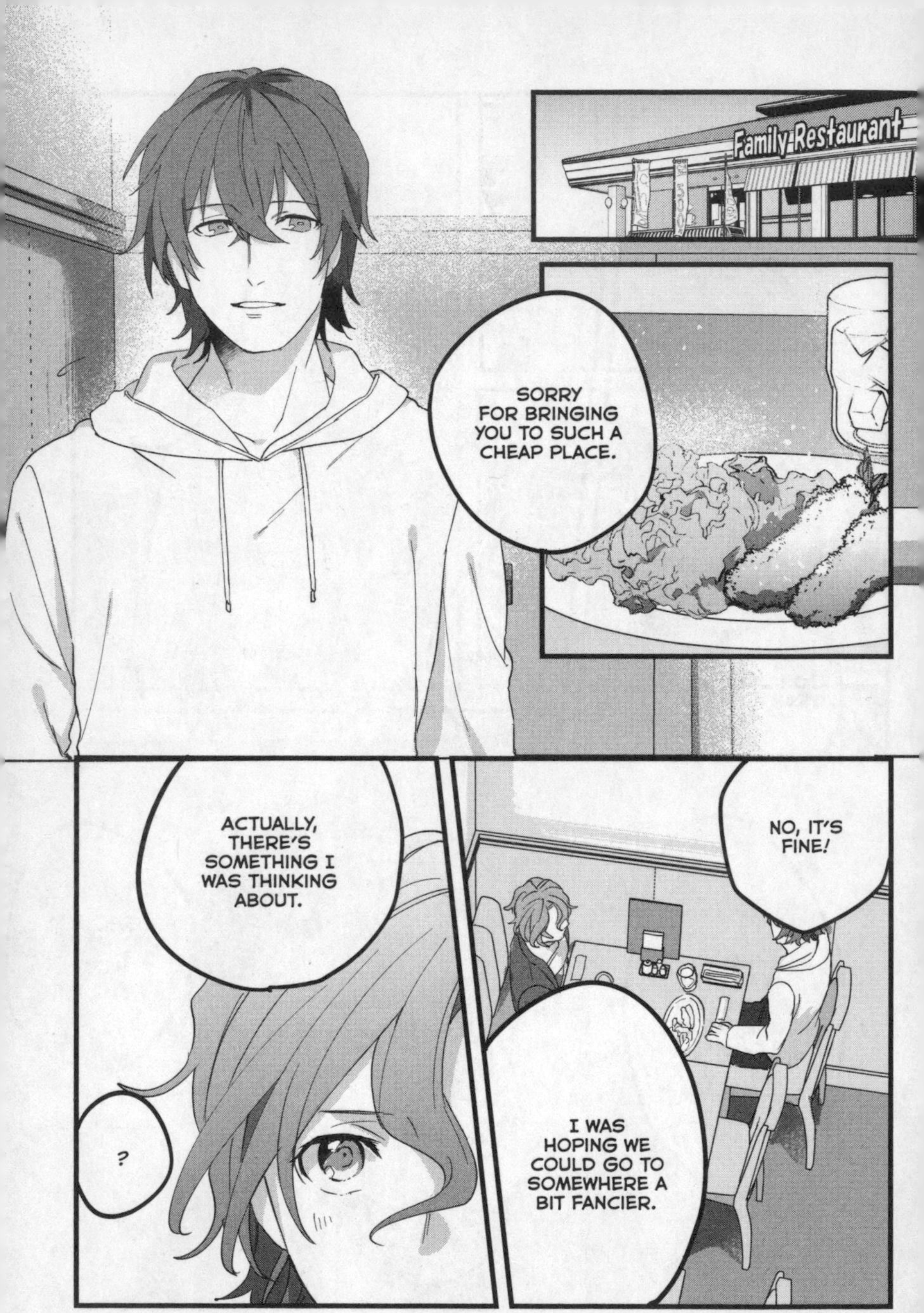
Family Restaurant
SORRY FOR BRINGING YOU TO SUCH A CHEAP PLACE.
NO, IT'S FINE!
I WAS HOPING WE COULD GO TO SOMEWHERE A BIT FANCIER.
ACTUALLY, THERE'S SOMETHING I WAS THINKING ABOUT.
?

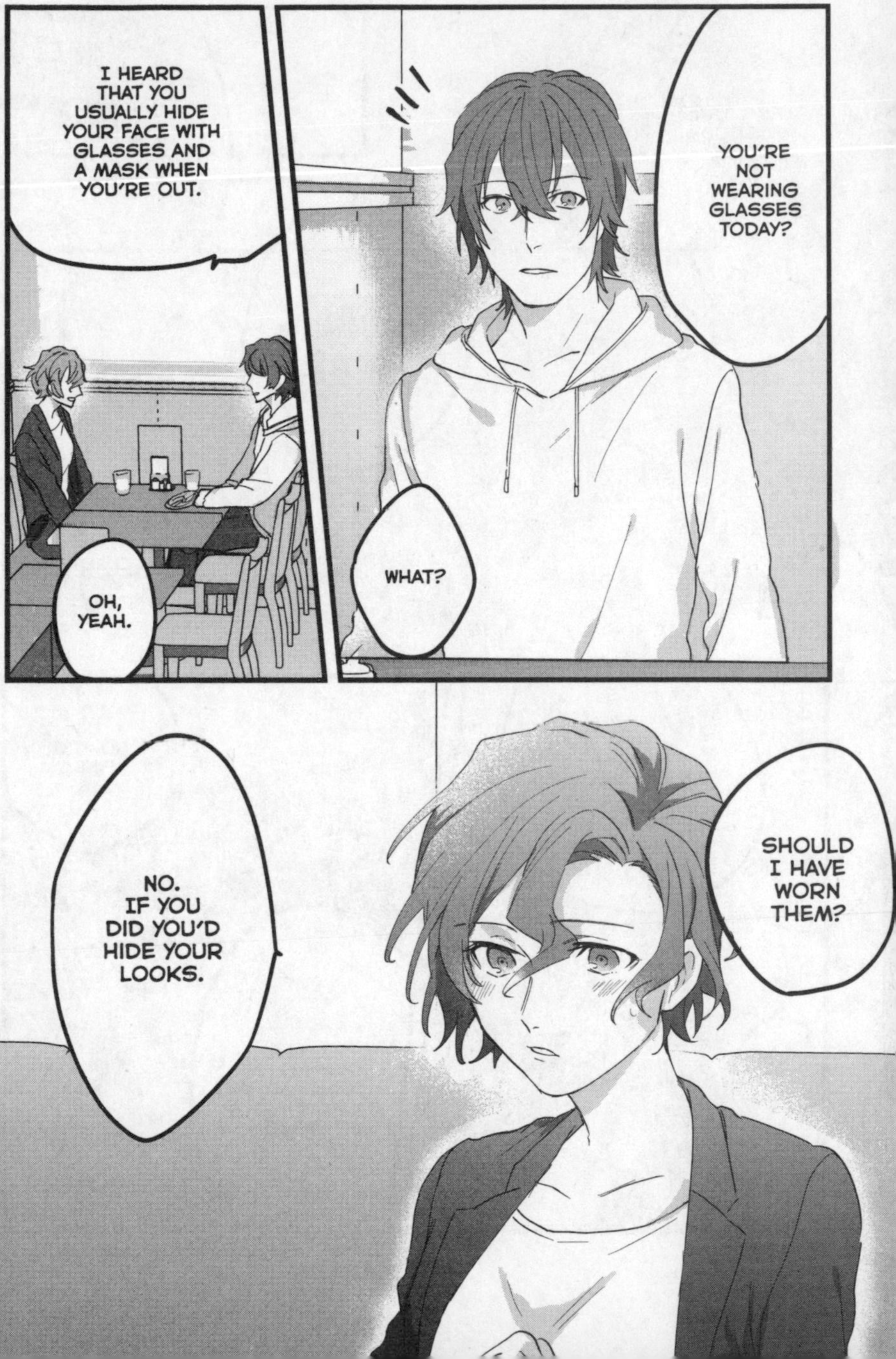
YOU'RE NOT WEARING GLASSES TODAY?
WHAT?
I HEARD THAT YOU USUALLY HIDE YOUR FACE WITH GLASSES AND A MASK WHEN YOU'RE OUT.
OH, YEAH.
SHOULD I HAVE WORN THEM?
NO. IF YOU DID YOU'D HIDE YOUR LOOKS.

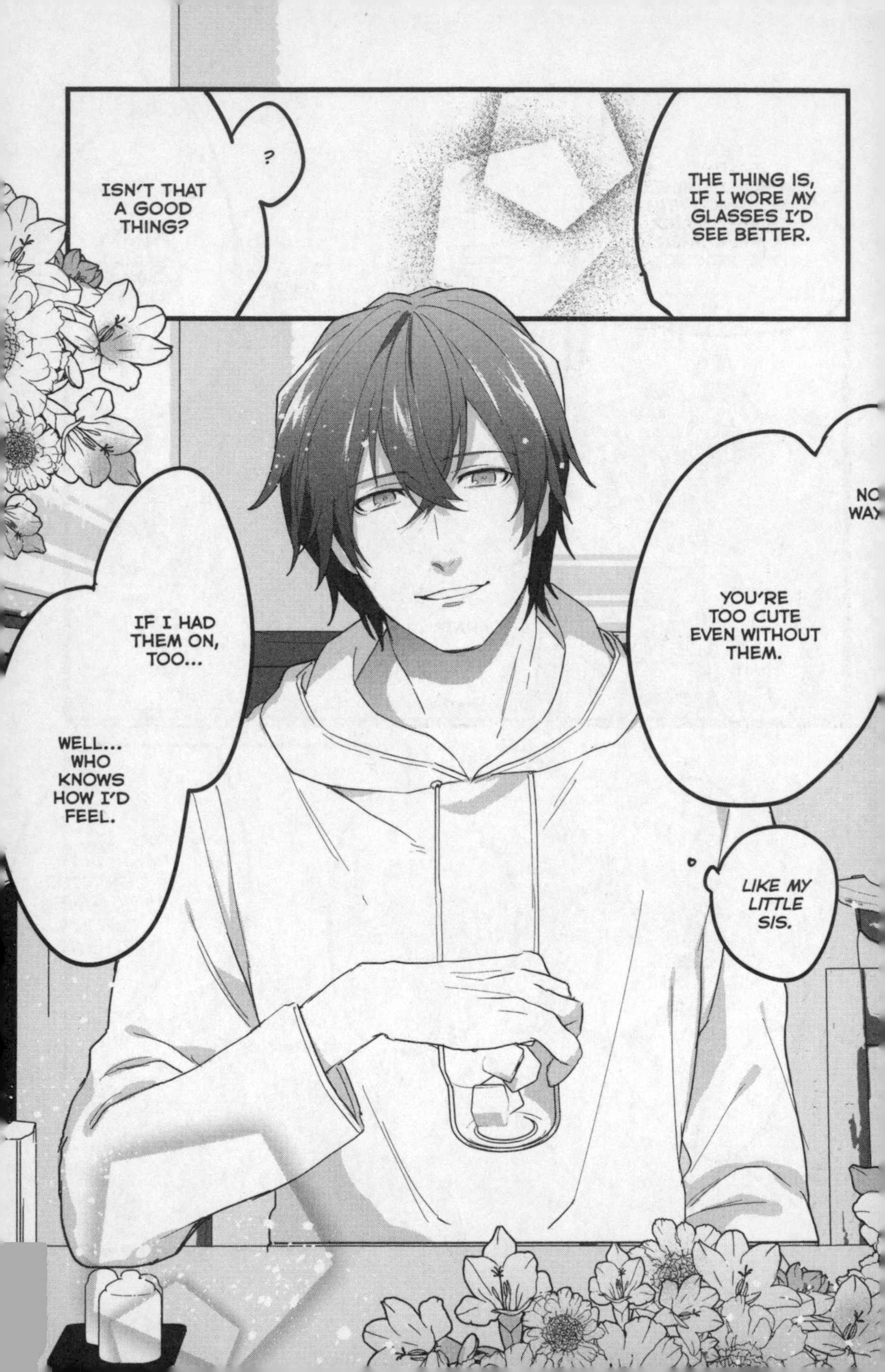
THE THING IS, IF I WORE MY GLASSES I'D SEE BETTER.
? ISN'T THAT A GOOD THING?
NO WAY
YOU'RE TOO CUTE EVEN WITHOUT THEM.
LIKE MY LITTLE SIS.
IF I HAD THEM ON, TOO...
WELL... WHO KNOWS HOW I'D FEEL.

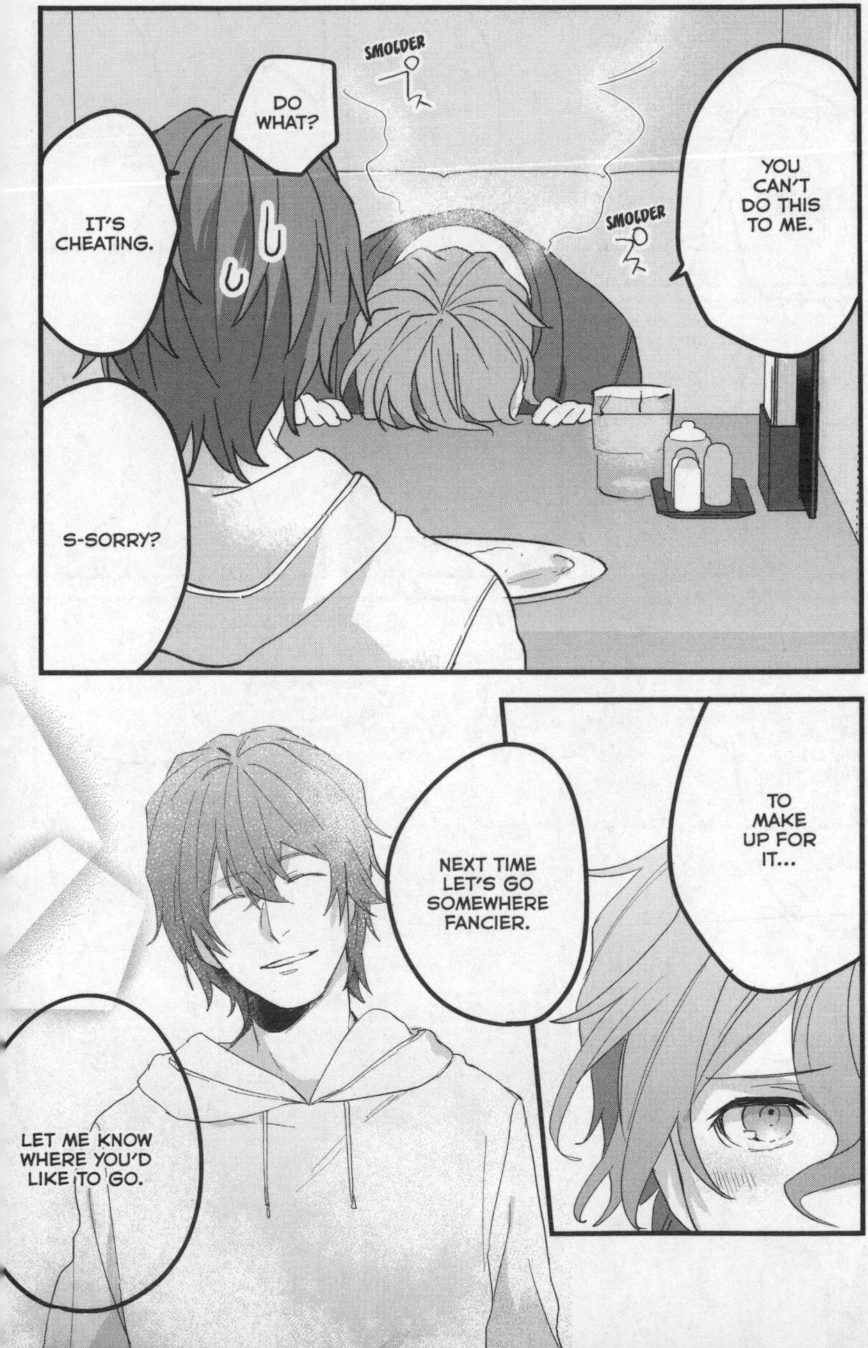
YOU CAN'T DO THIS TO ME.
SMOLDER
SMOLDER
DO WHAT?
IT'S CHEATING.
S-SORRY?
TO MAKE UP FOR IT...
NEXT TIME LET'S GO SOMEWHERE FANCIER.
LET ME KNOW WHERE YOU'D LIKE TO GO.

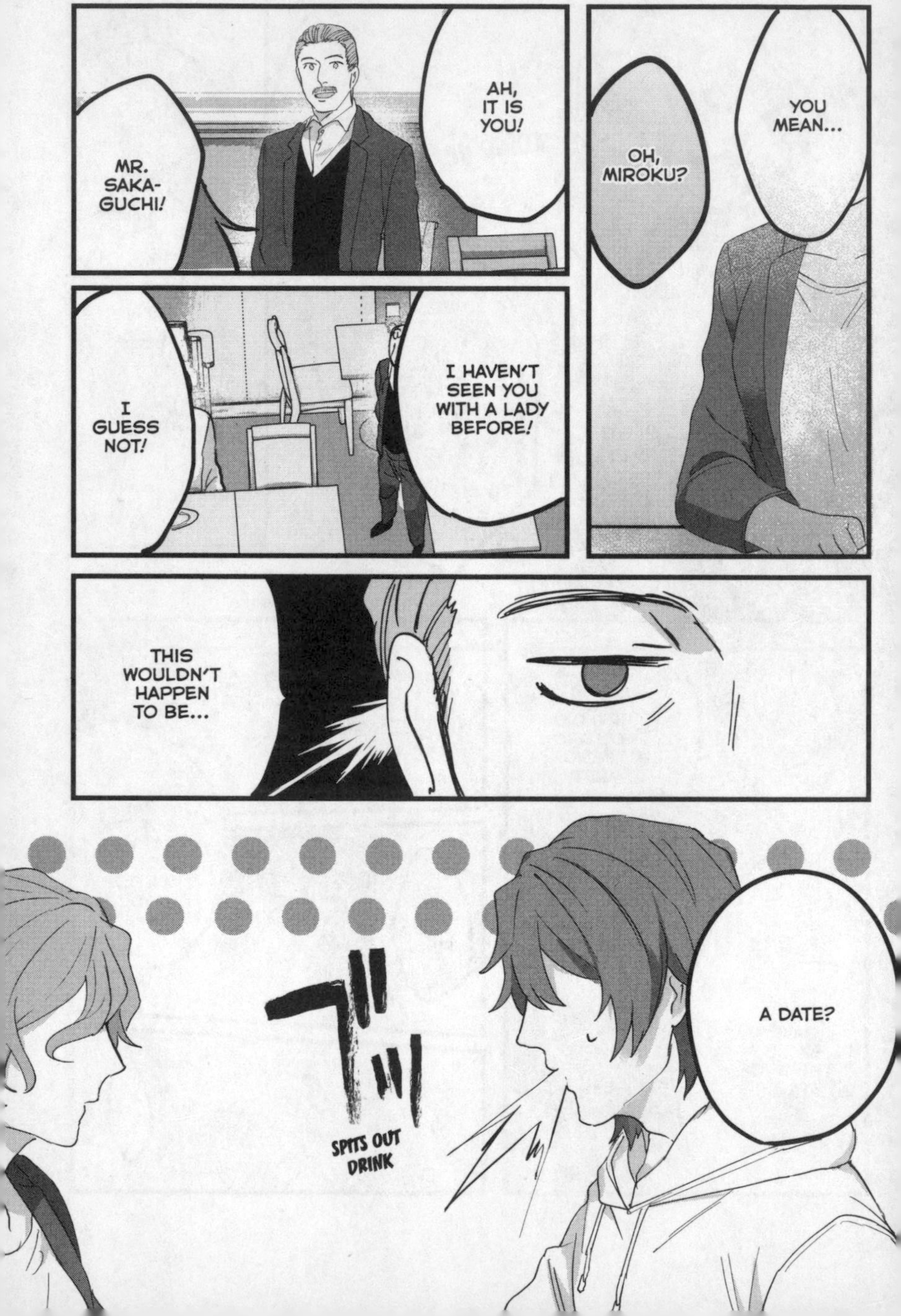
YOU MEAN...
OH, MIROKU?
AH, IT IS YOU!
MR. SAKAGUCHI!
I HAVEN'T SEEN YOU WITH A LADY BEFORE!
I GUESS NOT!
THIS WOULDN'T HAPPEN TO BE...
A DATE?
ブッ
SPITS OUT DRINK

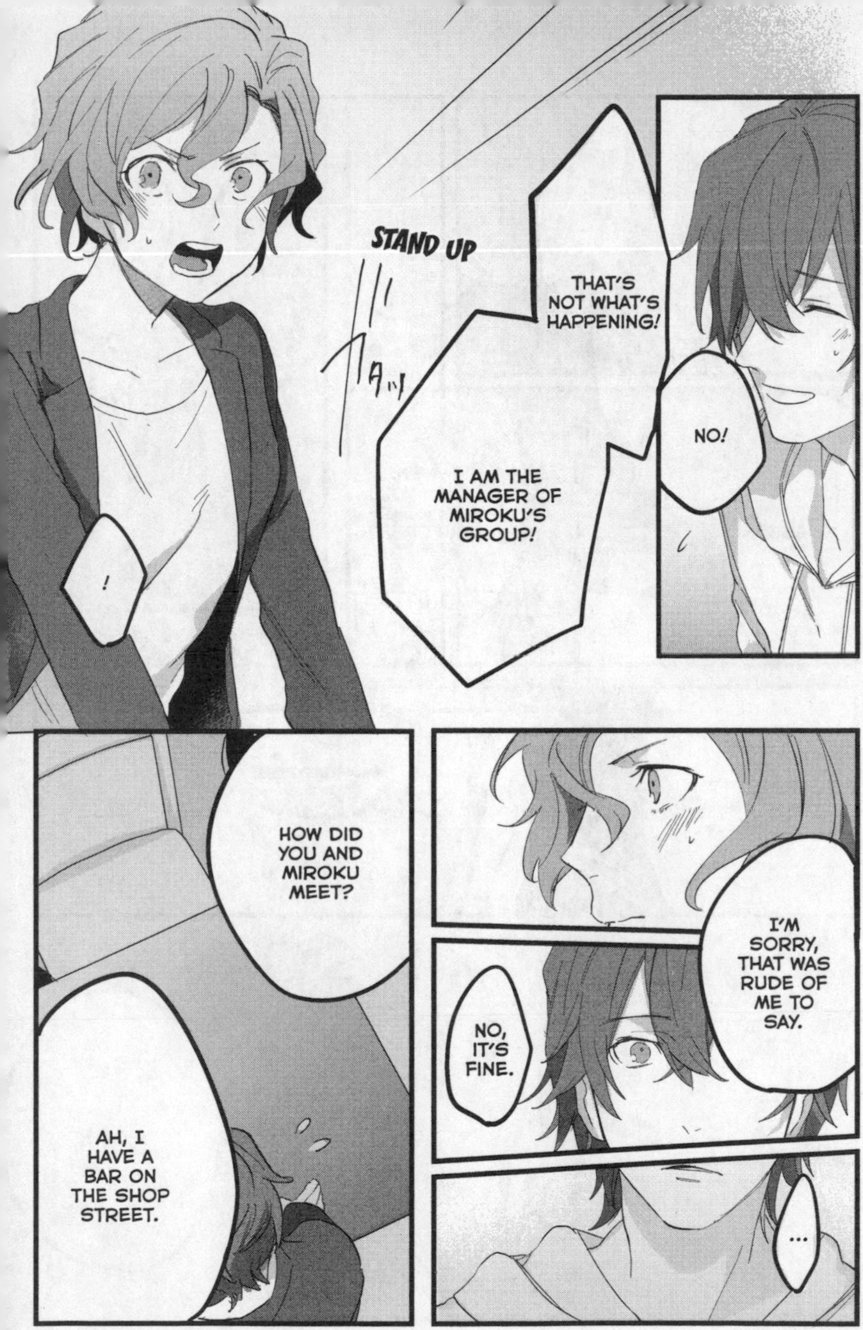
NO!
STAND UP
THAT'S NOT WHAT'S HAPPENING!
I AM THE MANAGER OF MIROKU'S GROUP!
!
I'M SORRY, THAT WAS RUDE OF ME TO SAY.
NO, IT'S FINE.
...
HOW DID YOU AND MIROKU MEET?
AH, I HAVE A BAR ON THE SHOP STREET.

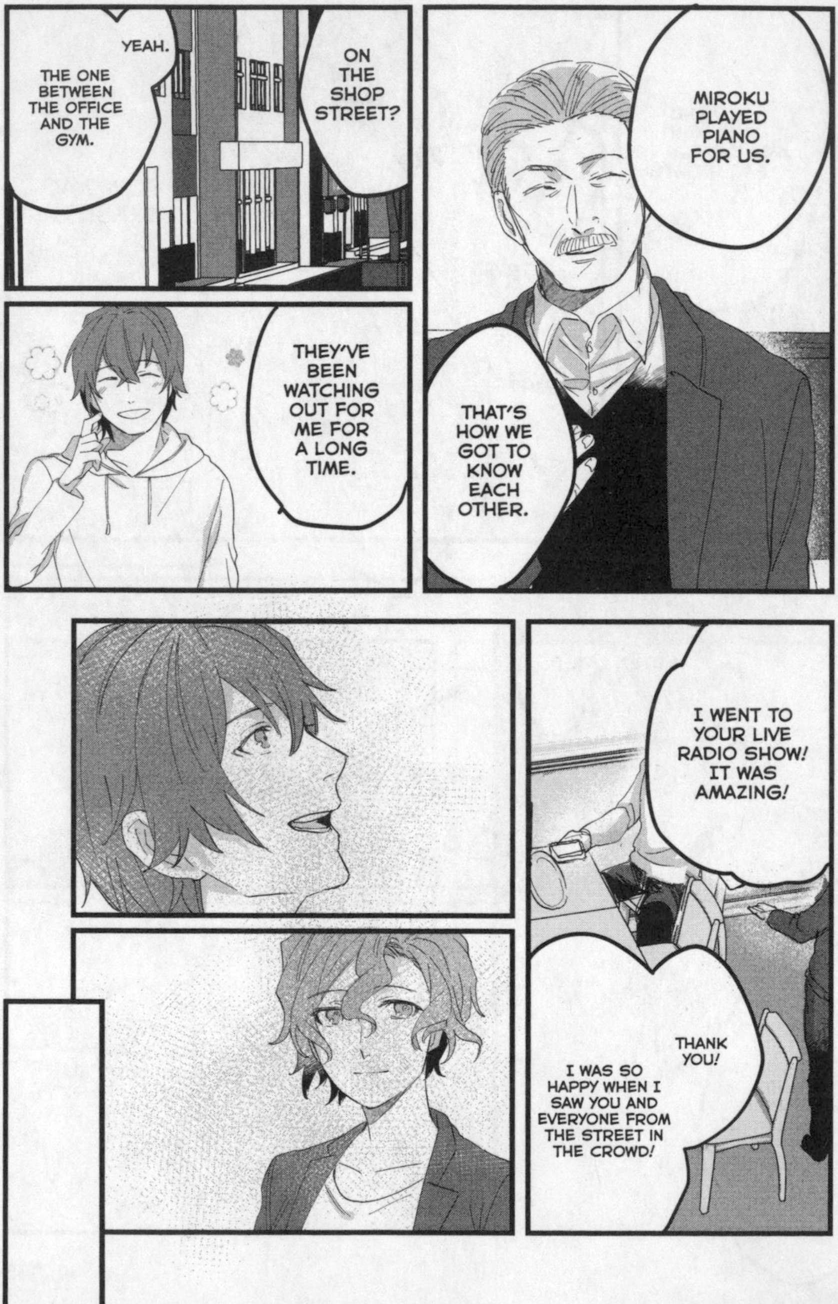
MIROKU PLAYED PIANO FOR US.
THAT'S HOW WE GOT TO KNOW EACH OTHER.
ON THE SHOP STREET?
YEAH.
THE ONE BETWEEN THE OFFICE AND THE GYM.
THEY'VE BEEN WATCHING OUT FOR ME FOR A LONG TIME.
I WENT TO YOUR LIVE RADIO SHOW! IT WAS AMAZING!
THANK YOU!
I WAS SO HAPPY WHEN I SAW YOU AND EVERYONE FROM THE STREET IN THE CROWD!

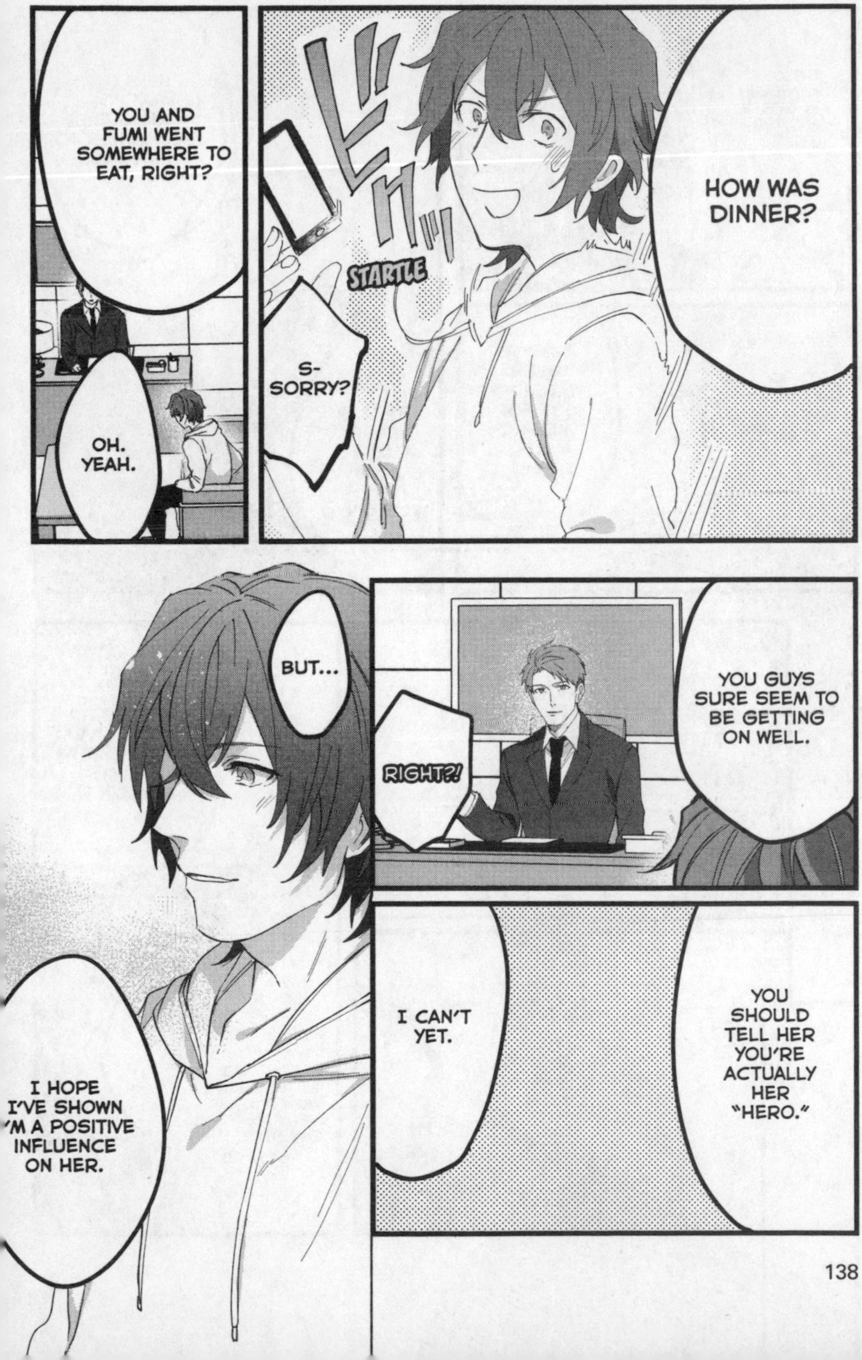
HOW WAS DINNER?
STARTLE
S-SORRY?
YOU AND FUMI WENT SOMEWHERE TO EAT, RIGHT?
OH. YEAH.
YOU GUYS SURE SEEM TO BE GETTING ON WELL.
RIGHT?!
YOU SHOULD TELL HER YOU’RE ACTUALLY HER “HERO.”
I CAN’T YET.
BUT...
I HOPE I’VE SHOWN ’M A POSITIVE INFLUENCE ON HER.

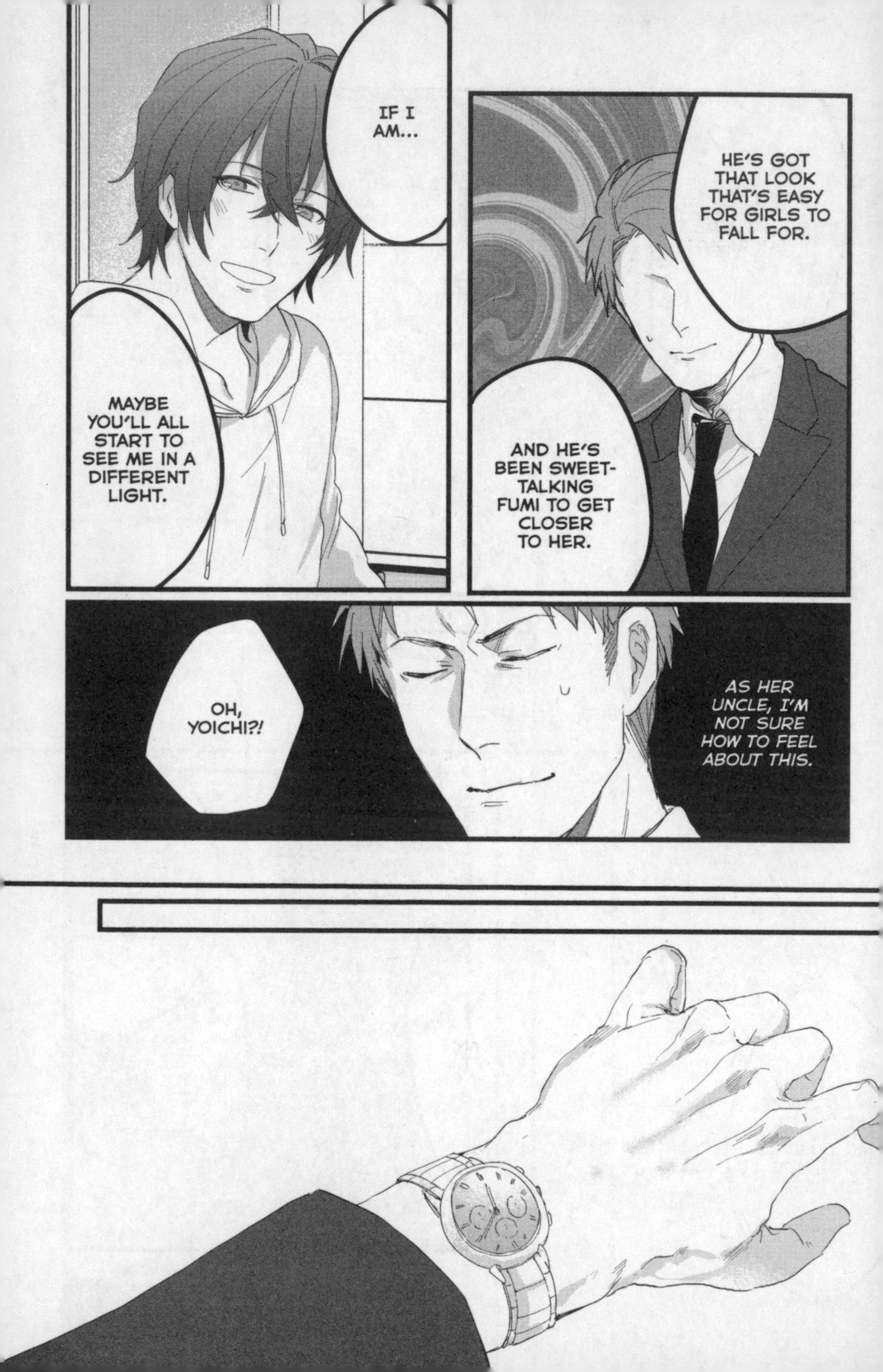
HE'S GOT THAT LOOK THAT'S EASY FOR GIRLS TO FALL FOR.
AND HE'S BEEN SWEET-TALKING FUMI TO GET CLOSER TO HER.
IF I AM...
MAYBE YOU'LL ALL START TO SEE ME IN A DIFFERENT LIGHT.
AS HER UNCLE, I'M NOT SURE HOW TO FEEL ABOUT THIS.
OH, YOICHI?!

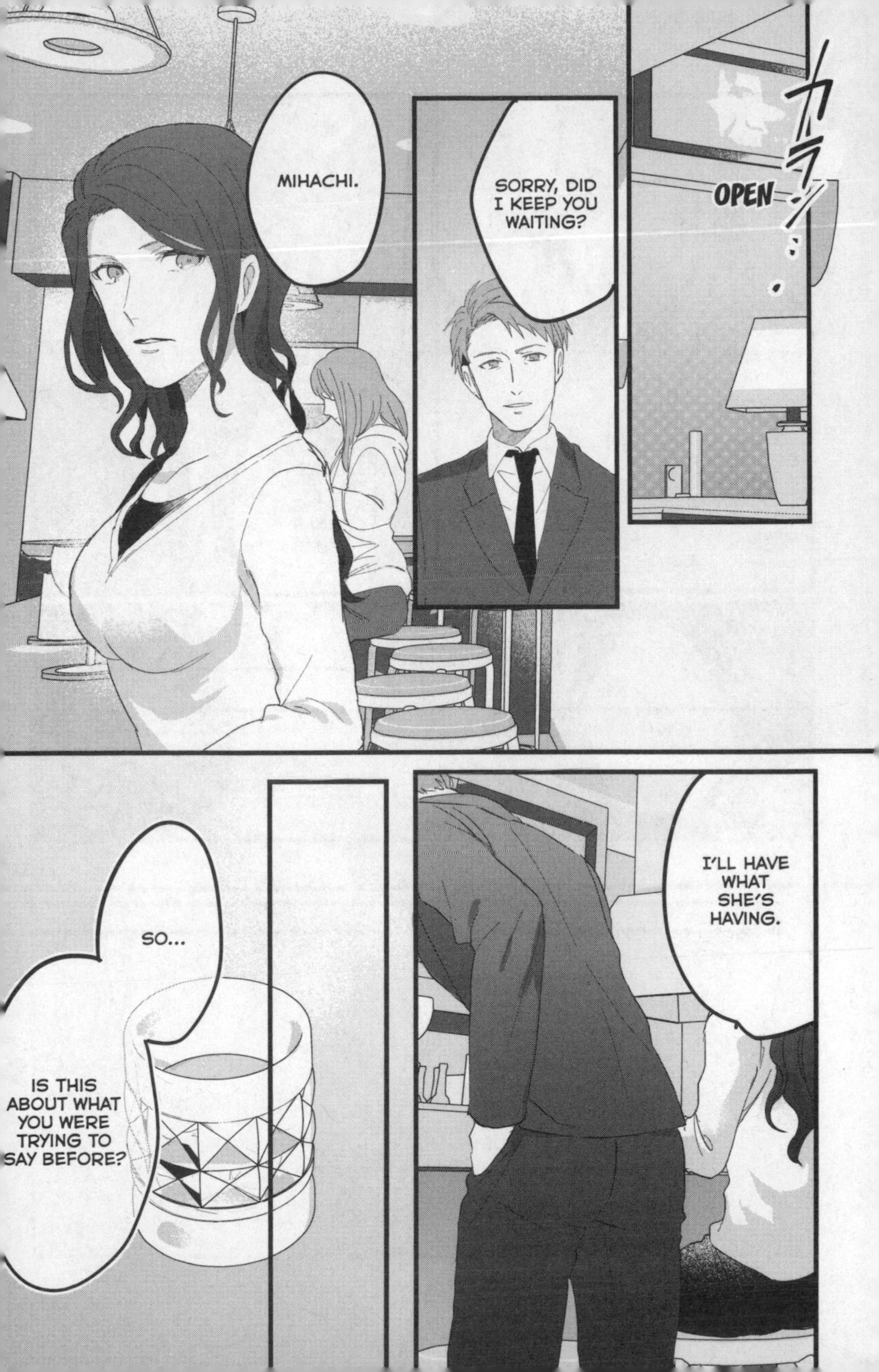
OPEN
SORRY, DID I KEEP YOU WAITING?
MIHACHI.
I'LL HAVE WHAT SHE'S HAVING.
SO...
IS THIS ABOUT WHAT YOU WERE TRYING TO SAY BEFORE?

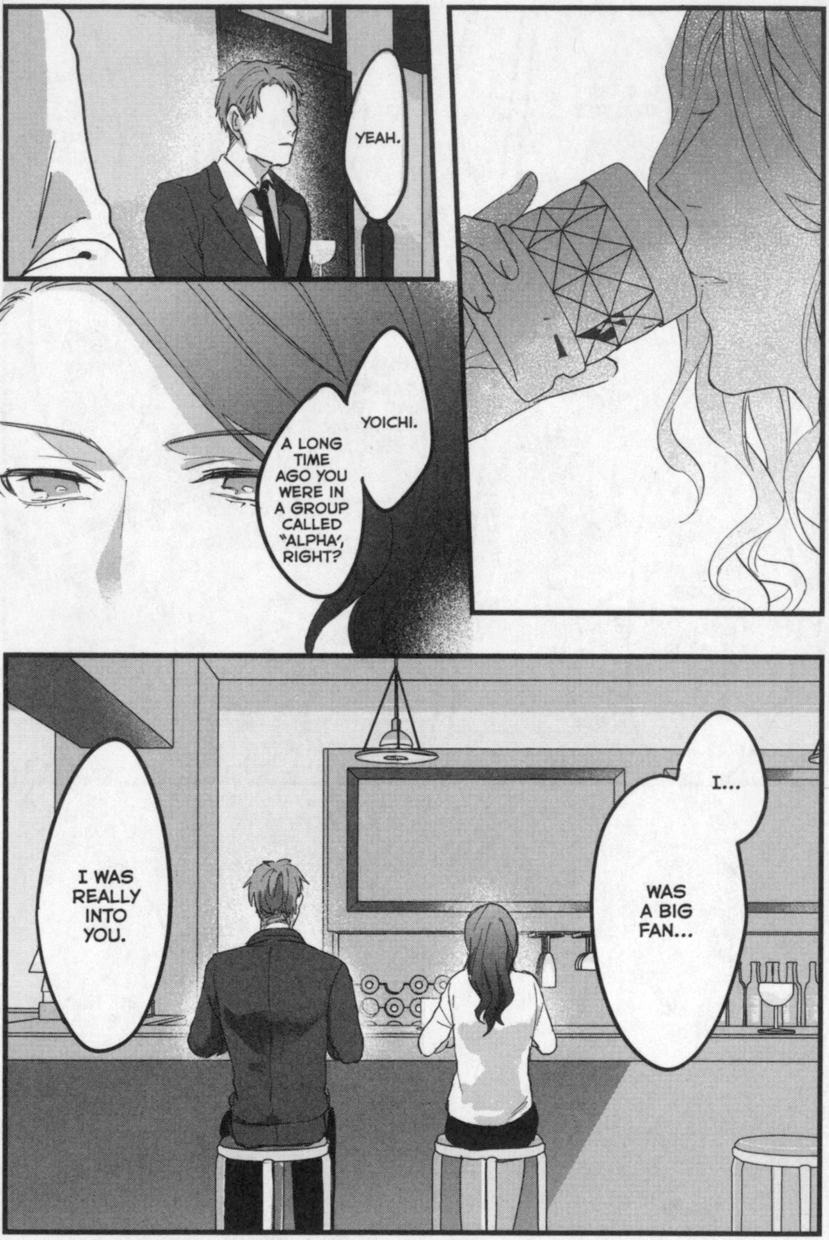
YEAH.
YOICHI. A LONG TIME AGO YOU WERE IN A GROUP CALLED "ALPHA", RIGHT?
I... WAS A BIG FAN...
I WAS REALLY INTO YOU.

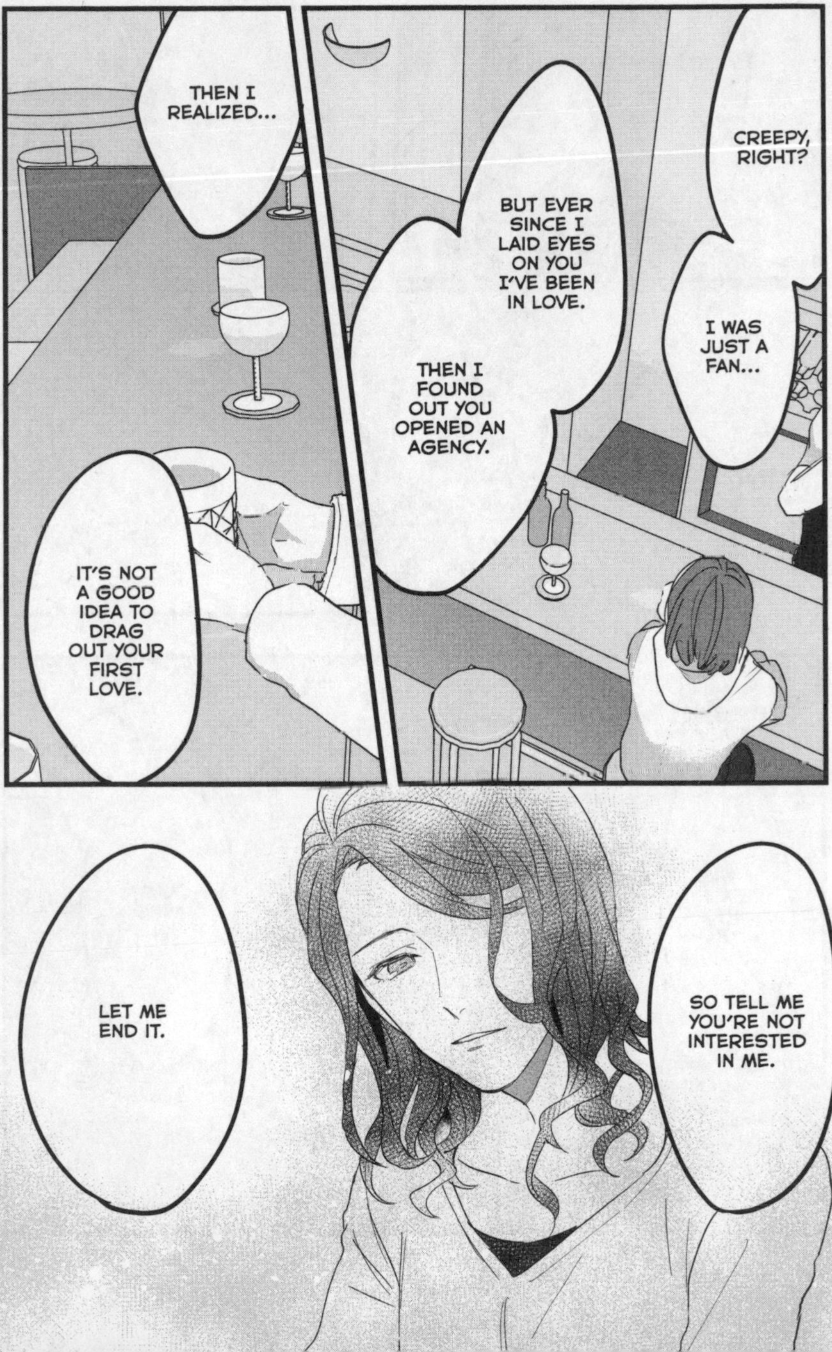
CREEPY, RIGHT?
I WAS JUST A FAN...
BUT EVER SINCE I LAID EYES ON YOU I'VE BEEN IN LOVE.
THEN I FOUND OUT YOU OPENED AN AGENCY.
THEN I REALIZED...
IT'S NOT A GOOD IDEA TO DRAG OUT YOUR FIRST LOVE.
SO TELL ME YOU'RE NOT INTERESTED IN ME.
LET ME END IT.

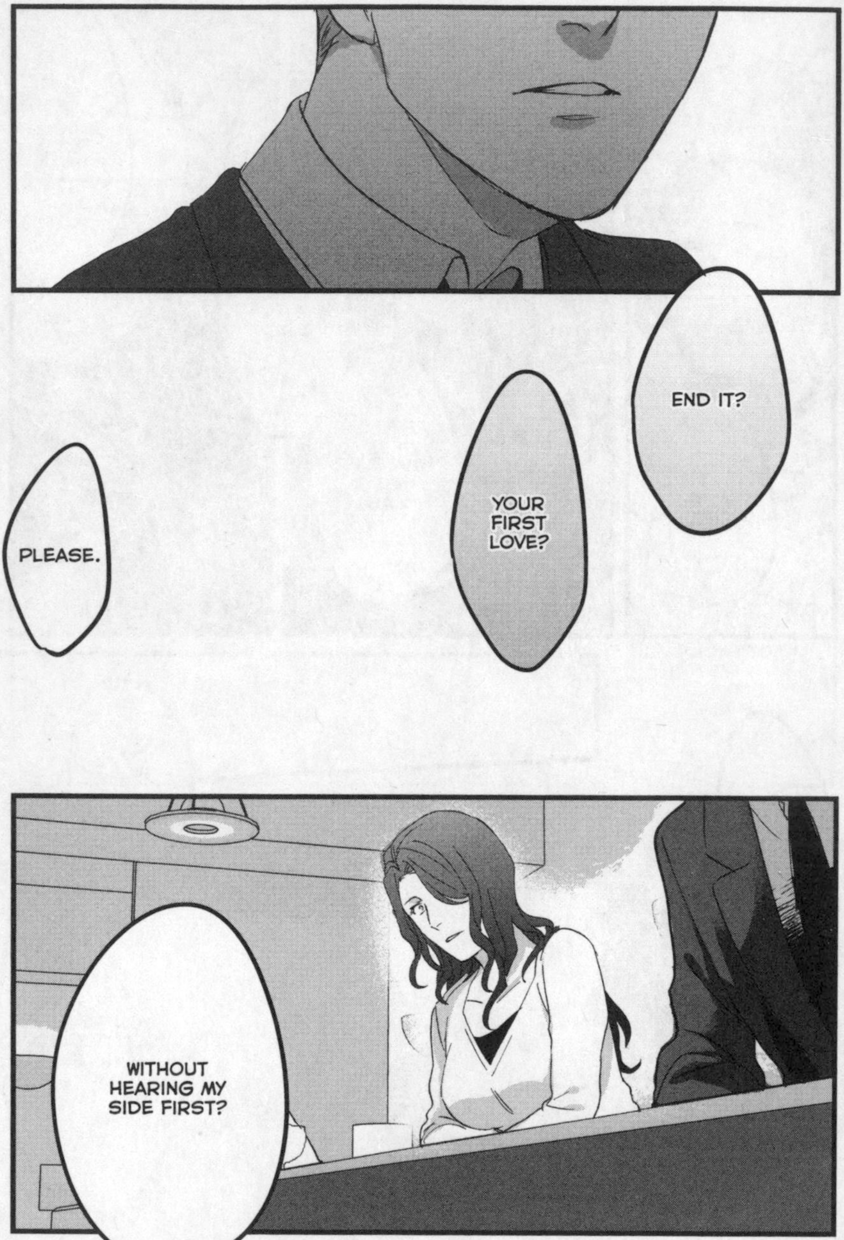
END IT?
YOUR FIRST LOVE?
PLEASE.
WITHOUT HEARING MY SIDE FIRST?

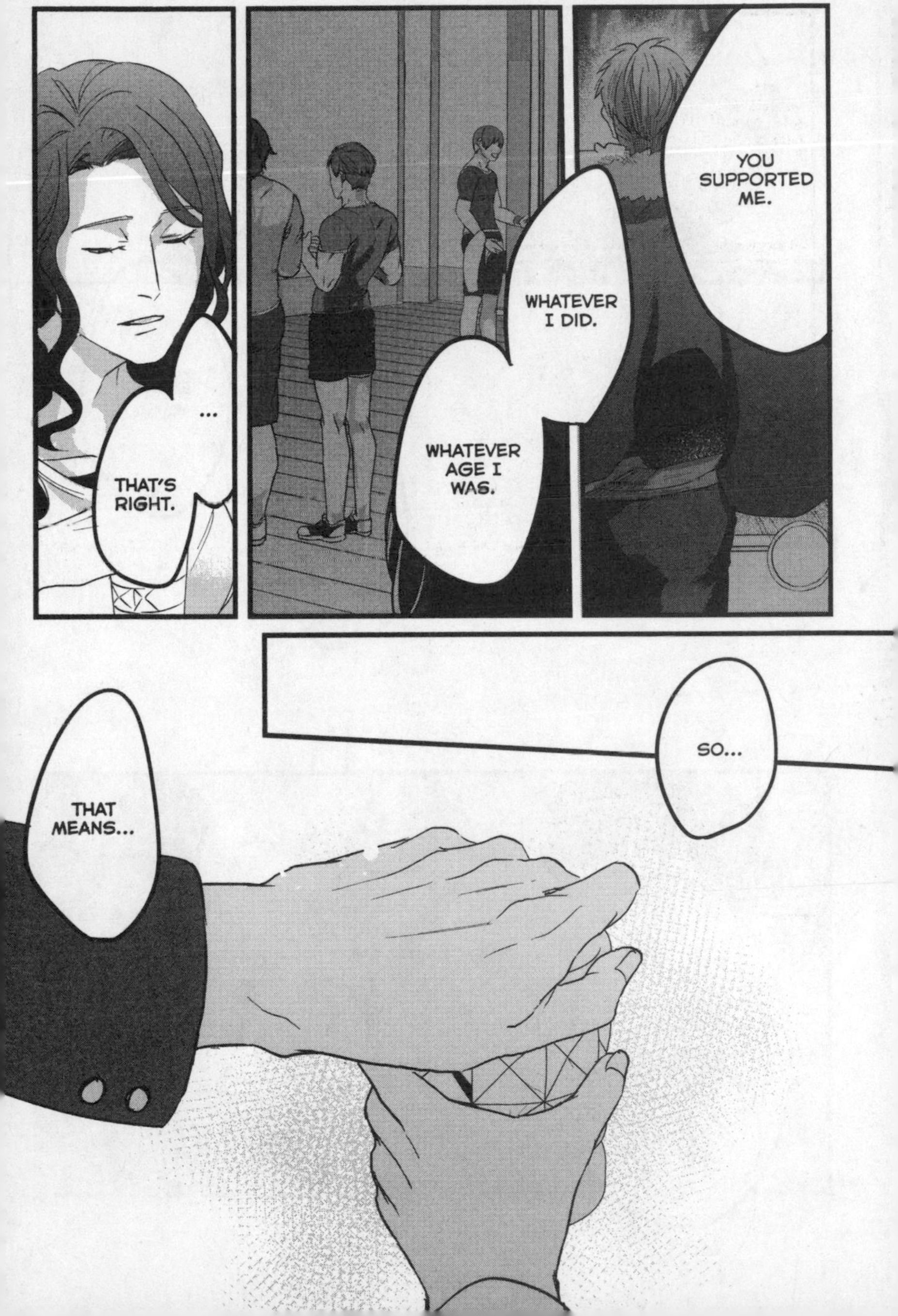
YOU SUPPORTED ME.
WHATEVER I DID.
WHATEVER AGE I WAS.
...
THAT'S RIGHT.
SO...
THAT MEANS...

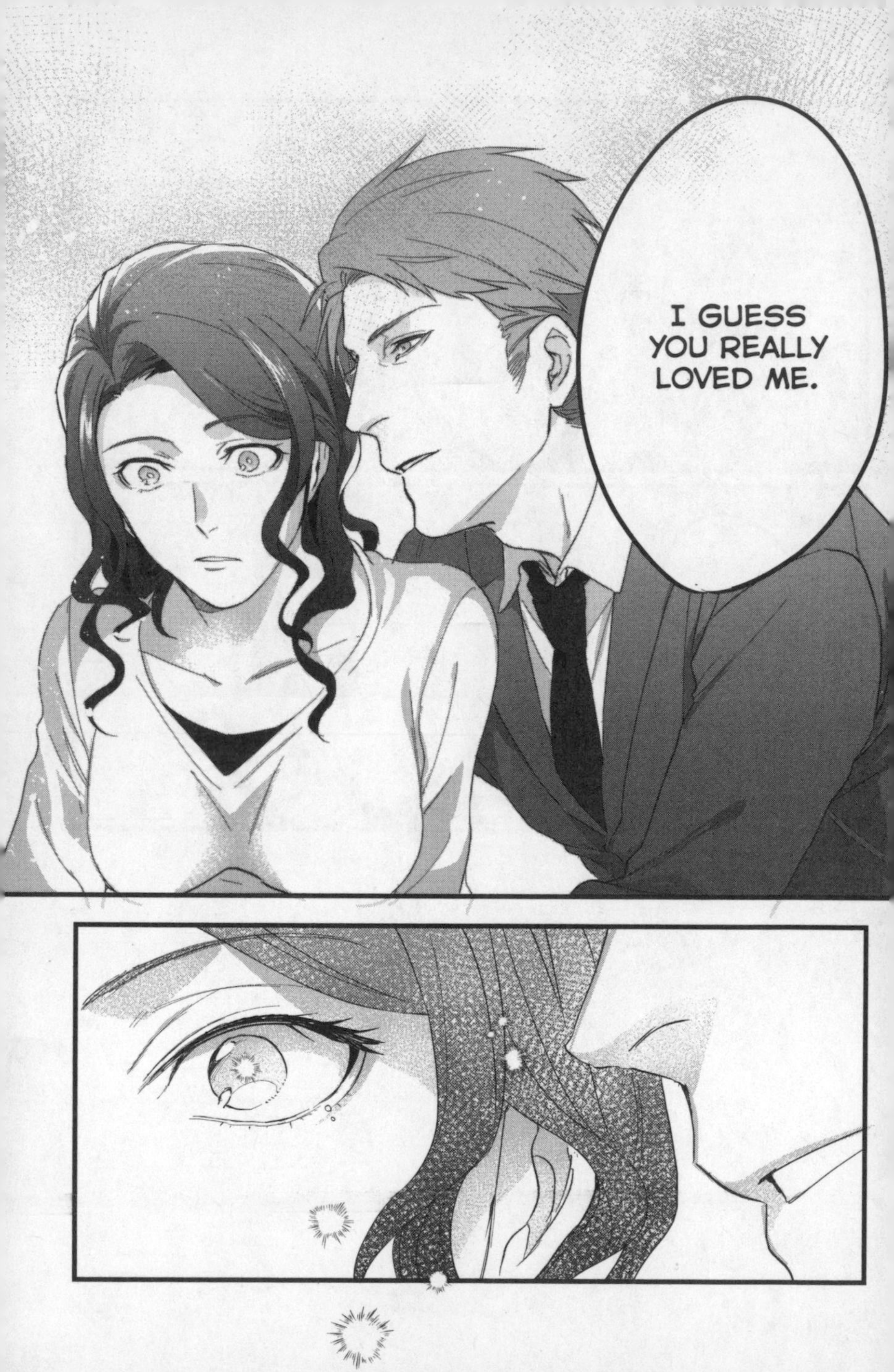
I GUESS YOU REALLY LOVED ME.

TO HAVE SUCH A PERSON IN MY LIFE...

IS A CHANCE I WON'T LET PASS ME BY.

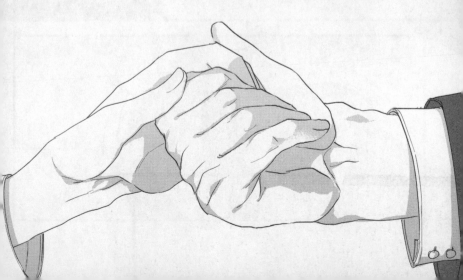

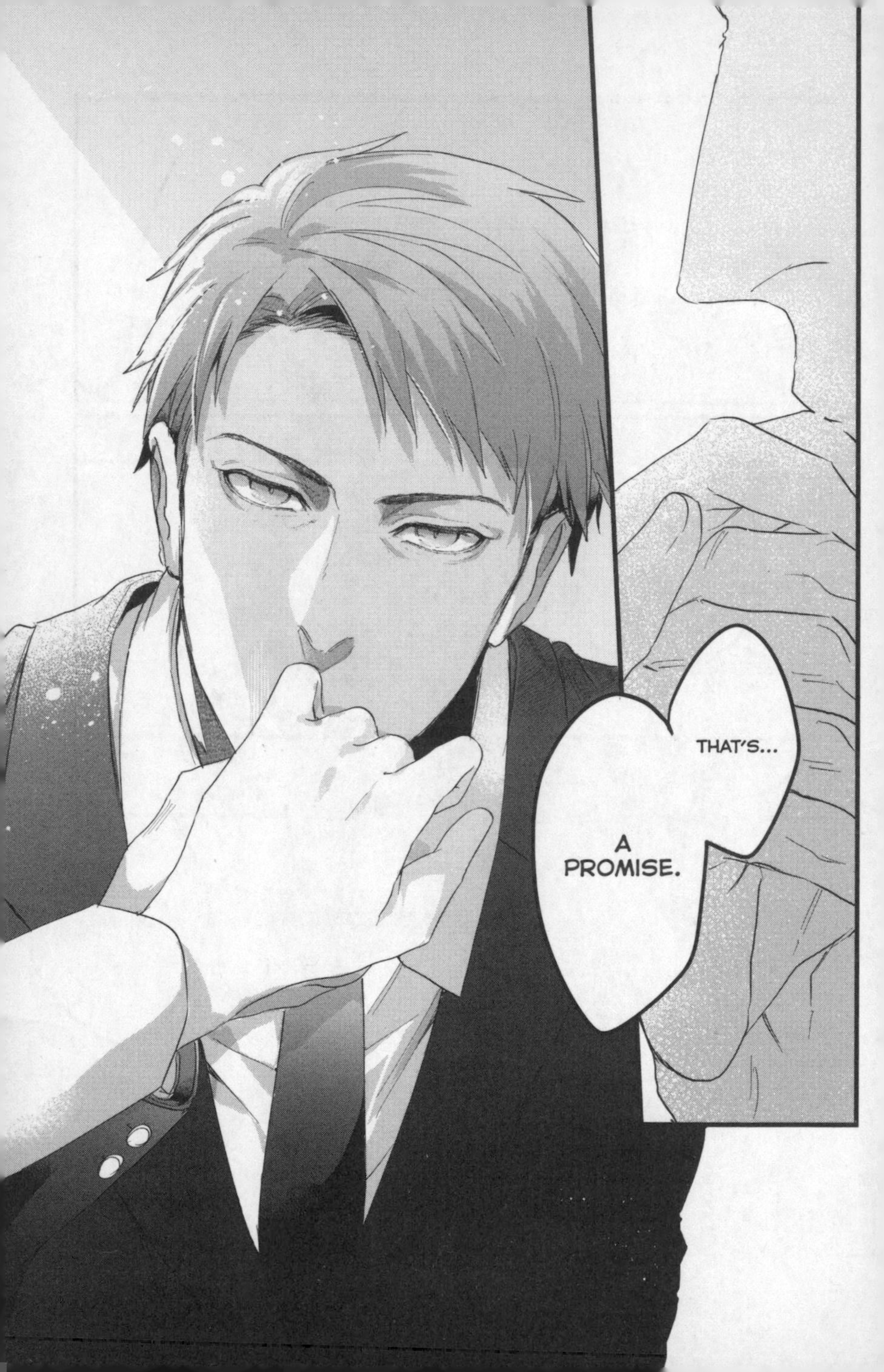
THAT'S...
A PROMISE.

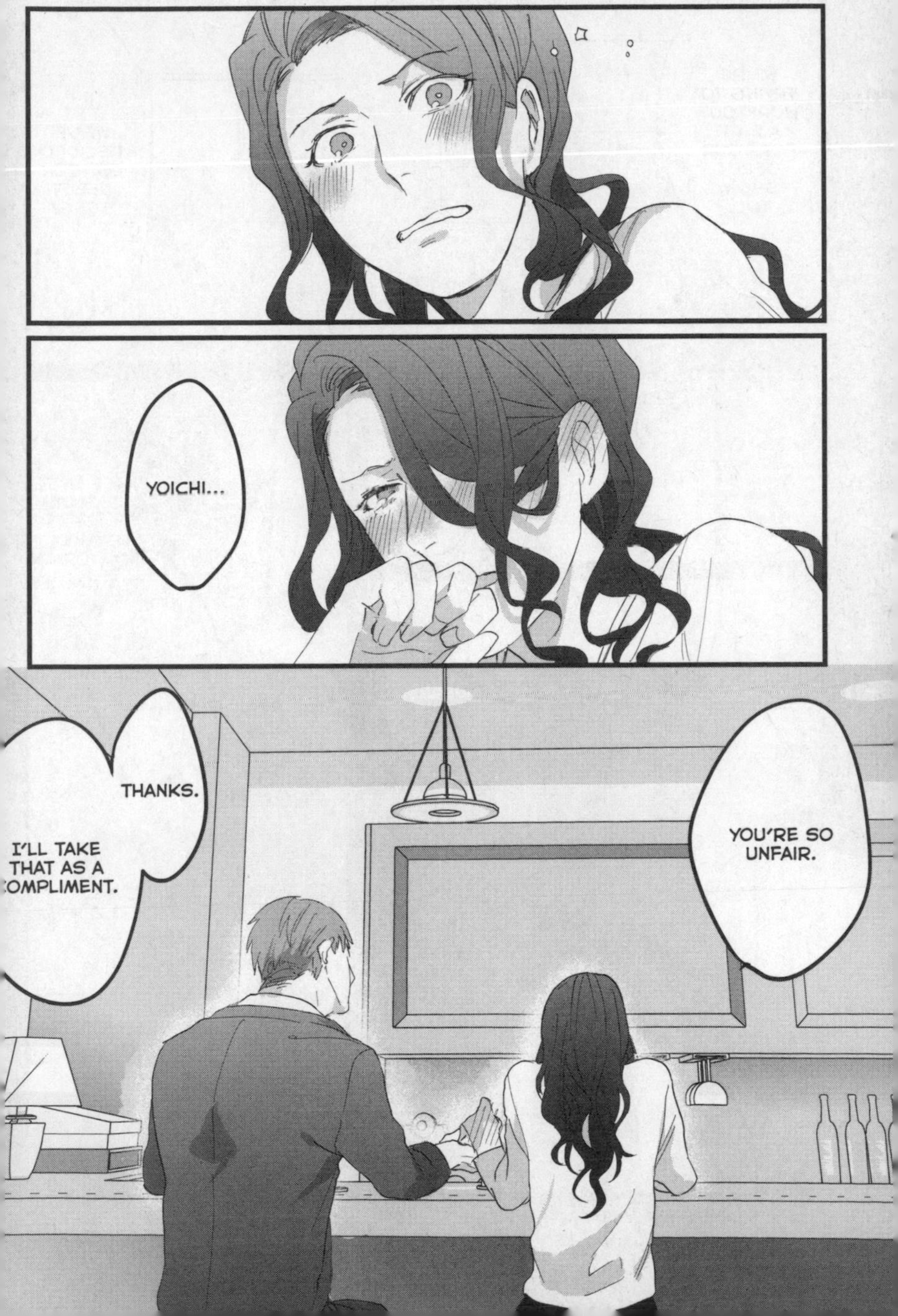
YOICHI...
YOU'RE SO UNFAIR.
THANKS.
I'LL TAKE THAT AS A COMPLIMENT.

Chapter 11

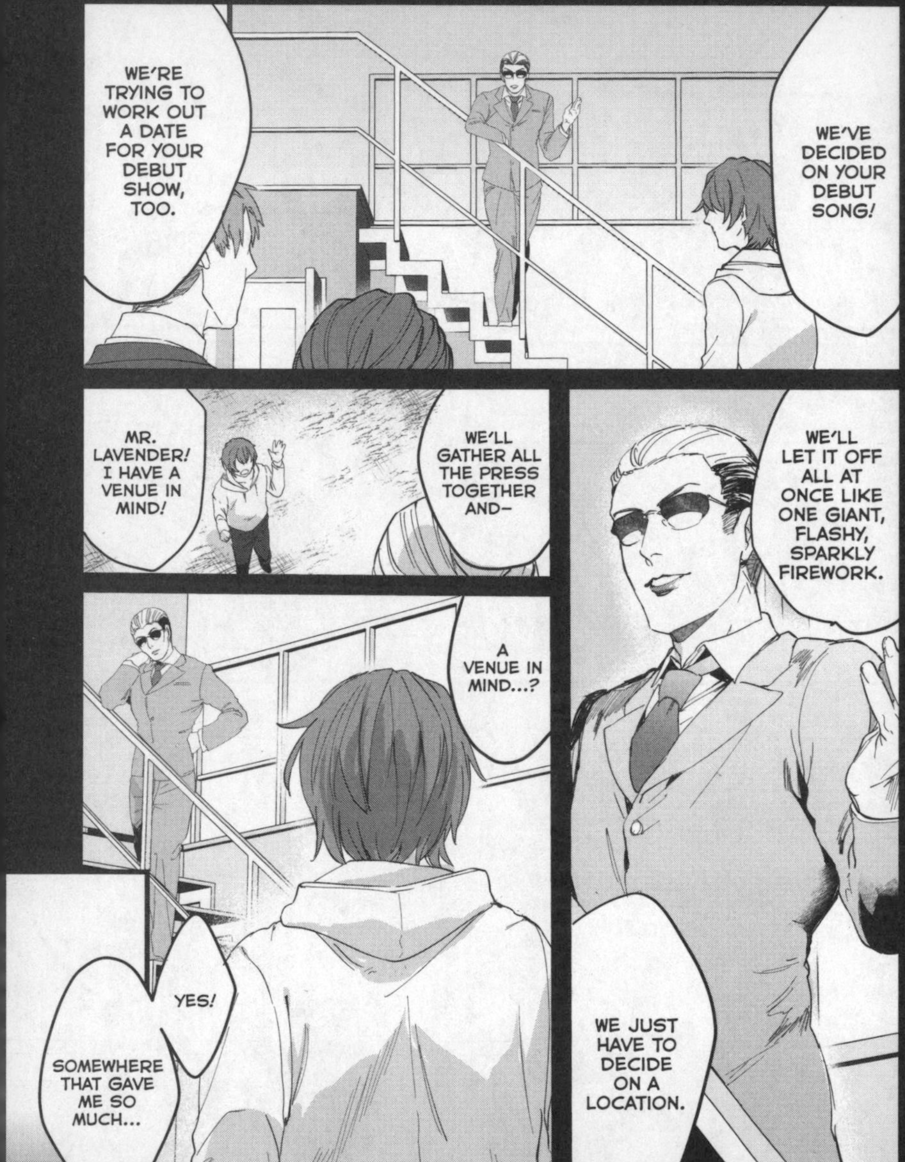
WE'VE DECIDED ON YOUR DEBUT SONG!
WE'RE TRYING TO WORK OUT A DATE FOR YOUR DEBUT SHOW, TOO.
WE'LL LET IT OFF ALL AT ONCE LIKE ONE GIANT, FLASHY, SPARKLY FIREWORK.
WE JUST HAVE TO DECIDE ON A LOCATION.
WE'LL GATHER ALL THE PRESS TOGETHER AND—
MR. LAVENDER! I HAVE A VENUE IN MIND!
A VENUE IN MIND...?
YES!
SOMEWHERE THAT GAVE ME SO MUCH...

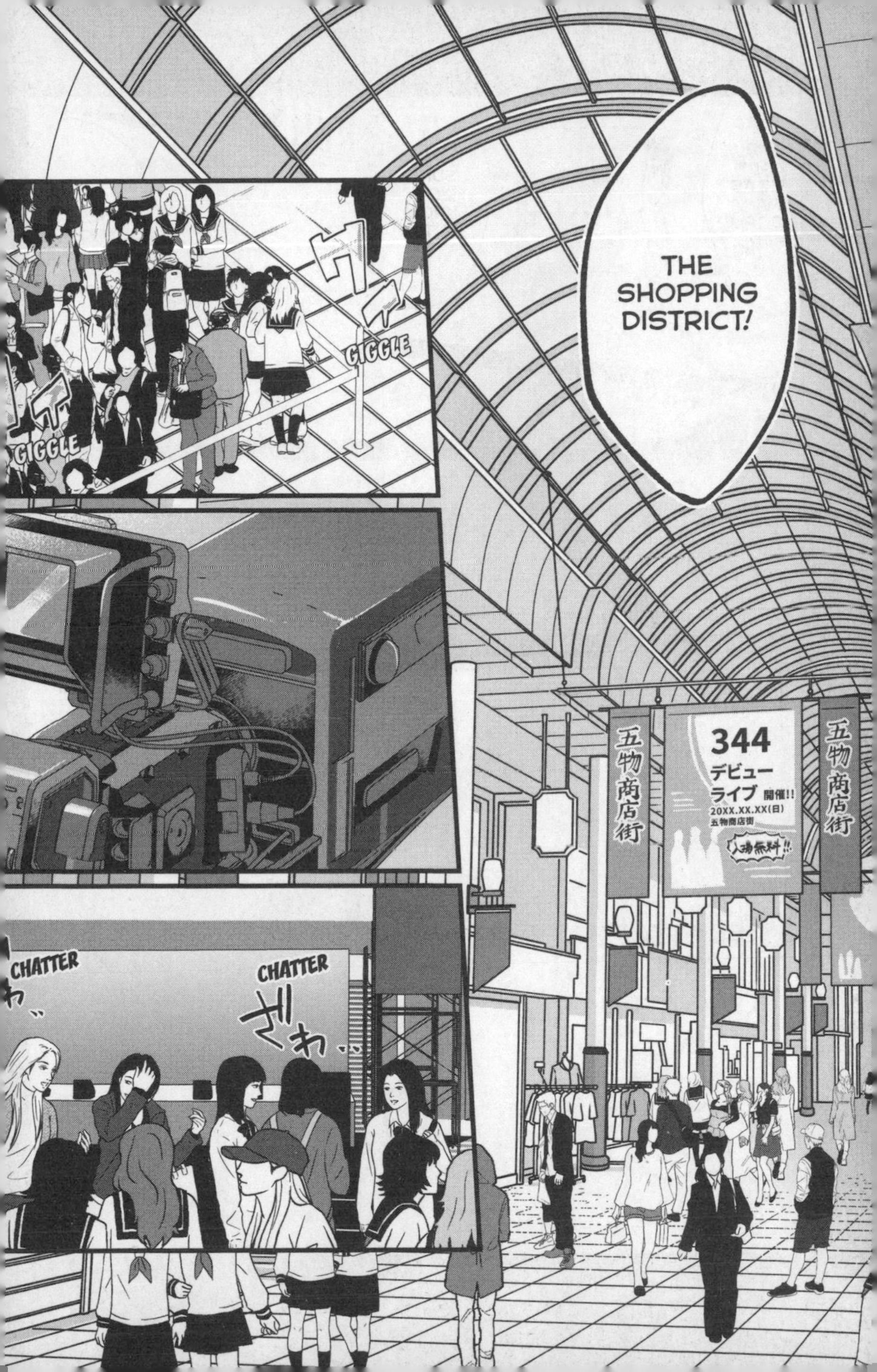
THE SHOPPING DISTRICT!
五物商店街
344
デビュー
ライブ 開催!!
20XX.XX.XX(日)
五物商店街
入場無料!!
五物商店街
GIGGLE
GIGGLE
CHATTER
ざわ
CHATTER

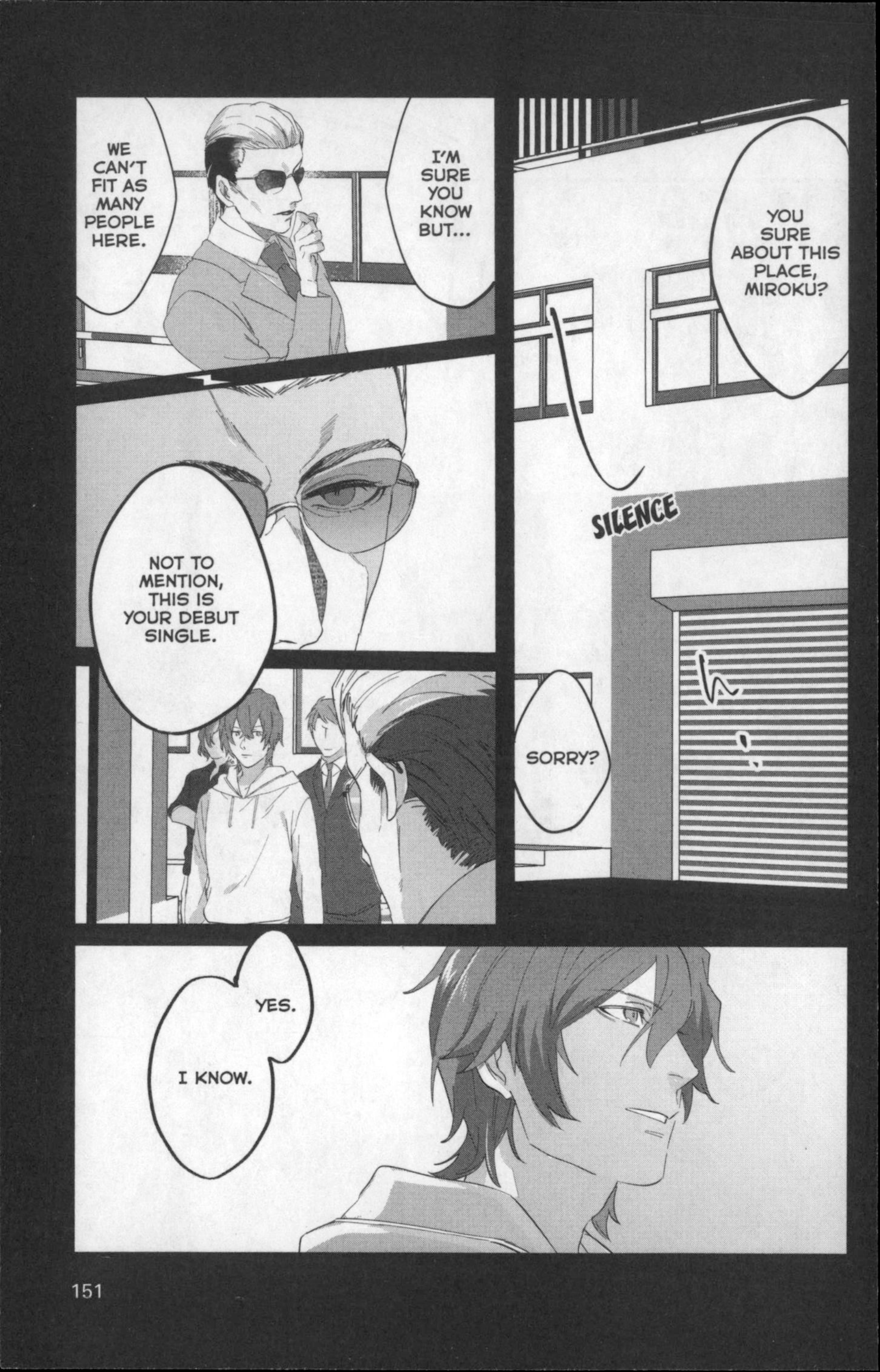
YOU SURE ABOUT THIS PLACE, MIROKU?
SILENCE
SORRY?
I'M SURE YOU KNOW BUT...
WE CAN'T FIT AS MANY PEOPLE HERE.
NOT TO MENTION, THIS IS YOUR DEBUT SINGLE.
YES.
I KNOW.

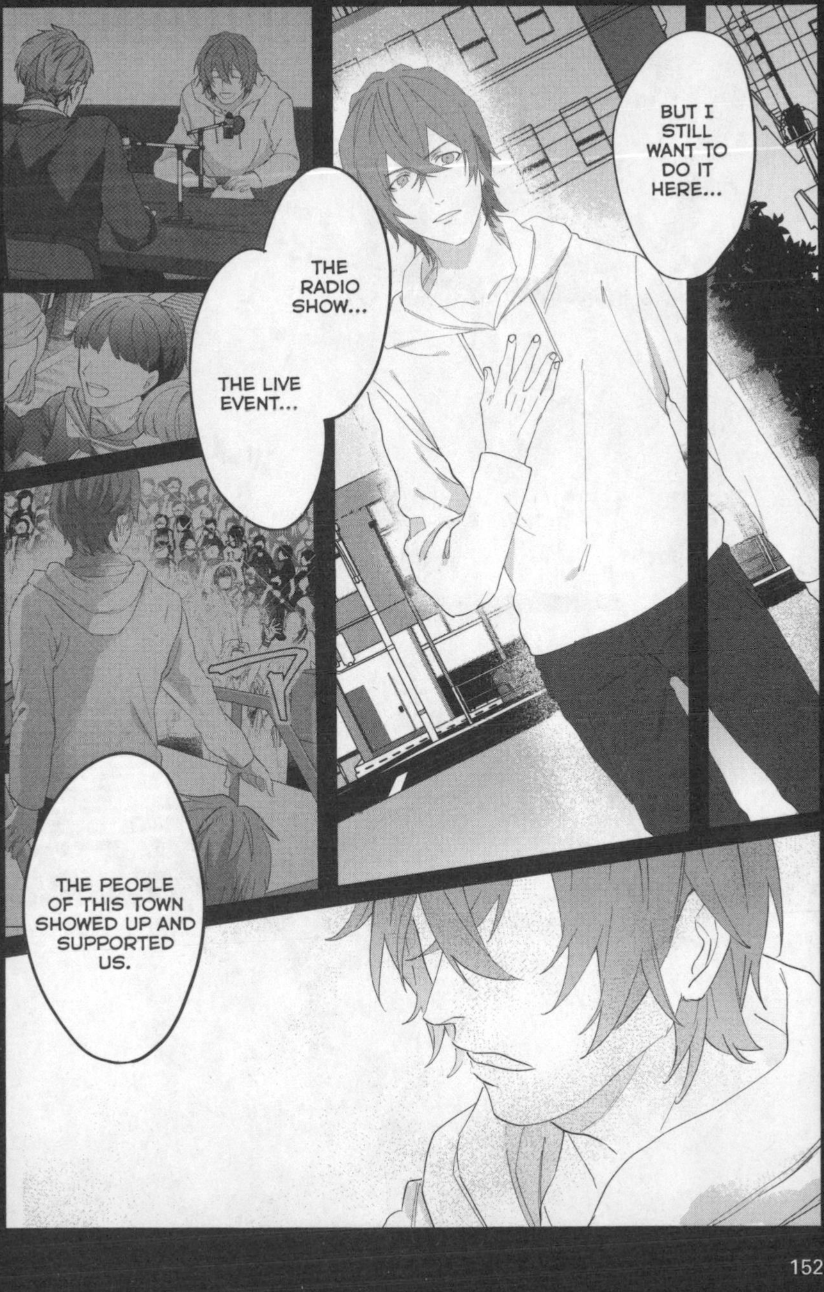
BUT I STILL WANT TO DO IT HERE...
THE RADIO SHOW...
THE LIVE EVENT...
THE PEOPLE OF THIS TOWN SHOWED UP AND SUPPORTED US.

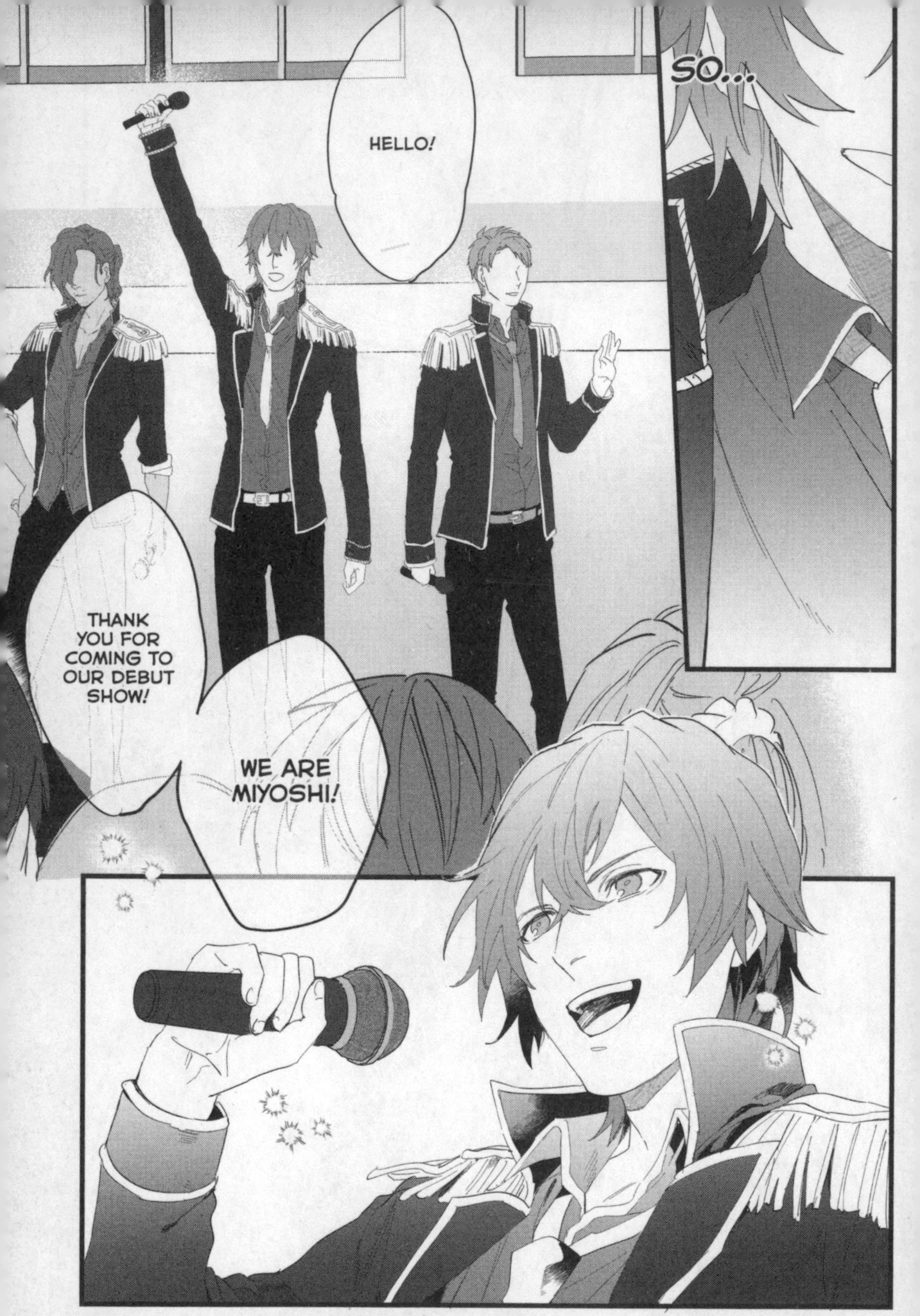
SO...
HELLO!
THANK YOU FOR COMING TO OUR DEBUT SHOW!
WE ARE MIYOSHI!

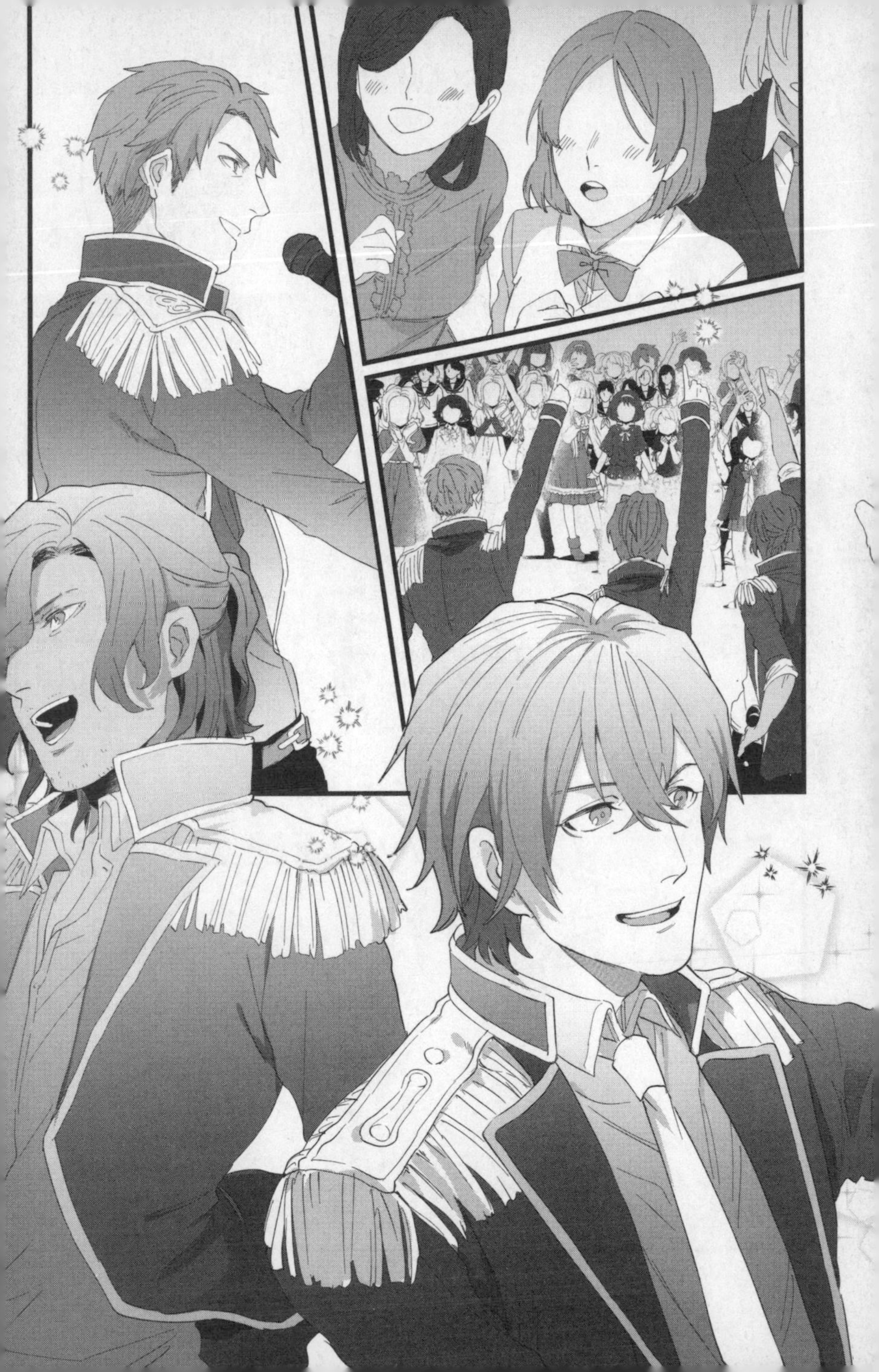

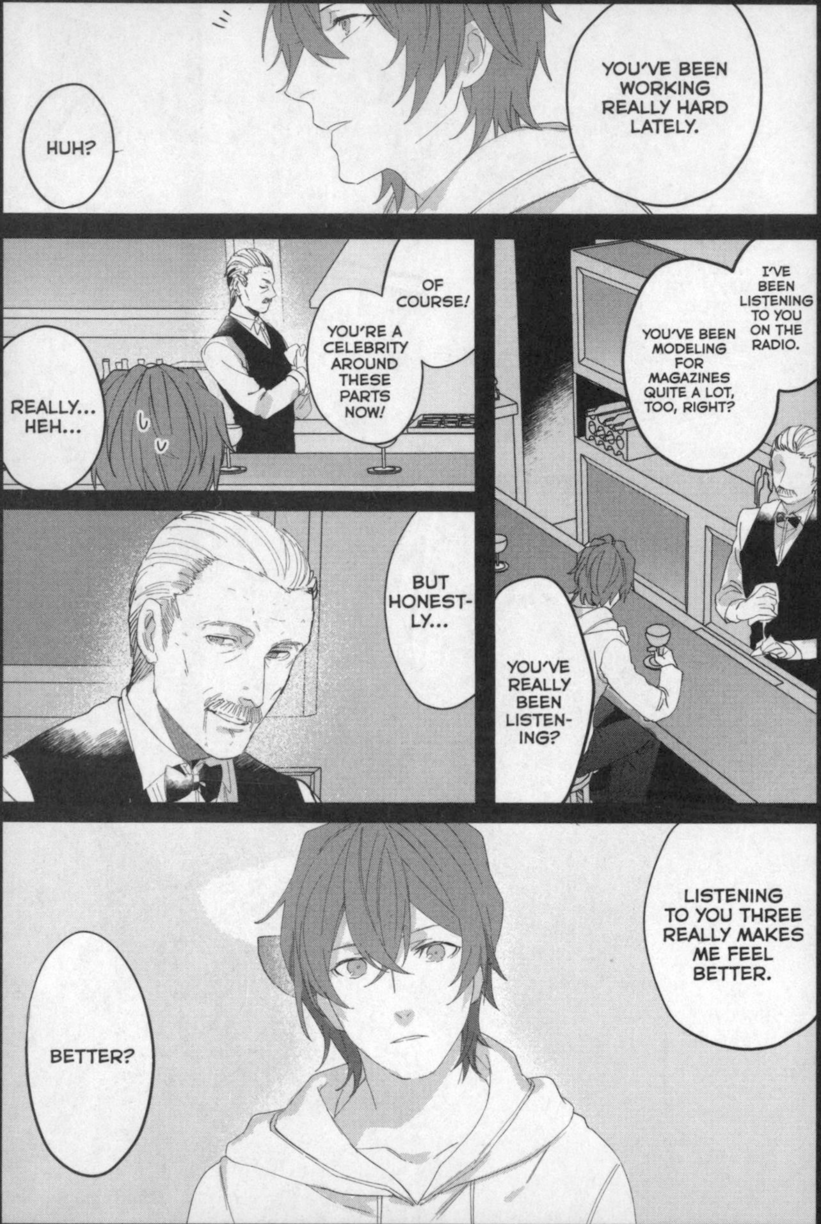
YOU'VE BEEN WORKING REALLY HARD LATELY.
HUH?
I'VE BEEN LISTENING TO YOU ON THE RADIO.
YOU'VE BEEN MODELING FOR MAGAZINES QUITE A LOT, TOO, RIGHT?
YOU'VE REALLY BEEN LISTEN-ING?
OF COURSE!
YOU'RE A CELEBRITY AROUND THESE PARTS NOW!
REALLY... HEH...
BUT HONEST-LY...
LISTENING TO YOU THREE REALLY MAKES ME FEEL BETTER.
BETTER?

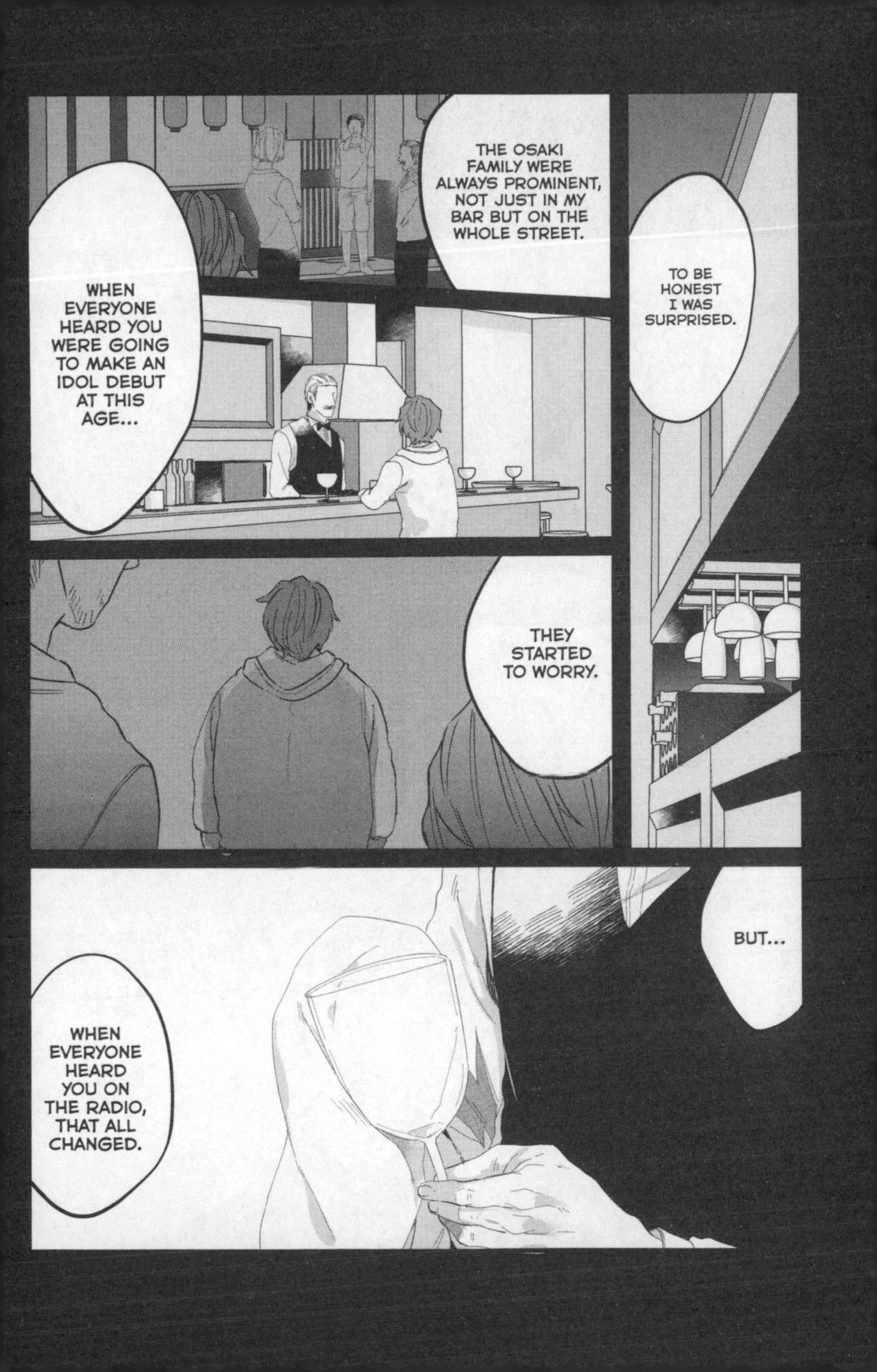
TO BE HONEST I WAS SURPRISED.
THE OSAKI FAMILY WERE ALWAYS PROMINENT, NOT JUST IN MY BAR BUT ON THE WHOLE STREET.
WHEN EVERYONE HEARD YOU WERE GOING TO MAKE AN IDOL DEBUT AT THIS AGE...
THEY STARTED TO WORRY.
BUT...
WHEN EVERYONE HEARD YOU ON THE RADIO, THAT ALL CHANGED.

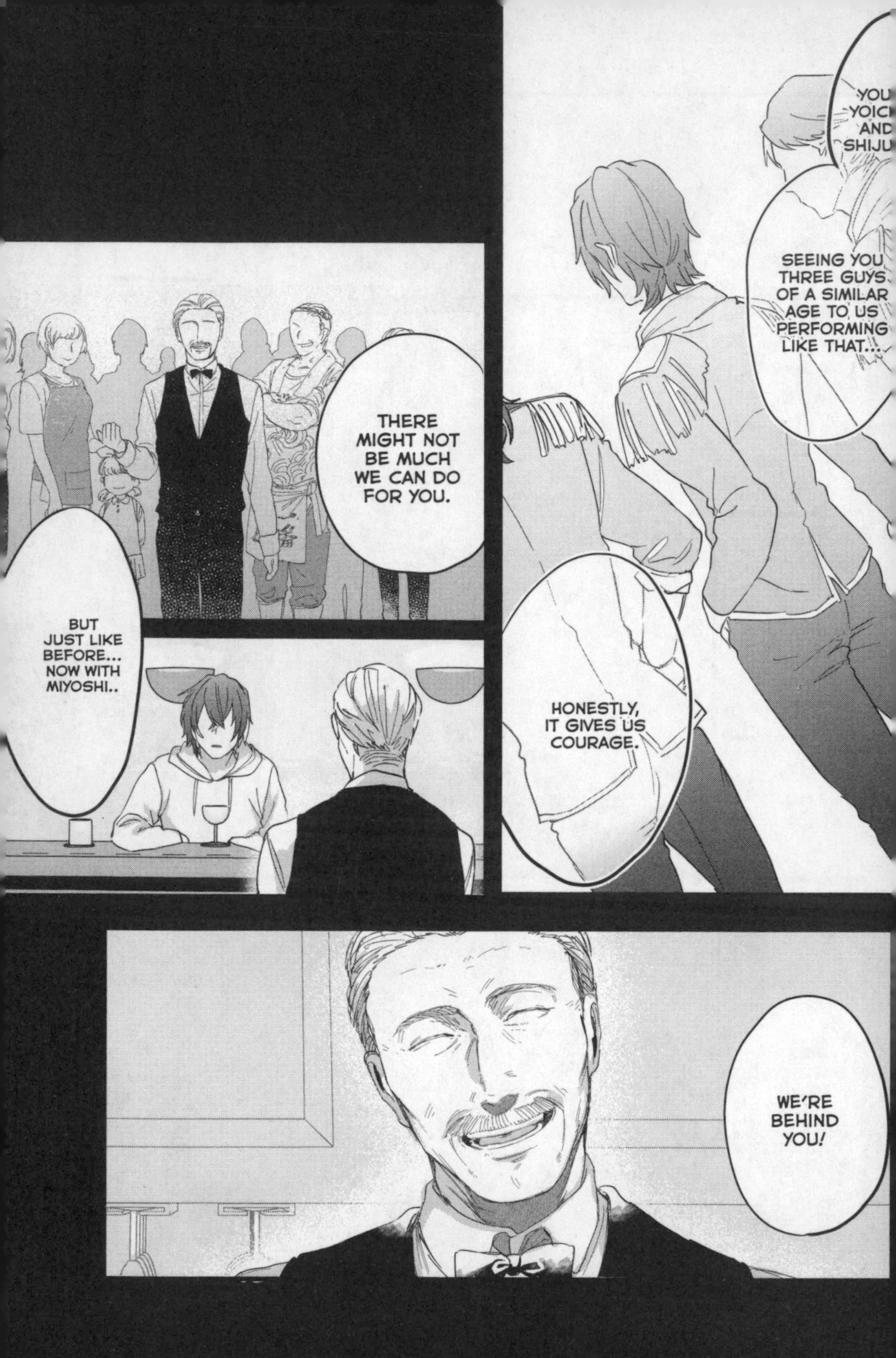
YOU YOIC AND SHIJU
SEEING YOU THREE GUYS OF A SIMILAR AGE TO US PERFORMING LIKE THAT...
HONESTLY, IT GIVES US COURAGE.
THERE MIGHT NOT BE MUCH WE CAN DO FOR YOU.
BUT JUST LIKE BEFORE... NOW WITH MIYOSHI..
WE'RE BEHIND YOU!

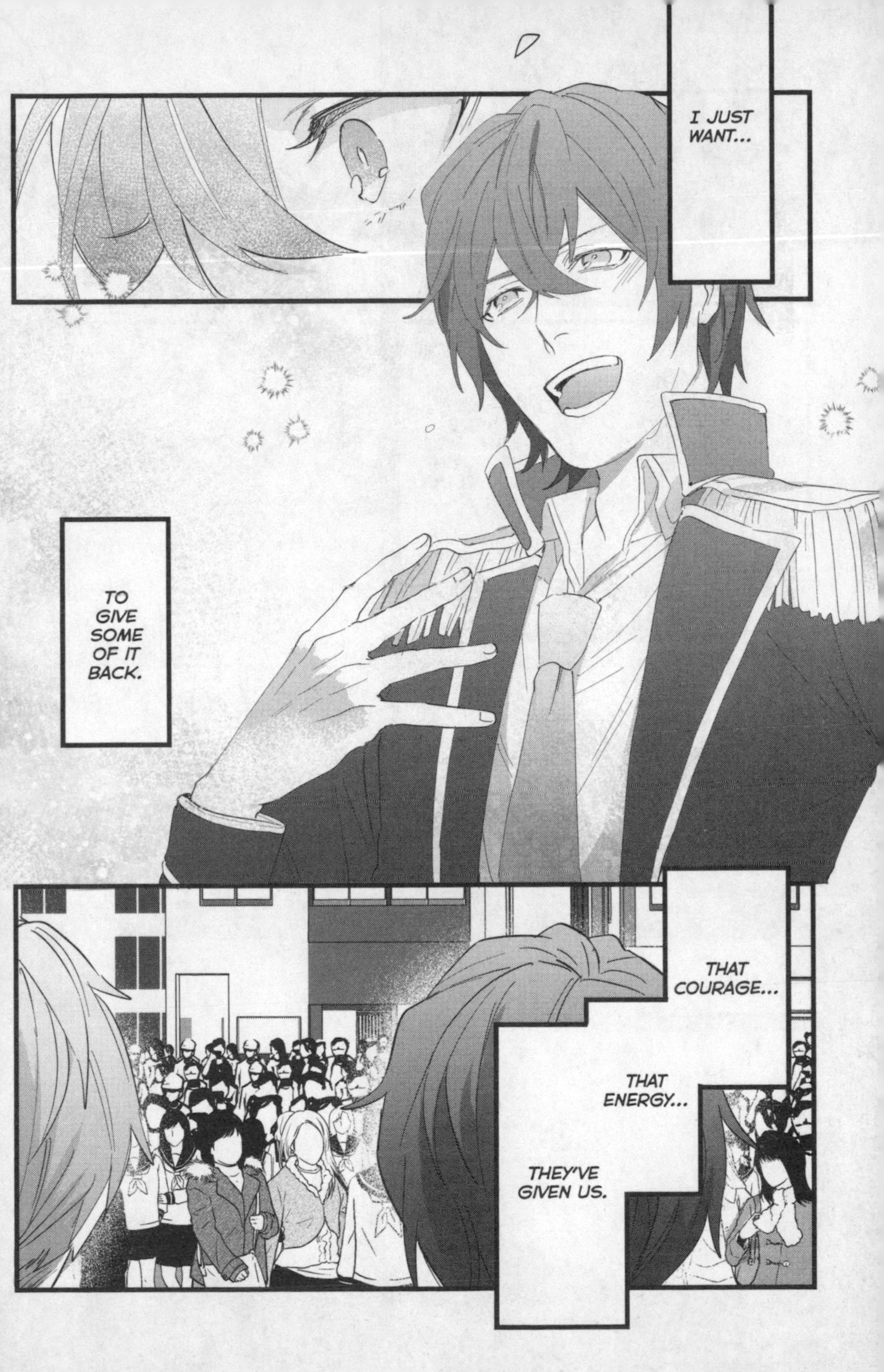
I JUST WANT...
TO GIVE SOME OF IT BACK.
THAT COURAGE...
THAT ENERGY...
THEY'VE GIVEN US.

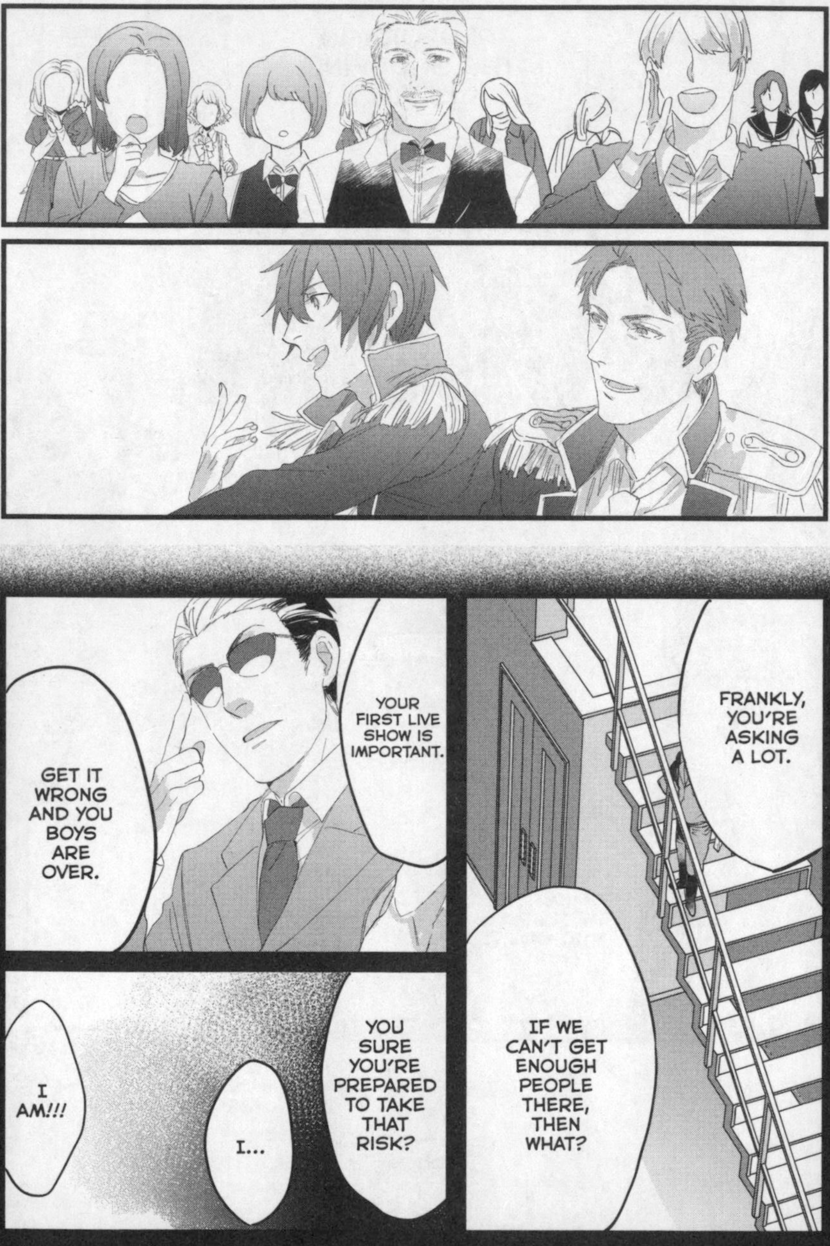
FRANKLY, YOU'RE ASKING A LOT.
IF WE CAN'T GET ENOUGH PEOPLE THERE, THEN WHAT?
YOUR FIRST LIVE SHOW IS IMPORTANT.
GET IT WRONG AND YOU BOYS ARE OVER.
YOU SURE YOU'RE PREPARED TO TAKE THAT RISK?
I...
I AM!!!

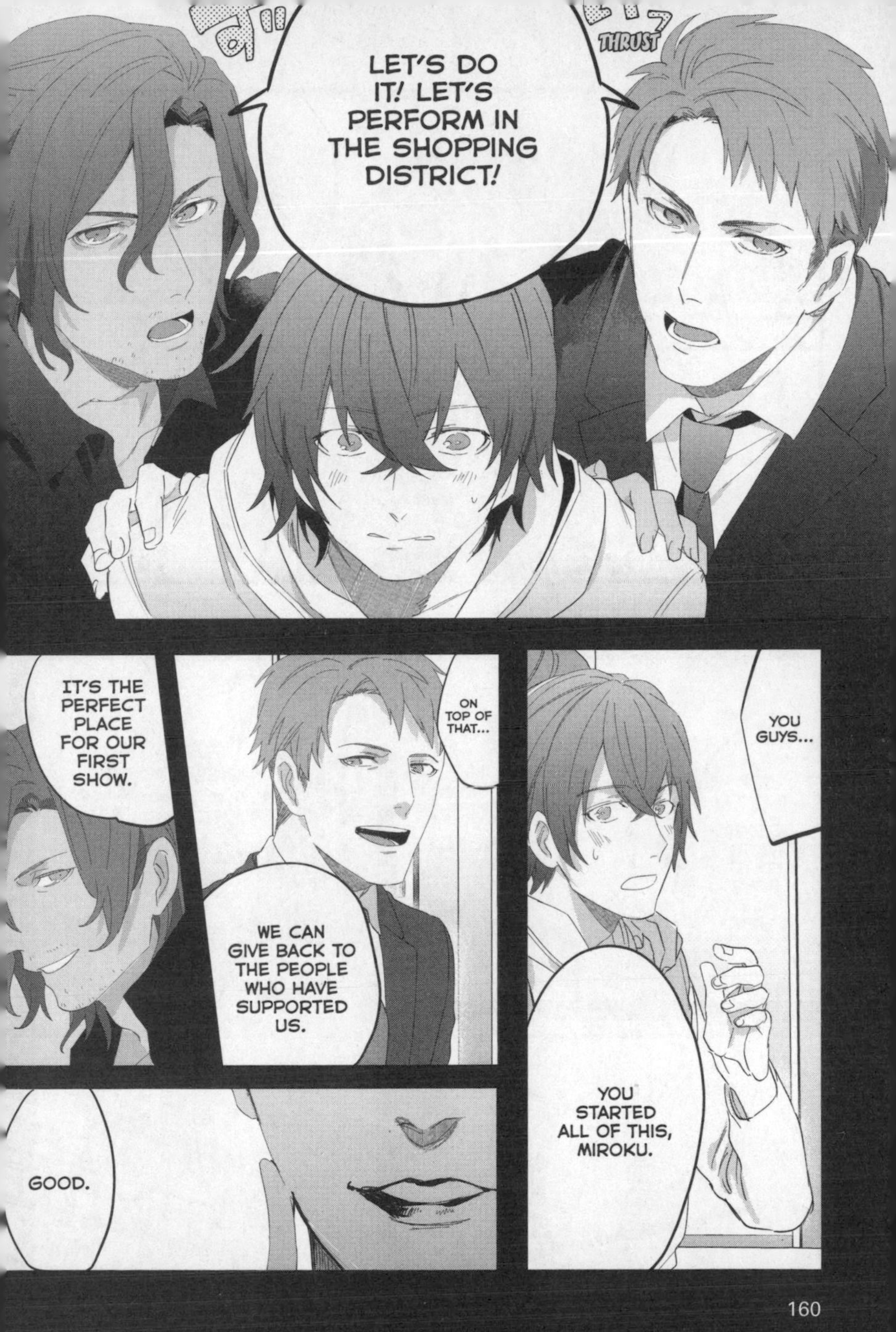
THRUST
LET'S DO IT! LET'S PERFORM IN THE SHOPPING DISTRICT!
YOU GUYS...
YOU STARTED ALL OF THIS, MIROKU.
ON TOP OF THAT...
WE CAN GIVE BACK TO THE PEOPLE WHO HAVE SUPPORTED US.
IT'S THE PERFECT PLACE FOR OUR FIRST SHOW.
GOOD.

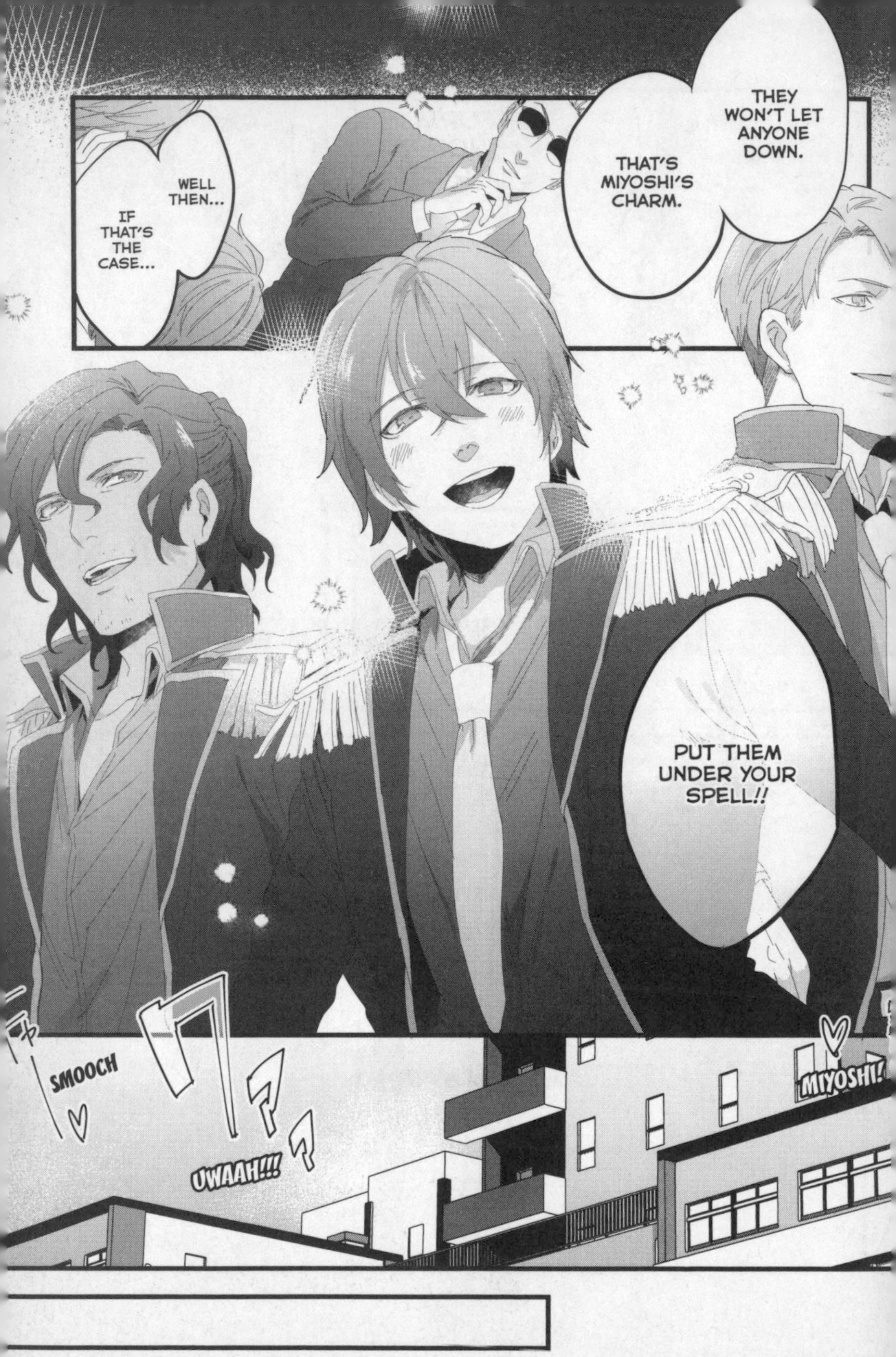
THEY WON'T LET ANYONE DOWN.
THAT'S MIYOSHI'S CHARM.
WELL THEN...
IF THAT'S THE CASE...
PUT THEM UNDER YOUR SPELL!!
MIYOSHI!
UWAAH!!!
SMOOCH

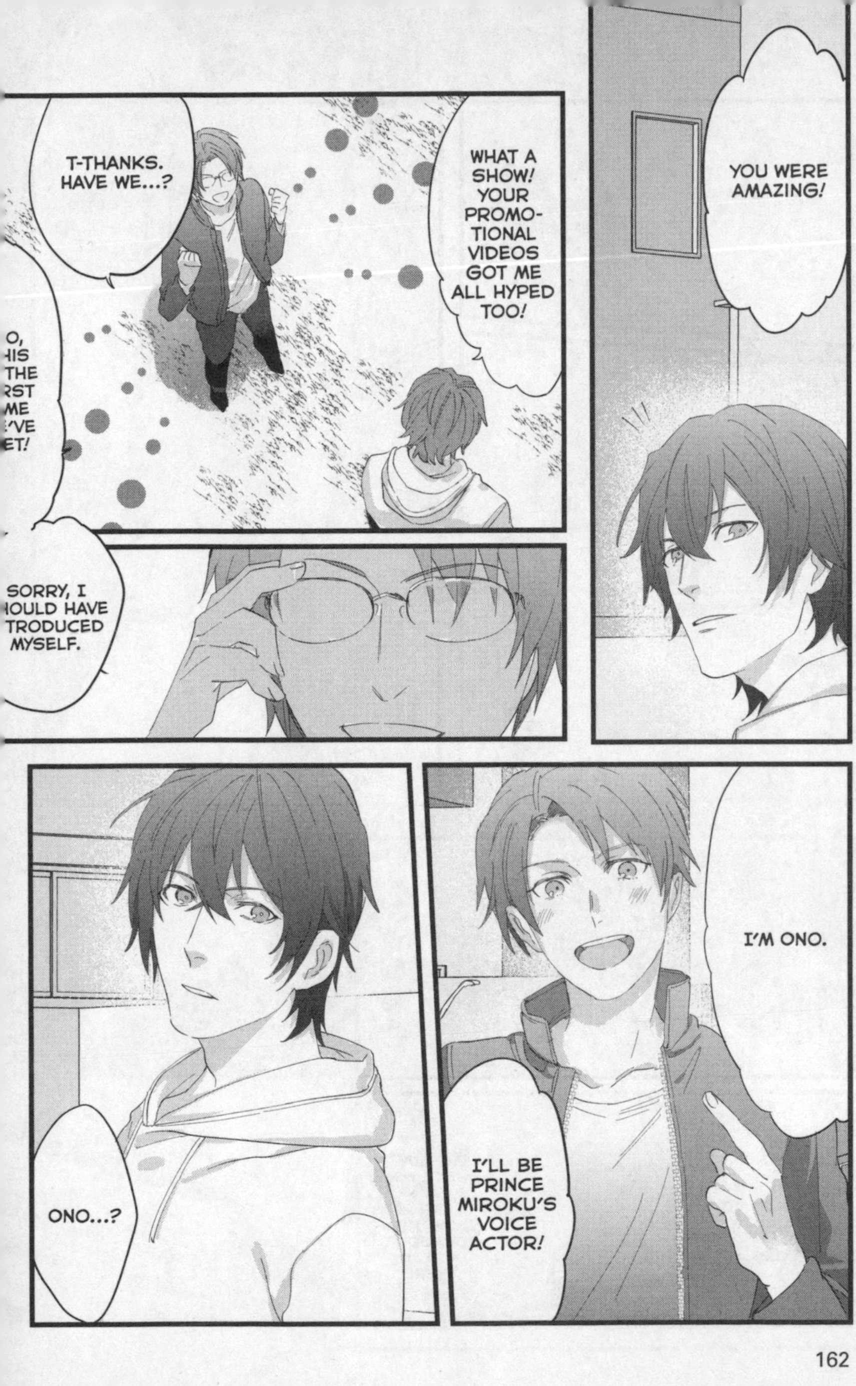
YOU WERE AMAZING!
WHAT A SHOW! YOUR PROMOTIONAL VIDEOS GOT ME ALL HYPED TOO!
T-THANKS. HAVE WE...?
O, HIS THE RST ME 'VE ET!
SORRY, I HOULD HAVE TRODUCED MYSELF.
I'M ONO.
I'LL BE PRINCE MIROKU'S VOICE ACTOR!
ONO...?

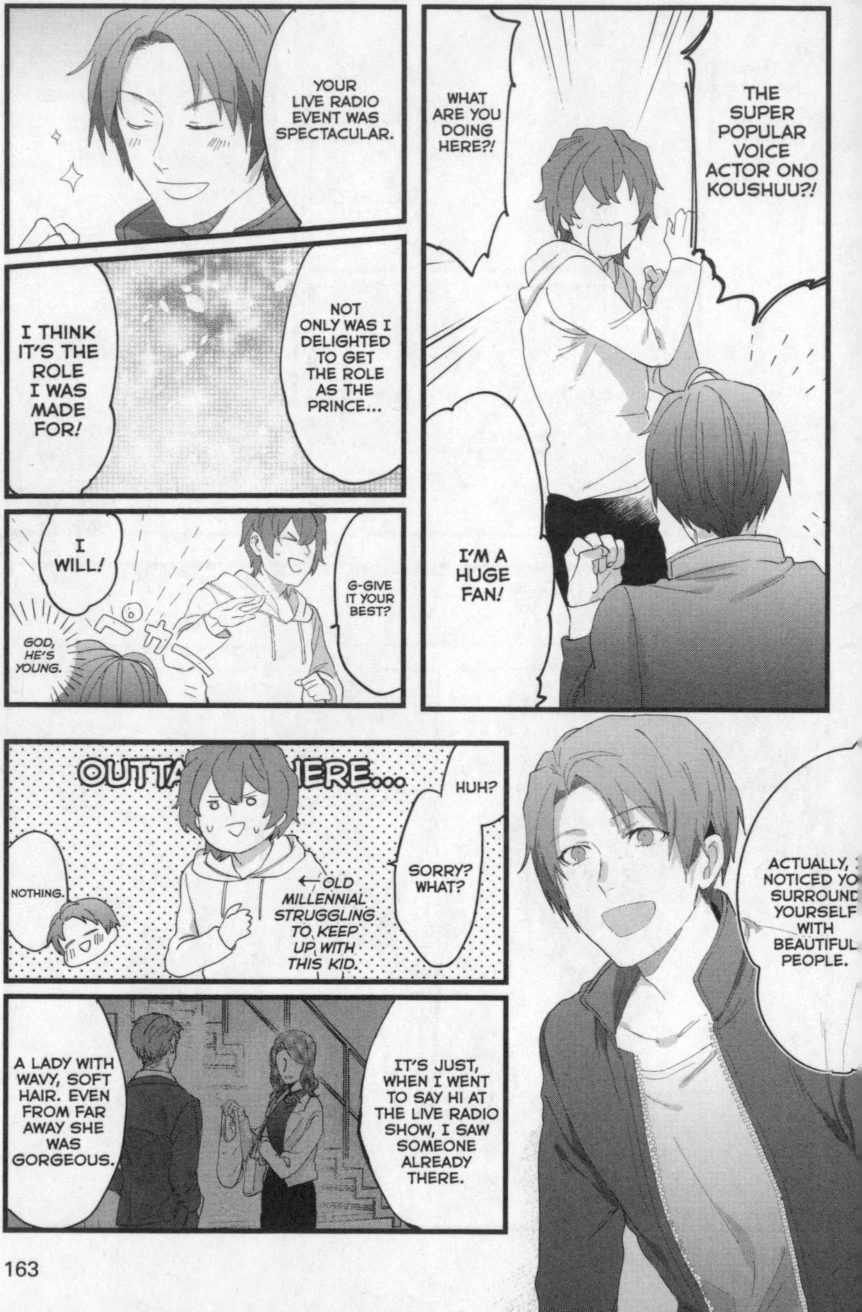
THE SUPER POPULAR VOICE ACTOR ONO KOUSHUU?!
WHAT ARE YOU DOING HERE?!
I'M A HUGE FAN!
YOUR LIVE RADIO EVENT WAS SPECTACULAR.
NOT ONLY WAS I DELIGHTED TO GET THE ROLE AS THE PRINCE...
I THINK IT'S THE ROLE I WAS MADE FOR!
G-GIVE IT YOUR BEST?
I WILL!
GOD, HE'S YOUNG.
ACTUALLY, NOTICED YO SURROUND YOURSELF WITH BEAUTIFUL PEOPLE.
OUTTA HERE...
HUH?
SORRY? WHAT?
←OLD MILLENNIAL STRUGGLING TO KEEP UP WITH THIS KID.
NOTHING.
IT'S JUST, WHEN I WENT TO SAY HI AT THE LIVE RADIO SHOW, I SAW SOMEONE ALREADY THERE.
A LADY WITH WAVY, SOFT HAIR. EVEN FROM FAR AWAY SHE WAS GORGEOUS.

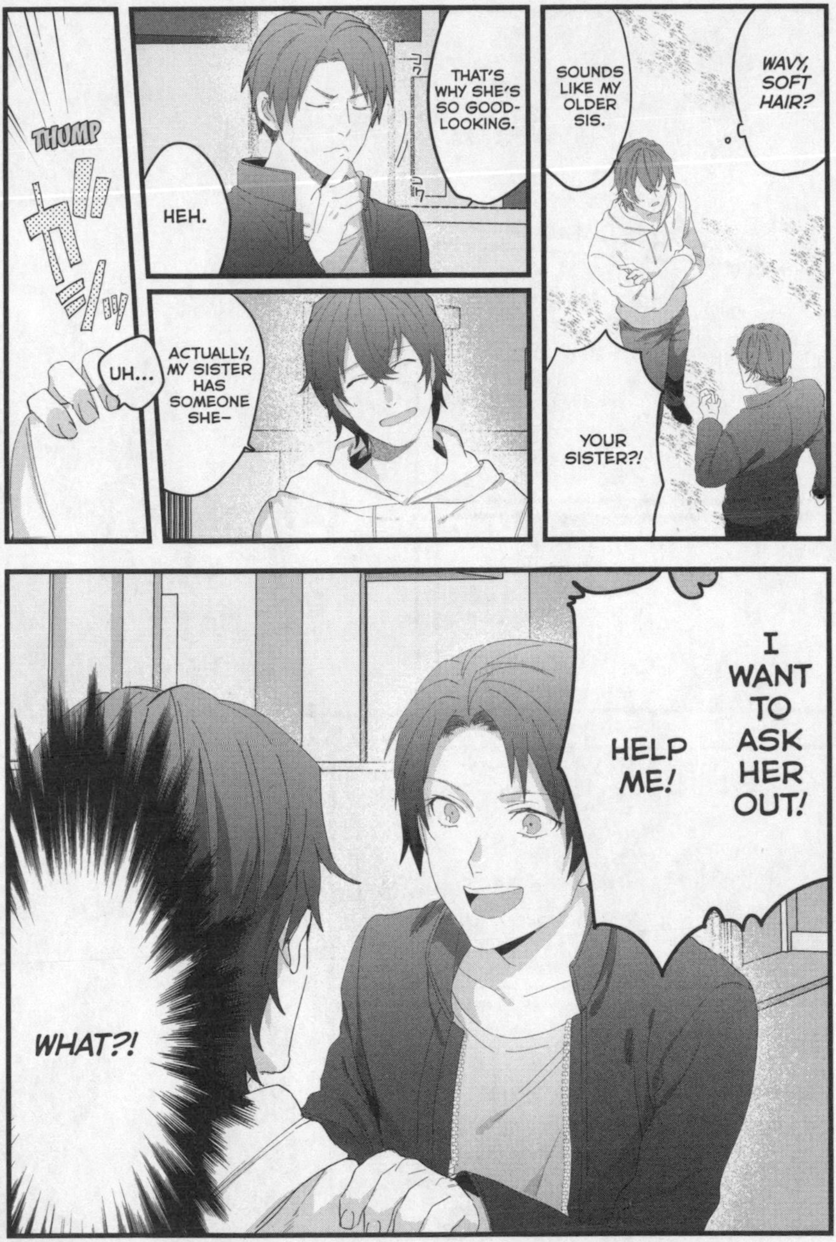
WAVY, SOFT HAIR?
SOUNDS LIKE MY OLDER SIS.
YOUR SISTER?!
THAT'S WHY SHE'S SO GOOD-LOOKING.
HEH.
ACTUALLY, MY SISTER HAS SOMEONE SHE–
THUMP
UH...
I WANT TO ASK HER OUT!
HELP ME!
WHAT?!

To be continued...

OSSAN IDOL!

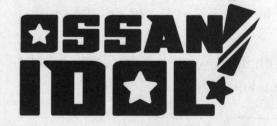

MiYoShi and I Went On A Date!
Written by Mochiko Mochida

I'm standing in front of the fountain when Miroku, wearing a hoodie and jeans, comes running towards me with his dazzling smile. Below are things that Miroku said while we were together.

"Sorry, did I make you wait?"

"I was really looking forward to this date, so I put on my favorite hoodie. Look, it's a soft marshmallowy doggy! Cute, right?"

"First, let's hit up the arcade! After that, how about a book store? Maybe pick up a light novel... Ah, sorry. Forget about me, where do you want to go?"

"Huh? Wherever I usually go is okay? You sure?"

"Well then... Let's do some karaoke! We can have fun, just the two of us."

"C'mon, try singing! You don't want to? You're no good? Don't be silly. Can't you sing just once, for me?"

"Oh no, you're shy. How about we sing together? I just want to hear your voice. You have to let me hear it next time, okay?"

"Your voice is really cute, I want to listen to it all day. Can I take a video just for me? No? Are you embarrassed? Haha, you're too cute."

"I guess I'll have to sing. Of course, I can't sing without dancing. I use my karaoke booth time slot to get in as much singing and dancing as I can!"

"Are you tired? I know this really nice cafe! Do you want to go there and rest?"

"I'm a big fan of their honey latte. It's sweet with just a touch of bitterness. Ah, it's so good."

"Ah, you want to try it?"

"Oh, your face has gone all red. Are you all right? Sorry! Could we have water, please?"

On a bench near the train station ticket gates, Yoichi is relaxing, still in his suit. Below are things that Yoichi said while we were together.

"Don't worry, you're not late. I just finished work early today."

"Did I make you rush? Sorry about that. Here, let me help you fix your hair since you were in such a hurry."

"Yeah, you look great!"

"Does the aquarium sound good? I try to come here when I can. You sure? You're too kind. Thank you."

"It's really dark in here. Hold onto my arm. No, no. Stay closer."

"You being shy is adorable, but you'll get mad at me if I continue to say such selfish things like that, right?"

"I can't come as often as I want, but the aquarium really is wonderful. Thank you for coming here with me."

"I booked a table at my regular haunt for after. Fancy something light to eat?"

"Do you drink? We could order some wine."

"Another? No way, if I drink too much, who knows what might happen? Especially with someone as pretty as you..."

"Can we order different dishes as our main? It will be more fun to share, don't you think?"

"Here, say 'aaaah!'"

"Was it too much? Do you want more? Haha, you don't have to be so embarrassed."

"It's your turn to feed me then. Make sure you get enough sauce on it. Ahh... Oh? Your face has gone all red."

"Sorry. Waiter, could we have some water, please?"

I go into the bar. On the far side of the counter sits a figure in a black shirt and jeans. He waves me over. Below are things that Shiju said while we were together.

"Sorry for making you come all this way. I got caught up practicing."

"Honestly, I'm really sorry. Today's on me."

"Huh? Really? It's fine if you're mad though?"

"Ah... You're trying to butter me up. I have a feeling you're up to something. That's fine. You're a good girl."

"Miroku is supposed to be playing piano here today. You've been supporting us this whole time so I thought today was a good day to come."

"Huh? I'm all you want?"

"Really... you trying to flatter this old ossan? You're very cute, so I'll give you a reward."

"Wow! You've gone totally red!"

"Hey now... You're mad an ossan kissed you on the cheek?"

"You're happy? Then I am, too. Ah no, it's nothing..."

"What's up? Are you tipsy?"

"Oh well. Here, hold onto me."

"Hey, let me take care of you more. You say it's fine, but I know you're just trying to go along with me."

"Huh? You fell asleep?"

"Well... I guess you won't mind if I kiss you once more. No one's watching us. Maybe twice more..."

"You smell amazing. I'm in trouble, you're too gorgeous!"

"Ah! What's with the red face? Y-You're awake?!"

"Can I get some water over here!"

Director:

"Okay, let's cut there! I think your date needs a moment to cool down! MiYoShi, take things a bit easier on them in the future!"

MiYoShi:

"What are you talking about?!"

OSSAN
IDOL
VOLUME
2

LET'S DECIDE ON THE COVER!

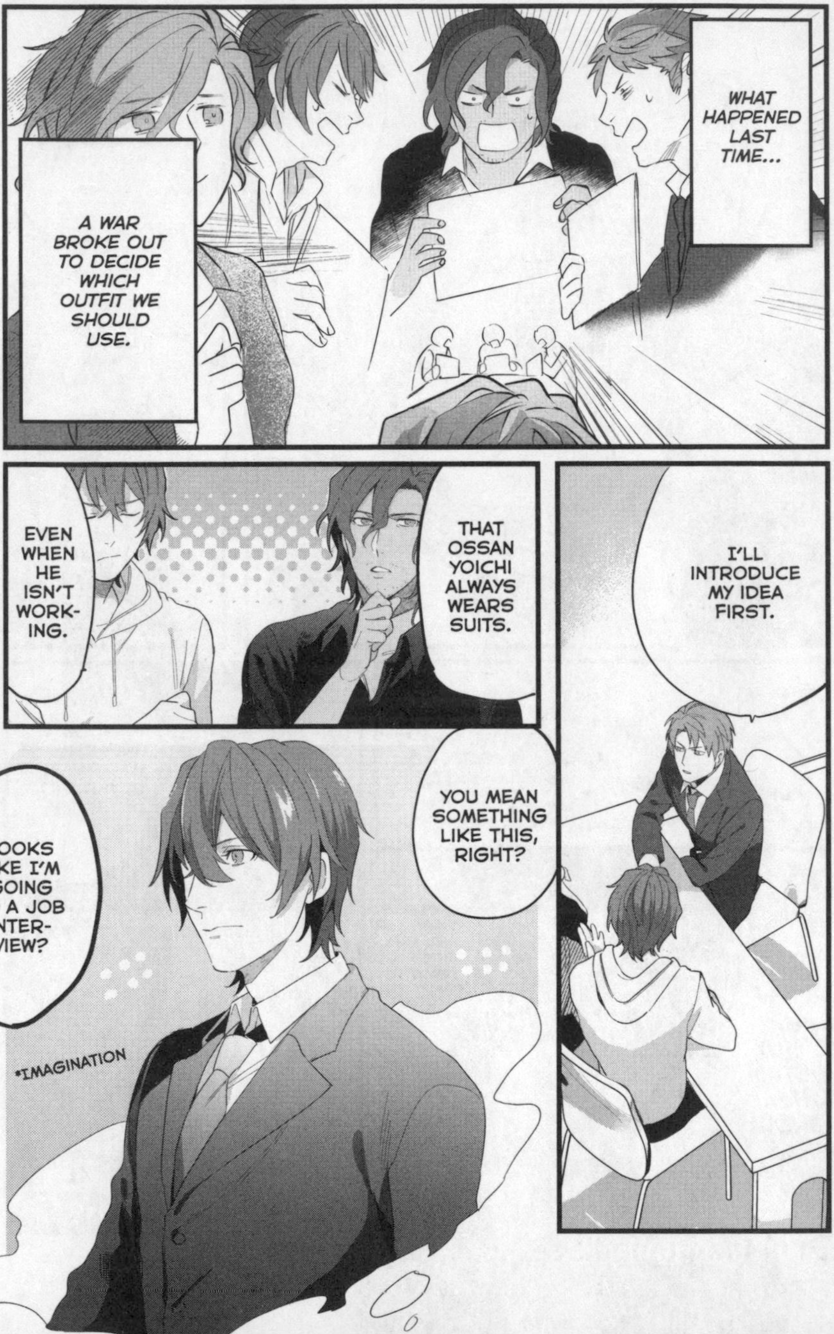
WHAT HAPPENED LAST TIME...
A WAR BROKE OUT TO DECIDE WHICH OUTFIT WE SHOULD USE.
I'LL INTRODUCE MY IDEA FIRST.
THAT OSSAN YOICHI ALWAYS WEARS SUITS.
EVEN WHEN HE ISN'T WORK-ING.
YOU MEAN SOMETHING LIKE THIS, RIGHT?
LOOKS LIKE I'M GOING TO A JOB INTER-VIEW?
*IMAGINATION

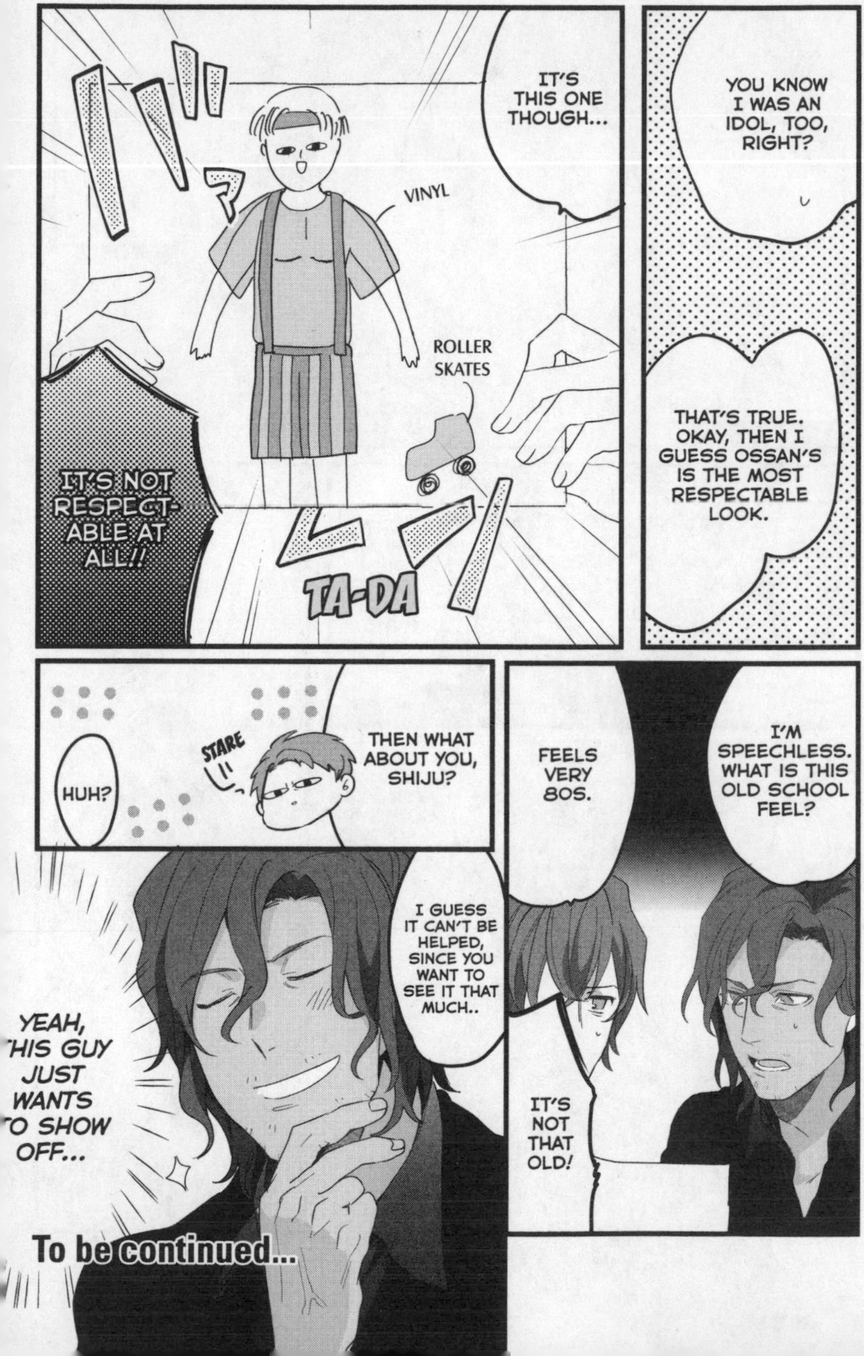
YOU KNOW I WAS AN IDOL, TOO, RIGHT?
THAT'S TRUE. OKAY, THEN I GUESS OSSAN'S IS THE MOST RESPECTABLE LOOK.
IT'S THIS ONE THOUGH...
VINYL
ROLLER SKATES
TA-DA
IT'S NOT RESPECT-ABLE AT ALL!!
I'M SPEECHLESS. WHAT IS THIS OLD SCHOOL FEEL?
FEELS VERY 80S.
IT'S NOT THAT OLD!
THEN WHAT ABOUT YOU, SHIJU?
STARE
HUH?
I GUESS IT CAN'T BE HELPED, SINCE YOU WANT TO SEE IT THAT MUCH..
YEAH, HIS GUY JUST WANTS O SHOW OFF...
To be continued...

3

4

4

END

Thank you so much!!

—Sakakibara

A huge thank you to all the designers and everyone involved. And you, dear reader!

—Mochida

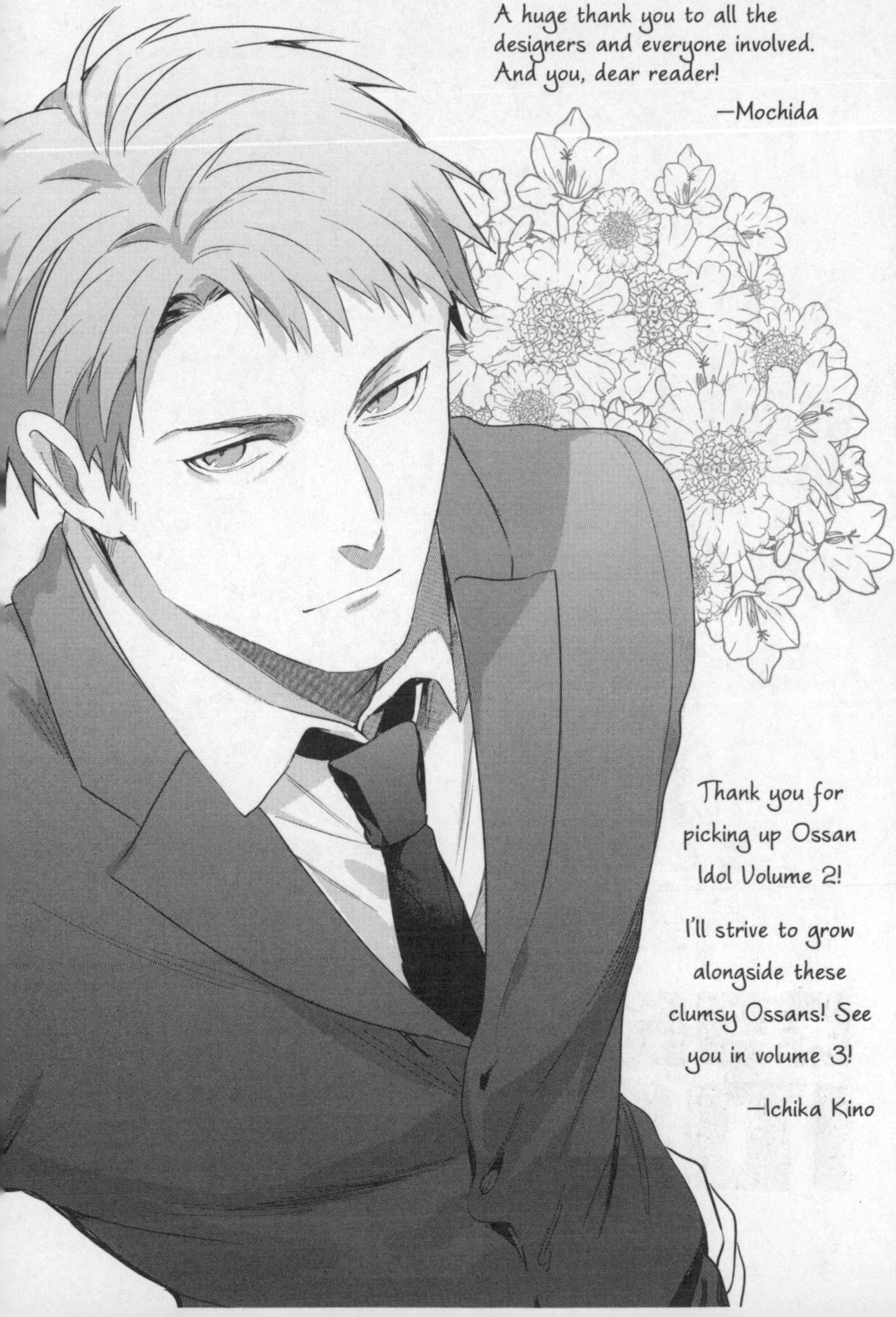

Thank you for picking up Ossan Idol Volume 2!

I'll strive to grow alongside these clumsy Ossans! See you in volume 3!

—Ichika Kino

OSSAN IDOL!

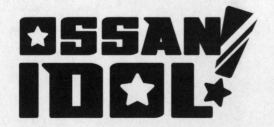

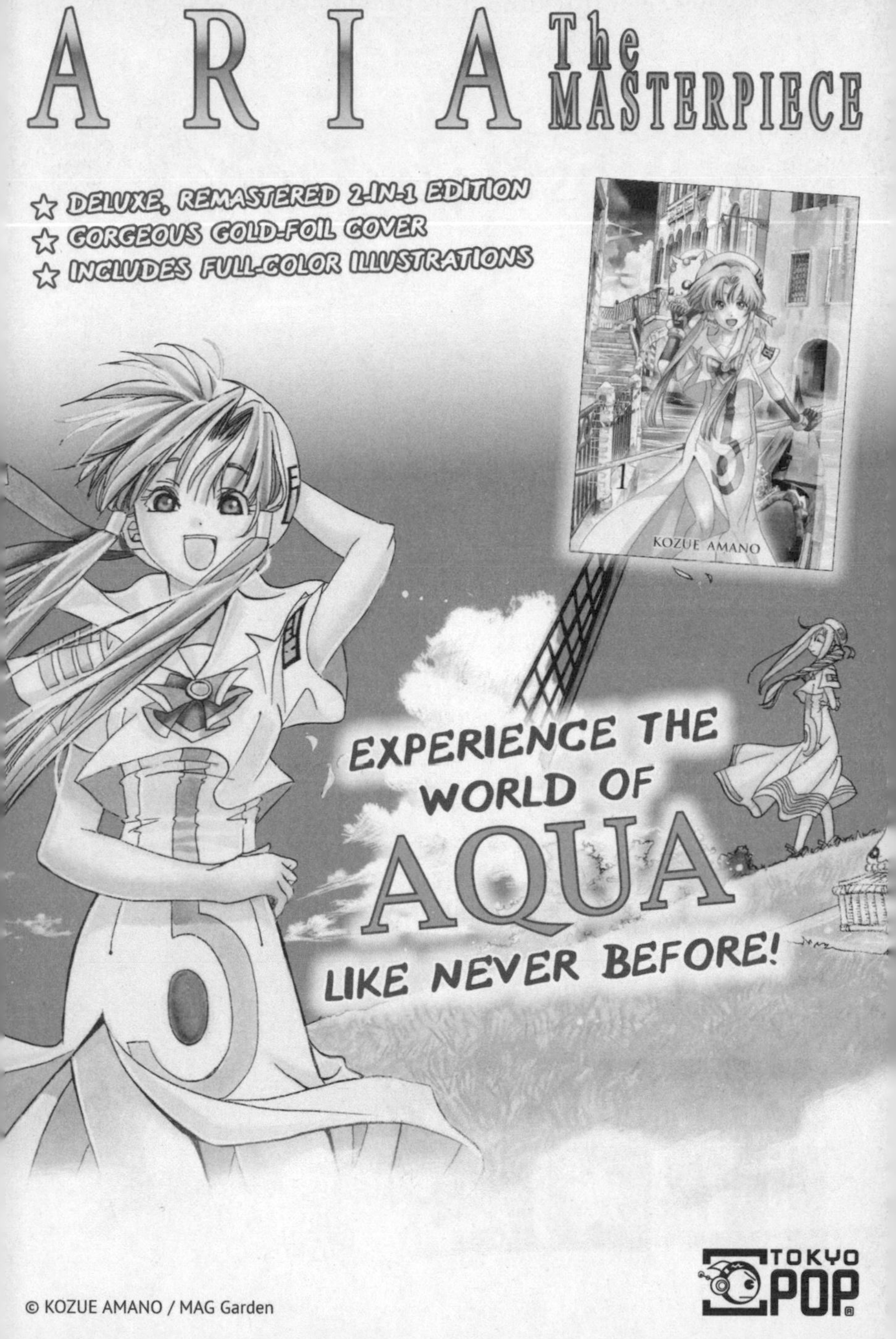
ARIA The MASTERPIECE
☆ DELUXE, REMASTERED 2-IN-1 EDITION
☆ GORGEOUS GOLD-FOIL COVER
☆ INCLUDES FULL-COLOR ILLUSTRATIONS
1
KOZUE AMANO
EXPERIENCE THE WORLD OF AQUA LIKE NEVER BEFORE!
TOKYO POP
© KOZUE AMANO / MAG Garden

Based on the smash-hit mobile game!

BanG Dream!
Girls Band Party!
Roselia Stage

Future World Fes is the biggest music event of the year, a world-famous spectacular that showcases only the best of the best. Do five high school girls have what it takes to rock their competition and secure a spot on the main stage?

TOKYOPOP

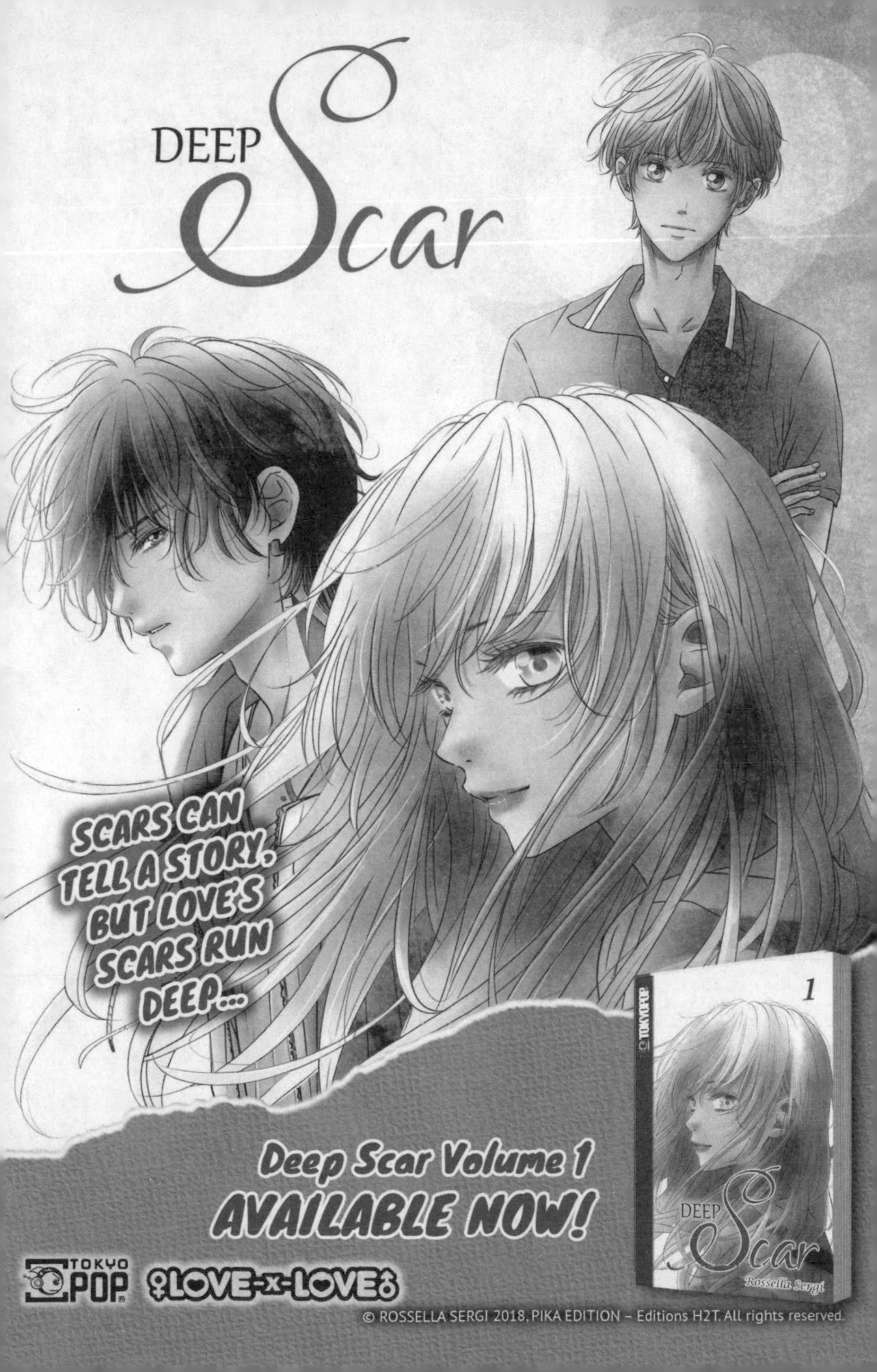
DEEP Scar
SCARS CAN TELL A STORY, BUT LOVE'S SCARS RUN DEEP...
Deep Scar Volume 1
AVAILABLE NOW!
TOKYOPOP
LOVE-x-LOVE
1
TOKYOPOP
DEEP Scar
Rossella Sergi
© ROSSELLA SERGI 2018, PIKA EDITION – Editions H2T. All rights reserved.

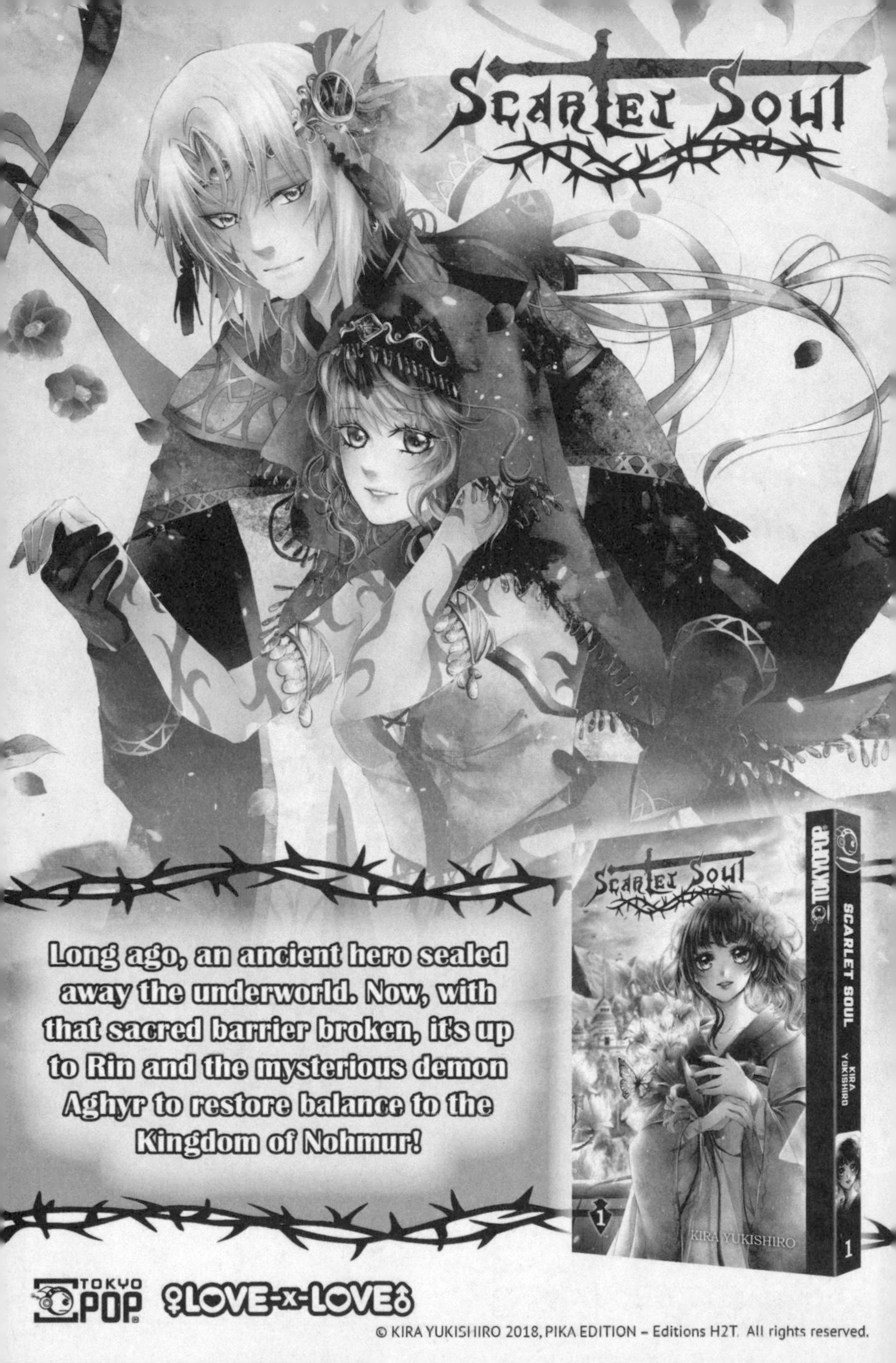
Scarlet Soul
Scarlet Soul
Long ago, an ancient hero sealed away the underworld. Now, with that sacred barrier broken, it's up to Rin and the mysterious demon Aghyr to restore balance to the Kingdom of Nohmur!
TOKYOPOP
SCARLET SOUL
KIRA YUKISHIRO
1
KIRA YUKISHIRO
1
TOKYO POP
LOVE x LOVE

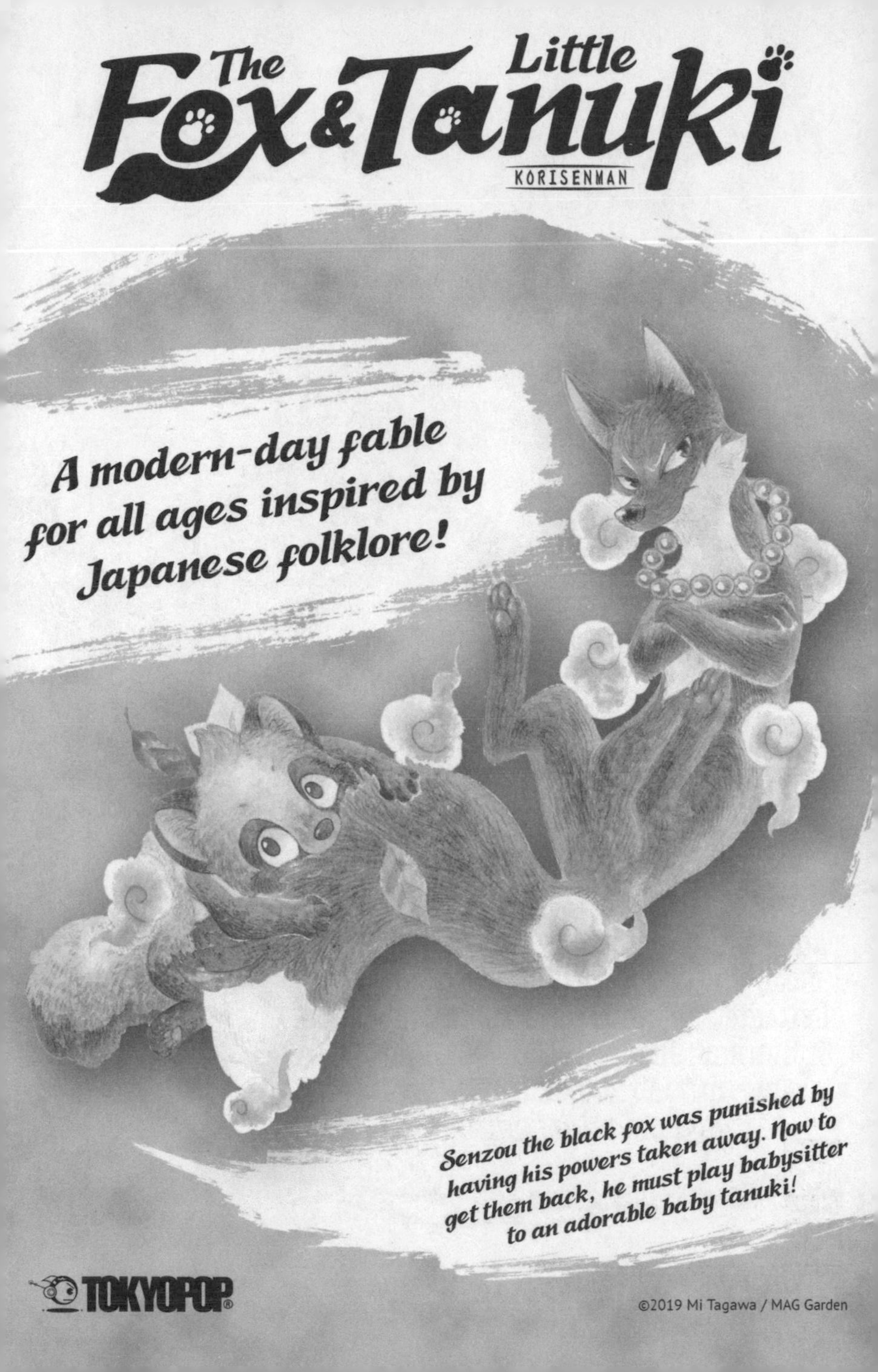
The Little Fox & Tanuki
KORISENMAN
A modern-day fable for all ages inspired by Japanese folklore!
Senzou the black fox was punished by having his powers taken away. Now to get them back, he must play babysitter to an adorable baby tanuki!
TOKYOPOP®
©2019 Mi Tagawa / MAG Garden

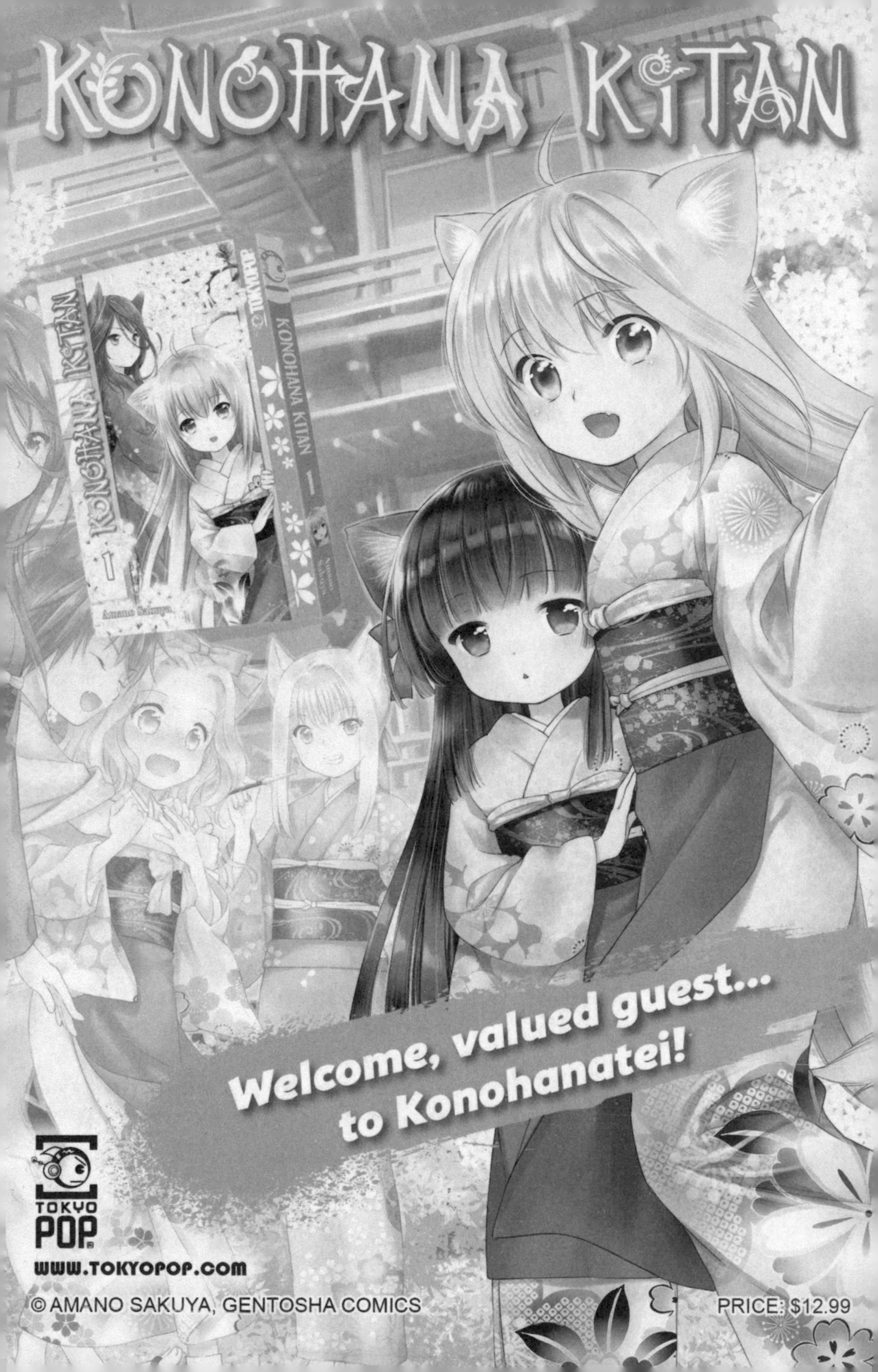
KONOHANA KITAN
KONOHANA KITAN 1
Amano Sakuya
Welcome, valued guest...
to Konohanatei!
TOKYO POP
www.tokyopop.com
© AMANO SAKUYA, GENTOSHA COMICS
PRICE: $12.99

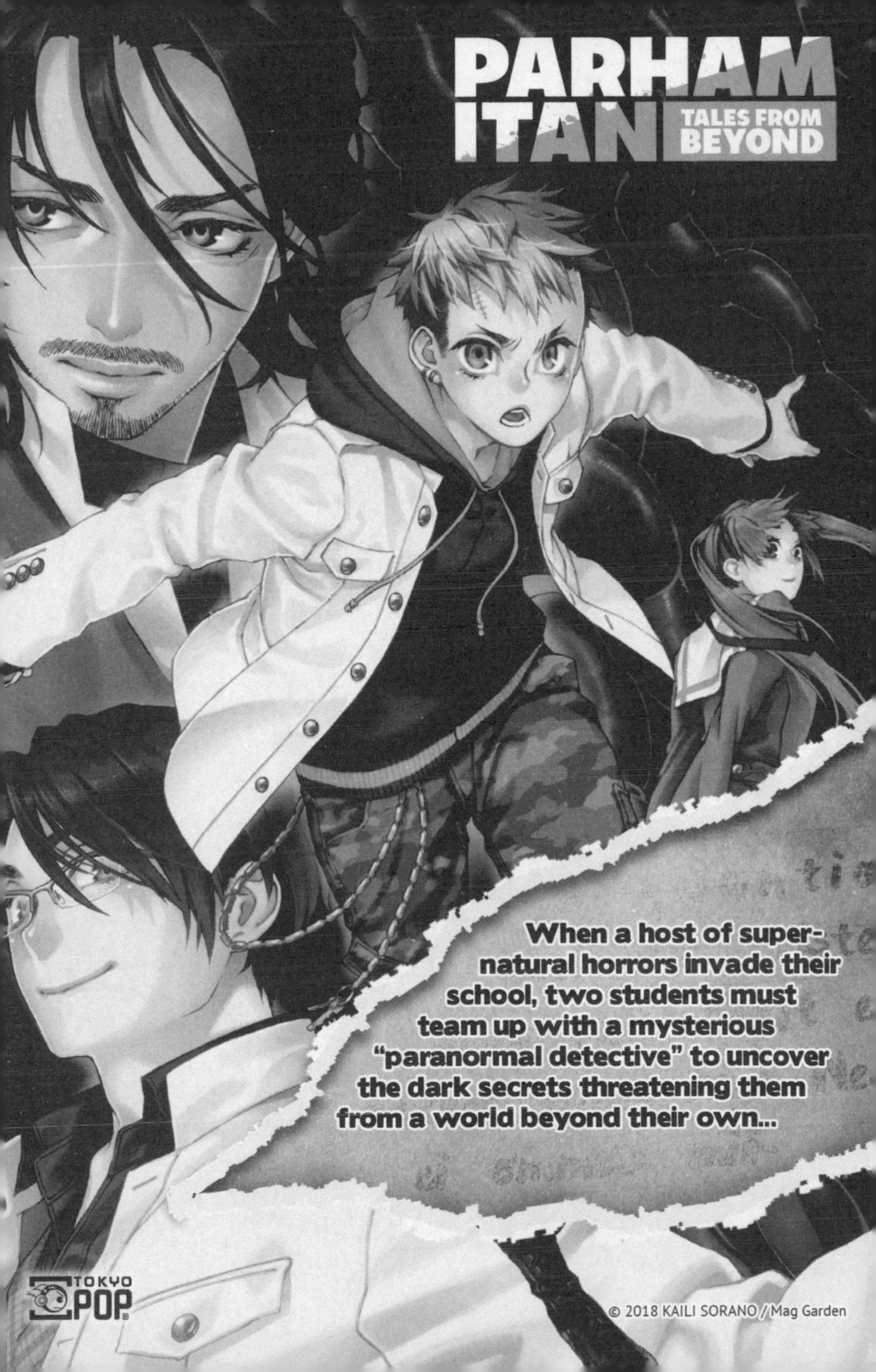
PARHAM ITAN
TALES FROM BEYOND
When a host of super-natural horrors invade their school, two students must team up with a mysterious "paranormal detective" to uncover the dark secrets threatening them from a world beyond their own...
TOKYO POP
© 2018 KAILI SORANO // Mag Garden

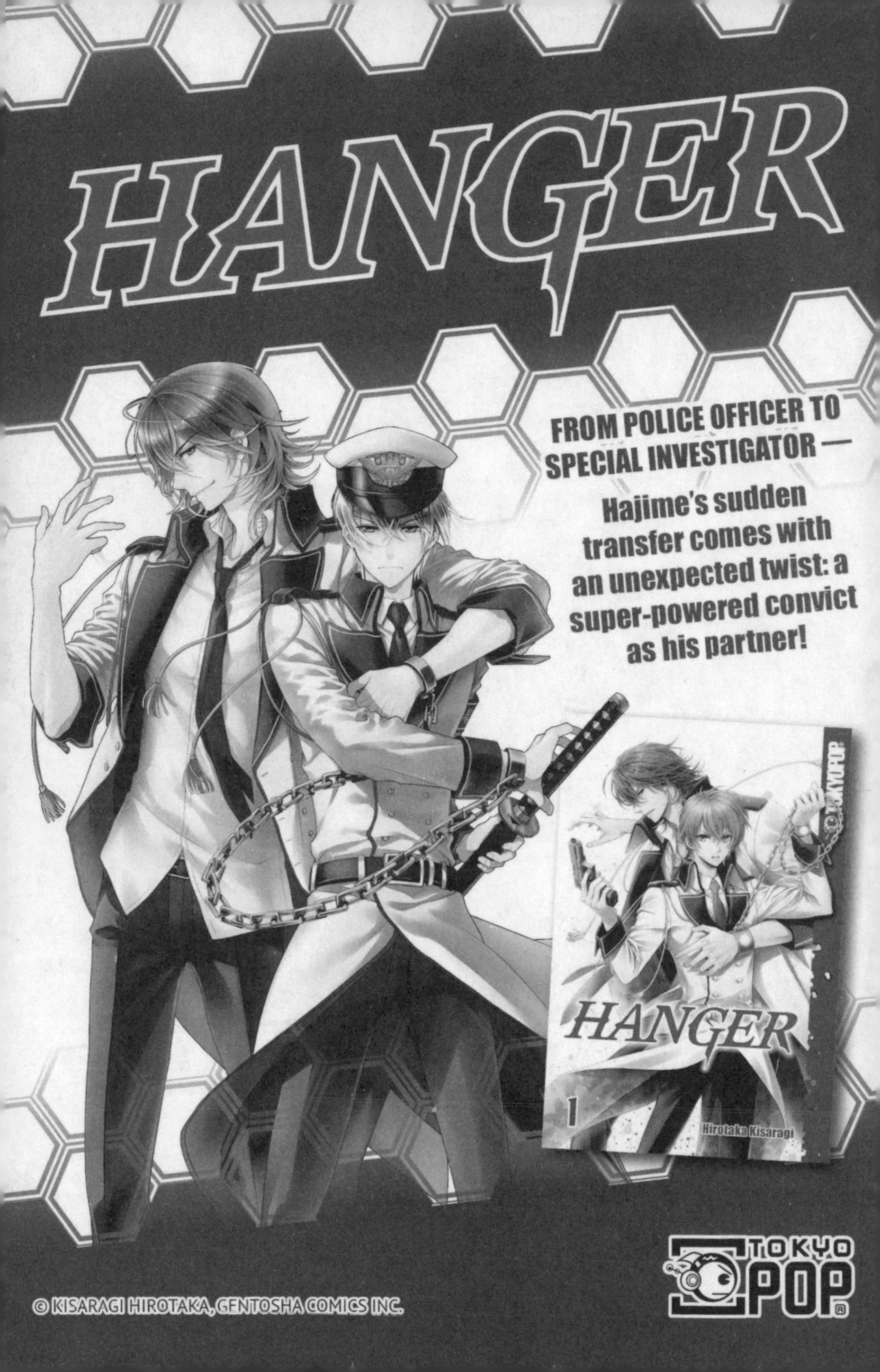
HANGER
FROM POLICE OFFICER TO SPECIAL INVESTIGATOR —
Hajime's sudden transfer comes with an unexpected twist: a super-powered convict as his partner!
TOKYOPOP
HANGER
1
Hirotaka Kisaragi
© KISARAGI HIROTAKA, GENTOSHA COMICS INC.
TOKYO POP

DON'T CALL ME DIRTY

Shouji is gay. Hama is homeless. Two men trying to make their way in a society that labels each of them as 'dirty' find a connection with one another — and a special relationship blossoms.

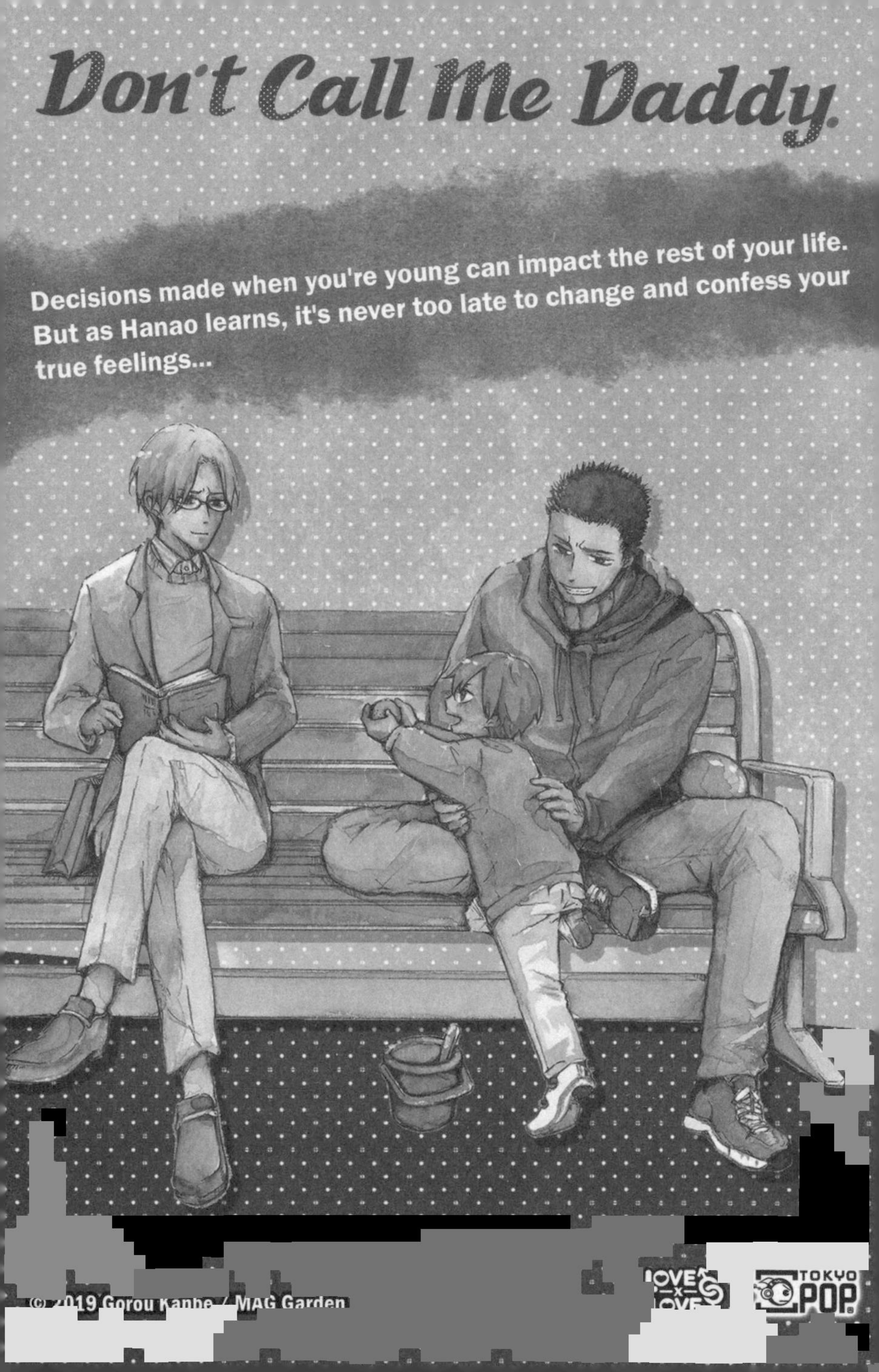
Don't Call Me Daddy.
Decisions made when you're young can impact the rest of your life. But as Hanao learns, it's never too late to change and confess your true feelings...
© 2019 Gorou Kanbe / MAG Garden

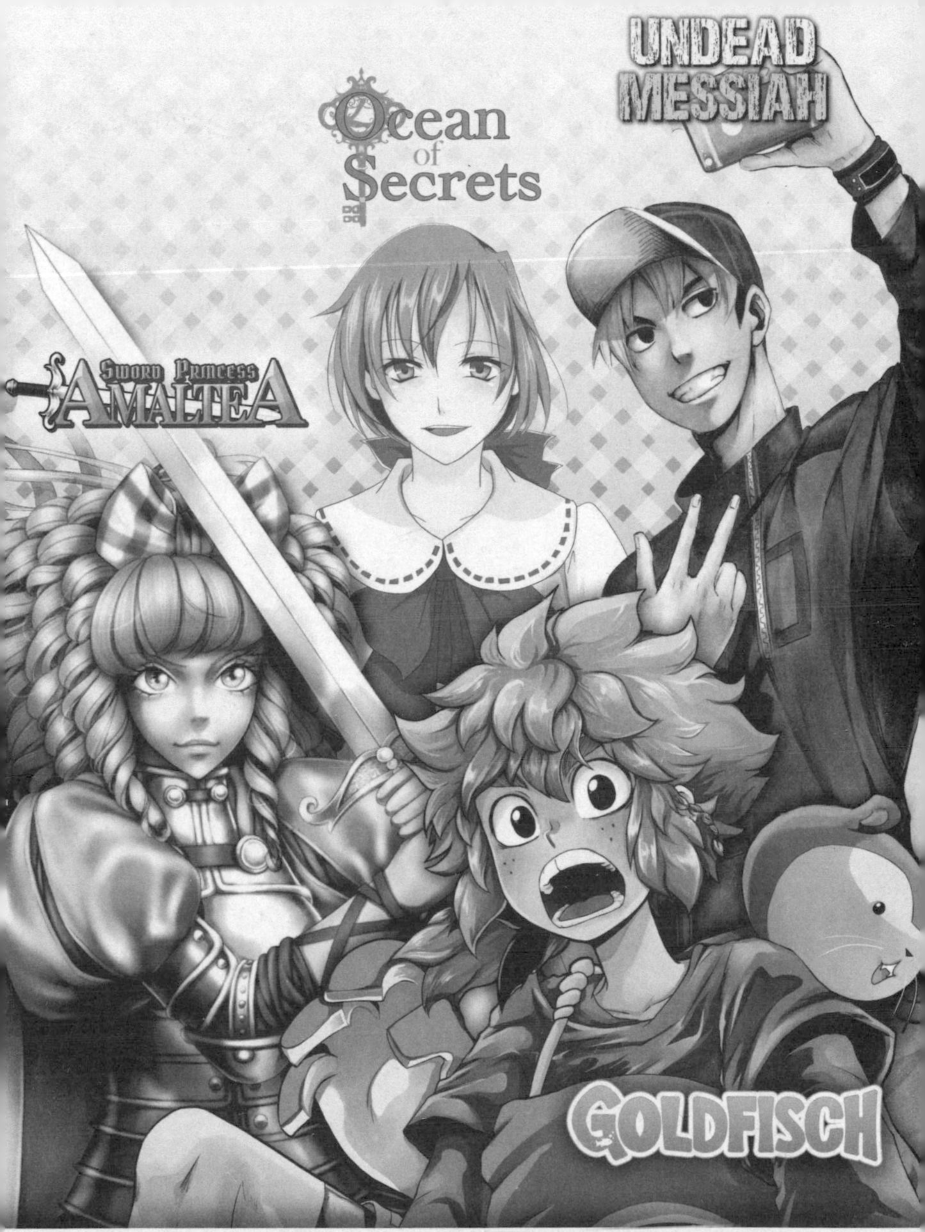
UNDEAD MESSIAH
Ocean of Secrets
SWORD PRINCESS AMALTEA
GOLDFISCH

STOP

THIS IS THE BACK OF THE BOOK!

How do you read manga-style? It's simple! Let's practice -- just start in the top right panel and follow the numbers below!

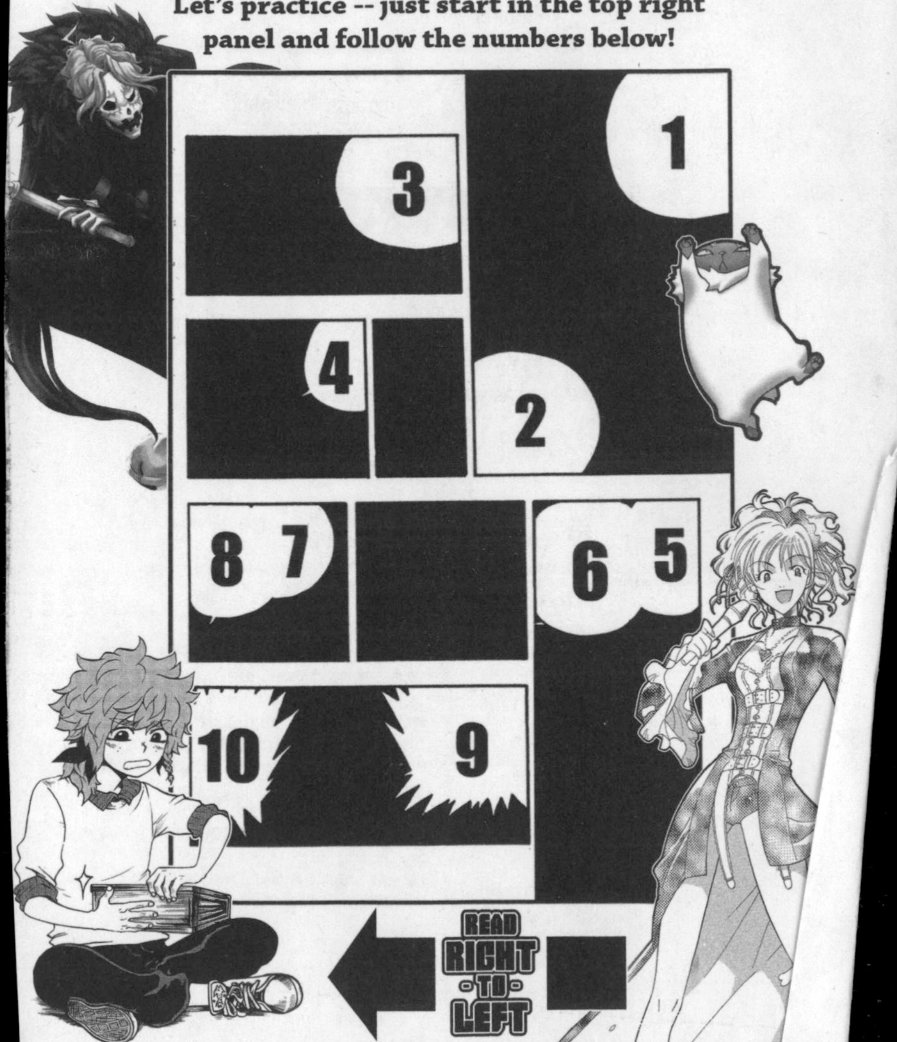
1
2
3
4
5
6
7
8
9
10
READ
RIGHT
-TO-
LEFT

Crimson from ***Kamo*** / Fairy Cat from ***Grimms Manga Tales***
Morrey from ***Goldfisch*** / Princess Ai from ***Princess Ai***

Ossani Idol! Volume 2
Manga by Ichika Kino
Original story by Mochiko Mochida

Editor - Lena Atanassova
Copy Editor - M. Cara Carper
Marketing Associate - Kae Winters
Translator - Ethan O'Brien
Proofreader - Kirin
Licensing Specialist - Arika Yanaka
Cover Design - Sol DeLeo
Retouching and Lettering - Vibrraant Publishing Studio
Editor-in-Chief & Publisher - Stu Levy

A  Manga

TOKYOPOP and 🐸 are trademarks or registered trademarks of TOKYOPOP Inc.

TOKYOPOP inc.
5200 W Century Blvd
Suite 705
Los Angeles, CA 90045 USA

E-mail: info@TOKYOPOP.com
Come visit us online at www.TOKYOPOP.com

f www.facebook.com/TOKYOPOP
🐦 www.twitter.com/TOKYOPOP
📌 www.pinterest.com/TOKYOPOP
📷 www.instagram.com/TOKYOPOP

OSSAN 36 GA IDOL NI NARUHANASHI 2
© 2019 Kino Ichika © 2019 Mochico Mochida

First published in Japan in 2019 by Shufu To Seikatsu Sha Co., Ltd.
English translation rights reserved by TOKYOPOP. under the license from Shufu To Seikatsu Sha Co., Ltd.

ISBN: 978-1-4278-6687-5

First TOKYOPOP Printing: February 2021
10 9 8 7 6 5 4 3 2 1
Printed in CANADA

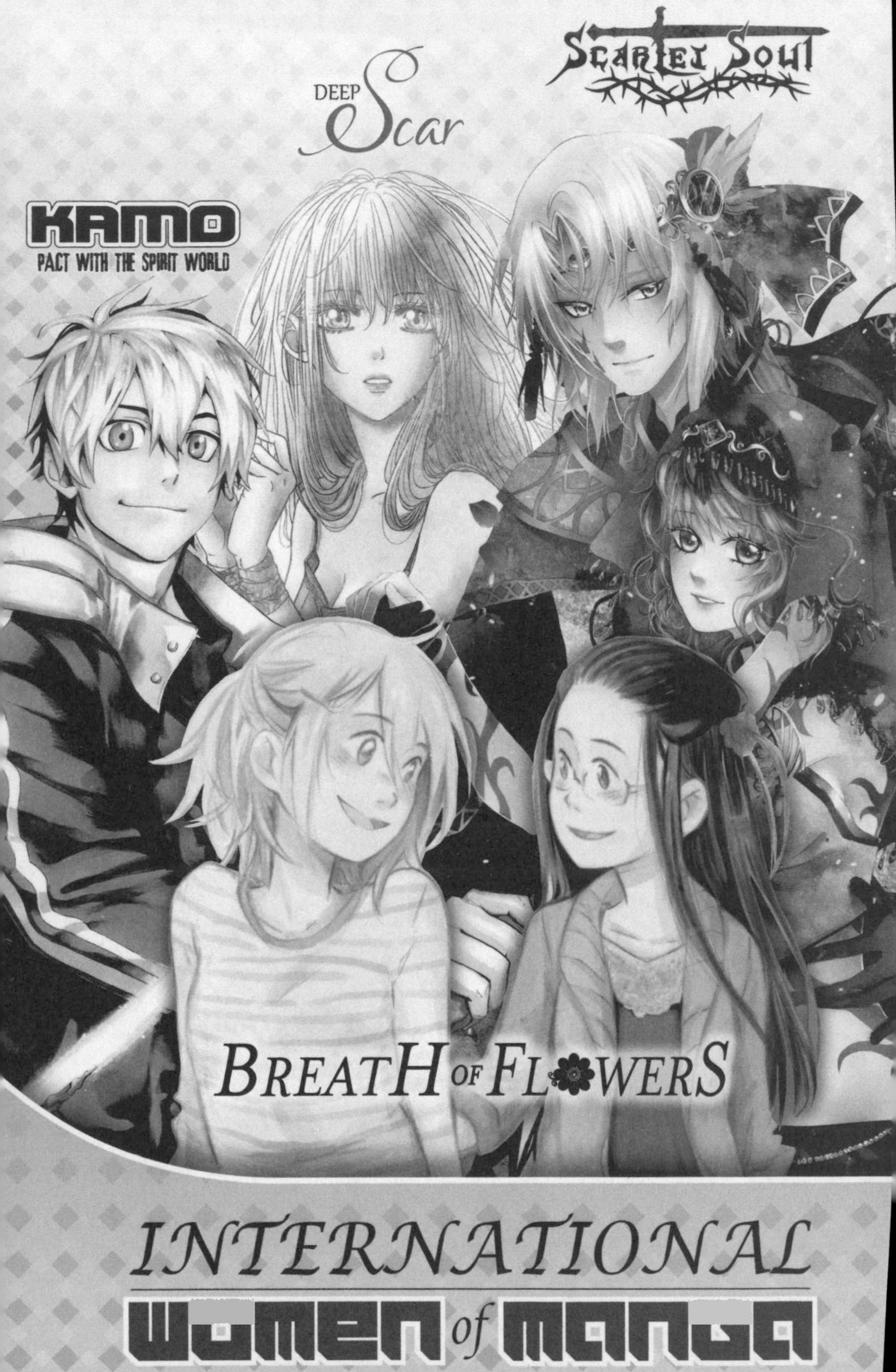
Scarlet Soul
DEEP Scar
KAMO
PACT WITH THE SPIRIT WORLD
BREATH OF FLOWERS
INTERNATIONAL
WOMEN of MANGA